C000046601

Race Relations in the
U.S. Virgin Islands

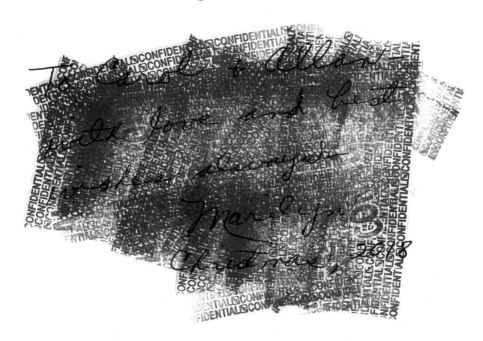

To Carol + Allan —
with love and best
wishes always —
Marilyn
Christmas, 2008

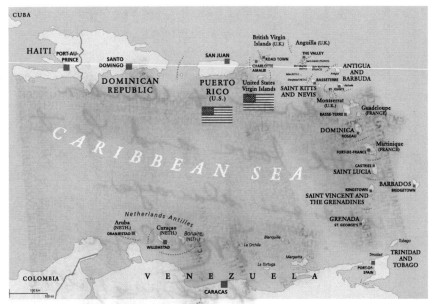

Caribbean Political Map courtesy of ©PeterHermesFurian via iStock.
United States flag courtesy of Wikimedia Commons.

Race Relations in the U.S. Virgin Islands

St. Thomas—A Centennial Retrospective

Marilyn F. Krigger

CAROLINA ACADEMIC PRESS

Durham, North Carolina

Library of Congress Cataloging-in-Publication Data

Names: Krigger, Marilyn F., author.
Title: Race relations in the US Virgin Islands : St. Thomas, a centennial
 retrospective / Marilyn F. Krigger.
Other titles: St. Thomas, a centennial retrospective
Description: Durham, N.C. : Carolina Academic Press, LLC, 2017. | Includes
 bibliographical references and index.
Identifiers: LCCN 2017012106 | ISBN 9781531002411 (alk. paper)
Subjects: LCSH: Saint Thomas (United States Virgin Islands : Island)--Race
 relations. | United States Virgin Islands--Race relations.
Classification: LCC F2105 .K78 2017 | DDC 305.80097297/22--dc23
LC record available at https://lccn.loc.gov/2017012106

eISBN 978-1-53100-458-3

CAROLINA ACADEMIC PRESS, LLC
700 Kent Street
Durham, North Carolina 27701
Telephone (919) 489-7486
Fax (919) 493-5668
www.cap-press.com

Printed in the United States of America

In Loving Memory

of

My Mother,
also a history teacher,
Mary Skelton Francis
(1917–2007),

My Husband,
Rudolph E. Krigger
(1934–2010),

and
three special CVI/UVI alumni,
Raymond Joseph
Dana Orie
Valentine Penha,

whose very impressive but shortened lives
did not allow their completion of all that
many had expected, but we remain thankful!

Contents

Part 2 · The First Half-Century of United States Sovereignty, 1917–1967

List of Illustrations and Tables

Illustrations

Tables

Preface

Many United States Virgin Islanders have been looking forward to the local unfolding of events in the year 2017, which marks the Transfer Centennial—the 100th anniversary of our beloved islands being transferred from the sovereignty of Denmark to that of the United States of America. Some events have already taken place, such as a spectacular Transfer Day Program on March 31st which featured, in addition to local dignitaries and performers and many visiting Danes, the Prime Minister of Denmark and the U.S. Secretary of Interior, who read a letter from President Trump. There are remaining expectations of continuing programs and forums, cultural exhibitions, colorful carnival parades, and picnics and social gatherings featuring great dining, story-telling, and grateful expressions of thanks to those, whether still living or not, whose labor and efforts have contributed positively to what we love and value about the U.S. Virgin Islands.

This book is a personal attempt by one Virgin Islander to contribute to the Centennial commemoration intellectually. It attempts to trace the relationships between the major racial groups—Whites and Blacks—and any involved others, that have shared St. Thomas since its colonization by Europeans in the late 1600s. It is hoped that it will motivate Virgin Islands residents, our fellow Americans, our fellow Caribbean peoples, and all interested others to consider more seriously, through the prism of race relations in one small society, how members and groups in societies have thought of, lived with, and treated each other, and to ponder how greater understanding, respect, and morality in human relations may be promoted.

The book stems from a doctoral dissertation on race relations in St. Thomas that was done in the early 1980s at the University of Delaware. My thanks to UD and my mentors there; to the University—then College—of the Virgin Islands, from which I was on sabbatical leave; and to the Virgin Islands Academic and Cultural Awards Endowment for the assistance it provided. The original dissertation has been revised and updated by recent research. In addition to the published works of Virgin Islands' and other scholars, major sources have been Virgin Islands newspapers, governmental reports, and interviews and conversations with many Virgin Islands residents, some of whom preferred anonymity, while most were willing to allow their names to be mentioned. The listed names are at the end of the bibliography, just before the index. Some have since departed, adding special poignancy to the study. I am deeply indebted to them all.

In keeping with the social reality of the Americanization of many aspects of Virgin Islands culture, the definitions of "black" and "white" used in this monograph are mainly those of the U.S. mainland, which are now in common use in the Virgin Islands. Thus, persons with any known African ancestry are referred to as black, even though that was not always the historical practice in the Virgin Islands. Black and white are not capitalized when used as adjectives (the black workers), but are when used as nouns (Blacks tend to be less wealthy than Whites).

I thank especially Dr. William Boyer, of the University of Delaware, for his publications during the last few decades on Virgin Islands history and political development. He has been not only a great professional model, but also a great friend. Other history professionals, whose works have added substantially to the recent written history of the U.S. Virgin Islands, include the late Dr. Neville Hall of the University of the West Indies-Jamaica; along with the late Dr. Isaac Dookhan and also Dr. Arnold Highfield, who were both my long-term colleagues at the University of the Virgin Islands.

Special thanks for assistance in procuring information to University of the Virgin Islands professionals and staff at its Paiewonsky and St. Croix libraries, the Eastern Caribbean Center, and the Offices of the President and Provost. Similar professional treatment was received at the Bureau of Economic Research of the Virgin Islands Government. The many weeks spent at the new Charles W. Turnbull Regional Library in eastern St. Thomas put it in a class by itself, and truly special thanks are due to Susan Lugo, the Territorial Archivist, and Beverly Smith, its Virgin Islands Collection Curator.

One's family usually plays substantial roles during research and writing efforts. I thank my son, Rudy Krigger, Jr. for his keen observations and his special assistance in numerous ways. I am also greatly indebted to my former student and now adopted daughter, Letetia Penn Rodgers, without whose persistence and computer skills, this work would not have been completed. My cousin, Ruth E. Thomas, a natural educator and the former principal of the

Charlotte Amalie High School, has been, as usual, an abundant source of general knowledge and wisdom. Additionally, to my many friends, former colleagues, and students who have been great sources of inspiration and knowledge over the years, special gratitude is extended. However, any faults and shortcomings of the work are mine, not theirs.

Marilyn F. Krigger
Professor Emerita of History
University of the Virgin Islands
St. Thomas, U.S. Virgin Islands
April, 2017

Part 1

The Danish Foundation, 1672–1917

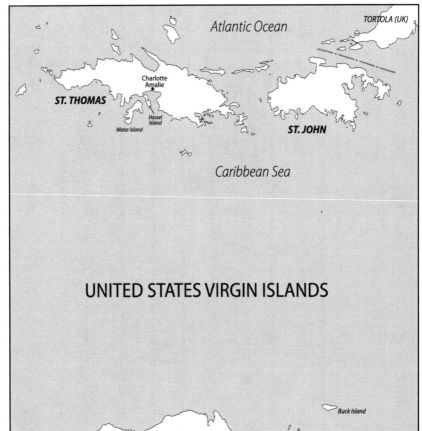

Atlantic Ocean

TORTOLA (UK)

Charlotte
Amalie

ST. THOMAS

Hassel
Island

Water Island

ST. JOHN

Caribbean Sea

UNITED STATES VIRGIN ISLANDS

Buck Island

Christiansted

• Frederiksted

ST. CROIX

0   5 mi.

Distance between St. Thomas and St. Croix (approximately 35 miles) not shown to scale

Chapter 1

Introduction to the Virgin Islands and Race Relations

The nation of Denmark effected permanent colonization of present-day St. Thomas, United States Virgin Islands, in May 1672. A prior Danish settlement in the mid-1660s had been short-lived, and Amerindian settlements that had existed many years earlier were also no longer in existence when the Danes made their second colonization attempt in 1672. Danish governance of St. Thomas thus lasted for 245 years, from 1672 until 1917, when the United States became the new sovereign power. Any assessment of St. Thomas' development under United States sovereignty, therefore, must begin with the island's long background of Danish rule, and the institutions, social groupings, and culture that had developed during that extensive pre-American period.

The geographical term "Virgin Islands" refers today to two small groups of islands located in the middle of the Caribbean island chain known as the West Indies. Although the Virgins now constitute two separate political entities, with the easternmost islands being the British Virgin Islands and the western ones forming the U. S. Virgin Islands, most of the islands are so close and look so similar (with tropical vegetation, hilly topographies, and white sand beaches) that Columbus seemingly considered them as one group. When he sailed by them, in November 1493 during his second voyage, their abundance (over 100 islands and islets) and untouched appearance apparently reminded Columbus of the Middle Ages legend of the martyred St. Ursula and her Eleven Thousand Virgins. He thus bestowed that name upon the islands, with the last word having become their permanent label.[1]

Over half of the Virgins—more than 60 islands—comprise the U.S. Virgin Islands today. However, as most of the islands are small cays, with many

far less than a square mile in size and uninhabited, the total land area of the
U. S. Virgin Islands is listed as 136 square miles. The 2010 population, according to the U.S. Census Bureau, was 106,405, which represented a two percent decrease from the 2000 figure of 108,612. The three largest islands by size
are St. Croix, St. Thomas, and St. John, in descending order. St. Croix is 84
square miles and had a 2010 population of 50,601. St. Thomas' 2010 population was 51,634 and its original 32 square miles have been expanded slightly
by the filling in of a few shoreline areas, such as the creation of its central "Veterans Drive" waterfront. St. John's 2010 population of 4,170 may seem small
for its 20 square miles. However, two-thirds of St. John's land area comprise
a United States National Park which, commendable in some ways and ques-
tionable in others, occupies two-thirds of the island, and therefore limits the
extent to which residential and other development may take place.[2]

St. Croix, far enough from the others that originally it was not considered
one of the Virgins, is 40 miles south of St. Thomas, St. John, and the British
Virgins. Today, most travel between St. Croix and the northern islands takes
place by air due to the greater frequency of air service and the comparative
traveling times (generally at least two hours by boat but only 20 minutes by
air). St. Thomas and St. John, however, are only three miles apart, with St.
John to the east, and there is frequent boat travel of twenty minutes between
the two, with some persons on each island even working daily on the other.
Similarly, there is boat travel several times a day between St. Thomas or St.
John, and the British Virgin Islands to the east. Tortola, the chief island of the
British Virgins, is separated from St. John by only a couple miles at their nearest point, and is the ancestral island-home of a sizeable percentage of present-
day St. Thomians. Additionally, St. Thomas, because of its bridge-type location
relative to the British Virgin Islands and the continuing chain of Lesser Antillean islands to the east, and its similar position with mainland Puerto Rico—
40 miles west—and the continuing Greater Antillean islands to the west, has
long served as the shipping and commercial center of the entire Virgin Islands
chain. As a result, St. Thomas is the site of the governmental capital of the U.
S. Virgins, Charlotte Amalie, even though St. Thomas is not the largest of the
Virgins nor was it the earliest to undergo European settlement.

In fact, St. Croix, the largest of the Virgins, was the first to have been colonized by Europeans, beginning in the 1630s. However, it suffered initially
from the rivalries of several different European settlements (English, French,
and Dutch); then later from administrative, labor, and population problems
under the French after they gained full control in the 1650s. The French finally
became so frustrated with failing attempts to make St. Croix successful that,

after over forty years of effort, they gave up on St. Croix and moved all of its colonists and their belongings, including their enslaved Africans, to the French colony of Saint-Domingue (present-day Haiti) in 1696, thus leaving St. Croix uninhabited.[3]

Meanwhile, St. Thomas had been colonized by Denmark in 1672, and therefore had been a Danish colony for over two decades at the time St. Croix was abandoned by the French. With St. Thomas as its base, Denmark undertook the settlement of St. John in 1718, and later purchased the mainly-unoccupied St. Croix from France in 1733, completing the political entity known as the Danish West Indies, which was sold to the United States in 1917. It was St. Thomas, therefore, that had the earliest and longest connection with Denmark, the full 245 years of Danish sovereignty, and thus provides the fullest record of race relations, the focus of this monograph, in the islands that were once the Danish West Indies and then became the Virgin Islands of the United States.

Race relations may be defined as all aspects of thought and behavior among interacting peoples which are influenced by awareness of each other's actual or attributed physical or other related differences.[4] The attributed differences may be real—wholly or partially, or may be substantially lacking in reality, but as long as they are believed to be true, they affect how persons think of and behave toward each other. Of course, there have been long-established human societies in which race was not a distinguishing factor, as all or practically all of their members had common origins and thus exhibited few or no factors that were considered important differentiations. However, the beginning of extensive worldwide travel in the Middle Ages (roughly A.D. or C.E. 500 to 1500) would result in persons of different countries and continents becoming aware of, and afterward closely residing with each other, leading to many of the well-known aspects and problems of race relations that characterize our nation and our world today.

Interestingly, contrary to what is often believed, race relations problems did not exist at first in some of the earliest European colonies in the Lesser Antilles. That was due to the fact that on a few of the earliest islands that were settled, such as Barbados and St. Croix, none of the pre-European Amerindian inhabitants of the New World were present. St. Croix had had Amerindian inhabitants at the time of Columbus's visit in 1493 and, in fact, they had presented Columbus's fleet with the first-known Amerindian military challenge to European presence. But by the time of European colonization of St. Croix in the 1630s, the Amerindians were no longer there.[5] However, there were racial conflicts—Amerindians vs. Europeans—on a number of other Lesser Antillean islands, such as St. Kitts, where Amerindians still existed at the time Europeans arrived to settle.[6]

Because of its late 1670s colonization, the course of European settlement on St. Thomas differed from many of the earlier-settled Lesser Antillean islands. By then, most other islands had been colonized for at least a couple decades, and the new European entrant—the Danes—knew of the lessons the others had learned. On St. Croix, and some other islands colonized before the middle of the seventeenth century, their early populations had been practically all European or, if there were Amerindians present, Whites and Amerindians. In islands lacking Amerindians, the earliest laboring class consisted of Europeans who came as indentured servants, having signed agreements to work for a period (generally three years), at the end of which, they would receive a pre-agreed compensation that they hoped would be sufficient to allow them to buy land and become planters themselves, or take up some other self-sufficient occupation. However, even though the purchase of white servants at first appeared cheaper than the later practice of purchasing Africans, who were generally twice the cost of getting indentured white laborers, planters soon learned that the purchase of Africans ended up being more profitable, as the enslaved Africans and their offspring were made, by law, property for life. Additionally, as word spread in Europe of the terrible treatment many of the indentured had to endure, it became harder and harder to recruit enough Europeans to meet the demand. Thus Africans ended up being purchased in numbers that brought them close to, or even greater than the white population of many of the islands being colonized.[7] The stage was thus being amply set for race-related issues in West Indian history.

Notes

1. Arnold R. Highfield, *Sainte Croix, 1650–1733: A Plantation Society in the French Antilles* (Christiansted, St. Croix: Antilles Press, 2003), pp. 18–22; J. *Antonio Jarvis, The Virgin Islands and Their People* (Philadelphia: Dorrance and Company, 1944), pp. 19–22.

2. United States Census Bureau, 2010 Census of the Virgin Islands, Census of Population and Housing. Washington, D.C., 2013, p.1. The population decline is thought to be due to the economic recession that had taken place on the mainland during the century's first decade, plus economic effects of the closing of St. Croix's oil-refining industry.

3. Arnold R. Highfield, *Sainte Croix, 1650–1733*, pp. 51–514.

4. Oliver C. Cox, *Caste, Class, and Race: A Study of Social Dynamics* (Garden City, New York: Doubleday & Company, Inc., 1948), pp. 319–320; G. Franklin Edwards and Thomas T. Pettigrew, "Race Relations," in David L. Sill, editor, *Encyclopedia of the Social Sciences* (New York: The Macmillan Company and the Free Press, 1988), pp. 268–272.

5. Arnold R. Highfield, *Sainte Croix, 1650–1733*, pp. 21, 111–112.

6. Ibid., pp. 44–46.

7. Ibid., pp. 84–85, 245–274, 453.

Chapter 2

Danish Settlement and Development of St. Thomas

Permanent settlement of St. Thomas was accomplished under the leadership of a Danish corporation named the Danish West India Company, which had been granted a royal charter in 1671 to colonize St. Thomas and possibly neighboring islands. (The Company's name was changed to the Danish West India and Guinea Company two years later, after receiving added authorization to engage in the African slave trade on West Africa's Guinea coast.) The Company's first ship to arrive, the *Faero*, "Pharaoh" in English, dropped anchor in St. Thomas' south central harbor on May 25, 1672. The harbor washes the shore of what would became Charlotte Amalia (now spelled as Amalie), the town on St. Thomas that was named in 1692 to honor the Danish Queen, and which is the present capital of the U.S. Virgin Islands. It has one of the best harbors in the Caribbean and is a well-known port in today's Caribbean cruise tourism.

Lessons that the late-arriving Danes learned from their knowledge of developments in earlier colonies were employed from the beginning. They did not strive for an all-Danish population. A substantial number of the *Faero*'s original 190 passengers were immigrant company employees who came as indentured servants, contracted to work for periods of three to five years. Some settlers had even been procured from prisons and other places of ill-repute in Denmark. A large number of the original passengers had died on the trans-Atlantic voyage or shortly after (common occurrences at that time), and their places were taken by Europeans from various nearby islands who were allowed to become a part of the infant colony. They included Dutch, French, German, and English nationals, and also some Jews. In July 1673, just slightly over a year after the new colony was established, St. Thomas had 98 white inhabitants, of whom only 28 were Danes.[1]

Another differentiating feature of the Danish colonization of St. Thomas was the rapidity with which the island's population became mainly black. On Barbados, St. Kitts, Antigua, Martinique, Guadeloupe, and other Lesser Antillean islands that had been settled during the first half of the 1600s, that transformation had usually taken at least a couple decades, as the pattern had been for the original European population to be supplemented by European indentured servants as more labor was needed. However, the much greater demands for labor spurred by the "sugar revolution" (the eventual change from tobacco or other earlier crops to sugarcane) as it took place on different islands, led to intensive importation of enslaved Africans to the degree that the black population overtook the white.[2]

In St. Thomas the process of population change took place in less than seven years. The white population in 1673, after one year of settlement, was ninety-eight; the black population, all enslaved, totaled fifty-five. Seven years later, in 1680, there were 156 Whites and 175 Blacks. Blacks had thus assumed the dominant numerical position in St. Thomas in far less than one decade. By 1691, just nineteen years after the Danes had arrived, there were 389 Whites, and the black population had grown to 555.[3]

Interestingly, the population change on St. Thomas took place without an accompanying sugar revolution. Of the 101 plantations on St. Thomas in 1691, only five were even partly planted in sugarcane. Cotton was the chief product on eighty-seven of the plantations, and tobacco, indigo, other dye woods were the other important exports. It was not until the beginning of the eighteenth century that St. Thomas became an island whose economy was dominated by sugar. The acceleration was amazing, for by 1715 forty plantations were solely devoted to sugar. The number of plantations had risen to 180 and there were still more cotton than sugar plantations, but cotton production was worth only about a third of sugar production. However, the population in 1715 left no doubt that in St. Thomas a sugar revolution-type effect had taken place: there were 3,042 Blacks and 547 Whites.[4]

The degree to which Whites became outnumbered in the West Indies was looked upon with derision by many Whites in Europe and in the English colonies in North America, that were themselves in the process of being settled by Europeans and would later become the United States of America. The reduction of Whites to a small minority of the populations in many West Indian islands would result in some Whites being unable to conceive of the islands as places for stable European family life, and led to the consequent development of a European get-rich-quick or profligate life style in the islands. Some scholarly works have discussed that European point of view which thus considered many of the West Indian islands as disastrous social failures, as far as Europeans were concerned.[5]

However, the determination of its Danish administrators to ensure the profitability and permanency of their new colony led to their acceptance of conditions that differed substantially from those employed in the earlier-settled West Indian colonies. There was not only an earlier predominance of Blacks than had happened elsewhere, but an interesting variety of mixtures in the population of Whites and their cultures. A St. Thomas census in 1688, when the colony was 16 years old, showed that the white population had grown to 317, of whom 148 were engaged in agriculture. Of the 148 in agriculture, 66 were Dutch, 31 were English, 17 were Danes and Norwegian (at that time Denmark and Norway constituted one country), 17 French, 4 Irish, 4 Flemish, 3 Germans, 3 Swedes, 1 Scot, 1 Brazilian, and 1 Portuguese.[6]

The variety of European languages spoken in the new colony was so great that instead of the development of a slave creole or patois based on the language of the "mother country," which happened in the English and French islands, the creole that developed among the Blacks in the Danish colony of St. Thomas was a Dutch creole, being that the Dutch were the most numerous of the planters. It came to be labelled as Negro Dutch Creole, and was the major spoken language in St. Thomas through the early decades of the 1800s. However, England took over and occupied the Danish islands for about nine years during the Napoleonic Wars. By the time war ended in 1815 and Denmark regained control of her colony, the English language was becoming quite popular and increasing British and United States commerce and influence led to the English language and an English creole being the major languages by 1850. English, therefore, was the language of the Danish West Indies long before their purchase by the United States.[7]

Notes

1. Westergaard, *The Danish West Indies Under Company Rule (1671–1754)* (New York: The Macmillan Company, 1917), pp. 38–39.

2. J. H. Parry and P. M. Sherlock, *A Short History of the West Indies* (Third Edition; New York: St. Martin's Press, 1971), pp. 88–89; Edmund S. Morgan, *American Slavery, American Freedom: The Ordeal of Colonial Virginia* (New York: W. W. Norton and Company, 1973), chapter 15.

3. Jens Larsen, *Virgin Islands Story* (Philadelphia: Fortress Press, 1950), pp. 41, 122.

4. Westergaard, *The Danish West Indies Under Company Rule*, pp. 41, 122.

5. See, as examples, Richard S. Dunn, *Sugar and Slaves: The Rise of the Planter Class in the English West Indies, 1624–1713* (Chapel Hill: The University of North Carolina Press, 1972) and Carl Bridenbaugh and Roberta Bridenbaugh, *No Peace Beyond the Line: The English in the Caribbean, 1624–1690* (New York: Oxford University Press, 1972).

6. Larsen, *Virgin Islands Story*, p. 19; Westergaard, *The Danish West Indies Under Company Rule*, pp. 121–122.

7. Larsen, *Virgin Islands Story,* chapter 9; Eddie Donoghue, "British 19th century occupations of Danish West Indies fueled big advances in slaves' quest for freedom," Daily News (St. Thomas, V.I.), November 23, 2015, p. 27.

Chapter 3

The Institution of Slavery on St. Thomas, 1672–1848

Slavery existed on St. Thomas for 176 years—from the colony's inception in 1672 until the institution was outlawed in the entire Danish West Indies in 1848. On August 8, 1672, less than two and one-half months after arrival, Jorgen Iversen, the 33-year-old Danish governor who established the colony, issued its first set of laws. The laws defined clearly the religious, military, and civic duties and positions of all of the colony's inhabitants. The thirteenth of the fourteen orders clearly established the relationship between persons of the black (African) and white (European) races on St. Thomas. It read:

> No man must let his negro leave the estate after sunset, without good cause, that he may not get to his neighbor's estate and do injury; and whosoever at night observes a strange negro on his estate, shall catch him and carry him in the morning to the fort, where he shall be punished.[1]

This ordinance reveals at least two very important facts. The first is that at that time, when the colony was only two and one-half months old, Blacks were already present. There were no Blacks listed in the initial group of settlers who had arrived in May, and several sources have stated that the first shipload of enslaved Africans (who numbered 103) did not arrive until 1673. What apparently happened during the first couple months was that some enslaved Africans were purchased from passing ships or from nearby already-settled islands.[2]

The other revelation is that it was already established, at that early date, that the black inhabitants of St. Thomas were in a category completely apart from and lower than any other group. The other laborers (the indentured servants)

Fort Christian, governmental center since 1672, in pre-automobile days. Courtesy of the Virgin Islands Government's Archival Collection at the Charles W. Turnbull Regional Library. (This and all pictures following, unless noted otherwise, are by courtesy of the Virgin Islands Government's Archival Collection at the Charles W. Turnbull Regional Library.)

were referred to in the ordinance as "white servants" or simply "servants," and there was no prohibition on their being out after sunset, with the threats of instant seizure and later punishment. St. Thomas' late settlement meant not only that there was no substantial period of white numerical superiority; it also meant that there was no period of ambiguity in regard to the relative status of black and white laborers, which some scholars have found for some colonies established during the first half of the seventeenth century. In St. Thomas, Africans occupied a position of unmistakable legal and social inferiority from the very beginning. (The fort, at which the enslaved were punished, referred to the earliest section of Fort Christian, which was expanded over the years and remains today as the premier historical landmark of Charlotte Amalie.)

The Role of Moravian Missionaries

The inconsequential position of the enslaved in the young Danish colony was evident in other aspects of relationships between them and the Europeans. The first and second of Governor Iversen's orders of 1672 mandated attendance at a religious service for all Danish speakers every Sunday morning, and for "persons of all other nations" every Sunday afternoon.[3] The category of "persons of all other nations" did not include the Africans; apparently they were not thought of as human beings who merited religion. Thus, for several decades, as stated by historian Isaac Dookhan, the "various Christian denominations concentrated on the needs of the white minority. No direct effort was made to incorporate Negroes into the Christian fold."[4]

The deplorable early record of the Lutheran Church, the established religion of Denmark and, therefore, of the colony, illustrated the stark contrast pointed out by some historians of Latin America regarding the inclusive nature of Catholicism in those countries vis-à-vis the black-excluding nature of some of the northern European denominations.[5] As a result, Spanish authorities in nearby Puerto Rico, using to their advantage the Danish neglect of the spiritual welfare of the Africans, often refused to return enslaved Africans who had run away from St. Thomas in the early 18th century, proclaiming that they had come to Puerto Rico to be baptized and would not be able to practice their faith if returned.[6]

The first systematic efforts to extend the faith of Europeans to the enslaved Africans on St. Thomas were not undertaken until 1732 and they were by a faith that had not been present among the diverse early European groups on St. Thomas. Significantly, the person who spearheaded the movement was an enslaved African, named Anthony Ulrich, who had been taken from St. Thomas to Denmark by his master, a Danish nobleman. Anthony's master and a German nobleman, Count Nicholas von Zinzendorf, were both guests at the 1731 coronation in Copenhagen of Danish King Christian VI and, somehow, Anthony, who had accompanied his master to the coronation, ended up speaking with the German Count. Count Zinzendorf was the leader of a group of Moravians to whom he had granted refuge at his estate in Germany, as they were Protestants who had fled from their homeland of Moravia in Czechoslovakia to avoid religious persecution. Anthony informed him graphically of the hardships and religious need of the enslaved Africans in St. Thomas. The Count was very touched and, on his return to the Moravian settlement in Germany, informed the group of Anthony's report and his plea for help. The Count and the Moravian settlers were moved to act, and chose two members to go as missionaries to the enslaved Africans of St. Thomas. Leonard Dober and David Nitschmann arrived in December, 1732.[7]

The two Moravian missionaries got to St. Thomas on a Dutch ship, as the Danish West India and Guinea Company opposed their mission to the slaves and refused them passage on a company ship. However, the missionaries received the support of the new Danish King and other members of the Royal Family, who were known to be very religious. Additional opposition in St.

Thomas came from a number of the planters, who considered the mission absurd and a danger to white colonists, especially since Moravian practice stressed the need for converts to learn to read the Gospel themselves. In fact, the first known acts of race relations on St. Thomas that exhibited an apparent belief of Whites in some degree of racial equality, were those of Moravian missionaries in regard to the enslaved Africans to whom they ministered. To the amazement and derision of the other Whites, the missionaries insisted that the slaves had the ability to understand the Christian religion, and asserted that "Christ had died for blacks as well as for whites."[8]

When in November of 1733, less than a year after the missionaries arrived, some of the Africans enslaved on nearby St. John carried out a substantial rebellion (resulting in the deaths of about 50 of the 200 Whites on St. John, and in African control of parts of the island for months), some Whites claimed that the uprising had been influenced by Moravian teachings. However, there had been no Moravian activity on St. John. Instead, what had provoked the St. John revolt was a severe set of laws issued by the Danish Governor on St. Thomas, in September, 1733, due to a drought and other natural disasters whose destruction of crops made the enslaved Africans hungrier and angrier than usual. Those circumstances, and the growing advantage that Blacks had in population growth over the Whites (5 to 1 on St. John) made the Whites believe that it was necessary for the Blacks to understand clearly that any actions against Whites would be met by severe punishments. Thus, the 1733 laws included: (1) any slave who raised his hand to hit a white person would be pinched three times with a hot iron, and additionally lose the offending hand or be hung, as preferred by the offended White; (2) the testimony of any reputable white person was sufficient evidence of the guilt of a slave; (3) a slave meeting a white person on a road had to step aside and allow the White to pass; failure to step aside resulted in whipping; (4) slaves who attempted to poison their masters were to be tortured with hot irons and afterward killed; (5) leaders of runaway slaves were also to be tortured with hot irons and then hanged; slaves guilty of planning conspiracies were to lose a leg, but if their owners requested leniency (as owners were inclined to do in order to preserve the slave's ability to work), the punishment was reduced to 150 lashes and the loss of both ears; (6) slaves who did not report conspiracy plans they knew of were to be branded on their foreheads and receive 100 lashes; (7) Free Negroes who harbored slaves or thieves or were in any way involved in runaway plots were to be flogged, deprived of their property, and sold into slavery; (8) Informants of any plots were to be given cash awards and their secrecy would be protected.

The 1733 laws also repeated ordinances that had already been proclaimed in 1684, such as forbidding the enslaved from carrying knives and sticks, from practicing witchcraft, and from dancing and feasting to African drum music. No wonder that some of St. John's enslaved Africans had decided to rebel! However, the subsequent official Danish investigation of the rebellion reported that only 14% of the enslaved had taken active roles in the uprising, not surprising based on the harshness of the publicized punishments.[9]

The Moravians' greatest statement of racial equality was made in 1738, when one of the white missionaries on St. Thomas married a free mulatto woman who had become a faithful Moravian convert. All three—the missionary who had performed the wedding, the missionary groom, and the bride—were imprisoned at Fort Christian in St. Thomas. The marriage, in the opinion of many local Whites, supported their view that the Moravians were fanatics and, even worse, were planning a social revolution. The marriage was declared invalid and the white husband was sentenced to be sold as a slave. However, they were all released in January 1739 due to a visit to St. Thomas by the Moravian leader, Count Zinzendorf, and the influence he possessed as a relative of the Danish royal family.[10]

Even Zinzendorf, however, could not completely escape the wrath of the Whites in their displeasure with the acts of the Moravian missionaries. He and some slaves who were following him were attacked one night in February 1739 by an armed mob of Whites who also proceeded to destroy the furnishings in the Moravian mission house. The white planters shortly after sent the Governor a memorandum expressing their fears that if the Moravians were allowed to continue "to spread their harmful doctrine … our slaves might revolt against us and murder us."[11] But Zinzendorf, on his arrival back in Europe, went to Copenhagen to plead for protection for the missionaries, who had been experiencing various attacks of violence. He also presented to the Danish King a petition from some of the Blacks. The King ordered, in August 1739, that the Danish West India and Guinea Company should give liberty and protection to the Moravian missionaries as long as their activities stayed within the limits of the law.[12]

In their efforts to minister to the slaves, the Moravian missionaries purposely learned the Negro Dutch Creole, which by the 1730s had become the mother tongue of the enslaved on St. Thomas. It had only been a spoken language, but in order to be able to teach the reading and writing of the Gospel, the missionaries ended up creating a written version of the language. By 1740 they were translating German and Dutch hymns into the Creole for the enslaved, and in the 1760s published a Creole hymnal, which also contained prayers and the liturgical services for baptism and communion.[13]

Unexpected Results of the Moravian Mission

An unexpected result was also taking place. The behavior of Moravian converts became so impressive that both the planters and government officials ended up realizing that their interests were enhanced by the work of the missionaries. Enslaved Moravians had become noticeably more industrious and obedient, and not as inclined to react to their bondage by running away or violence. By the 1750s, therefore, the extension of religion to the Africans was viewed by the white community on St. Thomas with great favor.[14]

As a result, the established Lutheran Church finally decided to work arduously with the enslaved Africans, and two Lutheran missionaries arrived in St. Thomas in 1757 to initiate the work. It proceeded very slowly as the missionaries were using Danish, which was not the language of the Africans. On realizing that their success would be dependent on their use of the Negro Dutch Creole, the Lutherans endeavored to learn it and started preparing translations of religious and other instructional materials for publication. With the patronage of the Danish government, in the 1770s several books were published in Copenhagen for use in St. Thomas and the other two islands. They included "Luther's Small Catechism," two A-B-C books, a hymnal, and a "Grammar of the Creole Language." Then in 1781, a New Testament in Creole was published and hundreds of copies were sold in the islands. Thus, in the latter half of the eighteenth century, enslaved Africans in St. Thomas and the two other Danish West Indian islands were being taught by white missionaries to read and write as part of their religious training.[15]

In 1787 an interesting development in educational history took place. An ordinance in Denmark mandated the first public schools for black children, both free and enslaved. That was forty years after the first school for white children on St. Thomas had been established by the Dutch Reformed Church. A school for the Blacks was established in the town area of St. Thomas and, as specified in the ordinance, had a free black schoolmaster chosen from the Lutheran mission congregation, and was jointly supervised by the Government and the Lutheran Church. Children of free parents were expected to pay a small monthly fee, and enslaved parents who were able could volunteer to pay for their children. A revealing comment on the inability of Europeans who were unacquainted with slavery to understand its effects is the fact that the instructions from Denmark, in stating that enslaved parents could volunteer to pay, referred to "wealthy slave parents."[16]

It is not possible to assess with accuracy the overall effect of the missionary and educational efforts on the black population of St. Thomas during the 1700s. There is evidence that great discrepancies existed between the printed law and actual practices. The research of historian Neville Hall does not support the claims of scholars Eva Lawaetz and Jens Larsen that the school which was opened in St. Thomas for Blacks was supported by public funds. Its reliance on mission collections must have greatly restricted its effectiveness.[17] Nevertheless, some available statistics suggest that a substantial percentage of Blacks did become literate. The Moravian missionary historian Christian G. A. Oldendorp, who lived on St. Thomas during the late 1760s, recorded that from the arrival of the first missionaries in the 1730s up to 1760, a total of 1,249 Moravian black converts had been baptized on St. Thomas.[18] That number represented about one-third of the enslaved population in St. Thomas. If the Moravian missionaries adhered in most cases to their principle of allowing baptism only to those who could practice their faith by reading the Gospel, it would appear that the enslaved black population on St. Thomas, from the mid-eighteenth century, must have consisted of a substantial percentage of literate persons.

The work of the Lutheran missionaries in the second half of the century, plus the publication of books in the Negro Dutch Creole, further increased the literacy of the Blacks. In 1800 the Lutheran mission congregation in St. Thomas numbered about 1,000 — half free and half enslaved, and many were receiving the same instructions the Moravians offered. Thus St. Thomas must have led the West Indies and other slave societies of the Americas at that time in its degree of literacy.[19]

Contradictory Aspects of Slavery in Early St. Thomas

One wonders how a slave-based European colony was willing to allow the development of a fairly literate slave population. There are three explanations. One was the influence and role played by the religious and humane concerns of the Danish royal family, which supported the Moravian mission. A second was that the products of Moravian persistence truly convinced the Whites that it was to their benefit to have a devout, Bible-reading slave population. The third and greatest was that the Africans' literacy was limited to their own peculiar language — the Negro Dutch Creole. Thus, the only reading materials they could utilize were those especially prepared for them and, under those circumstances, the usual fears of slave owners regarding slave access to seditious or revolutionary literature did not apply.

In spite of their unusual literary endeavors and results, the Moravian and Lutheran denominations in eighteenth century St. Thomas were characterized by racial separation. Based on the terms by which the Danish King had agreed to permit their mission to St. Thomas, the Moravians could not attempt to convert persons of any other Christian denomination, meaning Whites. Thus, except for the missionaries themselves, the Moravian congregations were all black. The Lutheran Church, after it began proselyting among Blacks, maintained two separate congregations — the mission congregation was all black and conducted in the Dutch Creole, while the white congregation had its service in Danish. On orders issued by church authorities in Copenhagen in 1771, the Lutheran black congregation was not allowed to use regular choir robes nor could their officiants use regular ministerial vestments. The missionaries were directed not to have "anything to do with marriage relations of the slaves, either to betroth or marry them."[20] The black and white Lutheran congregations were not joined until the 1850s, several years after slavery had ended. During the decade prior to that, however, other denominations such as the Dutch Reformed and the Roman Catholic were racially integrated, though sitting in separate pews was the common practice.[21]

Racial intermarriage was forbidden, as already illustrated by the prosecution of the Moravian missionary and his mulatto bride in 1738. However, half a century later, in the 1780s, Thomas de Malleville, a Dane who had been born on St. Thomas, became the Commandant of St. Thomas — the highest governmental official on that island — and found himself in a similar position. He was guilty of two great socio-political crimes — he was a Moravian convert and he had fallen in love with a mulatto Moravian woman he wished to marry. The first was easy to hide; he simply did not publicly admit his new faith for years. However, as he could not legally marry his desired partner, they lived in a common-law relationship and parented four children, whom he sent to a Moravian school in Denmark to spare them the racism of the separate schools in St. Thomas.[22]

Interestingly, de Malleville, who was originally a member of the Dutch Reformed Church, had been converted to the Moravian faith in a most unusual way — by a former slave named Cornelius with whom he had developed a close friendship. Cornelius had been able to purchase the freedom of his wife, himself, and their six children due to his skills, and was a person whose great intellectuality permitted him to transcend some of the prevailing boundaries of race relations. He was known for his architectural and construction skills and was an eloquent speaker with the ability to speak, read and write five languages — not only the Dutch Creole, but also Dutch, Danish, German and English. Cornelius thus became the highest ranking black leader of Moravian activities in the Danish West Indies, and was very much respected by a number of prominent Whites.[23]

In the 1780s de Malleville sought the aid of the Moravian Church in his desire to enter into legal marriage. On his behalf, a high-ranking Moravian official from Germany posed this question to the Danish West Indies Government: "Was a white person allowed to marry a colored person belonging to the Moravian congregation?" The official response from the Government was:

> It happens, although seldom, that a religious white man wants to marry a baptized negro woman, because he thinks it will be easier for him to consult with her than with a nonreligious white person. In such cases it ought to be considered, if such a connection should be completely forbidden. But as the laws of the country prohibit that a white man marry a Negro or Mulatto woman—whether slave or Free—according to the rites of the congregation, then the children from such a marriage could never be considered legitimate neither are they allowed to have their father's name. Consequently under these circumstances it can only be expected that the man sooner or later leave his Negro or Mulatto wife. Therefore it might be better to advise against such marriages as strongly as possible, and to prohibit them, if possible.[24]

De Malleville and his common-law wife thus never married. However, in 1796 he became the Governor General of the entire Danish West Indies, at which time he had to move to St. Croix, as Christiansted had become the capital of the Danish West Indies. He was the first and would be the only native-born Governor of the Danish West Indies. He then publicly confessed to being a Moravian convert, which greatly enhanced the status of the denomination. When he died in 1799, he was buried, based on his wishes, in accordance with the traditional Moravian burial service instead of the elaborate rites he merited as Governor General, and he became the first white person, except for the missionaries who had died in the islands, to be buried in a Moravian cemetery.[25]

De Malleville, however, embodied the contradictions that make black/white relations of his lifetime and other periods so difficult for many to understand. In spite of his willingness to become the first white lay member of the Moravian mission, his desire to marry his consort and his love for their children, he was a slave owner with a plantation at Estate Dorothea on St. Thomas and owned over eighty slaves. Moreover, he did not object to the slave trade, he did not favor the emancipation of enslaved Africans, and he was annoyed by the growing number of Free Blacks on St. Thomas.[26]

Similar contradictions were exhibited by some of the Moravian and Lutheran missionaries and other Christian denominations that admitted the injustice of

African enslavement during its existence in the Danish West Indies and else-where in the Western Hemisphere from the sixteenth through the nineteenth centuries. Their explanations have focused on the centrality of slavery to the economies and ways of life of the countries and colonies involved. The Mora-vians, for example, came to minister to and improve the lives of the enslaved Africans on St. Thomas at the urging of one who had been taken to serve in Denmark. The missionaries who valiantly undertook the challenge would prob-ably have denied vehemently and earnestly any suggestion that their mission would itself become a slave-holding enterprise, but that is just what happened.

The missionaries posited that the slave-holding development of their mis-sions came from their realistic realization that the entire political, social, and economic order of Danish colonization rested on slavery and its supplier, the slave trade. The Danish Crown, known for its religious support and benevo-lence in some areas, itself engaged in the slave trade and maintained planta-tions that were dependent on slave labor. The most influential persons and movers in the society were generally slaveholders, and profitable occupations unconnected with slavery were almost non-existent. The Moravian mission-aries to St. Thomas, after trying other avenues of making a living to support themselves and the mission, concluded that it would not have been possible for them to remain and to affect the lives of the enslaved if they did not have the income and the access to the slaves that only plantations afforded at that time. Thus, in 1737, five years after the first missionaries had arrived, new ones who had since arrived (missionaries suffered from a high death rate, as did many other settlers) were aided by a friendly planter to purchase an estate east of Charlotte Amalie that they named New Herrnhut (in honor of Herrn-hut, the name the Moravians gave to the settlement in Germany that Count Zinzendorf had granted them as a refuge). New Herrnhut was a large estate, with 800 enslaved Africans whom the missionaries figured they would proba-bly not have had access to if they did not own the estate. The missionaries de-cided to maximize their new situation by managing the estate in a humane manner, which they hoped would serve as an example to other plantation own-ers for better treatment of their slaves. They were very gratified when they began receiving requests from other plantation owners for extending their mis-sion work because of the "good" reputation that enslaved Moravians were ac-quiring. A second estate was acquired by the Moravians in 1771; it was west of Charlotte Amalie and named Nisky. In reports to their headquarters in Ger-many, the missionaries pointed with pride to their converts' progress in liter-acy and in their belief in the Gospel's promise of eternal life.[27]

Another result of the Moravian mission to the Danish West Indies was a study of the origins and varieties of the enslaved Africans. Even though the early records of the Danish colony spoke of the many different European peoples and languages, nothing similar was recorded for the Africans—neither in the Danish nor most other colonies. Apparently, such knowledge was unnecessary for the successful management of agricultural colonies. However, the Moravians, after more than three decades of work in the colony, wanted a formal assessment of their efforts and the changes they had brought about, and sent two Moravian missionaries to carry out that assignment. One was a teacher-missionary, Christian G. A. Oldendorp, who spent about one and one-half years (1767–1768) on the three Danish islands, learning as he much as he could about the enslaved and other local issues. Even though, in typical European thinking about Africans, he wrote of "the overwhelming ignorance of these people, together with their lack of ability to form their ideas properly and express them clearly," he recorded dutifully whatever he was able to find out about the Africans' geographical origins, governments, languages, and their moral and social systems. As best as he could figure, he thought they had come from almost thirty different African nations. Oldendorp's work was published in 1777, is considered an outstanding pioneer work in ethnography, and was translated into English by two UVI professors in 1987.[28]

St. Thomas never became a classic plantation society, characterized by many large plantations, with large numbers of enslaved workers producing sizeable amounts of one or a couple very profitable crops. That St. Thomas was not well suited for intense agricultural development became evident by the 1720s, just half a century after Danish colonization had begun, and it began to look toward trade. In 1724, the Danish West India and Guinea Company opened St. Thomas to trade with ships from all nations (except for the slave trade, which it retained for itself). However, neither the Company nor the Danish Crown (which assumed full control of the islands in 1754 by buying out and dissolving the Company) was consistent in allowing the promised free trade, thus St. Thomas's economy hardly benefitted during the rest of the century. Another step, however, that had been taken by the Company in search of economic improvement would prove to be a bonanza—the purchase of St. Croix from France in 1733.[29]

As hoped, the Danish West Indies underwent dramatic changes during the latter half of the eighteenth century due to the acquisition of St. Croix. St. Croix developed very rapidly under Danish rule, attracting settlers from other Caribbean colonies, many of whom were British, and also from St. Thomas and St. John, with planters from the latter who had suffered losses in the rebellion anxious to start anew elsewhere. St. Croix's agricultural growth was such that in two decades, by 1755, it had become the most profitable of the Danish West Indian islands, and Denmark designated the city of Christiansted on St. Croix as the new capital instead of Charlotte Amalie. Four decades later, by the mid-1790s, St. Croix was one of the top sugar producers in the Caribbean and had a total population of almost 29,000, of whom about 24,000 were enslaved, while St. Thomas' total population was about 5,000, with the enslaved comprising about 4,000.[30] These figures show that St. Thomas' population hardly grew during most of the eighteenth century, and indicate why, not having served in a fully developed plantation society, most of the enslaved on St. Thomas probably did not experience the harshest elements of slavery for which plantation societies were known. That is often cited as a possible reason why, contrary to St. John and St. Croix, no slave rebellion ever took place on St. Thomas.

The transfer of the Danish West Indies, however, from the rule of the founding company to the Danish Crown in 1754, did bring some legal changes in the relations between Blacks and Whites. A new law regulating slave conditions was passed in Copenhagen in 1755, placing restrictions on owners that had not existed before. Previously, owners had been free to punish their slaves as they saw fit and, if death occurred, it was considered mainly as a loss for the master. The new law prohibited the killing of a slave by an owner, and torturing or maiming of a slave by an owner could result in the loss of the slave. Owners were also prohibited from forcing slaves to marry, but neither could slaves get married without the consent of their owners. Married slaves were not to be separated, and neither could young children be separated from their parents. However, the prohibition against separating married couples, instead of strengthening marriage, actually decreased its occurrence, as many owners would not grant permission, for fear it might interfere with their future desires to sell slaves.[31]

Other changes contained in the laws of 1755 required that masters feed slaves properly, provide them with sufficient clothing, and be responsible for the care of old and sick slaves. As was already in practical effect, the Crown encouraged religion among slaves and allowed missionaries to preach on the estates. Historian Neville Hall, however, revealed that most of the new royal code was unenforced as the first royal governor was given the authority to promulgate it at his discretion, and he chose not to do so. Thus, the terrible laws that had inspired the St. John rebellion of 1733 remained in effect officially until the early nineteenth century, even though by the last decade of the 1700s the most brutal provisions were generally no longer employed.[32] However, that was probably very little consolation for the suffering enslaved!

Notes

1. J. Antonio Jarvis, *Brief History of the Virgin Islands (St. Thomas: The Art Shop, 1938)*, p. 35.

2. Larsen, *Virgin Islands Story, p. 18;* Westergaard, *The Danish West Indies Under Company Rule*, p. 40.

3. J. Antonio Jarvis, *Brief History of the Virgin Islands*, p. 34.

4. Isaac Dookhan, *A History of the Virgin Islands of the United States* (Epping, Essex, England: Caribbean Universities Press in association with the Bowker Publishing Company for the College of the Virgin Islands, 1974; reprinted in 1994 by Canoe Press of the University of the West Indies, Kingston, Jamaica), p. 61.

5. Frank Tannenbaum, *Slave and Citizen: The Negro in the Americas* (New York: Alfred A. Knopf, 1947), pp. 63–64, 82–84.

6. John P. Knox, *A Historical Account of St. Thomas, W.I.* (New York: Charles Scribner, 1852; reprinted in 1966 by the College of the Virgin Islands, St. Thomas), p.65; Westergaard, *The Danish West Indies Under Company Rule*, p. 161.

7. Eva Lawaetz, *Black Education in the Danish West Indies from 1732 to 1853: The Pioneering Efforts of the Moravian Brethren* (St. Croix, U.S. Virgin Islands: St. Croix Friends of Denmark Society, 1980), p. 22; G. Oliver Maynard, *A History of the Moravian Church: Eastern West Indies Province* (Port-of-Spain, Trinidad: Yuille's Printeries Limited, 1968), pp. 5–6.

8. Dookhan, *A History of the Virgin Islands of the United States*, pp. 186–187.

9. Lawaetz, *Black Education in the Danish West Indies*, p. 22; Knox, *A Historical Account of St. Thomas, W.I.*, p. 147.

10. Lawaetz, *Black Education in the Danish West Indies*, p. 16.

11. Larsen, *Virgin Islands Story*, pp. 67–68.

12. Knox, *A Historical Account of St. Thomas, W.I.*, pp. 150–151.

13. Lawaetz, *Black Education in the Danish West Indies*, p. 58.

14. Dookhan, *A History of the Virgin Islands of the United States*, p. 191.

15. Lawaetz, *Black Education in the Danish West Indies*, pp. 43–45; Larsen, *Virgin Islands Story*, pp. 112–117.

16. Lawaetz, *Black Education in the Danish West Indies*, pp. 24–28; Larsen, *Virgin Islands Story*, pp. 97–98.

17. Neville A.T. Hall, "Establishing a Public Elementary School for Slaves in the Danish Virgin Islands, 1732–1846," (Paper delivered at the Tenth Conference of Caribbean Historians, St. Thomas, V.I., March, 1978), pp. 5–7, ii.

18. Figures cited in Lawaetz, *Black Education in the Danish West Indies*, p. 20.

19. Larsen, *Virgin Islands Story*, p. 137; Lawaetz, *Black Education in the Danish West Indies*, p. 45.

20. *Larsen,* Virgin Islands Story, pp. 87–88.

21. Ibid., pp. 200–201.

22. The Commandant was then the highest official on St. Thomas because, after the acquisition of the islands by the Danish Crown in 1754, the seat of government was transferred to St. Croix from St. Thomas. The Governor-General thus lived in St. Croix and the second highest official of the islands was the Commandant of St. Thomas.; Lawaetz, *Black Education in the Danish West Indies*, pp. 48–53; Dookhan, *A History of the Virgin Islands of the United States*, p. 192.

23. Dookhan, *A History of the Virgin Islands of the United States*, pp. 196–197; G. Oliver Maynard, *A History of the Moravian Church: Eastern West Indies Province*, p. 12.

24. Quoted in Lawaetz, *Black Education in the Danish West Indies*, p. 53.

25. Lawaetz, *Black Education in the Danish West Indies*, p. 54.

26. Lawaetz, *Black Education in the Danish West Indies*, p. 51; Neville A. T. Hall, "Slavery in Three Danish West Indian Towns: Christiansted, Fredericksted and Charlotte Amalie in the Late Eighteenth and Early Nineteenth Century" (Mimeographed, [1980]), p. 14.

27. G. Oliver Maynard, *A History of the Moravian Church: Eastern West Indies Province*, pp. 8–9.

28. C. G. A. Oldendorp, *A Caribbean Mission*. Ann Arbor: Karoma Publishers, Inc., 1987. (Edited by John Jakob Bossard. English edition and translation by Arnold R. Highfied and Vladimir Barac.) *See* "Translators' Introduction," pp. xvii–xxix; the quotation is on p. 159.

29. Dookhan, *A History of the Virgin Islands of the United States*, pp. 44, 66.

30. Dookhan, *A History of the Virgin Islands of the United States*, pp. 79–82, 148; Marilyn F. Krigger, "A Quarter-Century of Race Relations in the U.S. Virgin Islands: St. Thomas, 1950–1975" (unpublished Ph.D. Dissertation, University of Delaware, 1983), pp. 449–450.

31. Neville Hall, "Slave Laws of the Danish Virgin Islands in the Later Eighteenth Century," in Vera Rubin and Arthur Tuden, editors, *Comparative Perspectives on Slavery in New World Plantation Societies* (New York: New York Academy of Sciences, 1977), pp. 178–181.

32. Ibid.

Chapter 4

Free Blacks and Free Trade in St. Thomian Slave Society

The economic sugar boom St. Croix experienced in the latter half of the eighteenth century was paralleled by St. Thomas's commerce boom in the first half of the nineteenth; its population grew from about 5,000 in the 1790s to 14,000 in 1835. The fastest growing group was a special class of persons of African descent—the Free Blacks. And it may be that, most realistically, the most prudent way of assessing race relations in a slave society is looking at the relations between the two groups of free persons, Free Blacks and Whites. For slaves were legally just chattel or simply the "money of their owners," the description used in the 1733 laws that had contributed to the St. John rebellion.[1] Thus, it may be too unrealistic to expect any semblance of "normal human relations" between free persons and persons who were legally nothing more than their property or "money" in human form.

The Growth of Free Blacks in St. Thomas

From the first decades of Danish colonization, St. Thomas had begun to acquire what would eventually become a sizeable population of racially mixed persons, referred to as "colored." The European parent of such persons was almost always the father, while the mothers, at least of the first generation of coloreds, were enslaved Africans. A number obtained freedom as a special gift from their fathers, or became able to purchase their freedom due to special advantages they enjoyed because of their partially white ancestry. As time went by, their numbers increased substantially as more were added by the original method and as the offspring of free colored women augmented the group.

Old Danish Bank on southwestern corner of the market square. Courtesy of the Virgin Islands Government's Archival Collection at the Charles W. Turnbull Regional Library.

There was another class of free non-white persons, generally referred to as Free Negroes. They were persons, usually of full African ancestry, who had obtained freedom in various ways—as gifts or rewards for special deeds, by purchase, or through manumission at the death of their masters. As time passed, some acquired varying degrees of racial admixture. As used in the Danish West Indies, "Negro" was reserved for persons of all or predominantly African ancestry; "colored" referred to mulattoes or other light-complexioned persons of obviously mixed ancestry. The combination "Free Colored," however, was often used collectively to include all free persons with any non-white ancestry.[2]

Free Blacks, including the "Negroes" and the "Coloreds," increased rapidly in the early nineteenth century. By 1835 they comprised the most numerous segment of St. Thomas's population of 14,000, which consisted of approximately 2,500 Whites, 5,000 enslaved, and 6,500 Free Blacks.[3] The Free Blacks accounted for 45% of the population, and their large number was due to the overwhelmingly commercial nature of St. Thomas' economy. By the 1820s it was the foremost trade and shipping center of the West Indies. The movement of former estate owners to the port town of Charlotte Amalie had decreased their need for slaves, and various opportunities in the town had enabled many of the enslaved to accumulate enough to purchase their freedom. Thus, in contrast to most other slave societies of the time, in St. Thomas the enslaved Blacks were outnumbered by the Free Blacks.

Relationships of Free Blacks and Whites

The relationships between Whites and Free Blacks during the slavery era in St. Thomas were marked by two contradictory tendencies. On one hand, there was a determined effort by Whites to ensure that persons with any degree of African ancestry would not enjoy the full degree of liberties and economic well-being available to persons of pure European descent. Little was left to chance: between 1747 and the 1830s there were more than thirty decrees in regard to the Free Colored. In addition to the ever-present threat of the loss of liberty for various forms of cooperation with enslaved persons and the requirement of special respect to white persons, they were forbidden to have land holdings in certain areas and restricted from a number of professions and trades. An ordinance in 1786 no longer permitted them to wear lace, silk stockings, or jewelry of gold, silver, or precious stones. Free black men were compelled to hunt runaway slaves and, from 1776, all free non-white persons were required to obtain from the Governor General and carry with them at all times a "letter of freedom." Failure to secure the letter meant banishment from the colony or sale into slavery.[4]

These degradations and limitations notwithstanding, Free Coloreds and Negroes were very proud of their status and zealously protected it. Considering the ever-present threatened alternative, otherwise could not realistically be expected. There was thus the desired or willing participation of many of the colored women in cohabitating relationships with white men. These relationships provided them with economic security, no small consideration in a system that limited these women to domestic or other meagerly-rewarded occupations, Moreover, they made possible the production of offspring who would be "whiter" than their mothers, and thus eligible for greater social and economic opportunities than offspring of black fathers. Such relationships were thus insurance for both a woman and her children.

For white men, interracial cohabitation was the natural solution in a society where they greatly outnumbered white women, as a result of regular migration patterns and also of the custom of many government officials and soldiers to leave their wives and children at home in Europe, which was considered to have better standards of living and educational facilities for children. Interracial cohabitation, therefore, was practiced from the highest levels of white officialdom downward, as already illustrated by the case of Commandant, then Governor General de Malleville. It formed the other—the contradictory tendency—in the maintenance of an uncrossable line and an unassailable white superiority over Blacks, even the free ones. The ban on intermarriage served to ensure that universal human sentiments would not surmount the legal constraints.

Except in cases where behavior was clearly recorded, as in diaries or trave-logues, it is somewhat difficult to gauge what may have been the day-to-day social relationships in a slave society between Whites and Blacks, both the free and the enslaved. On plantations that had a sizeable number of slaves, close contacts and conversations were probably quite minimal between the two races, except for those Blacks who were house slaves or had positions such as coach drivers which involved frequent contact with Whites. On the other hand, St. Thomas's "Golden Days" as a trade emporium, from 1820 to the 1850s, led to the ascendance in its economy of shipping and trading. The harbor of Char-lotte Amalie was always filled with ships, as over 2,000 ships visited each year, laden with passengers, goods, mail, and agents from the United States, Den-mark, France, England, and other countries. Similarly, purchasers came from throughout the Caribbean and Latin America to take needed merchandise, mail, and passengers in transit back to their islands or countries of destina-tion. The main street of Charlotte Amalie and the alleyways leading from the shore to the street were thus lined with stores, warehouses, and the offices of shipping, banking, and insurance agents.[5]

With the plantations failing, many planters willingly made agreements with businessmen in the town for the employment of some of their slaves. Thus, many enslaved males moved to Charlotte Amalie and became seamen, cargo handlers, porters, and building tradesmen. The opportunities in the town to make extra money allowed many to them to save and purchase their freedom from their masters, thus becoming regularly paid employees. Many enslaved females likewise became house servants, cooks, and nannies in town homes, then later moved on to independent careers as laundresses, seamstresses, food vendors, or bakers for the town's population.[6]

The Childhood World of the Fathers of Impressionism and Pan-Africanism

In urban circumstances, race relations were often characterized by greater social interaction, informality and camaraderie than existed in the plantation or agricultural setting. In fact, from the late eighteenth century, government officials had found it necessary to legislate against both Whites and the en-slaved in the town areas attending dances and other similar activities held by Free Blacks.[7] Charlotte Amalie became known for its variety of social rela-tionships, and some of the racial interactions during St. Thomas's "Golden Days" are illustrated by the early history of two St. Thomas-born youngsters who both became world famous in later life. One was Camille Pissarro, born in St. Thomas in 1830 on Main Street, where his Jewish parents owned one of the town's many stores. As was typical, the family lived in the second story of the building, while their store was on the street level. Due to differences between the local Jewish congregation and herself, Camille's mother decided not to have him schooled with the other Jewish children, but sent Camille and his siblings to the Moravian Town School, where they were the only white students. The school was a new elementary school, established by the Moravians in the early 1840s to cater to their members who had moved to the town. It was located on the street directly north of Main Street (now known popularly as Back Street), thus only a short walk from the Pissarro home and store. It must have been quite an interesting experience for young Camille, and his family's biographical novelist asserts that his school years influenced him to be sympathetic to those who were not highly considered in society. Years later Camille Pissarro relocated to France, where he would eventually become a world-renowned leader of the Impressionist art movement. Some of his early paintings included scenes of St. Thomas which featured black persons.[8]

The other "Golden Days" St. Thomian youngster, Edward Wilmot Blyden, was born in 1832, two years after Camille Pissarro. His parents were free Blacks, his father a tailor and his mother a teacher; his birthplace, the family home, was a few blocks north of Main Street, on a street called Long Path. The family worshipped at the Dutch Reformed Church, which had both black and white members, and was (still is) about halfway between Main Street and the Blyden residence. The Synagogue in St. Thomas was (still is) near to both the Reformed Church and the site of the Blyden family residence, and as the Jewish congregation on St. Thomas numbered about 400 at that time, many of whom lived in Charlotte Amalie and in the vicinity of the Synagogue, young Edward Blyden mixed freely with them. Many decades later, recalling his childhood on St. Thomas, he wrote:

> For years, the next door neighbors of my parents were Jews. I played with Jewish boys, and looked forward as eagerly as they did to the annual festivals and fasts of their Church. The Synagogue stood on the side of a hill; and, from a terrace immediately above it, we Christian boys who were interested could look down upon the mysterious assembly, which we did in breathless silence.[9]

Edward was intellectually gifted and also very interested in religion (as his quote above shows). Both qualities were recognized by his pastor, the Rev. John P. Knox, a white American, who thus became a special mentor to young Edward. When Edward had gotten as much education as was available on St. Thomas, Rev. Knox wrote to his alma mater, the Rutgers Theological College in New Jersey, to recommend Edward for studies for the ministry. Rev. Knox, apparently, had not mentioned that Edward was black, for which reason Edward was refused admission when he arrived at the college in 1850, even though he was accompanied by Mrs. Knox, the wife of the pastor. Edward tried staying in the United States, searching for an institution to admit him—to no avail. He also became afraid for his safety on realizing that, based on the Fugitive Slave Act of 1850, a number of innocent Blacks in northern United States were being falsely arrested, charged with being runaway slaves, and sent to slavery in the South. He therefore decided to go to Liberia to get the education he desired, which he did, and ended up having an outstanding career as an educator, linguist, diplomat, and author. Among the many positions he would hold were the Presidency of Liberia College and being the Liberian Ambassador to Great Britain. His efforts to educate persons of African descent throughout the world about their common heritage earned him the title of "Father of Pan-Africanism." Dr. Blyden and the Knox family corresponded for decades after he left St. Thomas.[10]

Notes

1. Poul Erik Olsen, "Slavery and the Law in the Danish West Indies," in Arnold R. Highfield & George F. Tyson, *Negotiating Enslavement: Perspectives on Slavery in the Danish west Indies* (St. Croix Virgin Islands: Antilles Press, 2009), p. 4.

2. Larsen, *Virgin Islands Story*, p. 162.

3. John Peter Nissen, *Reminiscences of a 46 Years' Residence in the Island of St. Thomas in the West Indies* (Nazareth, Pennsylvania: Senseman and Company, 1838), pp. 64, 75.

4. Larsen, *Virgin Islands Story*, pp. 163–65; Dookhan, *A History of the Virgin Islands of the United States*, pp. 144–146.

5. Dookhan, *A History of the Virgin Islands of the United States*, pp. 100–103.

6. Neville Hall, "Slaves' Use of Their Free Time in the Danish Virgin Islands in the Later Eighteenth and Early Nineteenth Century," in Hilary Beckles & Verene Shepherd, editors, *Caribbean Slave Society and Economy,* (Kingston, Jamaica: Ian Randle Publishers Ltd., 1991), pp. 335–343.

7. Ibid., pp. 338–343.

8. Axel Hansen. *From These Shores* (Nashville, Tennessee/St. Thomas, V.I.: Hansen and Francois, 1996), pp. 96–225; Hoffman, Alice. *The Marriage of Opposites.* (New York: Simon & Schuster, 2015), p. 365; Daily News (St. Thomas, V.I.), June 19, 2016, p. 1.

9. Quoted in Edward W. Blyden, *The Jewish Question* (Liverpool, England: Lionel Hart & Co., 1898, p. 5) in "A Black Nineteenth-Century Response to Jews and Zionism: The Case of Edward Wilmot Blyden, 1832–1912" by Hollis R. Lynch in Joseph R. Washington, Jr., ed., *Jews in Black Perspectives: A Dialogue* (London and Toronto: Associated University Presses, 1984), p. 42.

10. "Edward Wilmot Blyden" in Ruth Moolenaar, *Profiles of Outstanding Virgin Islanders, Third Edition (*St. Thomas: Department of Education, Government of the U.S. Virgin Islands, 1992), pp. 18–19; Hollis Lynch, *Edward Wilmot Blyden: Pan-Negro Patriot* (London: Oxford University Press, 1967).

Chapter 5

The Road to Emancipation

The perennial debate regarding which has the greater impact in bringing about profound historical changes—great men or the overall temper of their times—finds support for each in the characters of Peter von Scholten, the Governor-General of the Danish West Indies, and John "General Buddhoe" Gottlieb, the leader of the enslaved Africans on St. Croix, and in the course of race-related events in the West Indies and Europe during the first half of the nineteenth century. The facts of the Danish West Indies seem to argue for a synthesis of the impact of leaders and the temper of their times.

Peter von Scholten's History in the Danish West Indies

Peter von Scholten was born in Denmark in 1784 and arrived in St. Thomas in 1804 as a new lieutenant in the Danish army. His father, a career military man, had been stationed in St. Thomas for years and was the Commandant of St. Thomas when Peter arrived. Thus, the young von Scholten advanced rapidly from one position to another; by 1823 he was the Commandant of St. Thomas, and in 1827 he became the Governor-General of the Danish West Indies, a position he held for the next twenty-one years.

On becoming Governor-General, von Scholten moved to St. Croix, where the seat of government was located. In keeping with the local custom, von Scholten had a wife and children in Denmark, and they had lived with him in St. Thomas for only a few years in the 18-teens before returning to Denmark. Thus, following another prevalent custom, von Scholten enjoyed the company of local ladies. In 1828, one year after moving to St. Croix, he started living with a free colored woman of St. Croix, a relationship that lasted for the remaining twenty years of his Governorship. His consort was Anna Heegaard, the daughter of a free colored woman and a white official—a customs collector. Before von Scholten had moved to St. Croix and met Anna, who was then 38, five years younger than Peter, she had already lived with two white men, relationships that left her, along with an inheritance from her mother, a wealthy woman with property and slaves. She and von Scholten purchased a magnificent home in 1834, where they entertained openly, regularly, and lavishly. The maintenance and renovations of their manor were apparently very costly and evidence indicates that, on the basis of her expenditures, she became the main owner of it. As one example, there is a record of a loan of $4,000.00, which Anna made to von Scholten in the 1840s. Descriptions of their relationship agreed that they were deeply devoted to each other, that he had been known for his commitment to improving the status of Blacks even before meeting her, and that she probably augmented his commitment to her racial group.[1]

International and Danish Factors Promoting Change

What was the temper of the times? On January 1, 1803, Denmark became the first European nation to outlaw its slave trade. A royally appointed Danish Slave Trade Commission had declared the trade inhumane, costing not only African lives but also deadly for European crewmen and, most important, the trade was no longer economically profitable. Its great concern about economic profitability was shown by the substantial attention the Commission report paid to recommendations that all possible efforts should be made to ensure that the end of the trade would not lead to fewer slaves for the sugar industry in the Danish islands. Thus, it recommended government loans to enable planters to purchase as many slaves as possible before the trade ended, and it urged better treatment of the enslaved, especially the females, in order to enable higher slave birth rates.[2]

Within five years of the Danish decree, the two largest slave-trading nations—Great Britain and the United States—also officially ended their slave trades in 1808. And while those countries were being wracked by the debates attending the end of their slave trades, the first black nation in the Western Hemisphere—Haiti—came into existence on January 1, 1804, spawned by its great slave revolution of the previous decade. Never again could Whites in societies with large numbers of slaves rest assured that a similar fate might not overtake them. Slave societies throughout the Caribbean thus sought to institute various measures aimed at ameliorating the most oppressive aspects of the institution of slavery.[3]

By the early years of the nineteenth century, a number of Coloreds in the Danish West Indies, in common with Anna Heegaard, had become quite wealthy (limitations on land owning were no longer operative) and resented greatly the various restrictions they suffered. In 1816 they sent two members of their group to Copenhagen to present to the Crown a petition, signed by 331 free persons of color, which delineated the injustices of their position and asked for the same legal position as Whites. The Crown was stingingly ungracious; the delegates were sent back to the Islands with a rebuke for having undertaken the journey without the permission of the Islands' authorities. However, the mission revealed the seriousness of the Free Blacks' insistence on a change in their status.[4]

Throughout the 1820s debates raged in the British Parliament and England over the proposition to abolish slavery in the British Empire. The British Emancipation Act finally passed in 1833, six years after Peter von Scholten had become the head of the Danish West Indies, and took effect in August, 1834. Emancipation in the British Virgin Islands, which are near enough to be clearly visible from St. Thomas and St. John, created quite a problem for the local Danish West Indian authorities. The running away of slaves to the British islands was so great that in 1840 the von Scholten administration established naval patrolling of the narrow channel that separates St. John from the British island of Tortola.[5]

From early in his governorship, however, von Scholten had acted to bring about changes in the relations of the races in the society. He employed, for the first time, free colored persons in clerical positions with the government, and invited outstanding colored persons, again for the first time, to attend social functions at the Governor's home and on official occasions. Many of the planters and other Whites protested these departures from customary protocol, but von Scholten enjoyed the support of the King, who liked and trusted him.[6]

In April 1830 a royal ordinance, based on a plan von Scholten had submitted, granted a packet of new privileges to the Free Coloreds. The "letter of freedom" requirement was abolished. The Governor-General was granted the discretion to declare as "white" those colored persons who "assimilate in color to the whites, and they otherwise, by a cultivated mind and good conduct render themselves deserving to stand, according to their rank and station in life, on an equal footing with white inhabitants."[7] Thus, persons of African ancestry who were sufficiently light-colored and considered sufficiently accomplished in other important aspects, could have their categorization changed from colored to white. Being declared "white," therefore, was the only possible way to have equal status with Europeans!

An aspect of the Ordinance of 1830 which limited its success was an elaborate plan for the division of the Free Coloreds into classes. The first class, which was further subdivided into three divisions, was to be comprised of the most accomplished persons of color, who were to receive from the Government and wear silver cockades as marks of distinction. The first division of this class would be entitled to receive licenses to engage in trade. Members of the second class, comprising all other Free Coloreds, were simply to receive certificates, which really did not make any substantial differences in their status. These divisions aroused so much dissatisfaction that the King in 1832 requested von Scholten to make additional proposals for amending the status of the Free Coloreds. Von Scholten, on submitting his proposal, stated:

> ... many of the free colored now stand on the same cultural level as the middle class of Europe, wherefore the old colonial decisions regarding difference based upon color ought legally to be abolished for all those who were free by April 10, 1830.[8]

The King accepted von Scholten's proposal, and on April 18, 1834, a new royal ordinance cancelled all previous restrictions and qualifications and proclaimed full equality from that date between Whites and Free Coloreds. For persons of color who would obtain freedom after the date of the ordinance, a reference to the enslaved, there was to be a three-year waiting period before the attainment of full equality.[9] With this measure the Free Coloreds achieved the undifferentiated legal recognition they had long been seeking. Complete acceptance by the Whites was, of course, quite another matter.

In another royal decree of 1834, again proposed by von Scholten, the enslaved received certain long-sought benefits. It was mandated that they could not be denied the right to buy their freedom if they so desired and were economically able, and that they could change owners if maltreatment occurred. They were also permitted full control of their earnings and possessions, and no longer could be required to work on Sundays. Additionally, it was forbidden to assign pregnant slaves to hard labor.[10]

The next result of von Scholten's humanitarianism occurred in education. The school ordinance of 1787 which had instituted public education for black children did not mandate attendance and applied only to the town area. Thus, children who lived on plantations or in rural areas or had masters or parents not interested in education, received no schooling. Von Scholten thought that enslaved children should be prepared for eventual freedom, and the Country School Ordinance of 1839 established free and compulsory education in the Danish West Indies for all children, free and enslaved, aged six through thirteen. Compulsory education already existed for white children and almost all free colored children were already in school, public or private. Thus the law was meant specifically to grant education to enslaved children, particularly those in rural areas. By prior agreement with the Moravian authorities in Germany, the new schools were to be staffed by Moravian missionaries, as there was already a large group of them in the islands, thus eliminating the need for recruitment of new teachers. To encourage cooperation from the planters, who were required to furnish the building materials for the schools, regular hours were kept to a minimum—three hours from nine to twelve every weekday for children under nine. However, children from ages nine through twelve were considered old enough to work full-time for their masters in various capacities, so they had school only on Saturday mornings. Due to financial difficulties, the first country school in St. Thomas did not open until the mid-1840s. However, the Danish ordinance was unique in New World slave societies for the establishment of compulsory free education for enslaved children.[11]

In 1834, inspired by emancipation that year in the British islands, von Scholten had proposed a plan for gradual emancipation in the Danish West Indies. It did not find favor with either the Danish government or the planters, and a similar plan from the King was again rejected by the planters in 1840. However, in the first half of the 1840s, there was increasing anti-slavery agitation in Denmark and other parts of Europe. And in the Danish West Indies, two influential religious denominations at last freed their slaves—the Moravian Church in 1844 and the Lutheran Church in 1845.[12]

Finally, the Danish Government decided to begin changing the status of the "unfree"—the euphemistic term by which the enslaved in the Danish islands were then officially called. On the occasion of the Queen's birthday, July 28, 1847, King Christian VIII issued a decree which stipulated that

> "… the right of possession by the owners of the unfree … shall cease after twelve years from the date of this proclamation, and henceforth, from date, all children shall be born free."[13]

The Crown thus tried to meet the conflicting demands that were being made: for the abolitionists, freedom was granted immediately to newborns, with the employment of a twelve-year delay to the already enslaved; for their benefit, the planters received a dozen years to make the necessary economic adjustments. The year 1859 was thus scheduled to be a historic year in the Danish West Indies.

The St. Croix Events and Persons That Brought about Emancipation

Von Scholten did not like the decree, thinking that twelve years was too long a wait to impose on the enslaved; they themselves expressed great dissatisfaction with the decree. A little less than a year later, on Sunday night, July 2, 1848, a rebellion of the enslaved, that apparently had been very well planned, began on the estates of western St. Croix. Its main leader, John "General Buddhoe" Gottlieb was known to be committed to ending slavery, but without violence or bloodshed. However, many of the long-suffering enslaved made it clear that their status would simply no longer be tolerated. Early the next morning, Monday, July 3, thousands of slaves from various estates in the west marched to the town of Frederiksted on St. Croix's western coast, went to the fort there, and demanded their freedom. The Whites, some of whom retreated to boats in Frederiksted's harbor while others barricaded themselves at home, waited anxiously for government action to suppress the rebellion.

Governor-General von Scholten had been on an official visit to St. Thomas and had just returned to Christiansted that Sunday night, only to receive the news a few hours later—in the middle of the night—of the rebellion's outbreak on the western area of St. Croix. From then on, during the remainder of the night and throughout the morning, he and other officials who had gathered at Government House assessed the reports being received, including some of violent attacks on the homes of certain hated white officials. He and an entourage left at midday for Frederiksted, 15 miles away, and arrived there about 4 p.m. As soon as they arrived at the fort, where several thousands of enslaved persons were waiting, von Scholten proclaimed to them that they were free. An official proclamation which was printed, in Danish and English, and distributed later that night began: "All unfree in the Danish West Indies are from today emancipated."[14] Thus did slavery in the Danish West Indies end on July 3, 1848, due to the courageous acts of enslaved Africans on St. Croix, after 176 years of continuous existence on St. Thomas and an exceedingly prosperous tenure on St. Croix.

(Consequently, in the U.S. Virgin Islands today, as a result of their acquisition by the United States, there are two very special consecutive holidays every year in early July: V.I. Emancipation Day on July 3rd and U.S. Independence Day on July 4th.)

Many of the Whites in St. Croix were extremely angry at von Scholten, charging that his action was in contradiction of the King's decree and thus exceeded his authority; that he had acted against the safety and economic interests of the Whites; and even that he had known of or been involved in the planning of the rebellion. The disorder in St. Croix that followed the emancipation and the abuse that the Whites heaped on von Scholten apparently affectedly him greatly; he resigned his position on July 6 and left for Denmark on July 14. In Denmark he was tried and found guilty in 1851 of dereliction of duty for not using military force to suppress the rebellion. However, he appealed to the Danish High Court, which unanimously acquitted him in 1852, ruling that his actions were in the general welfare of the colony.[15]

General Buddhoe, on the other hand, fared much worse! Because of his efforts to curb violence after the emancipation, he was not killed but imprisoned and then placed on a ship and exiled to Trinidad. There were later reports of him being sighted there, or on other West Indian islands or New York City, but none was ever verified.[16]

Some planters had asked the Danish Government to rescind the emancipation proclamation, but instead Denmark wisely confirmed it. However, as the planters had also requested, Denmark compensated the former slave owners in 1853 (fifty dollars for each slave they had owned). No similar provision was made for those whose physical labor had generated the prosperity of the slave owners and the colony. Von Scholten died in 1854, without seeing the islands or Anna again.[17]

Postscript

Anna Heegaard died five years after von Scholten, in 1859, in the home they had shared and owned together. However, she "lives on" in Denmark. She herself had no children, but had a sister who did. Her sister's descendants in Denmark are very proud of their "mixed" heritage, to the degree that one of Anna's great nephews (about six generations from Anna) decided in the early 1970s to come to the College of the Virgin Islands for a part of his college education. Thus, this author had the pleasure of teaching Virgin Islands history to Jens Willumsen in St. Thomas at that time.

On Jens' return to Denmark, he earned a doctorate in the agricultural sciences, and worked as a professional in that area until he retired. We have kept in touch, and Jens and his family are very active in the Danish West Indian Society in Denmark, whose members visit the Virgin Islands every few years and attended this year's Transfer Centennial ceremonies. A similar organization in the Virgin Islands, known as the Friends of Denmark Society, and whose membership includes descendants of Danes who once lived in the Virgin Islands and other interested Virgin Islanders, maintains similar ties with Denmark and also visits there every few years.

Notes

1. Neville A. T. Hall, "Anna Heegaard—Enigma," *Caribbean Quarterly*, Vol. 22, nos. 2 and 3 (June–September, 1976), pp. 62–73; Betty Van Toil, "Anna Heegaard and her Role in the Emancipation" in *Freedom's Flame* (The Bureau of Libraries, Government of the U.S. Virgin Islands, 1981), pp 106–112.

2. The chief reasons for Denmark's official prohibition of slave trafficking appear to be that it was not considered economically profitable and the expectation that England was about to terminate its slave trade, with which the Danish trade was intertwined. See Svend E. Green-Pedersen, "The Scope and Structure of the Danish Negro Slave Trade," *The Scandinavian Economic History Review*, Vol. 19, No. 2 (1971), pp. 176–177.

3. Parry and Sherlock, *A Short History of the West Indies*, pp. 182–183.

4. Neville A. T. Hall, "The 1816 Freedmen Petition in the Danish West Indies: Its Background and Consequences," (Paper presented at the Eleventh Annual Conference of Caribbean Historians, Curacao, Netherlands Antilles, April, 1979), pp. 15–19.

5. Dookhan, *A History of the Virgin Islands of the United States*, p. 165.

6. Larsen, *Virgin Islands Story*, p. 165.

7. Quoted in Dookhan, *A History of the Virgin Islands of the United States*, p. 147.

8. Quoted in Larsen, *Virgin Islands Story*, p. 167.

9. Larsen, *Virgin Islands Story*, p. 167.

10. Dookhan, *A History of the Virgin Islands of the United States*, p. 158.

11. Lawaetz, *Black Education in the Danish West Indies*, pp. 24–30; Neville A. T. Hall, "Establishing a Public Elementary School System for Slaves in the Danish Virgin Islands 1733–1846," pp. 13–16.

12. Larsen, *Virgin Islands Story*, pp. 179–186.

13. Quoted in Larsen, *Virgin Islands Story*, p. 187.

14. Jarvis, *Brief History of the Virgin Islands*, p. 51; Svend E. Holsoe, "The 1848 St. Croix Slave Rebellion: The Day of the Rebellion," in Arnold R. Highfield & George F. Tyson, *Negotiating Enslavement: Perspectives on Slavery in the Danish West Indies* (St. Croix Virgin Islands: Antilles Press, 2009), pp. 191–209; *St. Thomas Source*—Internet Explorer, "Von Scholten's Mistress Played Important Role in Emancipation," February 20, 2016, pp. 1–3.

15. Dookhan, *A History of the Virgin Islands of the United States*, pp. 176–178. Larsen, *Virgin Islands Story*, pp. 188–191.

16. Svend E. Holsoe and George F. Tyson, "A Chronology of Slavery and Emancipation in the History of the Danish West Indies," in Arnold R. Highfield, editor, *Emancipation in the U. S. Virgin Islands*. St. Croix, U.S. Virgin Islands: Virgin Islands Humanities Council, 1999.

17. Dookhan, *A History of the Virgin Islands of the United States*, pp. 176–178.

Chapter 6

Emancipation to Transfer, 1848–1917

The news of the Emancipation Proclamation arrived by ship to St. Thomas and St. John on the following day, July 4, 1848. In St. Thomas it was first announced to the roll of drums in the square in Charlotte Amalie known today as the Emancipation Garden. Some of the newly freed Blacks followed the announcer as he moved from area to area with the announcement, celebrating their new status with music and dancing in the streets.

The Economic Effects of Emancipation on St. Thomas

Emancipation did not have an overwhelming economic effect on St. Thomas, as it had long turned from dependence on agriculture to being a trade emporium. However, The Rev. John Knox, Blyden's former pastor at the Dutch Reformed Church, and who had members who still owned estates in the country, wrote a history of St. Thomas in 1852 in which he stated that after emancipation the remaining estates on St. Thomas had a very hard time getting their laborers to work and were forced to employ stringent measures, including "constant use of the whipping post." Rev. Knox opined, though, that he considered such methods better than allowing the laborers to do as they wished. However, in spite of such measures, emancipation led shortly after to the end of commercial agriculture on St. Thomas. A Labor Act of 1849, which was a legislated effort of the Danish West Indian Government to ensure that former agricultural slaves remained on the plantations, was very effective on St. Croix for 30 years as non-agricultural means of employment were hardly available there. Thus, it took another very destructive rebellion on St. Croix in 1878 to end the Labor Act. But the former agricultural workers on St. Thomas left the estates and were able to find work in the bustling trading and shipping activities of Charlotte Amalie and its harbor.[1]

St. Thomas continued to experience substantial prosperity for almost two decades after emancipation. However, by the mid-1860s, St. Thomas was undergoing economic decline. That was due to the fact that its earlier prosperity had been based on being the main trading and meeting center in the West Indies for sailing ships, with the tons of goods and mail brought to St. Thomas then being trans-shipped to other Caribbean islands and countries. However, by 1860 sail ships were being supplanted by steamships, whose power and speed made it easier for them to go to other ports, some of which were very actively encouraging their visits. As business on St. Thomas decreased and trading and shipping firms began to move away, Blacks were losing their jobs and finding themselves in want and misery.

Post-Emancipation "Descriptions" of Blacks and Whites in St. Thomas

The Rev. Knox and hotelier Dr. Charles Edwin Taylor, two Whites who lived on St. Thomas and authored books in the 1850s and 1880s respectively, wrote of the conditions of Blacks in St. Thomas and their relations with Whites in the latter half of the nineteenth century.[2] Both gentlemen appeared to have viewed the Whites as the only true or legitimate people of the island, for whose benefit everything was to be directed. Blacks were viewed as if they were present only to be a laboring class to furnish the economic base and services needed for the comfort of the Whites. Dr. Taylor frequently referred to the Whites on St. Thomas as West Indians or Creoles, but did not use those terms for Blacks, who were referred to by their race or economic condition. Neither author expressed the opinion that with the end of slavery, it became necessary to incorporate Blacks, who formed the majority of the population, into the social fabric in a more positive way.

Of course, the terms "lower order" or "humbler classes" that were used by Taylor to refer to the majority of Blacks were also used to describe the majority of persons in Europe and many other parts of the world in the nineteenth century, regardless of race. However, in St. Thomas and similar former slave societies, the singular fact of being a Caucasian elevated one to a position superordinate to the "humble classes" or "lower orders." One's standing in such communities, therefore, was not based on the socio-economic dis-

Saturday morning vendors and shoppers on Pollyberg and Bjerge Gade corner, to Kongens Gade (present "Education Street"). Courtesy of the Virgin Islands Government's Archival Collection at the Charles W. Turnbull Regional Library.

tinctions operative throughout the Western World, but mainly on one's racial categorization.

The Rev. Knox in 1851 catalogued the evils which he thought the institution of slavery had bequeathed to the community. First, in his estimation, was "the want of industry or ambition ... of the African race." He surmised that this had developed from the forced and unrelenting labor of enslavement, and said it had "entered into their very soul" and thus would persist for generations after slavery. The result, he said, was that only a "small proportion of our laboring classes, in town, are in active service," with the others choosing dependency on relatives rather than working. Another related evil he listed was the idea that labor was degrading, which he said was held not only by the former slaves but also by the "West Indian," apparently referring to Whites who had been locally-born, as he next proceeded to state that no one, white or black, wanted to be seen in the streets carrying even the smallest bag or package. He explained that even black working class men, if they could afford it, hired children to carry their tools to work for them.[3]

A third characteristic left by slavery that Knox discerned was "a love of dominion, a thirst of power, characterizing the lower classes. Such persons are the most exacting taskmasters, the most tyrannical husbands, the cruelest parents." He spoke of child abuse by Blacks as a serious problem. Knox reasoned that this resulted from a history of servitude in which one was unjustly dealt with, but having no redress, simply stored up feelings of revenge to be afflicted on whomever was weaker in power. Other perceived traits of Blacks which Knox related to slavery were: extravagance, particularly in dressing, with consequent destitution in sickness and old age, and licentiousness as evidenced in the high percentage of illegitimate births. Knox reported that three-fourths of all births were illegitimate, and lamented that they were not all "confined to the weak and ignorant; but we mourn to find those whose knowledge of duty should lead them to a better life."[4]

Knox's comments indicate that widely differing standards of behavior were sometimes utilized for Blacks and Whites. It is quite interesting, for example, while reading his criticism of the cruelty of Blacks, to realize that he was the same author who, several pages earlier, had voiced his approval of the whipping of grown persons to force them to continue as estate workers after emancipation. Apparently, in areas where the labor of Blacks was essential to the economy, tyrannical enforcement was a positive good. Knox also demonstrated that some Whites realized how deeply the slave experience had impacted negatively on the psyche, personality, and behavior of Blacks. However, any corresponding sense of white collective guilt or obligation for remediation was not apparent in his book.

Dr. Charles Edwin Taylor was originally from England but had been living in St. Thomas for two decades when he published a book in 1888 entitled *Leaflets from the Danish West Indies*. He claimed to be a physician and was so addressed, but the Danish Government refused to grant him a license based on Danish requirements. He thus had a varied career in St. Thomas as a bookstore proprietor, almanac editor, hotelier (Hotel 1829), and was also popular enough to be an elected member of the St. Thomas Colonial Council, the local legislature which had been instituted as a measure of political reform in the decades following the end of slavery.[5]

In describing life in St. Thomas three decades after Knox had done so, Taylor had some of the same concerns. He mentioned that a humane society had recently (1880s) been formed and "much good has been accomplished already among the lower order towards the prevention of cruelty to children." In discussing the biracial distaste toward manual work, he noted: "A lady (white) rarely goes out to shop as they do in Europe. It is easy to understand how dependent a lady must be upon her servants, if they do nearly all her marketing and shopping for her."[6]

Taylor, in general, tended to be less critical of the character of Blacks than was Rev. Knox. Careful reading of Taylor, however, shows that general white opinion of black industry and morality had hardly changed in the four decades since slavery had ended; Taylor was simply a man of much more liberal bent then Rev. Knox. Taylor wrote that domestic employees "as a rule are not much worse than elsewhere. They are civil and obliging when kindly treated, and very honest." He added, however, that the mistress often had "to act as a perpetual driver to get anything done properly."[7]

The employment by most white families of black women in domestic capacities such as house servants, cooks, and nursemaids tied a substantial portion of the white and black populations in relationships of personal dependence on each other. For many Blacks such employment was the means of livelihood for an entire family, and for that they were very grateful. Black men were also employed by Whites who owned or managed wholesale or retail businesses and the remaining harbor and shipping firms. Some Blacks were self-employed, but their businesses as produce vendors, fishermen, lottery vendors, or in the building or repair trades still made them partially dependent on white patronage. Almost all substantial governmental and professional positions were still occupied by Whites.

Taylor strongly championed one category of laborers who had not existed during Rev. Knox's service in St. Thomas—the coal carriers. After St. Thomas' prosperity in the first half of the nineteenth century as a trading and rendezvous center for sailing ships ended, St. Thomas tried to remain in the shipping business by becoming a coaling center for the new steam ships. That necessitated the unloading of supply ships which brought coal to the island, and the fueling of other ships which stopped there to obtain coal. The persons—mainly women—who performed those grueling tasks were the coal carriers. Taylor wrote:

> We have before alluded to the tendency of some authors to describe the negro of the Danish Indies, and especially some of them, as licentious and immoral, but we unhesitatingly challenge a comparison with the lower class of white population dwelling in the large cities of Europe or America. The hard working coal wharf labourers of St. Thomas would not lose by it. As a rule, they are orderly and industrious. The coaling of a steamer is a sight worth seeing. No sooner is it in port than a horn is blown. This is a signal for the coal carriers to assemble, and it is not long before a hundred or more of them come trooping into the coal yard. By-and-by they may be seen running to and from the shore and the steamer with the heavy baskets of coal upon their heads. The greater part of them are women, who enliven this severe labor with their songs.... It is wonderful how rapidly they can coal a large steamer. Four or five hours is sufficient.... We have

been informed, on good authority that the women work better than the men, and are more amenable to discipline, though, mostly, all are, to kind treatment. They are fond of dancing and masking.... They dwell chiefly in that part of the town known as the "Back of All," living alone in one small room, or with a female friend if unmarried. Their pay is one cent per basket of coal weighing from eighty-five to ninety-five pounds. Some carry as many as two or three hundred baskets during the coaling of a steamer. When not thus employed their pay is from sixty to seventy-five cents per day, for discharging coal from the steamer or sailing vessels which bring it to St. Thomas. It is a life of hardship and exposure to all sorts of weather.... Their lot is a hard one, the hardest perhaps of all those in St. Thomas who earn a living at the water's edge?[8]

Additionally, the coal carriers also showed, in perhaps the first recorded labor protest on St. Thomas, that they were bold enough to stand up to their white employers when being cheated of valid payment for their labor. On September 1, 1892, a coal carrier, who was also a bamboula dancer known as Queen Coziah, led her co-workers (about 200) in a protest march on Main Street, demanding that they be paid in genuine currency rather than the recent practice of payment by devalued tokens, which the banks were refusing to exchange at full value. The Government sent two groups (20 soldiers in each group) of armed soldiers, and the women in turn waved sticks and other homemade implements. However, a sudden heavy rainfall took place and scattered the crowd before the police started taking action against them. Their aborted protest still proved successful as the steamship managers, not wanting additional protests, decided to pay them in full-value currency.[9]

Life in St. Thomas during the "Doldrum Years"

The last four decades of Danish rule—the period from about 1880 to 1917—were marked by such continuous economic depression that Virgin Islands historian J. Antonio Jarvis labelled them "The Doldrum Years." One of the measures taken by the Danish Government to halt the economic decline was the transfer of the capital city from St. Croix back to St. Thomas in 1871, but no great improvement resulted. Major shipping and other business firms continued to move elsewhere. The population of St. Thomas declined by almost one-fourth from 14,389 in 1880 to 11,012 in 1901, as both Blacks and Whites left in search of better economic opportunities. A number of the old

The Market, Casimir Square, St. Thomas, D. W. I.

Market Square before 1917. Courtesy of the Virgin Islands Government's Archival Collection at the Charles W. Turnbull Regional Library.

European merchants went to South America or Europe, while Blacks generally went to the United States, Cuba, the Dominican Republic, or Panama.[10]

Great disparities marked the lives of the well-to-do, most of whom were white, and the poor, most of whom were black. In fact, had it not been for the entry of a new ethnic group to St. Thomas in the post-slavery period, almost all of the poor would have been black. However, beginning in the 1850s, French-descended natives of the island of St. Barthelemy, about 100 miles southeast of St. Thomas, began arriving on St. Thomas and soon formed a physically separate and culturally distinct community of their own. Though almost all of them were Caucasians, they were not thought of as being white, as that had traditionally meant privilege or economic well-being, and they had neither. As poor newcomers, they were viewed as the bottom class of the society, and derogatively came to be called "Cha-Chas." Though the origin of that term is not certain, one explanation was that it was a name given by the French fishermen to an insignificant fish, and another was that it was a sound made by the black natives of St. Thomas to indicate their contempt for the French fish-peddlers. The French settlers lived very frugally, often not wearing shoes, and earned their living by catching and selling fish, raising and selling fruits and vegetables, and making hats and other articles of straw.[11] Their presence therefore prevented the poor class from being all black.

In the latter half of the 1800s, there were no legal delineations of residential areas in Charlotte Amalie, but there were areas that were almost exclusively white, others that had a substantial percentage of well-to-do mixed families, and areas whose residents were mainly working class Blacks. The residents of Government Hill (extending back and upward to the Blackbeard Castle area) were generally white, and that was also true of Main Street (Dronnigens Gade). Part of the area referred to as Upstreet, stretching from the eastern end of Government Hill to the lower part of Bluebeard Castle Hill, also contained some Whites, along with well-to-do mixed families. That racial mixture was also true of the area from the western end of Government Hill northward, which came to be called Gordon or Garden Street, and its extensions. The area known as Down Street extended from the large covered gut (Gottets Gade) next to the present Enid Baa Library Building, westward past the Catholic Church, to the Western Cemetery (Kronprindsens Gade). It housed a number of middle class mixed and black families, along with working class families. The area known as Savan had been set aside by local Danish officials from the 1760s as a residential area for newly-freed Blacks who were leaving the failing plantations in the country to seek jobs in Charlotte Amalie. It was therefore dominated by working-class Blacks, but also contained some middle-class families. The definitions of the boundaries of Down Street and Savan are often disputed, but one common version has Savan as running northwest from the same large gut (Gottets Gade) where Down Street begins, but with Savan branching to the west and northwest of the gut, with Back Street being Savan's southern boundary. In the Upstreet neighborhood also, the areas commonly known by names such as Hospital Ground, "Round de Course," and "Round de Field," and the "Bayside" also had a preponderance of working-class families, along with a few middle-class ones.[12]

The Whites and well-off Blacks usually occupied substantial homes, many being of the traditional construction combination—the lower or first story of brick or masonry to offer protection against hurricanes, and the second story built of wood, which was thought to be safer in the event of earthquakes. As Taylor mentioned, anyone who was considered of worthwhile standing was expected to have at least one house servant, preferably more. The homes of the poor were usually small shingled wooden cottages, or long partitioned row houses in which each family rented single rooms, arranged around a "big yard" in which a number of activities took place, such as outdoor cooking and washing, children playing, and nighttime story-telling gatherings.[13]

Some of the working-class neighborhoods, most particularly Savan, developed certain African-influenced cultural traditions that have since become highly esteemed aspects of Virgin Islands and broader Caribbean culture. On holidays such as Christmas Eve, Christmas Second Day, New Year, Three Kings

King's Wharf, south of Emancipation Garden, about 1900, before the District Court Building and the Waterfront were built. Courtesy of the Virgin Islands Government's Archival Collection at the Charles W. Turnbull Regional Library.

Day, Easter Monday, and Whit Monday, groups and individuals would entertain their neighbors and other areas of the community by going from place to place—playing instruments, some improvised, singing, dancing, and/or masquerading in various ways. Groups from Savan often marched through their neighborhood and then went to other areas such as Main Street, Government Hill, and Upstreet. Although some Whites criticized some of the dances as being too lewd, many Whites looked forward to the entertainment, and went out on their porches to enjoy and applaud the performers before presenting them with money.[14]

There continued to be interracial domestic relationships which lacked legal sanction. However, with legal impediments no longer existing, interracial nuptials did take place. Of such marriages that took place in St. Thomas late in the nineteenth century and early in the twentieth, a substantial number involved members of the Danish military and police forces stationed on the island or other minor government officials. The local women they married were usually of mixed ancestry and, in some cases, the women had more to contribute to the marriage, culturally and materially, than did their new husbands, and thus their families were not completely happy about the matches. The husbands, however, had the esteemed passport of being white.[15]

In the immediate post-emancipation period, St. Thomas was sorely lacking in public education institutions. Despite the admirable compulsion edict of the von Scholten administration, little was done by subsequent administrations to implement it on St. Thomas. Thus, during the 1850s and 1860s there were periods when no public schools operated and when they did, attendance was not enforced so the education of many black children was being neglected. Families of means sent their children to private or parochial schools. In 1876 a new law revised the education system. Public education was placed solely under government control (it had been contracted to the Moravians before emancipation), and attendance was strictly enforced. The period of compulsory schooling, however, was decreased to four years—from ages six through ten, with optional schooling available to age thirteen.[16]

Whites were very much concerned that there was no high school for the advanced education of their children. Dr. Taylor lamented that the Danish West Indies stood,

> ... almost alone in the West Indies as having no high school for the children of its taxpayers and respectable citizens. The consequences are sad to contemplate for those who are not rich enough to send their children to Europe.[17]

The consequences, he explained, were that they would be unable to attain the highest offices in the government and the leading professions, as the locally-available schooling was inadequate for those.

There had been a public institution of secondary education, named the St. Thomas College, founded in 1878. It was open to students of all races and creeds. However, it was short-lived, closing in 1883. It has been suggested that the school did not survive because its curriculum stressed the physical sciences and so was not related to the social and economic conditions of St. Thomas.[18] However, within months of the demise of the first secondary institution, a second one, also named the St. Thomas College, was founded by Roman Catholic priests and lasted for about a decade. It was apparently not accepted by many in the community, maybe due to religious prejudice, as it was in existence at the same time that Dr. Taylor was complaining of the lack of a high school. Awareness of a public fear of the school based on its religious affiliation was shown by a newspaper announcement in 1892 which stated that "Christian doctrine would be taught only to Roman Catholic pupils." In addition to standard courses, it apparently endeavored to meet local needs and interests; among its electives were bookkeeping and Negro Literature. The latter course so influenced one of the students that he eventually became a world-renowned collector of literature by and about Blacks. His name was Arthur Schomburg and, though he had been born in Puerto Rico, his mother was a native of St. Croix.[19]

During the last years of Danish rule, there was a movement in the direction of providing the masses who attended the public schools with an education that had greater vocational content than before. It was the recommendation of a commission from Denmark that had spent two months studying conditions in the Islands in 1903. Also, the famed U.S. black leader, Booker T. Washington, visited Denmark in 1911 and stressed this long-held philosophy that industrial education was the best path to competence and economic independence for Blacks. O. Rubner-Petersen, the Dane who was the School Director in the Danish West Indies from 1901 to 1917, visited Hampton and Tuskegee Institutes, black colleges in the United States, to observe how they conducted their programs of vocational training. He initiated a few changes in the local curriculum, but he was hampered by a lack of funds and then the islands were sold before any great changes were made.[20]

One wonders, however, if anything of great significance, vocationally or otherwise, could have been done without a re-ordering of the priorities of the Danish West Indian governmental officials. The money spent for public education, which really meant black education, was scandalously low. It was one of the smallest items in the public budget. Governmental expenditures for services such as public roads, the judiciary and police, sanitation, postal and telegraph operations, and maintenance of public buildings all greatly exceeded the sum spent for the education of the majority of the colony's children.[21] It is difficult not to conclude that the public education which was provided was to insure a basically civilized and law-abiding population; it was not education for progress.

Notes

1. Knox, *A Historical Account of St. Thomas, W.I.*, p. 122.; Marilyn F. Krigger, "A Quarter-Century of Race Relations in the U.S. Virgin Islands: St. Thomas, 1950–1975" (unpublished Ph.D. Dissertation, University of Delaware, 1983), p. 44.

2. Knox, *A Historical Account of St. Thomas, W.I.*, chapters 9, 12; Charles Edwin Taylor, *Leaflets from the Danish West Indies* (Westport, Connecticut: Negro Universities Press, reprinted 1970; originally published in London: William Dawson and Sons, 1888), chapters 3–12, 14, 18.

3. Knox, *A Historical Account of St. Thomas, W.I.*, pp. 127–128.

4. Ibid., pp. 129–131.

5. Knox, *A Historical Account of St. Thomas, W.I.*, chapters 9, 12; Charles Edwin Taylor, *Leaflets from the Danish West Indies* (Westport, Connecticut: Negro Universities Press, reprinted 1970; originally published in London: William Dawson and Sons, 1888), Preface.

6. Taylor, *Leaflets from the Danish West Indies*, p. 77.

7. Ibid.

8. Ibid., pp. 96–97.

9. Jarvis, *Brief History of the Virgin Islands*, pp. 87–88; Harold W. L. Willocks, *The Umbilical Cord: The History of the United States Virgin Islands from Pre-Columbian Era to the Present* (Christiansted, St. Croix, 1995), p. 222.

10. Jarvis, *Brief History of the Virgin Islands*, chapter 11.

11. Taylor, *Leaflets from the Danish West Indies*, p. 95.

12. Eric E. Dawson, *Down Street, Saint Thomas and Beyond* (Bloomington Indiana: Author House, 2011), pp. 1–4, 37–39; Ruth Moolenaar, *Legacies of Upstreet: The Transformation of A Virgin Islands Neighborhood* (St. Thomas Virgin Islands: We From Upstreet Inc., 2005), pp. 3, 7, 12, 165–166.

13. Taylor, *Leaflets from the Danish West Indies*, pp. 74–76; Eric E. Dawson, *Down Street, Saint Thomas and Beyond*, pp. 2–3.

14. Robert W. Nicholls, *Old-Time Masquerading in the U.S. Virgin Islands* (St. Thomas, The Virgin Islands Humanities Council, 1998), pp. 60–63.

15. Jarvis, *Brief History of the Virgin Islands*, p. 124; interview with an offspring [anonymity requested] of one such marriage, in which the colored bride's family had not thought that her Danish suitor was good enough for her.

16. Ezra A. Naughton, "The Origin and Development of Higher Education in the Virgin Islands" (Ph.D. Dissertation, The Catholic University of America, 1973), pp. 106–107.

17. Taylor, *Leaflets from the Danish West Indies*, pp. 41, 60.

18. Naughton, "The Origin and Development of Higher Education," pp. 107–111.

19. Ibid., pp. 132–138.

20. Ibid., pp. 144–148, 161.

21. Ibid., p. 161.

Chapter 7

The End of Danish Rule

United States interest in acquiring the Danish West Indies first developed in the 1860s as a result of the U.S. Civil War. The U.S. Navy came to realize that the harbor of St. Thomas would be good as a much-needed coaling station. As soon as victory over the South was assured, Secretary of State William Seward began overtures to the Danish Government, which culminated in a treaty signed in October 1867. It called for the cession of the islands of St. Thomas and St. John to the U.S. for a consideration of $7,500,000 (St. Croix was not included as the treaty by which Denmark had purchased St. Croix required French consent to any future sale, and such consent was not deemed achievable at that time.) The treaty was ratified in Denmark but, to the great surprise of Denmark and its islands, the U.S. Senate, embroiled in the politics of the Reconstruction period, rejected the treaty in 1870.[1]

It took forces in the U.S. which favored the Islands' acquisition more than three decades before they were able to achieve the negotiation of another treaty in 1902. That the economy of the islands had declined precipitously during the intervening period was evidenced by the fact that all three islands were to be transferred for a reduced total of only $5,000,000. However, for the second time, a treaty failed to win approval, but this time it was the Danish Upper House that turned it down to retaliate for the U.S. rejection of the 1867 treaty.[2]

Americans who favored expansion in the Caribbean refused to give up on the Danish islands, and finally the outbreak of World War I in 1914 presented an opportunity for the U.S. to make a third bid. In the preceding decades, Germans had developed substantial business interests in St. Thomas, and the hesitancy of the Danish government to negotiate another treaty was shaken on receipt of the following communication from the U.S. Secretary of State in October 1915:

> ... there was danger that Germany, taking advantage of the upheaval
> in Europe, might absorb Denmark and that she might do it so as to

obtain a legal title to the Danish West Indies, which the German Government coveted for naval use. The continued possession of the islands by Denmark might, therefore, became a menace to Danish independence.... In the event of an evident intention of the part of Germany to ... compel Denmark to cede the islands to her, the United States would be under the necessity of seizing and annexing them and, though it would be done with the greatest reluctance, it would be necessary to do as we would never permit the group to become German.[3]

With this blunt threat of the seizure of the islands, the most sensible action for Denmark was to sell, with the aim of receiving as great a degree of remuneration as it could in a transfer treaty. Commendably, the Danish Government also made valiant attempts to secure in the treaty important rights for the inhabitants of the islands. Many persons in Denmark had voiced their concerns about the treatment of Blacks in the U.S., especially the practice of lynching and the fear that American acquisition of the islands might lead to similar practices there. The Danish Foreign Minister asked that the U.S. "give guarantees which would affect the kind treatment of the present inhabitants, principally Negroes." In response, the U.S. Ambassador to Denmark tried to assure him that, "Americans are so well acquainted with the true character of the negroes that they could make them more content than the Europeans."[4]

The extent to which the Blacks of the islands had the same concerns is hard to ascertain. It appears that the fact of segregation in the U.S. was generally known and detested, but there was not much knowledge about specific actions such as lynching. It had been seen, from experiences of visiting U.S. ships, that American sailors could be rude and racially abusive when intoxicated. But the other side of the coin was the much-needed infusion of money that those ships had always provided. The war had worsened economic conditions even further, thus transfer to the U.S. was viewed as the best economic solution for islands whose economy had hit rock bottom.[5]

The Danish Government also tried to get the U.S. Government to grant the right of U.S. citizenship to inhabitants who so desired, a feature which had been in the 1867 treaty. However, Secretary of State Robert Lansing replied that that could not be done as citizenship had not yet been granted to Puerto Ricans, who had been under U.S. control since 1898. Thus, future citizenship status and the rights of the inhabitants were left to the determination of the Congress.[6] Yet, there was sufficient ambiguity in the wording of the treaty, referring to the right of inhabitants to retain allegiance to Denmark or elect citizenship in the U.S., that many inhabitants thought they would be regular citizens of the United States. Based on that, Dr. William Boyer, in his com-

The Transfer ceremony during the lowering of the Dannebrog; the building at the left was the Danish barracks and now houses the Virgin Islands Legislature. Courtesy of the Virgin Islands Government's Archival Collection at the Charles W. Turnbull Regional Library.

prehensive history of human rights in the Virgin Islands, charged that the U.S. deliberately deceived the inhabitants into expectations of full citizenship, which it had no intention of immediately bestowing.[7]

The final treaty was concluded on August 4, 1916. After the necessary approvals by the legislative bodies of Denmark and the U.S. Senate, and the signings by the Danish king and U.S. President Woodrow Wilson, ratifications were exchanged by the two nations on January 17, 1917. Denmark was definitely successful in its remuneration of $25,000,000.00 from the U.S., considering that the amount in the 1902 treaty, just fifteen years earlier, had been five million; however, the completion of the Panama Canal in 1914 had greatly enhanced the value of the islands.[8]

On the afternoon of Saturday, March 31, 1917, official ceremonies of transfer took place on all three islands, with the major ceremony at the capital, Charlotte Amalie, at 4 p.m., on the grounds of the large Danish military barracks, now the home of the Legislature of the Virgin Islands. In the nearby harbor were military vessels of both nations, and salutes were fired during the ceremony. In front of the barracks were lines of the white soldiers of both nations, and in the surrounding outer areas were thousands of local residents, both Blacks and Whites, with tears being shed by some members of each group. Emotions were mixed between sadness at the loss of the known and the familiar, along with hopes of expected betterment, especially in economic affairs. As the respective national anthems were played, the Danish "Dannebrog" was lowered and the United States' "Stars and Stripes" was raised.[9] The Danish West Indies became the Virgin Islands of the United States of America.

Notes

1. Charles Callan Tansill, *The Purchase of the Danish West Indies* (Baltimore: The Johns Hopkins University Press, 1932), chapter 1, *passim*. The island of St. Croix was to remain in Danish possession.

2. Ibid., chapters 5, 6, 7.

3. Quoted Ibid., pp. 477–478.

4. Ibid., pp. 455, 473.

5. Interviews with Ada Battiste, St. Thomas, December 12, 1982, and Reginald Davis, St. Thomas, February 19, 1983.

6. Tansill, *The Purchase of the Danish West Indies*, pp. 491–492.

7. William W. Boyer, *America's Virgin Islands: A History of Human Rights and Wrongs*, 2nd ed. (Durham, North Carolina: Carolina Academic Press, 2010), p. 88.

8. Tansill, *The Purchase of the Danish West Indies*, pp. 496–515.

9. Dookhan, *A History of the Virgin Islands of the United States*, pp. 260–262. Also, for a personal account of someone who attended the Transfer Ceremony in Christiansted, St. Croix, read G. James Fleming's "Transfer Day, 1917: A Day mixed with sadness and joy" in the *Daily News* (St. Thomas, V. I), February 24, 1981, p. 6.

Chapter 8

The Danish Racial Legacy

The legacy in race relations which 245 years of Danish sovereignty bequeathed to the people of the Virgin Islands was a very tangled assortment of attitudes, traditions, and conditions. In some areas, it was the typical heritage of any New World society which had a long history of slave-based European colonialism. In other areas, there were differences that are somewhat difficult to understand and explain.

The basic social structure of the society at the end of Danish rule was that prevalent throughout the West Indies. It was a three-tiered stratification of Whites, Light Browns, and Blacks, the post-slavery counterparts of ruling class, free coloreds, and slaves. The Whites still exercised political, social, and economic dominance, and exhibited no doubt that they had a divine mandate to do so. Close on their heels, however, with some equal in everything except purity of racial ancestry and the improbability of holding certain offices reserved for persons of such ancestry, was a small, well-to-do class of persons of mixed ancestry. As a result of the white bias which prevailed in European-established and controlled societies, mixed persons generally demonstrated great pride in the European components of their ancestry, suppressed as much as possible any reminders of the African component, and often looked with disdain on persons of predominantly African descent. Their lifestyle was much the same as that of well-positioned Whites, usually consisting of nuclear family organization, servants, formal entertaining, and traditional trappings of comfort. If pressed to use a one-word term to identify themselves racially, "mixed" was used in preference to "colored," and Negro or black was never used. "Negro" was usually reserved for persons who were dark or poor, and "black" was then a rather pejorative term, which not even purely African persons of the darkest complexions willingly used to describe themselves.[1]

The third and largest class, most of whom were referred to as Negroes, consisted of the great majority of dark and poor people. There were some dark persons who were considered exceptional by reasons of substantial wealth, education, or position; they were often associated with the mixed and were generally not referred to as Negroes. But the great majority of this class was comprised of persons of the varying darker hues and varying degrees of poverty. The lives of many of them were defined by conditions which sprang from the legal and economic restrictions of the slavery and post-slavery periods: inadequate housing, poor nutrition, lack of more than a primary education, families lacking ties of legality, the persistence of work ethics spawned by slavery, and continuing acceptance of many of the same white racist stereotypes which functioned to keep them in a disadvantaged status.

This latter class was by far the most varied, actually comprising at least a couple subdivisions. It ranged economically from persons who lived in sordid poverty to some who were very comfortable and enjoyed a great deal of respect. Its racial span stretched from persons who appeared or were considered to be of pure African ancestry, to the mulatto children, often paternally unacknowledged, of liaisons between white employers or other solicitors and black lower-class women. Thus, racial lineage was not the sole determinant of mixed persons; Danish West Indian society had intricately weighted factors of class and race. Yet, the racial ingredient had a special potency which no other factor could quite equal.

As some scholars, such as Orlando Patterson, have pointed out, the colonial systems of race and class stratification which developed in the West Indies and parts of Latin America are really more vicious in their implications for people of African descent than the black-or-white system which developed in the United States. In the gradation systems such as that of the Danish West Indies, persons of partial African ancestry may, at some point, socially dissociate themselves from that ancestry and cease to care about the fate of others who share than ancestry to a greater degree. However, because of the advantages which accrued from their partial white ancestry in white-biased societies, such persons have often been the very ones best equipped to lead and help others of African ancestry. This system thus encourages the departure from the group of many of its most accomplished persons, and often the credited achievements of the group are continually kept low by the deletion of the attainments of such persons. On the other hand, in the black/white dichotomy of the U. S., persons of known African ancestry do not have the social option of divorce from that ancestry. So all such persons are usually more concerned with the welfare of the entire group and more willing to contribute to its progress, regardless of how strongly some of those who "have made it" may resent being identified with or associating with all strata of the group.[2]

In the Danish West Indies, the tradition was developed in which "mixed" persons generally did not identify with "Negroes" and showed little or no interest in movements concerning Blacks. As a matter of fact, the color gradation system which was established during the Danish period was known to be operative even within family groups. White Americans who moved to the islands after Transfer were often amazed at first hearing that some old colored families from the Danish period were known to show preferential treatment to light-complexioned offspring over dark ones.[3]

There is no doubt that the Danish period strongly instilled the principle of white superiority. Writings by Whites have revealed the subordinate status expected of Blacks. In 1916 a young Black, David Hamilton Jackson of St. Croix, led a successful strike of sugarcane workers on that island. Referring to it in his memoirs, more than four decades later, white planter Robert Skeoch stated:

> The strike created a bitter feeling, and there were disagreeable instances due to the disrespectful conduct of the negroes against the whites and I regretfully add, that the former respect has never been entirely restored.[4]

The principle of white superiority may have been so well implanted that some Blacks projected the impression that they completely subscribed to it. Two white Americans who spent time in the islands during the last months of Danish rule, gathering information for a book and doing archaeological research, wrote:

> The St. Thomian Negroes are far more polite than any other Negroes in the West Indies; they do not seem to wish to be on a footing of equal equality with their white fellow citizens. This is undoubtedly due to the excellent and kind training given them during the Danish rule, the results of which will show for many years. If in the future the same treatment is accorded the Negroes, there will be no troubles between the Whites and the Negroes.[5]

The "excellent and kind treatment" those authors alluded to is one of the most intriguing aspects of the Danish legacy—the widespread idea in St. Thomas at the time of their departing that the Danes had been very kind colonial masters. During the early 1980s, when initial research was done by this author on that topic, there was hardly to be found any older black persons in St. Thomas whose memory extended back to the Danish period, nor among those whose thoughts had been recorded in the past, who did not agree with that assessment. Contrary to many former colonial regimes for which the subjects did or do not generally retain any great love, the Danes were, at the time of transfer and continuing long after to a substantial degree, even considering the role of nostalgia, regarded with great affection by many of their former St. Thomian subjects. When evidence of racial prejudice in Danish rule was pointed to, older persons retorted that it was not overt during the last decades of Danish rule, and that the Danes treated persons of color with respect in everyday interactions. They also pointed to a number of intermarriages in the last decades of Danish rule. To the charge of the parsimony of the Danish government in its public education expenditures, its black defenders retorted that Denmark was a small and poor country; that the Danish West Indies were among the very few places in the West Indies with compulsory education, and that those who completed the available years of education received a good basic education.[6]

However, going further back to the slavery period of Danish rule and judging by the Danish laws and the findings of scholars of slavery such as Tannenbaum and Neville Hall, the Danish slave system was by no means a lenient one.[7] Even there, partisans of Danish benevolence pointed to mitigating factors such as the role of the Danish Royal Family in promoting religion among the slaves, efforts to educate black children from late in the 18th century culminating in the decree of compulsory education before emancipation, and the laudatory career of Peter von Scholten. Additionally, for more than a century before Denmark exited, the plantation system had ceased to be important on St. Thomas and thus most of its Blacks worked and lived under less arduous conditions, even though the plantation system was still dominant in most of the West Indies during the first half of the twentieth century, including St. Thomas' sister island of St. Croix. The overall effect was that at the end of the Danish period, many Blacks in St. Thomas appeared to have held no general feelings of rancor in regard to Whites. They appeared to simply think that each white person should be judged individually.

Another aspect of the Danish legacy is the tradition of toleration they established in the islands. Indeed, this is presently often referred to as the USVI becomes increasingly more diverse and torn by ethnic divisions. Denmark allowed various nationalities and ethnic groups to settle in the colony and all were allowed substantial freedom. There was no imposition of the Danish language, religion, or other cultural traits; each group was permitted to live its own way. It should be recognized realistically, however, that the willingness of the Danes to accommodate so many other peoples lay largely in the fact that they were unable to generate any great population movement from Denmark to the Danish West Indies. And, of course, the enslaved Africans were the great exception to their cultural liberality. For reasons of economic profit and European safety, it was considered necessary that the lives of the Africans be governed by the most effective profit-producing routines and that any cohesive aspects of their culture be obliterated. However, the early demise of the plantation system on St. Thomas functioned otherwise.

Thus, by the time of the Danish retreat from the islands, a number of the black people of St. Thomas had grown to believe that the Danes were a people who cared for them and were happy to reciprocate the affection. As most nineteenth-century labor on St. Thomas had been performed in a freer commercial and urban setting than the plantation environment, the sentiment had grown that Danes were really kind masters. The inability of the islands to support themselves during the last decades of Danish rule and the fact that Denmark spent on their upkeep, it was rumored, far more than Great Britain spent on her greatly more numerous West Indian colonies, gave the Danish nation a reputation for paternalism and benevolence. An additional comparison between race relations in St. Thomas and what was heard about the Jim Crowism in the American South, and between the widespread literacy in the Danish islands compared to the lack of educational opportunity for poor Blacks in many parts of the Caribbean area, made the Blacks of St. Thomas feel that their lot, as poor as most were, could have been much worse had they been somewhere else in this hemisphere. For that they were grateful to the Danes.[8]

There is also a great deal of truth in the idea, best articulated by now-deceased Welsh professor Gordon Lewis, who spent decades living and teaching in Puerto Rico, that the people of the Virgin Islands have been victims of a "myth" of liberal Danish rule and culture.[9] He posited that Danish rule was woefully deficient and illiberal in many respects. He considered the downtrodden condition in which they left most of the inhabitants as the best testimony of the inadequacy of their tenure. On the other hand, the most important factor in any type of group relations, such as those based on race which are the subject of this work, is how members of groups define and view members of other groups. Though there were discerning persons who would have agreed with Lewis, most inhabitants left in St. Thomas (a number had been emigrating during the period before the Transfer), seemed to have been steeped in the ideas of Danish benevolence and paternalism. Such ideas had been transmitted by government officials, and by prominent citizens and writers such as the Rev. Knox and Dr. Taylor.

For many St. Thomians, then, regardless of the accumulated historical facts, the reality which they perceived was the then-current Danish reputation for benevolent paternalism, and the fact that the Danes were not leaving as a result of colonial dissatisfaction or because they particularly wished to relinquish the colony at that time. They left under pressure from a greater power. And at the end, the Danish role appeared to be that of trying to secure guarantees of civil rights and humane racial treatment for the subjects they were about to surrender. Their subjects were appreciative and, as they bade farewell, many wanted to forget the negative and remember only the positive aspects of the Danish racial legacy.

Notes

1. Albert A. Campbell, *St. Thomas Negroes: A Study of Personality and Culture* (*Psychological Monographs*, Vol. 55, No. 5, Evanston, Illinois: The American Psychological Association, Inc., 1943), pp. 36–38; Jarvis, *Brief History of the Virgin Islands*, pp. 89, 94–95; Interviews with Clarissa Creque, St. Thomas, February 19, 1983, and Enid Hansen Frederiksen, St. Thomas, February 24, 1983.

2. This is explained elaborately in Orlando Patterson, "Toward a Future That Has No Past—Reflections on the Fate of Blacks in the Americas," *The Public Interest*, No. 27 (Spring, 1972), pp. 25–62; it was also the subject of a lecture entitled "The Black Experience in the New World," which Patterson delivered at the College of the Virgin Islands, St. Thomas, on March 7, 1975. A similar discussion is found in Harmannus Hoetink, *Slavery and Race Relations in the Americas* (New York: Harper and Row, 1973), pp. 135–138.

3. Campbell, *St. Thomas Negroes*, pp. 33–34; interview with Charlotte Paiewonsky, St. Thomas, February 15, 1983.

4. Robert Skeoch (as told to Irene Armstrong), *Cruzan Planter* (n.p., 1971), pp. 98–99.

5. Theodoor De Booy and John T. Faris, *The Virgin Islands: Our New Possessions and the British Islands* (Westport, Connecticut: Negro Universities Press, reprinted in 1970; originally published in Philadelphia: J. B. Lippincott Company, 1918), p. 71.

6. Interviews with Reginald Davis, St. Thomas, February 19, 1983, and Arona Petersen, St. Thomas, February 24, 1983.

7. Tannenbaum, *Slave and Citizen*, p. 65; Hall, "Slave Laws of the Danish Virgin Islands in the Later Eighteenth Century," pp. 174–188.

8. Naughton, "The Origin and Development of Higher Education," p. 159; Interviews with Reginald Davis, St. Thomas, February 19, 1983, and Arona Petersen, St. Thomas, February 24, 1983.

9. Gordon K. Lewis, "The Myth of Danish Culture," *Virgin Islands View*, Vol. 1, No. 3 (August, 1967), pp. 14–22; Gordon K. Lewis, *The Virgin Islands: A Caribbean Lilliput* (Evanston, Illinois: Northwestern University Press, 1972), pp. 38–41.

Part 2

The First Half-Century of United States Sovereignty, 1917–1967

Chapter 9

The Naval Regime, 1917–1931

The first fourteen years of U.S. rule—1917 to 1931—are referred to in Virgin Islands history as the naval period. Maybe it should not have been surprising that the U.S. Government chose its Navy to supervise its new possession in view of the fact that initial U.S. interest in the islands had been spurred by naval sources, with the strategic value of St. Thomas and its harbor having been a prime motive for acquisition. Additionally, the formal acquisition of the Virgin Islands took place at practically the same time that the United States entered World War I, with its declaration of war against Germany on April 6, 1917, just six days after the transfer. Thus, for the first decade and a half of United States rule, the people of the Virgin Islands experienced government in which "all military, civil and judicial powers necessary to govern" were vested in naval officers who were appointed by the Presidents of the United States to be governors of the Virgin Islands. There were seven naval governors in all: three Rear Admirals and four Captains.[1]

Naval Governance and Racial Influence

Professor William Boyer has characterized the naval period as an era of "poverty and prejudice."[2] Those were indeed two of the major characteristics of that decade and a half. Prejudice had not been entirely unexpected and though it probably did not affect the daily lives of most St. Thomians as acutely as did poverty, it played a major role in insuring a lack of substantial political progress during the period. The persistence of great poverty had not been expected, and the failure of American rule to bring about marked economic improvement, along with inaction in political matters, constituted sore disappointments regarding the new regime.

In respect to race relations, the choice of the Navy Department to administer the islands was a most unfortunate one. During most of its period of dominance in the Virgin Islands, the U.S. Navy was an all-white organization, having adopted such a policy in 1920.[3] Given the state of race relations on the mainland at the time, it is possible to argue that almost any government by white mainland Americans would probably have occasioned departure from the lack of overt discrimination which had characterized race relations on St. Thomas. But for white military men in a segregated service, unaccustomed to supervising a mainly black civilian population, the situation was truly problematic.

On the very first night, after the transfer ceremony, there was an incident which struck fear in the hearts of black St. Thomians. A black man, intoxicated but otherwise inoffensive, was cursed with racial epithets and kicked into a gutter by a marine.[4] Blacks wondered if such treatment would be their regular fate. Fortunately, that proved not to be the case. However, there were sufficient incidents of weaponry display and minor violence involving Navy personnel during the early years that no one doubted that the old order had yielded to a new. Some of the incidents which especially angered the public included the firing of guns by sailors and marines on the streets of St. Thomas on Christmas Eve nights in 1917 and 1918, with the latter year also involving the beating and searching of some civilians. In another distasteful occurrence in March 1921, marines were firing guns in various directions in the heavily-populated Savan area; some houses were pierced by bullets and a Salvation Army revival meeting ended with the fearful flight of those in attendance. From time to time, there were various altercations involving military personnel and civilians, some of which resulted in injuries to Virgin Islanders and/or military men.[5]

The Naval regime began the process (which is still somewhat ongoing) of transforming the old three-tiered racial hierarchy into a racial structure akin to the American black-white dichotomy. Even though the U.S. Census of the Virgin Islands taken in 1917 and subsequent censuses followed the local racial classifications of "White," "Negro," "Mixed," and added "Other," Americans from the mainland generally thought of both the "Negro" and "Mixed" as black. Mixed persons began to realize that even though they retained many of the social and economic advantages with which the old Danish gradation system had endowed them, their new rulers consider them in the same racial category with all others of African ancestry.

Most mixed persons resented the American attitude toward race and felt insulted by their new categorization. In the reminiscences of Arthur Mahlon Linqvist, who was born toward the end of the 1800s and of mixed ancestry, he contrasted the differing positions of the Danes and the Americans. He noted that his paternal grandfather was a Dane and his grandmother was half-Danish. During his childhood in the waning years of the Danish period, "The American notion that if you are not white you are a Negro did not exist at that time. Danes and natives lived together, socialized, and intermarried." By contrast, after he had finished his schooling in Antigua (where many well-off families sent their children for secondary education, which was not available on St. Thomas until the 1920s) and passed the Cambridge University senior examination, his father wrote to a well-positioned acquaintance in Washington to inquire about the best colleges for him. The reply was that he should apply to Booker T. Washington's school (Tuskegee in Alabama) where he could learn a trade. Thus did the Lindqvist family learn that "According to the Americans a man with the least amount of colored blood was a Negro and was therefore qualified for no better position than a tradesman."[6]

St. Thomas, therefore, during the naval regime became a considerably more race-conscious society than it had previously been. Every segment of the older society was affected. The Danes and other Europeans who had remained, and who were the only residents with whom the new American officials willingly socialized, got a renewed realization of the transcendent importance of being white in Western societies, regardless of national or political identity. Some even began modification of their behavior to conform to American customs. Mixed persons painfully realized that white Americans were not impressed with any racial status other than pure white: being light was not sufficiently significant. In order to avoid the possibility of humiliating incidents, mixed persons consciously limited their social contacts with Whites much more than they had during the Danish period.[7]

The "Negroes" knew that, in the local scheme of relationships, their position was practically unchanged, but many also realized that the newly-arrived Americans did not place mixed persons completely apart from them in the special and separate status that Danish custom had. In fact, a few dark-skinned persons of ability were employed by the naval regime in positions that would probably have been reserved for lighter-complexioned individuals during the Danish period. The new order also had positive vibrations for the "Cha Chas," who in Danish times had not really been ranked racially; they had simply been considered the lowest group on the socio-economic scale. It became known locally that some Americans, including the wife of a naval governor, were telling those St. Thomians of French descent that their race gave them distinction and that they should assert superiority instead of accepting the inferior status they had previously held in local society.[8]

The Navy's Effect on the Economy

In addition to its racism, the naval period proved disappointing to the majority of the inhabitants of the Virgin Islands in a number of other areas. There were no broad-based improvements in the economy. On the contrary, the economy was dealt a serious blow by the enactment of the Eighteenth Amendment to the U.S. Constitution and its extension to the islands in 1921. The "noble experiment" of prohibition completely outlawed the rum industry, which had been an important facet of the local economy.[9] The persisting lack of economic opportunity fostered a continuing emigration to the U.S. and other places. The population of St. Thomas thus retained its downward trend, declining from 10,191 in 1917, the year of the transfer, to 9,834 in 1930.[10]

Economic stagnation continued the patterns of personal economic dependency which many Blacks had in relation to Whites. Though white American women began to change old local customs by going shopping and carrying parcels on the streets, which no self-respecting lady had done in the Danish era, many of the new American families who moved to the islands, in common with the older European families, employed house servants of various kinds. A number of black women also made their living by doing the laundry, often at their own homes, of the naval personnel who were stationed on the island. Other black families were often dependent on income sent by relatives who were in the domestic employ of white families on the U.S. mainland or elsewhere. In ways such as these, a sizeable number of black St. Thomians grew up with the impression of a positive relationship between their personal well-being and the actions of Whites.

In 1920 naval personnel in St. Thomas, including officers, enlisted men and their dependents, numbered 561. That was a sizable number of new inhabitants in a community of 10,000 persons. The constant presence of marines and sailors, along with economic need, facilitated the practice of the oldest profession. Also, though there did not occur the long-term or open relationships which were characteristic of the Danish period, there were interracial liaisons which produced a number of mulatto children. Such children usually received neither the acknowledgement nor financial support of their fathers.[11]

The only area in which the naval regime departed from its all-white mainland character was in the formation of a local black musical unit. A band was enlisted into the Navy with the members receiving equal pay, but they were permitted to live at home, thus apart from the other personnel. Led by Bandmaster Alton A. Adams, a noted St. Thomas musician, the band exhibited great talent and discipline, and became an important local institution, both socially and economically. It was used to provide local entertainment and culture

The Bayside, a poor Upstreet living area, now the area of the Ron de Lugo Federal Building. Courtesy of the Virgin Islands Government's Archival Collection at the Charles W. Turnbull Regional Library.

through regular concerts, and was also sent on a tour on the mainland to promote the reputation of the Navy in its administration of the islands.[12] Some members of the band, maybe due to the specially favored position which they enjoyed, maintained, contrary to substantial evidence, that the naval period was very progressive and untainted by official racism. (Two of Bandmaster Adams's old instruments—a flute and a piccolo—are now being displayed at the Smithsonian's new African-American Museum in Washington, D.C.[13])

The Navy's Effect on Political Development

Of the disappointments attendant to the early years of U.S. rule, the ones that caused the greatest public concern were those of a political nature. Many St. Thomians and other Virgin Islanders were unable to understand the need, especially after World War I ended, for prolonged military government. The explanation of the naval governors, that the government was really civil in nature because they reported to the President, did not in any way satisfy those who were concerned.

A greater thorn, however, was the matter of citizenship. While the provisions of the treaty had not extended immediate citizenship, the wording of the treaty led Virgin Islanders to believe that, one year from the date of the ex-

Frenchtown, after the hurricane of 1924, with the new St. Anne's Chapel atop the hill. Courtesy of the Virgin Islands Government's Archival Collection at the Charles W. Turnbull Regional Library.

change of the ratifications of the treaty, all who had not by declaration chosen to retain Danish citizenship would "be held to have renounced it and to have accepted citizenship in the United States."[14] Based on such an interpretation, U.S. citizenship of all Virgin Islanders who desired it was to become effective on January 17, 1918. On that day, therefore, in the belief that automatic citizenship was now theirs, the people of the St. Thomas celebrated with a parade and sports events, and sent a telegram of loyalty to the President and the Congress of the U.S. They later learned, however, that the interpretation of the Department of State was that the terms of the treaty had not been intended to grant U.S. citizenship to all Virgin Islanders but only to those who had been Danish citizens. Apparently, those Virgin Islanders who were descendants of slaves had not been considered Danish citizens and were thus excluded from the citizenship provision of the treaty. The overwhelming majority of islanders, therefore, were classified simply as "inhabitants of the Virgin Islands entitled to the protection of the United States." Such American nationals lacked the civil and political status of U.S. citizenship.[15]

There were widespread feelings of betrayal among the people over their indefinite, anomalous political position. During the next several years there was constant political agitation for a change in their citizenship status. Journalists conducted newspaper campaigns, there were mass meetings, pressure-group associations were formed both in the Virgin Islands and among Virgin Islanders resident in New York, and appeals for help were made to national organizations such as the American Civil Liberties Union (ACLU) and other prominent civil rights groups and individuals. Local political and civic leaders also testified before Congressional committees several times.[16] Finally, on February 25, 1927, almost ten years after the assumption of the islands by the U.S., a Congressional act granted U.S. citizenship to the natives of the Virgin Islands.[17]

The battle for citizenship had not been a single-issue fight. It was part of a package for overall political reform, which also included civil rule and an organic act with a bill of rights, adult suffrage, and greater legislative powers. The need for these stemmed from the fact that Congressional legislation of March 1917, which provided a temporary government for the islands, made no attempt to institute an American-style democracy. It simply left in effect the old Danish Colonial Law of 1906 until such time as a new American constitution could be written and implemented. Hardly anyone complained at the time, believing that the interim period would be very short. It lasted for two decades — until the late 1930s.

The struggle for an American civil government in the Virgin Islands during the 1920s led to the most revealing statements of racial attitudes and relationships during the early American decades. The Danish constitution of 1906 had not included complete freedom of the press, and its economic requirements for voting were extremely restrictive. Under it, less than ten per cent of the population of St. Thomas voted during the naval period, as only males, aged 25 or over, with annual incomes of $300.00 and over could vote. Additionally, the powers of the legislature, known as the Colonial Council, were severely limited as the governor had the right to appoint more than one-fourth of its membership (four of fifteen) and could dissolve the Council at any time.[18]

The fight for a democratic government in which the majority of inhabitants could have a voice brought to prominence a number of local leaders, and was opposed by many of the naval officials and well-to-do forces — white and black — of the society. The methods used by the naval government against those who championed the cause of the Blacks were often ruthless, ranging from personal vilification and deprivation of government employment or contracts to deportation of non-nationals and imprisonment for libel or other charges of misconduct.[19]

The outstanding leader in the fight for civil democracy in St. Thomas was Rothschild Francis. Francis, a shoemaker by trade, was fearless and had a brilliant mind. In 1920 he was president of the Federal Labor Union of St. Thomas and was authoring articles on the political and economic conditions of the islands. One of his articles which was published in a New York newspaper caught the attention of Roger Baldwin, the director of the ACLU. Baldwin contacted

Francis, met with him in New York in 1920, and for the next decade and a half the ACLU played an important supportive role in the V.I. struggle for civil freedom. Through the assistance of Baldwin and the ACLU, Francis procured a printing press and in May 1921, began the publication in St. Thomas of a newspaper named the *Emancipator*. It became the outstanding local crusader for political, social and economic democracy. After reading the first issue, Baldwin wrote to congratulate Francis:

> If you follow the fearless course of championing the rights of the workers and of the black people in the Islands, of the Negro against white exploitation, you will render a great and needed service.[20]

Virgin Islands historian J. Antonio Jarvis wrote, in 1938, that Francis:

> ... did much to destroy the old spirit of resignation which had been fostered by Church and State.... He did more, perhaps, than all the discrimination practiced by the officials, to tell black people that blackness is a handicap which only militant unity can hope to overcome. He was an important factor in the change from Naval to civil government.[21]

However, the first Naval governor, Rear Admiral James H. Oliver, had written to the Director of Naval Intelligence in 1919 that Rothschild Francis was "a sort of half-witted negro ... apparently without an occupation ... constantly causing agitation amongst the ignorant class ..." Another activist for the rights of the people, Randolph A. Innis, was reported by Oliver to be "a negro without occupation, and is always with Rothschild Francis." James C. Roberts, also identified by Oliver as an "agitator," was further characterized as a "negro editor" who was one of several persons "causing much dissatisfaction by agitating the question of their citizenship status and the rights of the native born to govern themselves."[22]

The records of the naval period show, without doubt, that some of the governors and other naval officials were dedicated to white supremacy in the Virgin Islands, and that constituted the basis for their opposition to any political changes. The third naval governor, Rear Admiral Sumner E. Kittelle, wrote in 1922 to President Warren Harding:

> I cannot too strongly urge that there be no change made in the organic law until a full generation has elapsed ... and above all the white element must remain in the land and in supreme control.

Government Secretary C.C. Timmons likewise was against any extension of the suffrage due to the ensuing probability of all-black juries; he was wor-

Kongens Gade, facing east from lower Government Hill. Courtesy of the Virgin Islands Government's Archival Collection at the Charles W. Turnbull Regional Library.

ried that "a person of the Caucasian race might not be entirely safe before such a jury."[23]

Not only naval officials, but some other white Americans who lived in the Virgin Islands during the naval period advocated the retention of a governmental regime such as the Navy which would guarantee the supremacy of Whites over the largely black population. For example, in September, 1926, the Reverend Father Henry Whitehead, an Episcopal clergyman who had lived in the islands, published an article in a mainland journal in which he extolled the naval regime and denigrated the Blacks of the islands. Rothschild Francis reprinted it in the *Emancipator* so that St. Thomians could read it. Father Whitehead declared that "the two upper classes of V.I. society, both white and colored, are in favor of the present excellent policy" and spoke of local orators haranguing "the ignorant laborers to agitate for civil government." He continued:

> The V.I. 'bad darky' is an agitator. He is in no sense a menace to white
> women and girls, as is his confrere in the American South. He dreams
> of a V.I. future when black shall rule in black's interest.[24]

The Rev. Father ended his discourse by warning against any lessening of voting qualifications, predicting that extending the suffrage to more V.I. Blacks would transform the colony into another Haiti overnight.

Francis and other V.I. leaders who were *attempting to* arouse the majority
of people to press for political freedoms were often accused by naval officers
and certain upper-class elements of being "Reds," "Bolsheviks," "un-American,"
and of actively fomenting race hatred.[25] Every available means was used to in-
timidate and frustrate the efforts of Francis and his coworkers. Even when
Francis and a couple other reformers were members of the Colonial Council
in 1924, they were unable to get that body to express support for a civil government and extend suffrage, as the majority of the Council consisted of representatives of the upper class and the appointees of the governor.

The judicial branch of the Virgin Islands government operated similarly. In
1924 the person who became the U.S. District Court Judge in the V.I. was
George Washington Williams, originally from Baltimore. Before being appointed to the judgeship of the District Court, Williams had served the naval
government as government attorney, police judge, police chief, and member
of the parole and pardons board—all concurrently![26] He was a vociferous defender of the naval administration, "fought verbal battles with local 'agitators'
in newspapers and magazines," and, in general, was known to be contemptu-
ous of Blacks.[27]

Judge Williams especially disliked Francis because Francis had opposed his
appointment as a judge, based on Williams' well-known political position. Between 1925 and 1928, Francis was subjected to several trials by Williams, who
insisted on making the decision himself by refusing Francis' requests for trial
by jury. Francis was sentenced to several periods of imprisonment—for libel
against government officials, for contempt of court charges stemming from
the libel conviction, and for the other charges, at least some of which were believed to have been partly engineered by naval officials. Historian Isaac
Dookhan wrote: "There was probably no greater martyr for the Virgin Islands
than Rothschild Francis."[28] Francis ended up leaving St. Thomas and settling
in New York City, where he continued his efforts on behalf of the islands but
to a greatly curtailed degree.

The Navy's Effect on Education and Health

On the credit side, there were several areas in which significant improvements were effected by naval rule. And since many of those efforts were undertaken in areas which represented some of the more deplorable conditions
left by the Danes, Blacks were often the major beneficiaries as they were the
ones living under the worst conditions. The Medical Corp of the Navy reorganized and equipped the hospitals, conducted a hospital nursing school which

trained a number of black natives in health care specialties such as nursing and midwifery, and instituted several widespread public health programs. As a result, the death rate fell from thirty-five per thousand at the time of the Transfer to less than twenty per thousand in 1925. Two examples of nursing students who were initially trained by the Navy, and whose names signified outstanding professionalism in nursing in St. Thomas for decades afterward, were Ianthe Blyden and Eugenie Tranberg Forde.[29] Miss Blyden, who was originally from St. John, would serve as the Chief Nurse at the hospital in St. Thomas for many years, and Mrs. Forde, originally from St. Croix, was a midwife who delivered over 4,000 babies (including this author) on St. Thomas.

Public education was another area which witnessed great improvement during the naval period. New school buildings were constructed or acquired; schools were given the American presidential names of George Washington, Abraham Lincoln, Thomas Jefferson, James Madison, and James Monroe. The average annual expenditure per pupil climbed from $10 in 1918 to $33 in 1930. The minimum age for leaving school was raised from thirteen to fifteen. The Danish system had provided only elementary education; American administration introduced the junior high school grades in the early 1920s and the senior high grades toward the end of the decade.[30]

Educational content was greatly revamped during the fourteen years of naval rule. For some reason never made clear, the new American director of public education chose to use in the elementary and secondary schools of the V.I. the curricula developed in the states of New Mexico, Utah, and Arizona. Since very few of the native teachers had any higher education, a few white Americans were recruited to conduct the high school classes.[31] It should be noted, however, that due to the sore poverty of most of the population, very few students were able to continue in school beyond the minimum age. The dropout rate for public school students in the Virgin Islands in the years from 1920 to 1930 averaged a whopping 77.3 per cent.[32] The few students who were members of the first twelfth grade graduating classes in St. Thomas formed a very small fraternity. The first class in 1931 had only four graduates; the class of 1932 numbered six.

In spite of notable achievements in health and education, too many felt that the naval administration had failed in the most important tasks: that of developing a sound economy in the islands as a foundation for overall social and political progress, while also failing in showing respect for the racial composition of the territory. The head of the Bureau of Efficiency finally convinced President Hoover in 1930 that the islands needed a massive rehabilitation program and that the Navy should be withdrawn. Dr. Paul M. Pearson, a resident of Swarthmore, Pennsylvania and a former professor at Swarthmore College, was chosen to be the first civilian governor. Late in January 1931, Hoover announced his nomination of Pearson and the transfer of the administration of the government of the Virgin Islands from the Navy to the Department of Interior.[33]

Notes

1. Luther Harris Evans, *The Virgin Islands: From Naval Base to New Deal* (Ann Arbor, Michigan: J. W. Edwards) 1945, p. 52; the naval governors are also listed in Willocks, *The Umbilical Cord*, p. 474, and in Jarvis, *Brief History of the Virgin Islands*, p. 242.

2. Boyer, *America's Virgin Islands*, pp. 109–138.

3. Lewis, *The Virgin Islands*, p. 51.

4. Jarvis, *Brief History of the Virgin Islands*, p. 141.

5. Boyer, *America's Virgin Islands*, 2nd edition, pp. 113–115.

6. Albert A. Campbell, *St. Thomas Negroes—A Study of Personality and Culture* (Psychological Association, Inc., 1943), pp. 31–34.

7. Interviews with Mary S. Francis, St. Thomas, October 15, 1982 and Reginald Davis, St. Thomas, February 19, 1983; Karl Frederiksen, Indiana, April, 2017.

8. Ibid.; Darwin Creque, *The U.S. Virgins and the Eastern Caribbean* (Philadelphia: Whitmore Publishing Co., 1968), pp. 74–76.

9. Waldo Evans, *The Virgin Islands of the United States: A General Report by the Governor* (Washington: U.S. Government Printing Office, 1928), pp. 6–10; *Annual Report of the Governor of the Virgin Islands*, 1930, pp. 9–11.

10. Jarvis, *Brief History of the Virgin Islands*, p. 141.

11. Ibid., p. 132.

12. Isaac Dookhan, "The Search for Identity: The Political Aspirations and Frustrations of Virgin Islanders Under the United States Naval Administration, 1917–27" (Paper presented to the Tenth Conference of Caribbean Historians, St. Thomas, V.I., March, 1978) p. 21.

13. "Son on hand as band leader's story becomes part of national museum," *Daily News* (St. Thomas, V.I.), September 26, 2016, p. 7.

14. "Convention Between the United States and Denmark—Cession of the Danish West Indies," Article 6, found in Evans, *The Virgin Islands of the U.S.: A General Report*, p. 32.

15. Dookhan, "The Search for Identity," pp. 2–3; Boyer, *America's Virgin Islands*, pp. 136–38; U.S. Department of the Interior, "The Virgin Islands of the United States: Information on the Virgin Islands of the United States Transmitted by the United States to the Secretary-General of the United States to the Secretary-General of the United Nations Pursuant to Article 73(e) of the Charter" (Washington, D.C., 1947—mimeographed report), p. 5.

16. Isaac Dookhan, "Civil Rights and Political Justice: The Role of the American Civil Liberties Union in the U.S. Virgin Islands, 1920–1936" (Mimeographed paper, St. Thomas, V.I., 1982), *passim*.

17. Evans, *The Virgin Islands of the U.S.: A General Report*, p. 52.

18. Ralph M. Paiewonsky (with Isaac Dookhan), *Memoirs of a Governor: A Man for the People* (New York: New York University Press, 1990), p. 94.

19. Dookhan, "The Search for Identity," pp. 21–25.

20. Dookhan, "Civil Rights and Political Justice," pp. 1–3; quotation from Baldwin on p. 3.

21. Jarvis, *Brief History of the Virgin Islands*, p. 140.

22. All quoted in Boyer, *America's Virgin Islands*, pp. 114–115.

23. Quotations are in Boyer, *America's Virgin Islands*, pp. 115–116.

24. *Emancipator* (St. Thomas, V.I.), September 27, 1926, p. 1.

25. Boyer, *America's Virgin Islands,* 129–130.

26. Boyer, *America's Virgin Islands,* pp. 125–126.

27. Evans, *The Virgin Islands: From Naval Base to New Deal,* pp. 214–215; Letter, Herbert D. Brown to Governor Walter Evans, March 4, 1930, Records of the Department of Interior, Box No. 1242, Record Group 126, National Archives Building, Washington, D.C.

28. Dookhan, "Civil Rights and Political Justice," pp. 15–19, quotation on p. 19.

29. *Annual Report of the Governor of the Virgin Islands,* 1919, p. 4; Evans, *The Virgin Islands of the U.S.; A General Report,* pp. 36–7; Moolenaar, *Profiles of Outstanding Virgin Islanders,* pp. 20, 73.

30. *Annual Reports of the Governor of the Virgin Islands,* 1918–1931, sections dealing with the Department of Education.

31. Evans, *The Virgin Islands of the U.S.: A General Report,* pp. 58–60.

32. Charles Wesley Turnbull, "The Structural Development of a Public Education System in the Virgin Islands, 1917–1970: A Functional Analysis in Historical Perspective" (Ph.D. dissertation, University of Minnesota, 1976), p. 208.

33. Boyer, *America's Virgin Islands,* pp. 142–46. Gov. Pearson was the father of national columnist Drew Pearson.

Chapter 10

Political Developments and Their Effects, 1931–1961

The years between the advent of civil government in 1931 and the outbreak of World War II in 1941 formed a short but eventful period in the history of St. Thomians and other Virgin Islanders. Many of the political rights which had been sought throughout the 1920s finally became theirs. The rehabilitation plans of the Hoover administration, New Deal programs, and preparatory military spending finally started an upward trend in the economy. And the very small but steady growth of a white, mainland American civilian population appeared to denote the permanent addition of new racial mores to those which the islands had historically known.

The Hoover Visit and the Pearson Administration

Dr. Paul M. Pearson was inaugurated as the first civil governor of the Virgin Islands on March 18, 1931, in St. Thomas. At that time, the only positive fulfillment of the list of expectations that Virgin Islanders had had at the Transfer was the attainment of U. S. citizenship, which had been granted only a few years earlier—1927—after a prolonged campaign. Pearson tried to give assurance that he had come "with the utmost good will toward the people of the Virgin Islands," and, in an obvious effort to appeal to the overwhelmingly black citizenry, spoke of Booker T. Washington and asked that they "let down your buckets where you are." But Pearson's assumption of office came at the worst possible time, when all of the untreated economic woes of the 1920s and before had been worsened by the beginning of the Great Depression. On the whole, his administration, in spite of some admirable intentions and deeds, did not go very well.[1]

The first misfortune of the Pearson administration took place just one week after his inauguration, when Herbert Hoover became the first incumbent President to visit the U.S. Virgin Islands. After five hours on St. Thomas, he returned to the *U.S.S. Arizona* and afterwards made a statement to the press expressing terrible disenchantment. According to *New York Times* reporter Richard Oulahan, the President said:

> The Virgin Islands may have some military value some time. Opinion upon this question is much divided. In any event, when we paid $25,000,000 for them, we acquired an effective poorhouse, comprising 90 per cent of the population. The people cannot be self-supporting, either in living or government without discovery of new methods and resources.... Viewed from every point except remote naval contingencies, it was unfortunate that we ever acquired these islands. Nevertheless, having assumed the responsibility, we must do our best to assist the inhabitants.[2]

In a follow-up article a few days later, reporter Oulahan stated that during his five-hour visit to St. Thomas, the President "was able to obtain an indelible impression of the character of the people." Hoover thought the economic plight of the V.I. was caused mainly by the dependence of the people on work furnished by activities from outside the islands such as shipping, and the neglect of home industries such as fruit-raising. The President "regarded their condition as hopeless." He and the officials who accompanied him "have little faith that the Virgin Islanders will react favorably to the principle of self-help."[3]

The article concluded with the revelation that President Hoover's trip to Puerto Rico (where he was more favorably impressed) and the Virgin Islands had caused his administration to become concerned about immigration policies. It was noted that the V.I. population decline was attributed to the lure of New York, where most emigrating islanders were said to settle. Administration officials began wondering why Virgin Islanders and the 100,000 Puerto Ricans living in New York should have been admitted without restrictions when quota limitations were placed on the admission of "immigrants from certain European countries who make especially desirable citizens."[4]

The hurt and humiliation that the islanders felt on hearing of Hoover's candid remarks can be gauged from the fact that up to today, over eight decades later, whenever Hoover's name is mentioned in any group of persons of Virgin Islands ancestry, someone inevitably says, "he's the one who called the Virgin Islands a poorhouse." Though his initial "poorhouse" statement did not

Frenchies selling their straw products. Courtesy of the Virgin Islands Government's Archival Collection at the Charles W. Turnbull Regional Library.

contain any basis for a racial interpretation, the follow-up article regarding the trip's effect on the administration's thinking about immigration and the special desirability of European immigrants, could not but convey the impression that there was indeed a racial bias for President Hoover's conclusions about the V.I.

There were widespread outcries about the statements. Many of the merchants and big landlords of St. Thomas, who had always wanted the Navy to remain and were experiencing decreased business due to the departure of the naval units (even the local band had been withdrawn), declared that Hoover's pronouncements would severely worsen the economy as potential investors and residents would be deterred. Some started a movement aimed at securing the return of the Navy and were responsible for much criticism against the Pearson administration.[5]

Pearson tried hard to initiate measures to promote the betterment of the black population. Having been a college professor, education was one of his chief concerns. Shortly after taking office, he was able to make arrangements for selected Virgin Islands teachers and high school graduates to begin college in the fall of 1931 on four-year scholarships offered by Hampton Institute and Howard University, black colleges in Virginia and Washington, D.C., respectively. The recipients had to pledge to return to the islands to teach. Each year more scholarships were secured from additional institutions, so that by the late 1930s over forty students from St. Thomas had attended or were in attendance at mainland colleges. A list of fifteen institutions of higher education which offered scholarships to V.I. students from 1930 to 1940 shows that all but four of them were historically black colleges, located mainly in the southern United States.[6] Other programs in education proposed by Pearson included adult education and greater in-service training for teachers through summer institutes. The Pearson administration also promoted the increased participation of islanders in the administrative and executive functions of the government. In 1931 only ten per cent of such positions were filled by natives; when he left office in 1935, natives occupied seventy-five per cent of such positions.[7]

The implementation of Hoover administration rehabilitation plans and of President Franklin Roosevelt's New Deal programs enabled Pearson to preside over a substantial amount of economic improvement in the Virgin Islands. Greatly needed employment was furnished by PWA public work projects, a CCC camp was established in St. Thomas, and food relief, at its peak, aided a substantial portion of the population. Federal grants provided funds for the construction of the Bluebeard Castle Hotel in St. Thomas to promote a tourist industry, and a cooperative which encouraged the production of locally made handicrafts for sale to tourists was put into operation. FHA funds accounted for the construction of the first housing project on St. Thomas (Berg Homes in the Hospital Ground area), and the Lindbergh Bay Estate of 508 acres was purchased and made available for homesteading; it included a golf course and a beach for recreation.[8]

Pearson seemed to have had a truly sympathetic attitude toward the poor Blacks of the Islands. In an address in June, 1932, he explained his opinion of Virgin Islanders and their problems. He felt that the background of slavery was significant. "The Negro has suffered great wrong and nothing that the white man can do will ever atone for it." He viewed Virgin Islanders as "an intelligent, friendly, law-abiding people, who [wanted] fair play and a chance to work out their problems without prejudice." They were "not to be bullied or patronized." He also believed that the overall poverty of the mass of the people made them "lacking in sufficient motives" to own their own homes and strive for other comforts of modern civilization. But he had faith that the children of the islands would be the great beneficiaries of economic reconstruction.[9] His human concern for the islanders was demonstrated by his special interest in encouraging cultural activities. He promoted the production of operettas and such activities as poetry readings. He was behind the arrangements for the solicitation in the U.S. and the distribution in the V.I. of over 100 pianos, and also the procurement of musical instruments for the high school band. However, such activities were criticized by some as being more show than substance.[10]

In spite of his achievements and a refreshingly different attitude toward the local population, Pearson generated an amazing degree of local opposition.

Grade at Charlotte Amalie High School in the early 1930s. Well-known musician Alwyn Richards is third from the right in the second row from the top. Courtesy of the Virgin Islands Government's Archival Collection at the Charles W. Turnbull Regional Library.

Some recent historians and political analysts think the opposition stemmed mainly from the old conservative elements who did not like the radical changes he was advocating. The St. Thomas merchant class resented his efforts to increase taxes and wanted the return of the Navy, whose rule had been profitable for them. Some felt threatened by his efforts to help the poor. There was, however, also a mass opposition headed by Morris Davis, a black St. Croix labor leader who was very active in St. Thomas with the Roosevelt-Garner Democratic Club (after March 1933, Pearson became a holdover Republican appointee). Davis charged that Pearson was an ineffective administrator, was trying to fool the people into believing that economic conditions were improving more than they really were, and that his administration had been dishonest in its distribution of local relief to the poor. Some residents were also offended by Pearson's moral disapproval of the high percentage of illegitimate births and his announced intention to reduce it.

Mass feeling against Pearson, fed by rumors and the allied sentiment of the upper classes, grew steadily and by 1934 mass meetings were being held in both St. Thomas and St. Croix to demand Pearson's resignation. On the night of October 16, 1934, when Davis and his followers staged a protest march on St. Thomas without a police permit and police attempted to arrest them, violence ensued in which the acting police director suffered a fractured skull and several policemen were beaten. The Davis group followed up with petitions to Washington, making serious charges and urging Pearson's removal. Pearson was finally persuaded to take a position on the mainland with the Roosevelt administration and resigned from the governorship in July 1935.[11]

One recent political analysis has suggested that the treatment Pearson received, despite his compassionate and noble motives, may have been an early case of the revolutions of rising expectations that were to take place in the Third World during the next decades. Maybe for a people emerging from the suppressed discontent of autocratic naval rule, the freer optimistic atmosphere of the Pearson administration may have created expectations it was unable to fulfill.[12]

However, a member of Pearson's governmental circle, his Chief Municipal Physician, suggested in a book published during the 1940s that some racially-biased practices of the administration may have played a substantial role in the public's turning against Pearson. Dr. Knud Knud-Hansen had been born in Denmark and had come to St. Thomas during the Danish period; while many of his countrymen had left at the time of the Transfer, he had elected to stay. He noted in his book, for example, that he was the only "St. Thomian" (the quotation marks were his) invited to the luncheon Governor Pearson had held when President Hoover visited. He also explicitly stated:

> I shouldn't wonder if it was his pet child, the Blue Beard Castle Hotel, that touched off the fire when the people realized it was going to be run as a hundred per cent white establishment for the sake of the continental tourists.... We had met the American prejudice against the negroes under the naval regime, but now popped up this child of Governor Pearson's, the much-looked-to Blue Beard's Castle, a symbol of his efforts in education. And the child was white and to be kept at a sacred distance from ninety-five per cent of the population. High on the hill stood this temple for race prejudice, flanking our beloved old tower of Blue Beard.... Yes, I shouldn't wonder if this was the spark that touched off the conflagration.[13]

Dr. Knud-Hansen also remembered that, even though Virgin Islanders were employed in government positions in greater numbers than ever before, Governor Pearson brought with him a number of former co-workers and friends who were given the top positions.[14] And some of these persons did not display as much liberality as Pearson himself projected; in fact, at least a couple were outright racists. One such was Hamilton Cochran, who served in Pearson's cabinet as the head of public welfare and also was placed in charge of cooperatives. Cochran's book on the Virgin Islands, published a couple years after he left office, testified as to the utter contempt with which he regarded the majority of the people:

> One might suppose that with the equitable climate and splendid environment typical of all the Caribbean isles, their dusky inhabitants would be the most delightful people on earth. Alas! They are not. They possess none of the lovable traits of our own dark citizens below the Mason and Dixon line. American negroes are famous for their sunny disposition, easy laughter, and happy-go-lucky attitude toward life. The West Indian, however, while just as improvident, seems to have shut the sun out of his soul. He is often somber and brooding, sullen when angry, and not given to frequent laughter. He is sensitive to a degree and seems to be constantly on the lookout for slights and insults.[15]

When the governor failed to invite any Blacks to a reception for the officers of a visiting German cruiser, an editorial of the St. Thomas *Daily News* (which had been founded in 1930 by two local Blacks-J. Antonio Jarvis and Ariel Melchoir) expressed the opinion of the majority of the people that governmental affairs should not be lily-white and that such prejudice was unpardonable. Cochran could not abide with such "negro newspaper nonsense" and wondered:

> How can one account for this unfortunate attitude, which contrasts so sharply with the comfortable and harmonious relations that exist between our southern negroes and their white neighbors?[16]

Cochran answered his own question with two "facts." One was that "a large proportion of West Indian negroes originated in different African tribes from those who reached the mainland" and the other was:

> ... West Indian negroes have gradually assumed more and more political and economic power during the past fifty years, as white men have relinquished their interests in the islands and have moved elsewhere in search of wealth. In St. Thomas, for example, hardly any native American white men have business interests on the island. Of the

three richest merchants, two are mulattoes and the third is a Latin American. The few white men in business are Europeans ...

This slow rise to power has naturally enhanced the negro's price and ego to a point where he actually believes that he should be permitted to rule his own islands according to his own ideas. But with the tragic example of Liberia and Haiti still before us, it will evidently be a rather long time before the negro is considered to work out his own destiny unaided by the white man's brains and money.[17]

As liberal and progressive as the Pearson administration was in some areas, it was therefore not as impressive in the sensitive area of race relations.

The Organic Act of 1936 and Its Effects

Pearson's departure in 1935 deprived him of presiding over the fulfillment of one of his greatest political objectives. Since the early 1920s, as already noted, island reformers led by Rothschild Francis of St. Thomas, David Hamilton Jackson of St. Croix, and Casper Holstein, who was residing in New York City, had been working to bring about an American constitutional document for the Virgin Islands. The ACLU had been part of this struggle, and it had later been joined by the National Association for the Advancement of Colored People (NAACP), the National Urban League, and other civil rights groups and spokesmen. After Pearson became governor in 1931, his Lieutenant Governor, Lawrence Cramer, drafted a constitution which was introduced in Congress in 1932 and which embodied many of the major proposals the islands' leaders had made. The final compromise document agreed upon by the Congress was essentially what Pearson had submitted in 1932. On June 22, 1936, the signature of President Roosevelt at last made "The Organic Act of the Virgin Islands of the United States" a reality.[18]

The Organic Act of 1936 laid the basis for a socio-political revolution in the Virgin Islands. Its most significant provision was the extension of the suffrage:

... the franchise shall be vested in residents of the Virgin Islands who are citizens of the United States, twenty-one years of age, or over, and able to read and write the English language ... no property or income qualification shall ever be imposed upon or required of any voter, nor shall any discrimination in qualification be made or based upon difference in race, color, sex, or religious belief.[19]

Included also was a bill of rights which insured to the people of the V.I. the rights which other Americans had enjoyed under the national Constitution. The legislatures, which became designated as Municipal Councils, were to have no appointed members, could no longer be dissolved by the Governor, and could override vetoes of the Governor, although such bills were then to be forwarded to the President for final disposition. The Governor and Government Secretary (the local position comparable to a lieutenant governor) were still to be appointed by the President.

Incorporated into the Organic Act were some important economic provisions. All federal taxes collected in the Virgin Islands—income taxes, customs duties, passport fees and such—were to remain in the respective local treasuries of the two separate government entities—the Municipality of St. Thomas-St. John and the Municipality of St. Croix. It is still a matter of debate by some as to whether these financial arrangements were indicative of New Deal thoughts that, with such help, the V.I. might eventually become financially self-sustaining, or if they were more reflective of Hoover's opinion of insular hopelessness and permanent dependence.[20]

The first election governed by the Organic Act, held in November 1938, occasioned the development of new methods of political organization and the emergence of new political leadership. Due to the extremely small electorate previously, there had been no real organized political parties. In 1937 the Virgin Islands Progressive Guide was formed in St. Thomas as a civic association to begin educating the masses in regard to their new privileges and opportunities under the Organic Act. Its founders were all young black men (including some who were noticeably mixed), most of whom were not highly regarded by the old ruling class. They included Omar Brown, Carlos Downing, Roy Gordon, Oswald Harris, Valdemar Hill, Sr., Aubrey Ottley, and Henry Richards, Jr. They ended up realizing that any actual improvement of the conditions of the majority of the people was contingent on the wielding of power in the interests of that majority, and that would not be done by the then-incumbent legislators. They, therefore, were persuaded to seek political office and the Progressive Guide became the first political party organization in the Virgin Islands.[21]

In the election of 1938, only three of the Guide's candidates were elected and representatives of the business and landed interests still remained a majority in the Municipal Council of St. Thomas-St. John. However, in the election of 1940, a Progressive Guide slate of candidates, pledged to enact labor and other needed legislation in the interest of the masses, won all seven seats in the legislature. From thenceforth those who aspired to elective office in the V.I. had to seek the support of the masses. That knowledge had been quickly discerned and applied by a native-born son of a Lithuanian immigrant who had become economically and socially prominent since arriving in St. Thomas in the late 1890s. Ralph Paiewonsky, who would become governor during the 1960s, had been elected to the Council in 1938 as a member of the old conservative clique; by 1940 he had switched to the Progressive Guide and retained his seat as a member of its all-triumphant team. Virgin Islands historian-economist Darwin Creque stated that the impact of the Organic Act represented a "changing of the old reactionary order which had existed in the islands for more than two-and-a-half centuries."[22] It represented the beginning of political democracy in the Virgin Islands, and made many residents feel that the territory was at last truly a part of a democratic country.

Significant also was President's Roosevelt's appointment of Blacks to positions in the Virgin Islands. Of great impact was William H. Hastie's arrival in St. Thomas in 1937 as the new U.S. District Court Judge. Hastie was the first Black to hold a federal judgeship in the United States. He had become known as a lawyer of great ability, was active in the NAACP and, as a former assistant solicitor in the Interior Department, was popularly thought of as a member of Roosevelt's "Black Cabinet." Blacks in the U.S. were elated with the appointment, though it was not well-received initially among some of the established leaders of the V.I. In July, 1936, the appointment of James A. Bough to the post of U.S. District Attorney for the V.I. was also a distinctive step. Bough, a native of St. Croix, was the first Virgin Islander to gain appointment to such a significant federal post in the islands. Another black native, Cyril Michael, became Clerk of the District Court shortly after. Hastie and Bough were both concerned about the needs of the local masses and acted as informal advisors to the organizers of the Progressive Guide. When Hastie resigned in 1939 to accept the deanship of the Howard University School of Law, Roosevelt appointed another U. S. Black to the V.I. District Court bench—Herman E. Moore of Chicago.[23]

Those appointments all vividly illustrated to Virgin Islands Blacks and others that Blacks could aspire to lofty positions, if they possessed the necessary education and talents. Then, in January, 1946, the ultimate took place when President Harry Truman appointed to the governorship of the Virgin Islands the same mainland Black, William H. Hastie, who had had prior experience in the V.I.

Hastie's nomination for the governorship was applauded by the local press, prominent black West Indian leaders such as Norman Manley of Jamaica, and, of course, by U.S. Blacks and civil rights leaders. However, a number of Whites and some upper-class Blacks in the V.I. opposed the appointment. Cables were sent to Washington, asserting that the islands were not ready for a Negro governor and that confirmation of such an appointment would lead to a catastrophe and the ruination of the islands. Some of the protesters felt insulted at the possibility of being governed by a Black and believed that it exemplified what little regard Truman had for the Virgin Islands. Some were also greatly concerned with its financial implications, feeling that a black governor would not be able to procure as much congressional funding as a white could, and that local government positions and contracts might no longer be available mainly on the basis of pigmentation.[24]

Hastie's inauguration as Governor of the Virgin Islands on May 17, 1946, established another racial precedent for him and for the Virgin Islands. From 1937 to 1939, he had served in the islands as the first black federal judge in U.S. history and now he had returned as the first black governor. His prior tenure of service made him much more knowledgeable about the islands than the great majority of his predecessors had been; additionally, during the time between the two positions, he had married Beryl Lockhart, a member of a wealthy and prominent mixed St. Thomas family.

Hastie's success, however, in bringing about what he viewed as desired changes in governmental administration and attitudes was uneven. He was successful in urging the enactment of the Merit System Law, which provided for the classification of governmental positions and a standardization of examination or qualification of government employees and the determination of their salaries. The law took effect in 1948 and meant that eventually the majority of employment in the V.I. civil service would be based on provably relevant qualifications rather than on the old qualifiers of family connection, race, or complexion.[25]

On the other hand, Hastie met with disappointment in his efforts to make Virgin Islanders more conscious of the need for greater self-government. His term of office included presiding over the year-long centennial commemoration of the emancipation of slaves in 1848; the festivities included a visit from President Truman in February 1948. Hastie thought that after a century of freedom and from what he had observed of the people of the V.I., they were ready for and would benefit from increased self-government. From his first year of office he embarked on a public campaign, hoping that both Virgin Islanders and the Congress would be convinced that "the people should elect their own Governor, as is done in all democratic societies." However, in a referendum in the November 1948 election, the voters who cast referendum ballots (forty per cent of the voters did not) rejected the popular election of their own governor by a three to one majority.[26] Hastie had not correctly gauged islands psychology and the force of history. A large number of Virgin Islanders still did not feel confident that one of their own should govern. Someone appointed from the outside and preferably white—the type of governor the islands had always had before—was considered more acceptable. Hastie probably felt relieved when Truman again tapped him in 1949 for yet another precedent-setting appointment—to be a judge of the Third Circuit Court of Appeals in Philadelphia.

Following Hastie, the next appointed governor of the Virgin Islands, in 1950, was considered a white "native." He was Morris F. de Castro, the son of a Jewish family that had long resided in St. Thomas; however, the term "native" is placed in quotation marks because he was actually born in Panama during a period of residency there by his family, which returned to St. Thomas during his early childhood. Since the 1930s, de Castro had held several administrative positions in the V.I. government and was fully prepared to be governor, understanding both the political situation and racial sensitivities very well. However, he was economically very conservative, and his reluctance to promote programs needed by the masses, if there was business opposition, made him a disappointment to many Blacks, and that was effectively vocalized. Governor de Castro resigned from the position in 1954 to join a new local bank formed by the Paiewonsky family and their associates.[27]

The Revised Organic Act of 1954 and Its Effects

During de Castro's governorship, popular local politicians kept urging the need for greater measures of self-government; bills were introduced in the Congress and in 1952 Congressional hearings were held in the V.I. A local referendum in 1953 had very different results from the one five years previously. It resulted in the majority of voters (as a result of overwhelming support in St. Thomas, though not St. Croix) favoring an elected governor, unification of the two island legislatures, and a resident commissioner for the V.I. in Washington. However, the 1954 Congressional bill establishing a new constitution was a great disappointed to many Virgin Islanders as it contained only one of the three changes requested in the referendum: it provided for a unified legislature, but no elected governor or resident commissioner in Washington. Consequently, Congressman Adam Clayton Powell of New York, a black rights advocate, and well known organizations such as the American Civil Liberties Union (ACLU) and the National Association for the Advancement of Colored

Peoples (NAACP) were planning to campaign against the measure. Skilled lobbying by St. Croix Councilman Walter Hodge and other V.I. legislative representatives, Ralph Paiewonsky, Sidney Kessler, and others who had gone to Washington to represent the Virgin Islands, persuaded the opponents that the financial benefits of the bill argued for its immediate acceptance, while the disappointments could be amended later. Two major provisions of the financial benefits included U. S. return of internal revenue taxes on V.I. products such as rum, and allowing U.S. citizens resident in the V.I. to pay income taxes on all their sources of income into the V.I. treasury.[28]

Thus, on July 22, 1954, exactly eighteen years and one month since its first Organic Act, the Virgin Islands received a new constitution, known as the Revised Organic Act of the Virgin Islands — 1954 (and which still remains today, with many revisions, as the official constitution of the U. S. Virgin Islands). It unified the governance of the islands by eliminating separate legislatures for St. Thomas-St. John and St. Croix, and established one Legislature of the Virgin Islands, headquartered in the capital, to promote greater governmental economy and efficiency. The eleven members of the Legislature, to be called Senators, were to be elected from all three islands and were provided with the low salary of $600.00 per year, which implied that persons without other means of support should not become senators. It also removed the English language requirement of the Organic Act of 1936, which brought Puerto Ricans and other non-English language citizens into the voting fold.[29]

Interestingly, in the U.S. Senate, a racial factor was injected into the discussion on the potential makeup of the new unified V.I. Legislature. It apparently took place because there was no white member in the St. Thomas-St. John Municipal Council from 1946 to 1952, as Ralph Paiewonsky, who had served continuously in the body from the mid-1930s through 1946, had stopped running in 1946. The lack of a white person in the legislature apparently did not sit well with at least one U.S. senator, and a provision that each voter could vote for only two of the six at-large senatorial positions was explained by the Senator as being necessary to guarantee minority (meaning "white" in the Virgin Islands) representation. A 1978 doctoral dissertation on the V.I. by a mainland American noted that similar colonial policies had been applied by the U.S. in its dealings with Hawaii and Alaska, whereby "the rights of the minority have been guaranteed without similar concerns expressed for the majority."[30]

In spite of the racist and other restrictions, the new Organic Act gave rise to a three-island party system, and increased popular interest in politics and the local government. With only one legislature, previously localized politicians realized the need to form tri-island organizations, and thus during the 1950s island politics became characterized by the territory-wide expansion of the two American parties, the Democratic and Republican, plus a local third group, the Unity Party, which was formed in 1953. The Republican Party never attracted a large following; thus the battles for domination were between the Democratic and Unity parties.[31]

"New Type" Governors of the Late 1940s and 50s — Hastie and His Successors

As already mentioned, the governorship of Hastie in 1946 was revolutionary — he became the first black governor of the Virgin Islands. Then, for the next decade and a half, all of the governors seemed to represent new types of persons for the position. Hastie was followed by Morris de Castro, who was considered as the first "native" in the American period, even though he had not been actually born in the territory. Then the appointments of President Eisenhower following the Republican victory in the U.S. in 1952 seemed to demonstrate that that party had noticed how pleased American Blacks had been about Truman's nomination of Hastie to the governorship of the Virgin Islands. Thus, Archibald A. Alexander, a black engineer from Iowa who was reputed to be a big contributor to the Republican Party, was appointed Governor in 1954. He became unpopular even before his arrival for having reputedly made the statement that President Eisenhower had selected him to teach Virgin Islanders "how to live and how to earn a living." When he did not work out well, another mainland Black, Walter A. Gordon, a California lawyer, was appointed the next year, 1955.[32]

Governor Gordon, too, was unsuccessful, even though his term lasted two years longer than Alexander's. Both Governors seemed to have had very little understanding of the history and culture of the people of the Virgin Islands; both got rid of qualified local persons who were in substantial government positions, and replaced them with persons imported from the mainland. They were unable to develop working relationships with the Legislature, and both ended up being the subjects of protest marches involving thousands of persons who called for their resignations. Alexander complied, citing his health as a reason; Gordon was able to obtain an appointment to the judgeship of the District Court of the Virgin Islands.[33] Both demonstrated also that in addition to race, as dominant and crucial as it has been in affecting human development, there are other factors that may serve to prevent human beings from in-

President Harry S. Truman, visiting St. Thomas in February 1948, being greeted by Gov. William Hastie. Courtesy of the Virgin Islands Government's Archival Collection at the Charles W. Turnbull Regional Library.

teracting constructively. Of course, the argument can also be made that, had there been greater regard for the majority of persons in the territory, greater care may have been taken in making those administrative appointments.

By 1958, the Eisenhower administration had apparently learned the perils of granting gubernatorial appointments, based on race, to persons who had no knowledge or empathetic understanding regarding their assignments. Thus, in 1958 the President's third appointment of a Virgin Islands governor went to a white native, John D. Merwin of St. Croix. Merwin was a member of an old landed family, often spoken of as one of the "Royal Families" of St. Croix. He was very well prepared for the governorship, having attended college at Yale and law school in Washington, D.C., having been a former member of the V.I. Legislature, and having served in the second-highest V.I. administrative position, Government Secretary, during Governor Gordon's term. As a Republican, Governor Merwin was more conservative than most members of the Legislature, but he worked hard at getting along with them, appointed quali-

Governor Hastie showing President Truman Magens Bay and a virgin Peterborg peninsula in 1948. Courtesy of the Virgin Islands Government's Archival Collection at the Charles W. Turnbull Regional Library.

fied local persons to high level positions, and made significant initiatives in areas such as tourism and higher education that the next governor could continue.[34] Being a Republican, however, meant that the Democratic victory of John F. Kennedy in 1960 brought Merwin's governorship to an end in 1961, after three years in the office.

Notes

1. Jarvis, *Brief History of the Virgin Islands*, p. 158.

2. Richard Oulahan, "Porto Rico Gaining; Virgin Isles A Lose, Hoover Concludes," *New York Times*, March 27, 1931, p. 1, col. 3 and p. 23, col 3.

3. Richard Oulahan, "President Returns From the Caribbean; Vigorous for Tasks," *New York Times*, March 30, 1931, p. 10, col. 2.

4. Ibid.

5. Boyer, *America's Virgin Islands*, p. 149.

6. Naughton, "The Origin and Development of Higher Education in the Virgin Islands," pp. 197–201. The black institutions were Atlanta, Dillard, Fisk, Hampton, Howard, Lincoln (Pennsylvania), Morehouse, Saint Augustine, Spelman, Talladega, and Tuskegee. The others were M.I.T., Swarthmore, University of Michigan, and Polytechnic Institute of Puerto Rico.

7. John Frederick Grede, "The New Deal in the Virgin Islands, 1931–1941" (Ph.D. dissertation, University of Chicago, 1962), p. 133.

8. Grede, "The New Deal in the Virgin Islands," pp. 131–134.

9. Evans, *The Virgin Islands: From Naval Base to New Deal*, pp. 296–297.

10. Grede, "The New Deal in the Virgin Islands," p. 106; *Annual Report of the Governor of the Virgin Islands, 1933*, p. 2; Interview with Mary S. Francis, St. Thomas, October 15, 1982.

11. Jarvis, *Brief History of the Virgin Islands*, pp. 166, 178–179; Alex Joseph, "187"; Centennial Countdown"; Alex Joseph, "Paul M. Pearson: The Rehabilitation Program," *Daily News* (St. Thomas, V.I.), May 19, 2016, pp. 10–11.

12. Boyer, *America's Virgin Islands*, pp. 149–161 (Boyer's 'rising expectations' analysis is found on pp. 160–61); Grede, "The New Deal in the Virgin Islands," pp. 135–141. After Pearson's death in 1938, his ashes, as he had requested, were scattered over the Caribbean Sea.

13. Knud Knud-Hansen, *From Denmark to the Virgin Islands* (Philadelphia: Dorrance and Company, 1947), pp. 122–124.

14. Knud-Hansen, *From Denmark to the Virgin Islands*, p. 120.

15. Hamilton Cochran, *These are the Virgin Islands* (New York: Prentice-Hall, Inc., 1937), p. 52.

16. Cochran, *These are the Virgin Islands*, p. 56.

17. Cochran, *These are the Virgin Islands*, pp. 56–57.

18. Boyer, *America's Virgin Islands*, pp. 179–181; Dookhan, "Civil Rights and Political Justice," pp. 28–36.

19. Section 17 of the "Organic Act of the Virgin Islands," 1936, in James A. Bough and Roy G. Macridis, editors, *Virgin Islands, America's Caribbean Outpost: The Evolution of Self-Government* (Wakefield, Massachusetts: The Walter F. Williams Publishing Company, 1970), p. 48.

20. Boyer, *America's Virgin Islands*, p. 183.

21. Earle B. Ottley, *Trials and Triumphs: The Long Road to a Middle Class Society in the U. S. Virgin Islands* (St. Thomas, V.I., 1982), pp. 38–40; Valdemar A. Hill, Sr., *Rise to Recognition* (St. Thomas, V.I.: St. Thomas Graphics Inc., 1971), p. 92.

22. Darwin D. Creque, *The U.S. Virgins and the Eastern Caribbean* (Philadelphia: Whit-

more Publishing Co., 1968), pp. 112–113; Valdemar A. Hill, Sr., *Rise to Recognition: An Account of U.S. Virgin Islanders from Slavery to Self-Government* (St. Thomas, V.I., St. Thomas Graphics, Inc., 1971), pp. 92–96. Founders of the Progressive Guide included Carlos Downing, Valdemar Hill, Omar Brown, Henry Richards, Oswald Harris, Roy P. Gordon, and Aubrey Ottley.

23. Jarvis, *Brief History of the Virgin Islands*, pp. 231–232; Creque, *The U.S. Virgins and the Eastern Caribbean*, p. 112.

24. Grede, "The New Deal in the Virgin Islands," pp. 50–51; Creque, *The U.S. Virgins and the Eastern Caribbean*, p. 125. Hastie's predecessor, Charles Harwood, had been able, through friends in Congress, to secure in 1944 a $10 million appropriation for various public projects in the Virgin Islands, for which the islanders bestowed on him unprecedented accolades. However, according to Robert Morse Lovett, his feeling about living in the Virgin Islands was such that he considered any time spent there as "punishment" and spent about half of his tenure of office away from the islands. During the last year of his administration, he was in the islands for only ninety days; this fact supposedly led President Truman to ask for his resignation. (Lovett, *All Our Years*, New York: The Viking Press, 1949, pp. 296–297; 328.)

25. Creque, *The U.S. Virgins and the Eastern Caribbean*, pp. 128–129.

26. Boyer, *America's Virgin Islands*, pp. 207, 209; Hazel May McFerson, "The Impact of a Changed Racial Tradition: Race, Politics, and Society in the U.S. Virgin Islands, 1917–1975" (Ph.D. dissertation, Brandeis University, 1976), pp. 91–92.

27. Earle B. Ottley, *Trials and Triumphs*, pp. 95–115, 212.

28. Ralph M. Paiewonsky, with Isaac Dookhan. Memoirs of a Governor: A Man for the People. New York: New York University Press, 1990, pp. 143–149.

29. Paul M. Leary, ed. *Major Political and Constitutional Documents of the United States Virgin Islands, 1671–1991.* (St. Thomas: University of the Virgin Islands, 1992.) pp. 168–192.

30. James A. Bough, "General Introduction to the Constitutional Evolution of the Virgin Islands," in Bough and Macridis, *Virgin Islands: America's Caribbean Outpost*, p. 124; McFerson, "The Impact of a Changed Racial Tradition," p. 183.

31. Earle B. Ottley, *Trials and Triumphs: The Long Road to a Middle Class Society in the U.S. Virgin Islands.* St. Thomas, U.S. Virgin Islands, 1982, pp. 93–115; William W. Boyer, *America's Virgin Islands: A History of Human Rights and Wrongs*, second edition. Durham, North Carolina: Carolina Academic Press, 2010, pp. 231–237.

32. Earle B. Ottley, *Trials and Triumphs*, pp. 116–117.

33. Ralph M. Paiewonsky, *Memoirs of a Governor*, pp. 150–151.

34. Ruth Moolenaar, *Profiles of Outstanding Virgin Islanders*, Third Edition, 1992, p. 155; Paiewonsky, *Memoirs of a Governor*, pp. 151–153.

Chapter 11

The Social Framework of Race Relations, 1930s–1960s

The political administrations of the 1940s through the 1960s faced quite different and more optimistic societies that those of the preceding decades. Economic conditions on St. Thomas had been so bad that the population had continuously declined from 1880 through the 1930s, as residents kept leaving to seek employment elsewhere—most often the United States mainland, and also the Dominican Republic, Cuba, and Panama. However, President Roosevelt's New Deal programs to prime the depression economy during the middle of the 1930s and the beginning of military activities in the late 1930s had a remarkable effect on the population of St. Thomas. From a high of 14,389 in 1880, the population had dwindled steadily each decade and reached a low of 9,834 in 1930. The census of 1940 showed that for the first time in the twentieth century, the population reflected an increase—of almost one and a half thousand persons over 1930—and registered 11,265 residents in St. Thomas.[1]

Early Effects of Defense Spending and Military Personnel

The acceleration of defense activities during the early 1940s, as World War II became a reality, presented even more lucrative employment opportunities. Construction workers who were paid twenty cents an hour on military projects in 1942 had received only nine or ten cents an hour before 1940.[2] Not only did such conditions keep in St. Thomas some natives who might otherwise have migrated, but hundreds of workers were attracted to St. Thomas from nearby islands, particularly the British Virgin Islands and Puerto Rico. In addition to those West Indians who had come in search of employment, St. Thomas's population was increased during the war years by a couple hundred white servicemen from the mainland who were stationed there.[3]

During the 1920s the overwhelming majority of white mainland Americans on St. Thomas had been there on temporary military assignment, and most such residencies ended with the withdrawal of the Navy in 1931. However, due to the civil administration of the 1930s there took place a slow but steady accretion of white Americans from the mainland, who were coming to establish permanent residence. In 1938 newspaper editor and educator J. Antonio Jarvis, who was the first Black to write a history of the Virgin Islands, observed:

> Because of the immigration there are more white and brown people now than at any other time in the immediate past. By the middle of this century, the native Negro will be outnumbered, unless some interruption in the visible trends make a change.[4]

Immigration did not continue at the pace Jarvis had envisioned, however, because the cessation of military construction after 1942 and the end of the war in 1945 led to slowdowns in economic activity.

In 1940 a white American psychologist, Albert Campbell, spent eight months studying the people of St. Thomas. He wrote a monograph which remains invaluable for its keen perception of the mentality and status of each socio-racial group on the island.[5] Campbell observed that Continentals, the term which was becoming popular for white persons from the U.S. mainland, constituted a small group that he estimated at considerably less than 100. However, almost all of them held positions of prestige and responsibility. In 1938 one had even gotten elected to the Municipal Council and, in conjunction with the older local Whites, they were able to exert great influence. The group tended to associate only among themselves or with the military officers and upper-class white St. Thomians and Europeans. Campbell wrote:

> Most of them bring to St. Thomas the characteristic American attitude toward race, and while they do not feel free to express their prejudices in the domineering manner they might regard as appropriate on the mainland, they make an effort to avoid all unnecessary contact with the colored natives, no matter their intellectual or economic pretensions.[6]

Those Continentals who acted with benevolence toward the Blacks, in contrast to the foregoing attitudes, were found to be unusually few.

Campbell also noted that the older, non-Continental St. Thomas Whites had different attitudes toward color and were able to mingle more easily with other groups, particularly well-to-do mixed persons. However, he detected that:

A certain degree of diffusion of American attitudes is taking place, and St. Thomas whites tend to imitate their American visitors in this regard.

They do not have sufficient strength in the community to introduce discriminatory laws or Jim Crow practices, but in their social contact they have tended to withdraw within the limits of their own race.[7]

The research conducted by Campbell pinpointed two developments in 1940 that were serving to make race a very conscious concern of a number of persons on St. Thomas. One was the growth of a tourist traffic since the mid-1930s and the growing tendency to provide segregated accommodations for the tourists. The other was the realization and resentment of Whites that political power was changing hands. The civil administrations of the 1930s had placed Blacks in many government jobs and the Organic Act had placed control of the legislature in the hands of the black majority. Whites confided their observations that some of the young black natives were refusing to treat them with the deference to which Whites had been accustomed, and bitterly resented the new atmosphere. Campbell was told, "St. Thomas was a charming place under the Navy. The Negroes were happy but they were kept in their place." Some Whites were looking forward to a period when white supremacy would be restored.[8] Campbell perceived that fear may have been a factor in explaining some of the antagonism the newer members of the white community felt toward the Blacks:

Prejudiced white individuals do not find it reassuring to be surrounded by a heavy preponderance of black people from whom they have been taught to expect hostility. The self-confidence with which they deal with Negroes in other areas frequently disappears in such an atmosphere…. Some of the more excitable Americans frighten each other with rumors of a black revolution …[9]

A number of incidents and developments showed how accurate Campbell's observations were. One incident even led to the removal of the Governor. In 1940, a white Continental named Jacques Schiffer was serving as a member of the Municipal Council from St. Thomas. He and Governor Cramer were not in agreement because the administration was trying to get the Rural Electrification Administration to provide power for the islands, but Schiffer, an employee of the West Indian Company, which was a private supplier of electrical power on St. Thomas, opposed any such move. Schiffer, hoping to discredit the governor and considering himself the spokesman for the Continentals on the island, went to Washington in the fall of 1940 and related to Interior Secretary Harold Ickes a frightening tale. Schiffer said that law enforcement in the islands had broken down and that residents were in great fear for their safety. He insisted that the islands were on the verge of a race war and that the Whites were arming. Schiffer disclosed that he himself had hired a bodyguard. The President and Secretary Ickes both became alarmed as the seeming approach of war made the security of the Caribbean important. Ickes sent an agent, a Mr. Kelly, to investigate and report what was going in the Virgin Islands.

Governor Cramer felt that the special investigation was totally unwarranted and did not hide his sentiments. On his next trip to Washington he insisted on seeing a copy of the report. Ickes had by then realized the trumped-up nature of Schiffer's charges and had refused to see him again, while Kelly had been dismissed after the submission of his report, which had relied too heavily on irresponsible sources. Nonetheless, Cramer wrote Ickes a strongly-worded protest of the investigation and report, which caused Ickes to ask for Cramer's resignation in December, 1940.[10]

Morris F. De Castro, a white St. Thomian who was serving as Commissioner of Finance and generally acted as the stabilizer and link between the various V.I. administrations, assessed the Schiffer-inspired investigation as follows:

> ... some newcomers who do not see why the Negroes should be given any special consideration, or rather any consideration, at all, are out to get the Governor's skin by any means. I have it from several sources that the race question is behind this — particularly from dislike on the part of certain Americans to meet colored persons like the Bornns, etc. at Government House.[11]

Increasing American Settlement and Racial Influence

Many of the Blacks on St. Thomas had very little idea of the racial politics which were transpiring. And the advent of new trends in race relations also was not seriously considered or admitted by many. Campbell found that upper and middle-class Blacks adjusted by simply avoiding interracial situations as much as possible, while he discovered that many lower-class Blacks did not even "recognize race prejudice when they encounter it; their inclination is to interpret any discrimination as springing from class differentiation.[12]

There were numerous indicators, however, that the American-style race relations were steadily infiltrating the islands. During the 1930s all three hotels on St. Thomas attempted the exclusion of non-white guests. In doing so, the

Virgin Isle Hotel, built in 1950 on a hill west of Charlotte Amalie, the first luxury hotel in the Virgin Islands. Courtesy of the Virgin Islands Government's Archival Collection at the Charles W. Turnbull Regional Library.

continental manager of the government-owned Bluebeard Castle Hotel defied government regulations, but his policy was widely approved by the resident Continentals. The Grand Hotel, which was the oldest such establishment on St. Thomas, followed suit with a similar policy. The third hotel, which was managed by white Americans from the mainland, relaxed its policies somewhat during the off-season but contrived to maintain an all-white policy at the height of the tourist season. Even a restaurant on Main Street labeled a room "For Tourists Only" and it was generally reserved for Whites. Such measures aroused the resentment of a number of local Blacks and in the case of the Grand Hotel, which was located right in the center of the town, protest was sufficiently strong to prevent any strict adherence to an all-white policy.[13]

That overt racist behavior was being adopted by the older white groups of St. Thomas was demonstrated in 1945, when a number of children of the French community known as Carenage (now called French Town) were withdrawn from the school there because the new teacher was black instead of French. The local *Daily News* warned the French against "aping the demagogues of the South" and further editorialized:

> It is unfortunate that in a community which is predominantly colored this shocking and indefensible action should be taken by the people

of Careenage … such action in order to keep up a pretense to a non-existent superiority is inexcusable.[14]

A substantial amount of racial friction was generated in the 1940s by the reported behavior of the white military personnel stationed on St. Thomas. There was intermittent press coverage of the public display of biased racial attitudes by members of the armed forces. A typical report was of an incident in October, 1942, which involved a black taxi driver and two white marines, who called the driver a "black liar." According to the news story, a marine shore patrolman became disturbed only when the driver retaliated and called one of the marines a "white liar"; the patrolman then held the driver so the marines could punch him in the face. Additionally, the police director (who was also a Continental) pressed charges of disorderly conduct against the taxi driver, but they were later dismissed by the police judge.[15]

In addition to the experience of offensive racial behavior from military personnel stationed in St. Thomas, many St. Thomian men who served in the armed forces themselves suffered discriminatory treatment on the mainland. The Selective Service Act was extended to the V.I. in 1943, partly at the request of Virgin Islanders; prior to that some islanders had joined the armed forces on the mainland or in Puerto Rico. Approximately 900 Virgin Islanders rendered military service during the war; about 600 returned home afterward. A sizeable contingent had been sent to an Army camp near to New Orleans, where they experienced the total segregation of Jim Crowism for the first time. Many were also assigned, because of their race, only to manual tasks. Active defiance of such humiliating racism by some of the Virgin Islands soldiers led to a number of incidents which involved "illegal" actions and physical confrontations. Army authorities finally realized that these men would not passively abide by a racial tradition so different to their own, and decided to avoid further incidents by sending them to Hawaii. By that time, those Virgin Islanders had come to understand first-hand the pervasive significance of race in certain areas of the United States.[16]

Perceived Need for Civil Rights Legislation

By 1943, there was sufficient concern in St. Thomas about the new attitudes and overt practices of racial segregation and discrimination that legislative action was taken. The Fifth Municipal Council of St. Thomas-St. John enacted an "Ordinance to Determine the Right of All Persons to Enjoy the Facilities Offered by Public Places and Businesses in the Municipality of St. Thomas and

St. John and other purposes," which became law on May 30, 1945. Fines or imprisonment were stipulated for violation of the ordinance, and licensed entities were to suffer suspension of the license for a second violation. Its basic provision was:

> No person shall be denied access to, service, equal treatment or employment in/or at any publicly licensed place of business (including public transportation), or benefits soliciting public patronage in the Municipality of St. Thomas and St. John because of politics, religion, race, color, or because of any other reason not applicable to all persons.[17]

A year and a half later, in December 1946, the Legislative Assembly of the Virgin Islands (which consisted of the joint Municipal Councils of St. Thomas-St. John and St. Croix) acted likewise and passed an "Act to Provide Equal Rights in Places of Public Accommodation, Resort, or Amusements." This enactment became applicable to the entire Virgin Islands, but it contained two significant differences from the ordinance which had earlier been enacted for St. Thomas and St. John. It specifically exempted private clubs and it left the question of whether business licenses should be suspended or revoked to the discretion of the governor. The latter provision was probably due to the fact that William H. Hastie had shortly before become the Virgin Islands' first black governor, and the Legislative Assembly trusted him to execute properly the spirit of the law.[18]

The overall achievements of the civil rights ordinance passed in 1946 varied considerably. It brought to an end the more blatant forms of prohibited discrimination, such as the refusal of hotels and restaurants to cater to non-Whites. However, there continued the steady growth of other discriminatory practices. As the law passed by the Legislative Assembly had exempted private clubs, such organizations operated with shameless insensitivity. The St. Croix Country Club, for example, which had always extended membership to Virgin Islands governors prior to Hastie, did not accord him that option. And on St. Thomas, the Contant Club, at the site of the old Contant Great House, also operated as an exclusive white institution.[19]

St. Thomas at the end of the 1940s, after about three decades of American rule, was displaying indications of a growing economic direction for its future—the accommodation of tourists. Sustained promotion was started in 1948 when the St. Thomas Tourist Development Board was established, even though it had only one full-time employee. During the decade, several guesthouses and hotels were added to those which had already been in operation. By the end of 1949 the number of tourist beds available in St. Thomas numbered over 500.[20]

From a long-term point of view, more important than the temporary residents and tourists of the late 1940s was the growing number of mainland Americans who were making the V.I. their permanent home. Some were servicemen who had been stationed in the islands during the war and decided to return to live. A few had initially come with only the thought of satisfying the six-week divorce requirement (which made Thomas during the late 1940s one of the well-known divorce destinations of the nation) and ended up thinking that it was a pretty good place to live. Some simply came on vacations and saw business opportunities, a more relaxed social pace, or a physical environment which lured them to return.

A number of publicists in the late 1940s actively tried to introduce or invite tourists and potential residents to the islands. Two St. Thomians, J. Antonio Jarvis and Rufus Martin, published their *Virgin Islands Picture Book* in 1946 with just that in mind. Its finale, written by Alvaro de Lugo, the local postmaster, stated:

> These are the Virgin Islands, and their people are not selfish about their beautiful islands. They welcome the visitor to share with them their beauty and climate. This picture book is your introduction to them and your invitation to visit with them.[21]

David Maas, a white American originally from Cincinnati and who would become Lieutenant Governor of the Virgin Islands in 1971, went to St. Thomas in the early 1940s as a special agent for the FBI. He resigned his position and moved to St. Thomas in 1945. In addition to his law practice, he was attracted by the possibilities of tourism and started with a few cottages for tourists. He ended up establishing the Sapphire Bay Beach Resort, one of the first beach hotels on St. Thomas, and became the publisher and editor of "The Beachcomber," a newsletter devoted to promoting tourism for the Virgin Islands.[22]

During the next two decades, the 1950s and especially the 60s, St. Thomas and the U.S. Virgin Islands populations experienced explosive growth, due not only to arriving Continentals but more so to Caribbeans from nearby islands seeking employment.

In the two decades from 1950 through the end of the 1960s, every important numerical indicator of social relations in St. Thomas underwent dramatic change. The population more than doubled, increasing from 13, 813 in 1950 to over 28,000 in 1969, as indicated by the Census of 1970.[23] The relative proportions of the various component groups also showed fundamental alteration. Whereas in 1950 about three-fourths (73.6%) of the population had been born in the Virgin Islands, that percentage had fallen to 63% by 1960 and then to 46% by 1969. Thus the outnumbering of native Virgin Islanders, which

Charlotte Amalie during the construction of the Waterfront in the early 1950s. Courtesy of the Virgin Islands Government's Archival Collection at the Charles W. Turnbull Regional Library.

Jarvis had predicted would happen by mid-century, actually took place during the 1960s, due mainly to the prodigious influx of two very dissimilar groups. The larger of the two was comprised of West Indians from eastern Caribbean islands, almost all of whom were black. The second largest group of newcomers consisted of Americans who had moved down from the U.S. mainland, most of whom were white, although an appreciable percentage was black.[24]

Renowned Caribbean historian Franklin Knight's theory of the difference between "settler" and "non-settler" societies in the Americas explains some of the changes which were taking place in St. Thomas and the rest of the V.I. in the middle of the twentieth century. Knight points out that in the societies of the New World which Europeans regarded as "settler" areas for themselves and became predominant in the population, best exemplified by the United States, the society came to be sharply divided along racial lines. In "non-settler" societies, such as the islands of the West Indies, where Whites did not envision themselves as living permanently in large numbers but came essentially to make fortunes and leave and were always a small proportion of the population, a more relaxed attitude developed towards race. Such white settlers, who formed a small elite, were forced by demographic conditions to think and act differently and somewhat more benevolently regarding race.[25]

To apply Knight's model and terminology, therefore, prior to 1950 the V.I. comprised a non-settler society for American Whites. Those whites living there expected to be part of a small, somewhat exotic group and generally were not engaged in economic activities which involved direct competition with Blacks. With the tourism growth of the 1950s and the industrial development of the 1960s, the V.I. began, belatedly, to become a white settler community, with substantial numbers of Whites from all walks of life attracted to the islands, many with seeming intentions to stay. Even though Whites would, for a time, remain a small minority, their growing presence would lead to increasing competition and sharpened racial lines.

Though it was probably realized at the time by only very few, 1950 appears to have been a watershed year—a dividing line between the white non-settler society that had prevailed in the V.I. throughout most of its recorded history and the beginning of a new order. Four events took place in the year 1950 which seemed to presage the major developments of the next half century. The first was the finding of the U.S. 1950 Census that the white population of the V.I. exceeded ten per cent, which is considered by some sociologists as a significant figure in the racial differentiation of societies.[26] In 1917, at the beginning of American rule, it had been 7.4%; in 1940 it was 9%; and the 1950 Census showed the white population to be 11%. By the 1960 Census Whites had increased to 16.7% and the 1970 count placed Whites at 18.2% of the V.I. populace. For St. Thomas alone, however, the white percentage had long been larger due to the presence of the French-descended communities. Thus, the figures for St. Thomas were 12.7% white in 1917, 16.2% in 1950, and 18% in 1960.

The significance of the 1950 above-ten per cent figure for the entire Virgin Islands, therefore, was that it indicated the growing presence of Whites from the U.S. mainland, whose background of race relations made them potentially more culturally discordant than the West Indian Whites of French descent, who had theretofore accounted for the greatest proportion of Whites in the V.I. In non-settler societies, the dominant group (power-wise) is often a small minority of less than ten per cent of the population. In settler societies the dominant group is frequently a large minority of about twenty per cent or more of the population and may grow to be a majority. The growing number of white mainland settlers in the V.I., as revealed by the Census of 1950, was a prognosticator of an impending rapid growth of a white settler society and the possible transformations in race relations which had attended such movements elsewhere.[27]

The second significant event of 1950 was the perceived necessity for a second civil rights law. Despite the civil rights ordinance of 1945, the growth of certain discriminatory practices, such as those of private clubs, and fear of the possible results of increasing tourism, prompted the Legislative Assembly of the V.I. to pass the Harris-Neaser-McFarlane Anti-Discrimination Act of 1950. Branded as the strongest civil rights law under the American flag, it was designed to "prevent and prohibit discrimination in any form based upon race, creed, color, or national origin, whether practiced directly or indirectly or by subterfuge ..."[28]

The third consequential occurrence of 1950 was the founding of the Antilles School in St. Thomas, a private, non-sectarian elementary and junior high institution. Even though there were several other non-public schools on St. Thomas and a sizeable percentage of children had always attended private or parochial institutions, the tuition fees of the Antilles School were so far above the others as to exclude even most middle class children. The Antilles School, therefore, began, and remained for its first few decades, a mainly white institution in a mainly black community. Many wondered if it represented the beginning of a somewhat segregated school system.

The fourth momentous event in St. Thomas in 1950 was the opening of the Virgin Isles Hotel, the first luxury hotel in the V.I. Its 130 rooms immediately increased St Thomas' bed capacity by one-third and gave to that island more than three-fourths of the tourist accommodation capacity of the entire Virgin Islands.[29]

Notes

1. U.S. Bureau of the Census, Census of Population: 1960. *General Population Characteristics*, Final Report PC (1)-B55 Virgin Islands (Washington: U.S. Government Printing Office) 1961, pp. 6–7.

2. Grede, "The New Deal in the Virgin Islands," p. 239.

3. Marilyn Krigger, "Attitudes and References to Immigrants in the St. Thomas Press, 1936–1942" (Paper presented to the Tenth Conference of Caribbean Historians, St. Thomas, V.I., March, 1978), p. 3.

4. Jarvis, *Brief History of the Virgin Islands*, p. 240. His reference to "brown people" probably meant Puerto Ricans and was occasioned by the migration to St. Croix in far greater numbers than was the case for St. Thomas.

5. Professor Campbell, also known as Angus Campbell, eventually became the Director of the Institute for Social Research at the University of Michigan, and was a leading researcher on racial attitudes in the United States during the 1960s and 1970s.

6. Campbell, *St. Thomas Negroes*, p. 33

7. Campbell, *St. Thomas Negroes*, p. 33.

8. Campbell, *St. Thomas Negroes*, pp. 81–82.

9. Campbell, *St. Thomas Negroes*, pp. 81–82.

10. Grede, "The New Deal in the Virgin Islands," pp. 229–233.

11. Letter from Morris de Castro to Robert Morse Lovett, September 25, 1940 (in the Lovett Papers at the Harper Library, University of Chicago), quoted in Grede, "The New Deal in the Virgin Islands," pp. 230–231. De Castro would become Governor of the V.I. in 1950.

12. Campbell, *St. Thomas Negroes*, p. 82.

13. Campbell, *St. Thomas Negroes*, p. 82; also interview with Enid Hansen Frederiksen, a mixed St. Thomian, February 24, 1983, who remembers that a restaurant in the Grand Hotel in the late 1930s initially refused service to herself and some friends because they were not white.

14. Editorial entitled "Cha Cha Town," February 10, 1948; found in Ariel Melchior, *Thoughts Along the Way: An Anthology of Editorials from the Virgin Islands Daily News, 1930–1978* (St. Thomas, Virgin Islands: Ariel Melchior, Inc., 1981), pp. 126–127.

15. "Editorial," *Daily News*, (St. Thomas, V.I.), October 29, 1942, p. 5.

16. Creque, *The U.S. Virgins and the Eastern Caribbean*, pp. 115–117; Boyer, *America's Virgin Islands*, p. 213.

17. Found in William W. Boyer, *Civil Liberties in the U.S. Virgin Islands, 1917–1949* (St. Croix, U.S. V.I.: Antilles Graphic Arts, 1982), p. 135.

18. Boyer, *Civil Liberties in the U.S. Virgin Islands*, pp. 135–136.

19. Ottley, *Trials and Triumphs*, p. 107.

20. Martin Garson Orlins, "The Impact of Tourism on the Virgin Islands of the United States" (Ph.D. dissertation, Columbia University, 1969), pp. 93, 103–4; Jarvis and Martin, *Virgin Islands Picture Book*, pp. 63–65.

21. Jarvis and Martin, *Virgin Islands Picture Book*, "Finale" by Alvaro de Lugo, pp. 112–13.

22. "Governor Evans Inaugural Journal," special edition of the *Home Journal* (St. Thomas, V.I.), January 1, 1971, Section F, p. 1; Speech by Henry Wheatley, presenting

David Maas at his inauguration as Lieutenant Governor in January, 1971, as recorded in the *Daily News* (St. Thomas, V.I.), January 5, 1971, p. 2.

23. U.S. Bureau of the Census, *1970 Census of Population: General Population Characteristics*, p. 55–16.

24. U.S. Bureau of the Census, *1970 Census of Population: General Population Characteristics*, p. 55–16.

25. Franklin W. Knight, *The African Dimension in Latin American Societies* (New York: Macmillan Publishing Co. Inc., 1974), *passim*, especially pp. 45–49; 70–136.

26. See, for example, Van den Berghe, Race and Racism, pp. 25–33.

27. U.S. Bureau of the Census, *1950 Census of Population: General Population Characteristics*, p. 54–85; U.S. Bureau of the Census, *1960 Census of Population: General Population Characteristics*, p. 55–12; U.S. Bureau of the Census, *1970 Census of Population: General Population Characteristics*, p. 55–16; Van den Berghe, *Race and Racism*, pp. 27, 29.

28. Marilyn F. Krigger, "A Quarter-Century of Race Relations in the U.S. Virgin Islands: St. Thomas, 1950–1975." Unpublished Ph.D. Dissertation, University of Delaware, 1983, p. 131; "Bill No. 1," *Daily News* (St. Thomas, V.I.), September 22, 1950, pp. 2, 4.

29. Orlins, "The Impact of Tourism on the Virgin Islands," p. 104.

Chapter 12

The Socio-Racial Groups, 1930s–1960s

The major groups of the society during the 1930s–60s are being referred to as socio-racial groups rather than just racial because, based on the findings of sociological research of the time and popular knowledge, a sizeable number of persons in the society did not readily classify themselves by race. Instead, they tended to classify themselves mostly by a mix of various social and racial factors such as class, complexion, occupational position, or wealth.

Components of the Black Socio-Racial Groups

Blacks in St. Thomas in 1950 numbered approximately 11,572 of a total population of 13,813. The U.S. Census of 1950 actually reported them as 10,278 "Negroes" and 1,294 "Mixed and other races." As there were hardly any Asians in St. Thomas at that time, practically all of the persons in the "mixed and other races" category were persons with some degree of African ancestry.[1]

In explaining differences between the settler and non-settler societies of the Americas, Professor Franklin Knight observed: "Where Afro-Americans form a majority of the population, and where they have political power, race seems to be a less important consideration than, color, social status, and economic position."[2] That was quite true of many Blacks in St. Thomas at the middle of the twentieth century. There was very little concern about any shared African ancestry; there was considerable concern about the differences in complexion and class which various historical fortuities had brought about. What Campbell had observed in 1940 was probably at least partially true ten years later:

St. Thomians are highly aware of color, but they feel almost no common bond based on the Negro ancestry which they share. The light-skinned people and some of brown complexion insist that they are not Negroes and try to repudiate all connection with the black race. The black people accept their racial identity as they must, but it has very little significance to them except in so far as their dark skin affects their lives locally. Only a few feel any interest in the history or present status of the Negro race in the world at large.... They feel very little relationship with the American Negroes and ... American Negroes who visit the island are not cordially received unless they are exceptionally prominent.... Several race conscious American Negroes have brought their equalitarian doctrines to St. Thomas during the last twenty years, and they have never failed to create a furor of resentment among the white colony and the upper- and middle-class colored groups.[3]

Based on his research, Campbell had also asserted that the majority of lower-class St. Thomians "regard the Negro as inferior to the white man.... People of this class are almost unanimous in their preference for white persons in positions of authority."[4] He found that not only in racial matters, but also in some other areas, black St. Thomians showed a lack of group identification and social cooperation. Interestingly, Campbell discerned that St. Thomians were aware of their weaknesses in social cooperation and lamented them, but efforts at change generally did not advance beyond that stage.[5]

Even in 1940, though, there had been signs of growing racial consciousness on the part of a small number of Blacks, and the number slowly augmented as time went by. Some were persons who had had exposure outside of the V.I. to mainland attitudes about race, and thought that any sizeable influx of white Continentals to the islands might pose serious threats to black Virgin Islanders, most of whom had not completed high school and worked in blue collar positions in governmental services, retailing, and tourist accommodations. Included among the concerned were some of the alumni of historically black colleges in the South, which had become well known locally due to scholarships they had given to Virgin Islanders in the 1930s. These colleges were attended even by Virgin Islanders who, in the islands, would not have classified themselves as "Negro." During the 1940s and 1950s these institutions, especially Hampton Institute and Howard University, continued to attract a considerable percentage of V.I. college students. A very large percentage of Virgin Islanders who earned medical or law degrees during those decades earned them at Howard University. One scholar has suggested that being educated at black institutions placed V.I. students in a "double-bind" situation: in order to take advantage of the educational opportunities offered in the U.S., they had to accept at least temporarily the mainland American view of themselves as inferior beings in a segregated educational system.[6]

During the 1950s the black St. Thomian population was overwhelmingly native-born. Of the non-native Blacks, the great majority were from St. Thomas's nearest foreign neighbor, the British Virgin Islands. However, because of a long history of social and economic interrelationships, and except for technical immigration purposes, the B.V.I. was not completely considered a foreign area. Present also was a small number of other British West Indians, most of whom had arrived in St. Thomas initially to work on defense projects in the early 1940s. To complete the black population of St. Thomas in the 1950s were two other small groups—those Puerto Ricans who were of noticeably African ancestry, even though some may not necessarily have classified themselves thusly, and Blacks from the U.S. mainland. The last group was very small but quite conspicuous, consisting mainly of Blacks who had been sent on federal political appointments or who had migrated to work in professional positions. In the early 1950s, therefore, it included such persons as the judge of the U.S. District Court, the Government Secretary (the second highest executive position) of the V.I., the principal of the only public high school on St. Thomas, and several school teachers.

Beginning in the late 1950s and accelerating throughout the 1960s was a large movement of Blacks from the British and other West Indian Islands and, to a lesser degree, Blacks from the U.S. mainland. The term "Continental," which had once been applied almost exclusively to Whites, by the 1960s had to be qualified by "black" or "white." (However, if not qualified, it usually referred to white Continentals.) Both the black Continentals and the aliens, as Blacks from the non-U.S. Caribbean were officially classified and popularly called, were pulled to St. Thomas by the growing tourist industry—its labor demands and the increased governmental services a growing populace needed. Most alien-status West Indians were in construction, tourism services, or domestic workers, while a sizeable percentage of black Continentals worked for the government or private industry in positions such as teaching or clerical areas.

During the 1960s therefore, the black population of St. Thomas was a composite of three different groups—native Blacks, Blacks from other West Indian islands (most were from the British Virgin Islands, Anguilla, Antigua, Dominica, Montserrat, Nevis, and St. Kitts), and Blacks from the mainland U.S. There were, however, substantial differences in the size of each group. Native Blacks accounted for over forty per cent of the total population, non-citizen Blacks comprised about one-third, and continental Blacks formed the smallest group, making up less than three percent of St. Thomas residents.[7]

Faculty of Charlotte Amalie High School in the early 1940s. L-R standing: Austin Donovan, Jane E. Tuitt, unsure, Mildred Anduze, Rupert Vanterpool, Elizabeth Michael, John P. Scott, J. Antonio Jarvis. L-R seated: Adina Kean, Emma B. Smith, Bertha C. Boschulte, Eldra Shulterbrandt, Ivanna Eudora Kean, unsure. Courtesy of the Virgin Islands Government's Archival Collection at the Charles W. Turnbull Regional Library.

A number of developments charted the relationship of the three black subgroups to each other. As both incoming groups charged, neither was particularly welcomed by the native Blacks. Due to the lack of racial identification, many native Blacks seemed to feel no greater affinity for the black Continentals than they did for the white. In fact, some native Blacks viewed black Continentals, especially those from the South, as inferior in a number of ways—partly because of stereotypes projected by U.S. entertainment media and from the knowledge that those from the South were products of lifelong segregation. Many black Continentals were surprised at the lack of sympathy they got from native Blacks and truly amazed at their perception that white Continentals often were accepted more readily than were they. Of course, there were exceptions: black Continentals who, from the beginning, met helpful neighbors, or those who arrived as spouses of V.I. Blacks they had met on the mainland and thus may have been a part of a supportive family group. But for many black Continentals, most of whom had stronger feelings of racial solidarity than most islanders, it was a sorely disappointing experience to find that their race provided no special acceptance or advantages in a community whose racial make-up was overwhelmingly black. However, the experience of residing in a mainly black political entity where some of the leaders were black was a new and especially pleasurable feeling for some continental Blacks.[8]

The entry of large numbers of non-American Blacks into the V.I. resulted from federal action in response to local business pressure. The Chambers of Commerce of St. Thomas-St. John and St. Croix realized in the early 1950s that the growing tourist trade needed labor beyond what was available in the U.S. V.I. They lobbied in Washington for special exemptions for the V.I. from the restrictive provisions of the 1952 Immigration and Naturalization Act, which banned non-immigrant labor except for jobs of a strictly temporary character. Accordingly, in 1956 a special foreign labor program was initiated, whereby alien workers from the British Virgin Islands could be issued temporary work permits by the Immigration and Naturalization Service to fill positions in the V.I. for which U.S. citizens were determined to be unavailable. Several hundred British Virgin Islanders were thus admitted in the late 1950s. In 1959 the program was extended to include all of the British, Dutch, and French Islands of the Caribbean. Each work permit was renewable repeatedly, as long as it was officially certified by the Labor Department that a citizen or permanent resident was not available. Under those conditions, over 7,000 Blacks from the eastern Caribbean, principally the British Islands, migrated to St. Thomas during the 1960s. And, in addition to legally-admitted persons, thousands more entered by various illegal and extra-legal means. By the late 60s, non-citizen West Indian Blacks comprised thirty per cent of the population and forty-five per cent of the labor force of the Virgin Islands.[9]

The non-citizen West Indians took the place which the "Cha Chas" had held in the past—that of the lowest socio-economic stratum. And, as if to signify that whatever group was in that position deserved a derogatory name, the non-citizen Blacks were popularly called "Garrots."[10] There has been much speculation about the origin of the term "Garrot." The most common explanation on St. Thomas was that it was used by Marcus Garvey in reference to some Antiguans as a result of unpleasant experiences on that island during efforts to promote his Universal Negro Improvement Association. Their position in the Virgin Islands was probably worse than that of any group since the enslaved, as they were lacking in job and thus residential security and also in political power, being non-citizens. Additionally, the legal regulations of the 1960s prevented most of them from bringing their families to the V.I. and denied them access to government services such as public education and housing.

One of the most painful of the conditions the alien-status Blacks experienced was simply the low esteem in which they were held by many native Blacks. In spite of the similarity of racial and historical backgrounds and certain West Indian cultural commonalities, some native Blacks refused to iden-

Sts. Peter & Paul graduating class of 1958—a racial mix! Courtesy of the Virgin Islands Government's Archival Collection at the Charles W. Turnbull Regional Library.

tify with the alien-status Blacks—racially, culturally, or otherwise. Continentals, black and white, sometimes listened in disbelief or amusement as they heard some native Blacks make the same charges of cultural and moral inferiority against non-citizen Blacks as racist Whites were known to make against Blacks. Some alien-status Blacks even thought that, on the whole, they were accorded kinder treatment by Whites in the V.I. than by the native Blacks. In fact, alien-status Blacks, continental Blacks, and continental Whites had a common bond in their agreement that some native Blacks did not willingly accept any of them.[11]

For their part, most St. Thomians claimed that they were not really against the alien-status Blacks as persons, but were resentful of the social and economic disruptions caused by the massive influx of so many workers within a short span of time—conditions that would cause bitter resentment in any society. Alien-status workers were viewed as greatly depressing wage levels in some areas and as exerting tremendous demands on those government services which were not denied them. As early as 1962, for example, and continuing for several consecutive years, statistics from the V.I. Department of Health revealed that the number of babies born annually to British West Indian fathers and mothers in St. Thomas exceeded the number born to native parents.[12] By 1966, a continuing insufficiency of housing, despite substantial building and reportedly caused mainly by alien immigration, was considered to be the greatest problem facing the Government of the V.I.[13]

Components of the White Socio-Racial Groups

The white population of St. Thomas was also comprised of three groups throughout the midcentury decades, during which great changes took place in the socio-economic status or numerical proportions of the sub-groups. The first group, both in chronological order of arrival and in the socio-economic power they possessed at the middle of the century, may be dubbed the Old Whites. This group included all Whites, or their descendants, who had been living in St. Thomas from the Danish period and had lived a Euro-American lifestyle. Their original nationality—whether Danish, other European, or American—made no difference. Their religious affiliation—whether Christian or Jewish—likewise did not matter. Though some scholars have referred to Jews as a separate social group, there has been no substantial basis in the history or general sentiment of St. Thomas for such a distinction. What distinguished the Old Whites, a sizeable portion of whom were Jews, was that they were the ruling class during the slavery era and the post-slavery decades, when their dominance was unchallenged. The socio-economic distance between them and the majority of the population had been so great that their status had seemed like a law of nature. They generally had established long-term residence, were viewed as integral members of the community, and their leadership and economic control were fully accepted. In fact, the more generous or socially-involved Old Whites used to be regarded by many Blacks with genuine affection as they had a history of having been major employers, and that role was often regarded with appreciation.

The second White group on St. Thomas, West Indians of French descent who had been migrating from the island of St Barthelemy since the second half of the nineteenth century, was not popularly spoken of as white before the

1960s. Its members were subdivided into two communities. One was located on the north-central hills of St. Thomas, overlooking the Atlantic, an area referred to as "Northside." Its economy was dominated by farming; in fact, it was the only substantial farming area left in midcentury St. Thomas. The other French community was located on the Caribbean shore west of Charlotte Amalie. Its economy at mid-century was based on fishing and straw handicrafts. It was called Carenage or Cha Cha Town.

When speaking in terms of definite racial categories, the majority of St. Thomians designated the un-mixed members of the two French communities as white. However, according to the socio-economic criteria which dominated St. Thomian mid-century thinking, most of the French stood very far from the Euro-American life style expected of Whites, and adhered to by the Old Whites and the Continentals. Thus, the French were generally just thought of and referred to as "Cha Chas," a term which most of them viewed as derogatory. Numerically, the local French had fallen from first place among the white groups (having been eclipsed by white Continentals), to a population of about 1,500 in the 1960s.

Continentals, as the newest Whites were called, referred to persons originally from the U.S. mainland who had relocated in St. Thomas since the Transfer in 1917. Since so few had moved to St. Thomas before the 1940s, some whose move had predated that decade were sometimes popularly identified as Old Whites. The term "Continental" was additionally sometimes applied to foreign Whites—from Europe, Canada, Latin America, who too were recent arrivals in St. Thomas. Even though the non-American ones were politically as alien as the non-citizen West Indian Blacks, race-conscious Blacks occasionally pointed out that the term "alien" which was popularly used for the West Indian Blacks was never used for the Whites.

The overwhelming majority of white Continentals were transplanted U.S. mainlanders; their island-born children were sometimes also referred to as Continentals. From having been a very small group in 1950, Continentals by the late 1960s had become by far the largest white sub-group. They had become so ubiquitous by the late 1960s that some Blacks used the terms "continental" and "white" interchangeably which, on some occasions, led to confusion when "white" was used to mean "continental" but was interpreted as being inclusive of the two older white groups. (Similarly, many Blacks and Whites used "native" and "black" interchangeably, though "native" properly included many of the Old and French Whites, but not black Continentals and the foreign-born West Indian Blacks.)

Not only had white Continentals become the most numerous white group by the late 1960s, but they had become the most powerful segment economically of the population of St. Thomas. They comprised the majority of the major entrepreneurial and managerial personalities on the island, and also maintained a growing number of civic, educational, cultural and other organizations.

Unifying forces were operative among the white groups to a much greater extent than similar forces among the Blacks. Common school experiences, religious fellowship (especially among the Jewish population, where a small dwindling synagogue was completely rejuvenated by the influx of continental Jews), marriages and various business ventures served to cement much of the shrunken Old White community and certain segments of the French group with the community of Continentals.

Race relations in St. Thomas during the midcentury decades, viewed in terms of strict racial categorization—an accelerating process during the period, became largely a black-white dichotomy. There were no other large, distinct socio-racial groups. In some U. S. mainland cities, and to some degree on St. Croix, a large Puerto Rican community had coalesced as a distinct third force. On St. Thomas, there had not been as much Puerto Rican migration as to St. Croix (where, before the influx of West Indian workers and Continentals in the 1960s, persons of Puerto Rican descent were estimated as comprising over forty per cent of the population). As a result, many of the Puerto Ricans on St. Thomas became quite integrated with the older groups through marriage or other associations and generally identified with one or the other of the main socio-racial groups. As the population was mainly black, many Puerto Ricans ended up mixing with that group, as indicated by an informal tally based on the St. Thomas portion of the 1975 V.I. telephone directory, in which most of the listed persons with Hispanic names were phenotypically black.[14]

Other Very Small Groups

There had been practically no other extant groups on St. Thomas in 1950, but the prosperity of the 1960s attracted people from everywhere. By the end of the 60s there were noticeable numbers of new ethnic components—mainly Asian—in the St. Thomian population. However, none was large enough to be considered a significant group. In fact, in the 1970 Census all of the new groups together totaled considerably less than one thousand persons.[15] The largest consisted of persons whose ancestors or who themselves had come from India. Most of those of Indian ancestry had arrived in St. Thomas from Trinidad or Guyana as part of the influx of workers from elsewhere in the Caribbean. As such, many of those East Indians, as they are known in the West

Indies, were in the same socio-economic range as the majority of Blacks. The other Indians, who had come directly from Asia, came manly as entrepreneurs of retail establishments geared towards tourists and thus were on an economic level with many white Continentals engaged in similar enterprise.

Another small group of new immigrants consisted of persons of eastern Asian background. A sizeable percentage were professionals in the medical fields and came from places such as the Philippines and Korea. A few went into restaurant or food retail businesses. An additional group of Asian newcomers was from western Asia and were solidifying in St. Thomas a business class that was already quite familiar in much of the Caribbean—Arab retail merchants. These small new ethnic groups added even more to the complexity of the diverse population strains St. Thomas had acquired over the course of three centuries.

Cross Perceptions of the Socio-Racial Groups

In spite of the growing diversity of the St. Thomas population, discourses about race relations focused mainly on the black/white dichotomy. That reflected, after all, the historic racial divisions of both the Virgin Islands and the United States. Yet, until after the middle of the twentieth century, most Blacks on St. Thomas had not been very race conscious and racial solidarity had not been conceived as a reason why they should have welcomed the other West Indian and continental Blacks who were arriving in substantial numbers. Yet, by the end of the 1960s, the old Danish gradation system which had placed a "mixed" group between Negroes and Whites had been gradually eroded by mainland American influence and continental definitions of race were largely accepted: persons with any known African ancestry were thought of as members of the black race, regardless of their complexions. Though there remained some who refused to acquiesce to the revised definitions and terminology, they seemed to realize that they were swimming against a tide that was growing increasingly stronger. As if in recognition of the evolution which had taken place, the U.S. Bureau of the Census deleted the term "mixed" from the 1970 census questionnaire used in the Virgin Islands. The 1970 choices for color or race were "Negro," White," and "Other," instead of the third category being "Mixed and other races," as it had been from 1917 through 1960.[16]

While many Blacks blamed Continentals for having imported stateside race relations patterns to the islands and for the increased racial consciousness, many Whites, on the other hand, expressed blameless amazement at some of the changes which they had noted between 1950 and the end of the 60s. A frequently expressed white opinion was that a considerable number of Virgin Islands Blacks, especially the young, had changed from being free of the "chips on the shoulder" attitude, by which mainland Blacks were often characterized, to having adopted the anti-white prejudices and physical behavior associated with black ghettoes on the mainland. By the late 1960s, the perceptions that Blacks and Whites in St. Thomas had developed of each other's racial evolution and views were very far apart.

The growing movement of white Continentals to St. Thomas in the early 1950s had been viewed with favor by most Blacks on the island. For a place which two decades earlier had seemed on a depopulation path, as decades of economic stagnation had persistently pushed many of its younger and more ambitious natives toward the U.S. mainland and elsewhere, the reverse was heartening. The movement of people to St. Thomas had meant hope! It attested to the fact that the economy was on the upswing. And the arriving Continentals, most of whom were presumed to have considerable money and hopefully also considerable knowledge, were expected to be the chief agents of change in ensuring a growing and prosperous economy.

The island's press and people generally paid due respect to the white Continentals who came to live and spend among them. Sydney Kessler became one of the most celebrated men on St. Thomas when he started the construction of the Virgin Isle Hotel in 1948. He and his wife, Frances, had moved to St. Thomas in 1945 (after having spent several years in Puerto Rico, where they had initially moved from New York). She became quite involved in local affairs, and was one of the founders of the St. Thomas USO in 1953, an organizer of the 1950s Hands Across the Sea Scholarship Fund which provided support for deserving local students to attend college, and also was very active in the Jewish congregation. The opening of the Virgin Isle Hotel on December 15, 1950, was a noted event in St. Thomas, with editorials and other effusive expressions of congratulations and gratitude to the owners. In April 1951, the Municipal Council of St. Thomas-St. John passed a resolution expressing the appreciation of the community to the hotel's owners—Sydney Kessler and Benjamin E. Bayne.

Ben Bayne, as the hotel's other principal was popularly known, had also become a well-known figure on St. Thomas. He and his wife, Irene, had arrived in 1944 from Brookline, Massachusetts. Mrs. Bayne had also plunged into civic activities, being one of the founders in 1948 of the Women's League, an organization which then provided various forms of material support and social services to the local hospital.[17]

The arrival of any Continental of note was usually extolled in the press. (Both of St. Thomas's newspapers were owned and managed by native Blacks during the 1950s through the early 1970s—the *Daily News* by Ariel Melchior,

Sr. and the *Home Journal* by Earle B. Ottley.) After the psychiatrist, Dr. Wein-stein, had arrived and was working with the Department of Health, a front-page newspaper story reported his presence and that he and Mrs. Weinstein, who had formerly lived in Bethesda, Maryland, had sold their country home in Phillipstown, New York, on moving to St. Thomas.[18]

The arrival of an author such as Herman Wouk would have made a splash in any community—he had won the Pulitzer Prize for fiction with his novel, *The Caine Mutiny*, in 1951. He bought property on St. Thomas in 1958 and then relocated with his wife and two sons. He was reported as saying that he found St. Thomas a good place to work, and wrote three books within the next six years. One of those books was *Don't Stop the Carnival*, published in 1965, a comic account of a Continental managing a hotel in the Caribbean, and clearly reflective of the experience of living in St. Thomas. Wouk received sev-eral appointments of honor during his residence in St. Thomas. In the early 1960s he served as cultural advisor to Governor Ralph Paiewonsky and was ap-pointed to the V.I. Board of Education and to the Board of Trustees of the new College of the Virgin Islands.[19]

Blacks in St. Thomas additionally realized that white Continentals could be very generous to the community on occasion. The example par excellence had been established in 1946 by Arthur Fairchild, who had deeded to St. Thomas the gift of Magens Bay Beach and its adjoining fifty acres, with the provision that it be permanently maintained for public use. Fairchild was a Wall Street financier and had acquired the property and maintained a home on St. Thomas for several decades before his death in St. Thomas in 1951. Magens Bay has been acclaimed as one of the most beautiful beaches in the world.[20]

During the two decades following 1950, several Continentals made sub-stantial philanthropic contributions to the people of the V.I. Howard Jackson, a retired Tennessee industrialist who had acquired the famous Blackbeard Cas-tle on St. Thomas and converted it into his private residence, contributed monies during the early 1950s to the Vocational Division of the Charlotte Amalie High School and provided scholarships for natives to further their ed-ucation at mainland institutions.[21]

Laurance Rockefeller, who owned the Caneel Bay Resort on St. John, per-sonally donated $100,000 to the College of the V.I. when it opened in 1963. Henry H. Reichhold, who had bought the Bluebeard Castle Hotel and was the head of a chemical firm on the mainland, donated to the College, within a two-year period in the mid-1960s two gifts of one million dollars each. The second million was earmarked for the construction and furnishing of a com-munity cultural center, now known as the Reichhold Center, sorely needed in St. Thomas.[22] The College received another great gift in 1966, when Harry L.

Etelman and his wife Elizabeth, presented their property at Estate Bonne Resolution in St. Thomas. It consisted of an impressive ten-room residence, and an astronomical observatory with a large telescope, located on seven acres of land. Etelman House is used for astronomy classes, special meetings and social functions, and for public astronomical observations.[23]

At least one Old White family, already known for its private generosity, also engaged in public philanthropy. In 1954 the Paiewonsky family established the Isaac and Rebecca Paiewonsky Golden Jubilee Scholarship Fund, to provide a four-year college award each year to a member of the graduating class of the Charlotte Amalie High School. The Paiewonsky family also made substantial donations to the College of the V.I., including $75,000 in 1963 to set up the Isaac Paiewonsky Memorial Fund.[24]

However, in spite of all the positive aspects and prospects of continental migration to the V.I., there was concern on the part of some Blacks about the possibly negative effects which such migrations and donations might have. Knowledge of the naval period, certain events after, and of race relations on the U.S. mainland could not but cause such wariness. And the occasional actions of Continentals which revealed negative thoughts about black islanders added to it. In 1952, as an example, when the U.S. House of Representatives Sub-Committee on Interior and Insular Affairs held hearings in the V.I. on a proposed new Organic Act, Mrs. Sally Milgrom, a white Continental who was a part-owner of the Hotel Flamboyant on St. Thomas, made a dramatic plea before the Sub-Committee for the Virgin Islands to be incorporated under Puerto Rico. She said that nothing Congress could put in the Organic Act would change the people of the V.I., whom she described as likeable but shiftless, lazy, dishonest, lacking in pride, and incapable of shouldering responsibility. Mrs. Milgrom explained to the Sub-Committee that her group had invested a million dollars in their hotel but regretted it because they got no local cooperation. She asserted that it was impossible to get a direct answer on any question from the V.I. government and that her workers at the hotel stole, often did not show up for work, and wanted maximum salary for minimum labor. Another white Continental, a Commander Harman, also testified to the Sub-Committee that, in his opinion, the people of the V.I. did not possess the moral and political responsibility to elect their own governor, which was one of the changes being proposed in the new Organic Act.[25]

Again, in 1953 the relationship between race and the new population growth became a public matter in St. Thomas. In March of that year, the *Daily News* carried a long front-page analysis entitled, "Says Racial Factor Complicates Growth of Island." Its main thesis was that among the white Continentals, there were many who genuinely loved the islands and were contributing positively to their way of life. But it said there were also those Continentals who were fighting desperately to maintain a white-dominated plantation-type economy. The group's headquarters in St. Thomas was said to be the exclusively white Contant Club and the owner of the club, Edward Bindley, was said to be one of the leaders in a campaign to vilify the incumbent governor, Morris de Castro, who was the first Virgin Islander (an Old White) to be appointed by the U.S. to that office. Those Continentals were said to be bitter about rising wages and their inability to hire subservient menials for ten dollars or less per month. They were also said to have opposed the new schools and hospitals, which were desperately needed, because such benefits for the people were deemed by them as wasteful.[26]

Another Continental on St. Thomas who was waging a campaign against Governor de Castro and other government officials was William Greer, manager of WSTA, the only radio station on St. Thomas. On St. Croix there were also local activists who were concerned about such Continentals. In November, 1953, a St. Croix legislator, Henry E. Rohlsen, delivered a speech on St. Croix radio station WIVI, on racial developments in relation to attacks on the government. He related that he had attempted to give the same speech on St. Thomas's WSTA, but had been prevented from doing so. The St. Thomas newspapers, however, gave full coverage to his speech. Rohlsen had said that those white Continentals who were causing concern:

> ... would like to bring the same restrictions upon our people that have been carried to Bermuda and other places. They do not want a native Governor. They do not want natives in top positions. They do not want wage and hour laws. They do not want anti-discrimination laws.... [They] cannot tolerate for one moment the idea, that here is an area under the American flag, where non-whites enjoy equality, dignity, self-respect, and run the affairs of their government.... Some of us believe that racial discrimination is applied only to the black. Don't be mistaken. A lighter shade of skin does not exempt you from being included. To be exempted, you will have to establish the fact that you are racially pure white and not many of us in the Virgin Islands, where the races have commingled for several hundred years, can meet those qualifications.[27]

In addition to the perception that some white Continentals were trying to bring the race relations of the V.I. in line with those of many places on the mainland, some islanders also feared the importation by Continentals of various practices which were considered immoral, anti-religious, criminal, or which simply ran counter to the traditional way of life. A local editorial in October 1950 was entitled "Odious Element" and was concerned with the "debased living of some visiting Continentals." It noted that so many strangers came to reform and preach to the natives that sordid behavior on the part of persons originally from elsewhere stood out:

> The more the Virgin Islands become known as a paradise the more the people can expect to have in their midst persons whose only contribution to their future will be more on the side of improved technics in vice and debauchery.... Our continental friends should assist in purging the community of the odorous element that clings to their society.[28]

One concern in this area was that of the open practice of homosexuality. Prior to the 1950s any such practice on St. Thomas and the supposedly involved persons were matters only for private conversation. Several white continentals who went to St. Thomas in the 1950s acted more openly. In 1957, a Continental bookstore proprietor was charged with 'unnatural' practices. He then wrote to the Legislature demanding that a commission be established to investigate homosexuality on the islands and make recommendations for new and liberal statutes on the matter. He also informed the Legislators that he had a list of "two dozen native men and boys" who had indulged in homosexual practices or who were so inclined. The Legislature took no action on the proposed commission, and the charges against the man were dismissed in the U.S. District Court of the V.I.[29]

In January 1963, a serious occurrence made supposedly imported homosexuality a matter of public concern for several weeks. A government official, a White originally from upstate New York who was serving as Deputy Commissioner of the V.I. Department of Commerce, was killed. It ended up being disclosed that homosexuality had been involved in the relationship between him and the native young man who was charged with the fatal stabbing. The local opinion was that youths were being financially lured into sexual deviancy by Continentals. There was a public outcry, including several newspaper editorials, for effective preventive action. Commissioner of Public Safety Otis Felix said that better laws were needed and that the Police Department suspected that there were certain night clubs in St. Thomas which were catering especially to these "undesirable elements." Governor Paiewonsky was reported to have been quoted as saying that homosexuals must be run off the island. The matter was even covered in a *Time* magazine article which, however, met with general objection in the V.I. because it exaggeratedly reported that deviates were "swarming to the islands."[30]

Another series of events in 1963 further added to the impressions of older residents that Continentals were importing activities detrimental to the morals of the community. It came to public attention that a club in downtown St. Thomas, the Coffee House, was featuring stripping in its shows. After outcries, the club was said to have started a practice of admitting only Whites. In April, 1963, the manager and two strip dancers, all Caucasian, were arrested and charged with indecent exposure and the presence of narcotics. In August, 1963, based on the results of a hearing, the operating license of the Coffee House was suspended.[31]

Continentals were also imputed with special responsibility for the deterioration of public attire. The Women's League conducted a campaign in the late 1950s to insist that the ordinance regarding public attire be enforced by the police. During the 1960s, when a sizeable percentage of the public school teaching staff came to consist of Continentals, concern was expressed at times about their classroom appearance.[32]

A number of St. Thomas Blacks developed a perception that an appreciable number of white Continentals who moved to the islands had been, in some way or another, failures or misfits, but did well in St. Thomas. Natives frequently said that the Virgin Islands guaranteed success to incoming failures.[33] What caused the resentment was the supposition, occasionally the definite knowledge, that such successes were at times based at least partially on the fact of whiteness. For in a society where there was a tradition of white and outside dominance and where key institutions such as banks remained under the control of Whites or other persons who identified more with Whites than Blacks, incoming Whites often enjoyed an edge over comparable Blacks in competition for credit, high-level positions, and other such keys to success.

Most Whites, in contrast, seemed to believe that any poverty, disabilities, or restrictions that Blacks suffered were due principally to black behavior and characteristics. In general, black Virgin Islanders had been viewed by the early-arriving Continentals as being a gentle, likeable, and easygoing people, but lacking in the overall knowledge, business skills and acquisitive drive necessary for success in twentieth-century America. Dr. Edwin Weinstein, a white continental who published the results of his psychiatric study of the Virgin Islands in 1962, had this passage in his book:

> An interesting example of the contrast between Virgin Island and Continental attitudes occurred in the case of a Continental who was brought to the hospital after he had slashed both of his wrists in a suicidal gesture. He had done so after hearing voices reproach him for not having lived up to his opportunities in life, for not having paid his debts, and for having visited prostitutes. It is not likely that the 'voices' would have spoken thus to a Virgin Islander.[34]

Blacks thus appeared as lacking in the urge to seek out opportunities and as being relatively unconcerned about meeting financial and moral obligations.

Dr. Weinstein disagreed with those who characterized black Virgin Islanders as lazy, but noted that his findings showed they did not esteem work as a virtue in itself.[35]

Patterns of family organization and sexual behavior which were evident among Blacks in the V.I. were often cited by Whites as indicative of social and financial irresponsibility and sexual immorality. Illegitimate births in St. Thomas-St. John, as a percentage of all live births during the 1950s and 1960s ranged from a high of 48.6% in 1952 to a low of 29.4% in 1962.[36] As a result, a substantial number of parents, mainly male, did not live with their children and some did not contribute significantly to their children's financial support. The restrictions on the non-citizen West Indian workers during the 1960s aggravated some of these conditions as the separation of many workers from their families on other islands occasioned the formation of various new relationships, some of which could not be legalized. Additionally, it appeared that some alien women were deliberately mothering children in the hope that the U.S. citizenship of the children would protect the mothers against the possibility of deportation. Regarding such local styles of living, St. Thomas author J. Antonio Jarvis had noted the following as far back as 1944:

> Observers have made out that the Virgin Islands are immoral, but it seems rather that they have no moral inhibitions, and that they regard their mores as absolutely natural. Education has here made only a trifling advance. Religion has been helpless.... It cannot be said that the Virgin Islanders spend much time worrying about their moral defects, their marital status, or the social implications of the folkways.[37]

By 1970 concern about the morality of such folkways seemed to be almost universally in retreat, but in the V.I. there was a great deal of thought about the socio-economic implications, as the Virgin Islands had become a more competitive society in the 1960s. It was pointed out by some Blacks and Whites that among the several factors which accounted for the inability of many Blacks to engage in successful economic competition were those stemming from the local patterns of sexual behavior and household organization. The implication was that unless substantial changes could be brought about in those fundamental areas of social behavior, many Blacks would be doomed by the effects to inadequacy for meaningful participation in the competitive society of the 1970s and beyond.

The area, however, in which Blacks and Whites generally had the most incompatible perceptions related to the views of each regarding the origin and extent of racism in the other. From a large-scale review of newspaper reports and correspondence and a sizeable number of interviews of both Blacks and

Whites, it was revealed that there existed between many persons of the two groups, and even within the black group, extremely different ideas regarding the development of racial problems in St. Thomas from the 1950s onward.

A large majority of Blacks and Whites agreed that at midcentury most Blacks on St. Thomas were not very race-conscious and harbored little, if any, animosity against Whites. Therefore, any perceptible amount of black racism which may have existed by the end of the 60s had to have developed during the previous two decades. Most Blacks and Whites agreed, also, that a substantial amount of Black racism did exist by the end of the 1960s, evidenced mainly by the expressions and actions of some young Blacks. After these points of agreement, however, there were great discrepancies in the assessment of attendant factors.

Most Blacks appeared to believe, as judged by the frequency of mention in newspaper expressions and in interviews, that the four greatest factors in the deterioration of race relations in St. Thomas had been (in declining order of importance): (1) increased white racism and black reaction to it; (2) increased white domination of the economy and black reaction to it; (3) the influence of black Continentals and the Black Revolution on the mainland; and (4) the influence of black Virgin Islanders who had served in the military, studied, or worked on the mainland.

It was in itself a revealing measure of what had become the state of race relations on St. Thomas that the expressed opinion of Whites, in accounting for it, ran exactly counter to those of Blacks. The four greatest factors perceived by Whites were (in declining order of importance): (1) the influence of black Virgin Islanders who had served in the military, studied, or worked on the mainland; (2) the influence of black Continentals and the Black Revolution on the mainland; (3) increased white domination of the economy and black reaction to it; and (4) increased white racism and black reaction to it. Some members of both groups mentioned the rapid and unplanned population growth that had taken place, but were unsure of its effect on race relations.

In general, many Blacks had perceived the development of black racism on St. Thomas as due mainly to what had been happening locally—the influx of white Continentals with the abhorred racial mores of the mainland and resentment over the growth of white economic control. The influence of the Black Revolution, black Continentals, and local Blacks who had lived on the mainland were thought to be important mostly in bringing about awareness and reactions to the basic reasons, but were not viewed by most as the principal causes of the development of black prejudice against Whites. Many Whites, on the other hand, did not view local developments—possibly increased white racism or economic control—as significant. They viewed increasing black consciousness and antagonism as stemming mainly from behavior learned elsewhere and taken to St. Thomas, without there being any great amount of justification in the realities of the Virgin Islands.

In addition to their opposite prioritizing of the contributory factors in race relations, there were other differences in the perceptions of Whites and Blacks. Among the most interesting was that no Black interviewed denied the existence of prejudice among some Blacks in St. Thomas by the end of the Sixties, though some stated it was understandable or even justifiable by the developments of the preceding two decades.

Additionally, there were Blacks (a small minority) who denied that any appreciable amount of white racism had been operative on St. Thomas. Their explanations ranged from statements that there had been racism during the naval period but that more recent Whites had not been racist, to the opinion that Whites who did not like black people or could not at least tolerate them would not choose to reside in a place like the Virgin Islands.

As was true of Blacks, no Whites denied the development of black racism in St. Thomas during the 50s and 60s, and several also said it was understandable. However, there was a response of Whites which had no black parallels in that several Whites denied the existence of white racism in St. Thomas or that it was a reasonable basis for black racism. One white Continental, a government employee, said that racist Whites would not last on St. Thomas because "people would scream bloody murder if the slightest tinge of racism came from any White." He thought black racism was due to the experiences of Virgin Islanders at Southern colleges and in the military. Another white Continental thought likewise and explained: "I don't think Whites brought racism with them. I think Blacks who went to the U.S. learned about racism and took it back to the islands." When asked if she thought that most Whites in the U.S. were prejudiced against Blacks, she replied in the positive but added: "They don't take those feelings with them—especially not to St. Thomas. They are quite aware that they're in a black community."

Another white continental, who had lived in St. Thomas for a few decades, seemed quite surprised at a question regarding whether Whites may have contributed to racial tensions by going to St. Thomas with prejudices from the mainland. She said that she had never considered that possibility and her conception of Whites in St. Thomas was focused on all the good they had done for the community. Several other Whites said they could not be definite, but they tended to believe that white racism was not operative on St. Thomas; a few stated that St. Croix was different and it definitely existed there.[38]

Without questioning the sincerity of those Whites and Blacks who believed, or tended to believe, that the white Continentals in St. Thomas were not carriers of prejudice against Blacks, research on racism has demonstrated that their opinions were not realistic. People do not choose whether they take life-long prejudices with them when they travel. And, however difficult it may be for some Americans to admit, multiple studies have shown that:

> Racial segregation and an ideology of racial superiority have been part of the American culture for generations and in some sense every White American is implicated in this aspect of the American way of life.[39]

Additionally, research has also uncovered that race prejudice also exists and operates even more as a functioning sense of a group's position than in terms of the individual feelings of members of the group. And, in a situation such as in St. Thomas, where continental Whites who had previously been part of a majority find themselves a minority, they become more conscious of their group's position and its meaning for them than they had been before.[40]

The inability of some Whites and Blacks to perceive white racism in St. Thomas was really not hard to understand. As black St. Thomian Edwin Hatch-ette realized, "Whites here don't see racism because the government structure is still mainly black." Glenn "Kwabena" Davis, a black St. Thomian educator, noted that many people did not think of racism in terms of exploitation or subtle actions based on unadmitted prejudices. They focused on speech and other readily-discerned behavior, which caused vocal black Continentals, college students, and military veterans to be given disproportionate blame for promoting racial tensions.[41]

The existence of these cross perceptions of the racial or socio-racial groups imposed severe restrictions on efforts to achieve meaningful and helpful dialogue on the many race-related problems which the mid-century decades brought to St. Thomas. Opinions often differed so greatly that attempts to discuss problems peacefully sometimes generated greater hostility than had existed before the efforts at verbalization had taken place. Let us now look at the Paiewonsky administration of the 1960s, whose great and effective efforts to improve the economy and society of the Virgin Islands, unintentionally also provided fertile ground for the intensification of the burgeoning race relations problems, a fascinating example of the "law" of unintended consequences.

Notes

1. U.S. Bureau of the Census, *1950 Census of Population: General Population Characteristics*, U.S. Virgin Islands, pp. 54–85, Washington, D.C., 1953.

2. Knight, *The African Dimension in Latin American Societies*, p. 135.

3. Campbell, *St. Thomas Negroes—A Study of Personality and Culture*, pp. 64–65.

4. Campbell, *St. Thomas Negroes*, p. 36.

5. Campbell, *St. Thomas Negroes*, p. 65–66.

6. Patricia Gill Murphy, "The Education of the New World Blacks in the Danish West Indies/U.S. Virgin Islands: A Case Study of Social Transition." Ph.D. dissertation, The University of Connecticut, 1977, p. 126.

7. U.S. Bureau of the Census, *1970 Census of Population: General Population Characteristics*, p. 55-16; Frank Mills, "A Household Survey of the Virgin Islands on Economic Development" (Prepared for the Economic Policy Council, V.I. Department of Commerce, 1978), p. 104.

8. Partly based on interviews with Emily Tynes, Delaware-Washington, D.C., telephone conversation, December 4, 1982; Marion Bray Hedrington, St. Thomas, February 13, 1983; Dr. Herbert Hoover, St. Thomas, February 16, 1983; Gloria Alexander Statham, Delaware-Pennsylvania conversation, May 8, 1983. All of these interviewees are continental Blacks who lived on St. Thomas during the 1960s or 1970s; two have since returned to the mainland.

9. E. Aracelle Francis, "The History of Social Welfare and Foreign Labor in the United States Virgin Islands: A Policy Analysis" (D.S.W. dissertation, Columbia University, 1979), pp. 325–328; U.S. Bureau of the Census, *1970 Census of Population: General Population Characteristics*, p. 55-17; Mark J. Miller and William W. Boyer, "Foreign Workers in the USVI: History of a Dilemma," *Caribbean Review*, Vol. XI, No. 1 (Winter, 1982), pp. 48–51.

10. A book published in 2009 by Dr. H. Akia Gore, who grew up in the U.S. V.I., but was Antigua-born, spells the term as "Garrote" and presents a painful account of the experiences of alien-status workers in the V.I.

11. Partly based on interviews with Dr. Frank Mills, St. Thomas, February 17, 1983; Dennis Richardson, St. Thomas, February 21, 1983; Ethiopia Tamara I (Anthony G. Leroy, St. Thomas, February 25, 1981). All are Blacks, originally from other West Indian Islands, who went to St. Thomas during the 1960s or 1970s.

12. "Babies born to British parents exceed islanders," *Daily News* (St. Thomas, V.I.), August 17, 1965, p. 1.

13. Krigger, "A Quarter-Century of Race Relations," p. 141. "New Approach Needed For Alien Housing: Gov.," *Daily News* (St. Thomas, V.I.), December 12, 1966, p.1.

14. Weinstein, *Cultural Aspects of Delusion*, pp. 173–186; Virgin Islands Telephone Corporation, *U.S. Virgin Islands Telephone Directory*, 1975.

15. U.S. Bureau of the Census, *1970 Census of Population: General Population Characteristics*, U.S. Virgin Islands, pp. 55–16.

16. U.S. Bureau of the Census, *1970 Census of Population: General Population Characteristics*, Part 55, Appendix B, page 21; page 16.

17. Krigger, "A Quarter-Century of Race Relations," pp. 113–114, 152. "Women's League Marks 25th Anniversary In VI," *Daily News* (St. Thomas, V.I.), May 14, 1971, p. 10.

18. The Weinsteins returned to the mainland in 1960.

19. "A Skyline Home and Workshop for a Noted Writer," *Daily News* (St. Thomas, V.I.), December 8, 1961, p. 10; "Herman Wouk: An Interview," *Virgin Islands View*, Vol. 1, No. 4 (September, 1965), pp. 9–13. The Wouk family returned to the mainland after the mid-1960s.

20. "Arthur Fairchild 65, Dies at Louisenhoj," *Daily News* (St. Thomas, V.I.), February 10, 1951, p. 1; February 13, 1951, p. 2; Creque, *The U.S. Virgins and the Eastern Caribbean*, pp. 126–127. Fairchild had also provided financial aid for several local students to attend college.

21. Krigger, "A Quarter-Century of Race Relations," p. 115. "Jackson Donates $250 for Home Economics," *Daily News* (St. Thomas, V.I.), June 20, 1952, p. 1; August 29, 1952, p. 3.

22. Ibid. "College Recipient of Rockefeller Gift," *Daily News* (St. Thomas, V.I.), August 1, 1963, p. 6; "Reichhold donates Another Million $ $ $ For Center," October 20, 1967, p. 1.

23. Ibid. *Daily News* (St. Thomas, V.I.), December 3, 1971, p. 1. The daughter of President Lyndon Johnson, Lynda Bird, and her husband Charles Robb, spent their honeymoon at Etelman House.

24. Ibid. *Daily News* (St. Thomas, V.I.), November 26, 1954, p. 3; "Donation To College Marks Creation of Memorial Fund," August 9, 1963, p. 1. A large number of the recipients of the Isaac and Rebecca Paiewonsky Golden Jubilee Scholarships returned to the Virgin Islands, after completing their education, and made significant contributions.

25. Ibid., p. 116. "Congressional Hearing[s] Shift to St. Croix," *Daily News* (St. Thomas, V.I.), January 15, 1952, p. 1.

26. "Says Racial Factor Complicates Growth of Island," *Daily News* (St. Thomas, V.I.), March 30, 1953, pp. 1, 4.

27. Krigger, "A Quarter-Century of Race Relations," p. 117. "Radio Address Of The Hon. Henry E. Rohlsen," *Daily News* (St. Thomas, V.I.), November 16, 1953, pp. 2, 4; November 17, 1953, pp. 2, 4; November 18, 1953, p. 2.

28. "Odorous Element," *Daily News* (St. Thomas, V.I.), October 12, 1950, p. 5.

29. Krigger, "A Quarter-Century of Race Relations," p. 118. "Sees Attempted 'Blackmail' In Combs' Letters," *Daily News* (St. Thomas, V.I.), June 6, 1957, p. 1; "Combs Freed on 'Morals' Counts, Case Dismissed," October 3, 1957, p. 1.

30. Ibid., *118*. *Daily News* (St. Thomas, V.I.), January 8, 1963, p. 1; January 10, 1963, p. 1; January 11, 1963, p. 1; January 12, 1963, p. 9; January 14, 1963, p. 9; February 3, 1963, p. 7.

31. Interview, *Daily News* (St. Thomas, V.I.), March 7, 1963, p. 1; "Night Club Entertainer Arrested; Manager Is Too," April 22, 1963, p. 1; "Result of Hearing On Club's License Pending," August 3, 1963, p.1; "Nightclub Owner Charged With Resisting Arrest," August 19, 1963, p. 1. Also interview with retired Chief of Police Ivan Williams, St. Thomas, February 18, 1983....

32. Krigger, "A Quarter-Century of Race Relations," p. 118. *Daily News* (St. Thomas, V.I.), March 27, 1963, p. 3; "League-Mawson in 'Decent Dress' Correspondence," August 12, 1957, p. 1; "Contrasts In Attire," July 6, 1963, p. 9; Juliette George Fahie, "Letter to the Editor," October 7, 1971, p. 7.

33. A good pertinent quotation is found in Norwell Harrigan and Pearl L. Varlack, "The U.S. Virgin Islands and the Black Experience." *Journal of Black Studies*, Vol. 7, No. 4 (June, 1977), p. 403.

34. Edwin A. Weinstein, *Cultural Aspects of Delusion: A Psychiatric Study of the Virgin Islands* (New York, The Free Press of Glencoe, Inc., 1962), p. 67.

35. Ibid., pp. 61, 64.

36. V.I. Department of Health; "Virgin Islands Vital Statistics; 1969," p. 19.

37. Jarvis, *The Virgin Islands and Their People*, p. 99.

38. This section was based on newspaper reports and correspondence from 1950 through 1975 and on interviews with 48 of the persons listed in Part D of the Bibliography.

39. The quotation is from Angus Campbell and Howard Schuman, *Racial Attitudes in Fifteen American States* (Ann Arbor: Institute for Social Research, The University of Michigan, 1969), p. 62.

40. See Herbert Blumer, "Race Prejudice as a Sense of Group Position," *The Pacific Sociological Review*, Vol. 1, No. 1 (Spring, 1958), pp. 3–7; Hubert M. Blalock, Jr., "A Power Analysis of Racial Discrimination," *Social Forces*, Vol. 39, No. 1 (October, 1960), pp. 53–59; Judy H. Katz, *White Awareness: Handbook for Anti-Racism Training* (Norman: The University of Oklahoma Press, 1978).

41. Interviews with Edwin Hatchette, St. Thomas telephone conversation, February 15, 1983, and Glenn "Kwabena" Davis, St. Thomas, February 25, 1983.

Chapter 13

The Paiewonsky
Administration and Its Effects,
1961–1969

President John F. Kennedy's nomination of Ralph M. Paiewonsky in 1961 to be the governor of the U.S. Virgin Islands was somewhat of a fairy tale knitting of the ultimate successes of two special European-American families. The story of President Kennedy's great grandfather's migration from Ireland to Massachusetts in the 1840s and the great economic and political accomplishments of the family he sired are widely known. Ralph Paiewonsky's family had a similar story: his father, Isaac, had arrived in St. Thomas from Lithuania in the 1890s, as a young teenager, along with other members of their Jewish family. The V.I. economy was so bad at that time that several family members left to seek better conditions in the Dominican Republic and elsewhere. However, Isaac stayed in St. Thomas, working with relatives, such as his cousin, I. Levin, who had migrated earlier and had established a dry goods store. A few years later, Isaac got married to Rebecca (who was recruited from Lithuania to become his bride), and with her encouragement, established his own dry goods business which eventually mushroomed into a number of diversified businesses (hardware, groceries, a bay rum factory, an apothecary) and well-located properties that made them very wealthy.[1]

The Background of a Privileged St. Thomian

Ralph, their son and the future governor, was born in November 1907 and was nine years old when he witnessed the Transfer in 1917, seated atop the ramparts of Fort Christian. Of course, Ralph was not only white, but a child of one of the richest white families on the island and, based on his family's interactions with the naval personnel, he "developed a favorable opinion of the naval administration." He expressed in his memoirs the opinion that there was no greater color or race prejudice during the naval period than had already existed. He even opined that continuation of class prejudices among the various levels of Blacks was practiced "more extensively and intensively" than racial prejudices. He admitted knowing, however, that the Navy had maintained a tennis court on St. Thomas at which only Whites and a few fair-complexioned Blacks were members. Paiewonsky also stated, gratefully, that there was no anti-Semitism in the Virgin Islands and that that was because the Jews had kept on friendly terms with the black population and tried to give them whatever assistance they could.[2] This author interviewed a number of persons who were acquainted with some of the numerous personal and business employees the Paiewonsky family usually had, and they remembered the kind and generous treatment spoken of by the employees.

Paiewonsky's family provided him with educational experiences then unavailable in the Virgin Islands. Up to the early 1920s, schooling beyond the elementary level did not exist, so his parents and other relatives procured a home in Brooklyn, New York, where their children could reside while attending high school. After graduating from high school in Brooklyn, Ralph attended New York University, from which he graduated in 1930 with a degree in chemistry, which would prove useful in the family's production of bay rum and liquor. He married two months later—to a Brooklynite—and returned to St. Thomas where, over the next three decades, he became an even greater businessman than his father had been—in areas such as rum production, shipping, movie theaters, insurance, real estate, liquor and gift shops, and banking. Additionally, Ralph entered the field of politics, serving as a Virgin Islands legislator from 1936 to 1946, followed by various other political positions, culminating with the governorship from 1961 to 1969.[3]

Illustrative of the special status enjoyed by the young Paiewonsky as a result of his race and wealth, and which set him very much apart from even other Whites in the Virgin Islands, was his long association with the Democratic National Committee. Even though there was no organized Democratic group in the Virgin Islands until the late 1930s, Ralph attended the Democratic National Convention in 1936, which nominated Roosevelt (FDR) for the second time. A St. Thomas Democratic Club was formed in 1939, designating Ralph as the Democratic National Committeeman, in which capacity he attended the next six Democratic presidential conventions, from 1940 through 1960.[4]

It may, therefore, not have been a great surprise to those in the know when the new President Kennedy nominated Ralph Paiewonsky in 1961 to be the next Governor of the Virgin Islands. The families were not strangers, as the new President and his wife, Jacqueline, had already been entertained by the Paiewonsky family during a 1958 visit to St. Thomas. Indeed, the Paiewonskies were known for their kindness and generosity in that regard. Not only the Kennedys, but all special visitors to the islands, including visiting black West Indian political dignitaries, were generally invited and treated warmly at the "Big House," the popular name for the upstairs living quarters of the Paiewonsky family's large home and business complex at the center of St. Thomas' Main Street. Just as they were known for treating their employees well, the family was quite dedicated to extending kindness and hospitality liberally, as an aspect of their personal and political ethics.[5]

Paiewonsky's inauguration took place on April 5, 1961. His inaugural address listed the following among the areas he planned to work on in order "to serve you and your welfare as your Governor": home ownership, year-round tourism, economic diversification, education, the development of a college, increased governmental representation through an elected governor and the right to vote for the President and Vice-president of the U.S.[6]

The Paiewonsky-Ottley Connection — The Election Code of 1963 and Its Effects

Except for the last item, the right to vote for the President, which still has not been realized and would apparently need a constitutional amendment, all of those objectives were substantially realized by the end of Paiewonsky's eight years in office. However, the political alignment that allowed the successful attainment of those objectives ended up being far different from what many had expected. The two contending local parties at the time were the Democratic and the Unity. The Governor, having been the V.I. Democratic National Committeeman for many years, had been expected by many to work closely with the Democratic senators. However, he apparently realized that many of the objectives by which he hoped to improve the lives of the working class masses were shared more by the Unity Party than the local Democratic Party, and thus he supported legislation that would bring the local parties more in line with the open membership operations of parties on the mainland. The special piece of legislation was known as the Election Code of 1963; it legalized political parties and established open procedures for party membership, registration and voting. It thus enabled the members of the Unity Party to take over the Democratic Party.

The rationale by which Paiewonsky and the Unity Party supported their actions, and which was eventually upheld by the U.S. Third Circuit Court of Appeal, was the right of American citizens to enroll in whatever political party they desired membership. It was known locally that Unity Party members identified with the national Democratic Party (as also did most Blacks nationwide as a result of FDR's New Deal programs), but some local Democratic Party members had attempted to keep its old character intact by denying membership to applicants as they chose. The Unity Party senators thus fashioned a bill (the Election Code) that allowed any citizen to enroll in his or her desired party, and the majority of a party's members would be able to elect the party's officers. The former Democratic Party leaders were shocked when Paiewonsky approved the Code (he had at first vetoed it, but then signed it after certain recommendations he made were included, and it thus became law). The former Unity members then registered as Democrats, outnumbering the former Democrats, and their choice of officers made the former Unity leaders, such as Earle B. Ottley, the leaders of the revised Democratic Party.[7]

It was transformative that the head of the new Democratic Party and legislative majority, who would be vital to much of Paiewonsky's gubernatorial success, was a Black whose early history epitomized the large Virgin Islands working class whose lives Paiewonsky wanted to make history by changing. Earle B. Ottley was born on St. Thomas in 1921 and grew up in the storied black community of Savan, the seventh child of Henry Ottley and Eulalia Queeman. His father was a joiner who died when Earle was only four, and two years later his mother migrated to New York City, as did many of her contemporaries, to support their families by taking care of other families far from home. She took the "girl children" with her, as mothers often did, but left the boys, including Earle, in the care of a cousin. Indeed, had Earle been born several years earlier, he would not even have had the benefit of a high school education, as that did not become available in St. Thomas until the late 1920s. But he was born late enough that he could attend the new Charlotte Amalie High School and was a member of its Class of 1939.[8]

Despite the many factors that could have worked against his success, "Earle B.," as Ottley became popularly known, would have a long and outstanding career as a newspaper journalist and publisher, a labor union organizer and leader, a political party founder and leader, the longest-serving V.I. legislator to date (32 years), an author, and probably the most powerful political leader of the Virgin Islands in the twentieth century. Many of the progressive changes that characterized the Virgin Islands by the time he died in 1999, compared to the conditions of his early life, were due to Ottley's untiring work and the support that his legislative coalitions furnished to Paiewonsky and other governors.

The Role of Race in the Paiewonsky Administration

However, just a few weeks after Paiewonsky took office, he was diverted from the goals stated in his inaugural address by a national article on race relations in the May 8, 1961, issue of *U.S. News and World Report*. The article, which was part of a survey on conditions in the Caribbean, reported:

> Racial trouble is growing in the Unites States Caribbean paradise, the Virgin Islands. The racial trouble is being imported with U.S. citizens who are moving there from the continent in growing numbers—and bring their segregationist customs with them.... Recent arrivals are financially able to outbid the Virgin Islander for the limited land and housing available in these densely populated islands.... Prices are going ever higher. Result is a tightening squeeze on native inhabitants. One problem you do not find here is nationalism. The people of the Virgin Islands want to stay close to the U.S. The big problem here, as in most other islands of the Caribbean, is one of race.[9]

The article brought about the first widespread territorial discussion of race relations in the V.I. and initiated a discussion that has never completely ended; it is simply subtle at some times and louder at other times.

Reactions ranged from complete agreement to indignant denials. Both St. Thomas newspapers—the *Daily News* and the *Home Journal*—had editorials that agreed threats did exist and should be nipped in the bud.[10] Governor Paiewonsky thought the article was exaggerated and said the writer was "looking for a needle in a haystack," but promised his administration would do all it could to end discrimination.[11] Novelist Herman Wouk, who was a resident of St. Thomas at the time and had been named by Paiewonsky as his Special Advisor on Cultural Affairs, stated: "the question of race just doesn't exist here ... the subject of integration or segregation is not even a concept here." Many of the islands' residents, especially the young, were thankful that the matters had been brought to light. The article's contents were even noted at the United Nations by the Nigerian representative, and a U. S. representative promised it would be probed.[12]

In late May 1961, a couple weeks after the article had appeared and due to the widespread local concern and considerable national publicity, Governor Paiewonsky appointed a seven-member Commission on Human Relations. His charge to it was:

> To study and promote good human relations in the Virgin Islands, and goodwill between all races in the Virgin Islands, to report your work back to the Governor on or before December 31, 1961, after holding such seminars with various groups in the Virgin Islands as you see fit.

Amazingly, however, the Governor also told the members of the Commission that:

> On the islands of St. Thomas and St. John there is no discrimination problem of any kind whatsoever. Equality of opportunity is total.... The whole work of this commission, therefore, turns on the situation in St. Croix.[13]

The situation on St. Croix to which the Governor referred was the known presence there of three white-only private clubs (one that had existed on St. Thomas had apparently closed by the 1960s). The unfortunate narrow mandate that the Commission was thus given made it easy for its members to overlook other forms of discrimination which it might otherwise have investigated.

The much-discussed article also led to legislative action. On June 1, 1961, the Legislature passed unanimously a new 11-page Civil Rights Act. The new law specifically prohibited discrimination in real estate and other sales, in employment, working conditions, and in private clubs as long as they had any type of government license, such as licenses for the sale of alcoholic beverages. The penalties were several times greater than those in the 1950 Anti-Discrimination Act, and additionally, victims could receive up to $5000.00 in civil suits.[14]

The strength of its provisions was disturbing to persons who were against strong civil rights enforcement. One such was Senator Barry Goldwater of Arizona, who was then a contender for the Republican presidential nomination of 1964. He criticized it on the floor of the U.S. Senate, stating on August 7, 1961: "The revisions of the Civil Rights Act of the Virgin Islands appear to this layman to be a rather destructive effort toward the right of association."[15] However, representing the other side of the controversy, the Anti-Defamation League of B'nai'B'rith, an international Jewish organization, called the act "the first serious effort by any legislature within the U.S. to cope with the practice of using the private club device to evade statutory prohibitions against racial or religious discrimination."[16]

Former governor Ralph Paiewonsky presents a plaque to Senator Earle B. Ottley, 1972. Courtesy of Mrs. Alma Ottley.

Early in 1962 the local ramifications of the Civil Rights Act took an astonishing turn. In January, half a year after the Act was passed, the Legislature was concerned that Jack Monsanto, who had been retained from the Merwin administration by Gov. Paiewonsky as Commissioner of the Department of Public Safety (the prior name of the present Police Department) had not yet chosen a panel of police officers to inspect places of business, as directed by the Act. It was then learned, early in February, that Commissioner Monsanto was himself a member of one of the "Whites-only" clubs in the Virgin Islands—the St. Croix Country Club, and that, in order to escape the consequences of the new Act, the Club had recently withdrawn its renewal request for the liquor license it had had for years.[17] (Commissioner Jack Monsanto was a member of an old white St. Thomas family. However, by the 1900s most of the other local Monsantos were black as a result of racial admixture. For example, a well-known member of the black Monsantos was David Monsanto, who was a vocational teacher at the Charlotte Amalie High School and a long-term leader of the St. Thomas

Community Band, which led to him being honored by the bestowal of his name on the Bandstand in the St. Thomas Emancipation Garden.)

Commissioner Monsanto stated that he had no intention of resigning and saw no conflict between his club membership and his governmental responsibilities. He explained that his club membership predated his government role and had taken place at a time when he had maintained a flying service, which necessitated spending a lot of nights on St. Croix, and so he was often invited to the club. He thought it better to stay in the club and correct things if they were wrong than to resign. However, he refused to say there was anything wrong with the club as it was and, when confronted with the statistic that of the club's 300 members, not one was black, he responded; "Has any asked to join?"[18]

The Legislature held a hearing on the issue, at which Monsanto again stated that, not knowing of the applications of any Negroes, he could not say whether or not the club was discriminatory; he also reiterated his decision not to resign. The Legislature voted to request the Governor to ask for his resignation, declaring Monsanto could no longer be regarded as a person fit to carry out his duties. A few days later, on February 13, 1962, Monsanto resigned after a conference with the Governor.[19]

The *U.S. News* article and the Monsanto affair greatly increased racial consciousness and awareness in St. Thomas and the rest of the Virgin Islands that all was not as well as had been projected before. For, based on a suggestion of President Kennedy, local tourism professionals had succeeded in projecting an image on the mainland of the Virgin Islands as an "American Paradise" and a "Showplace of Democracy," and thus there were U.S. government-sponsored programs that regularly sent foreign visitors to the V.I. to see racial democracy and equality at work in a part of the United States. Many Virgin Islanders were left wondering about the possibilities of bridging the realities and the projected images.

Achievements in Housing and in Education, Particularly CVI

Governor Paiewonsky remained determined to undertake the tasks of historical transformation of the Virgin Islands by elevating the society's substandard conditions to twentieth-century levels. With the solid legislative partnership of Ottley and the new Democrats, along with the Governor's own personal network of national political and business leaders, various areas of deficiency were tackled. There were many new housing developments. Some were federally-financed public housing, such as the 300 units erected at Harris Court on the eastern edge of Charlotte Amalie, and the higher-rental middle-income Warren Brown Apartments on Bluebeard's Hill. Others were privately financed, such as the 700 acres in Estate Anna's Retreat, known popularly as Tutu, developed by Sydney Kessler (who also owned the Virgin Isles Hotel) which offered complete homes for $13,500, with down payments of only a couple hundred dollars. The new housing developments took thousands of poor, mainly black Virgin Islands families from crowded primitive housing conditions that frequently lacked running water or flush toilet systems, into new homes with clean, sanitary, modern-day accommodations. The private developments also allowed many young newly-educated Virgin Islanders the opportunity of early home ownership for raising their families, instead of having to wait until middle-age or older, as many of their parents had had to do.[20]

In the area of education, there was substantial expansion of physical facilities, with over 160 classrooms added in St. Thomas alone during the Paiewonsky administration; many were needed because of the great population influx of new workers (and their children) for the growing economy. That mandated the employment of many new teachers, and teachers' salaries were raised. The minimum salary for teachers with bachelor's degrees was increased in 1963 from $4,000 a year to $4,600, and then again in 1965 to $5,100. To insure qualitative along with numerical increases, the Paiewonsky administration pressed for accreditation of the territory's three public high schools; two attained that status, with the Charlotte Amalie High School on St. Thomas being one. The governor also asked New York University, his alma mater, to come and assess the V.I. educational system and propose methods of improvement. One proposal resulted in the designation of a demonstration school that concentrated on new teaching and learning motivation techniques, supplementary instructional materials, and patterns for individualization of instruction that could also be employed in other schools. Several administrators of the V.I. Department of Education were selected to attend NYU for advanced training. Under that program, well-known educators such as Rehenia Gabriel and Arthur Richards earned doctoral degrees, while Vitalia Wallace and Mario Watlington earned master's degrees in their areas of specialty.[21]

This writer remembers, however, at least one grievous criticism resulting from the pace at which some changes in education were made. Apparently, a new recommendation for hiring teachers was that only college-educated persons should be employed. That had long been the local practice for high school teachers but, due to the absence of a local institution of higher education before the College of the Virgin Islands opened in 1963 and the financial inability of many to go away to college right after high school, the practice had been to employ highly-recommended high school graduates as elementary instructors, with the government offering after-school or summer sessions at which they began receiving college-level training. Many of the most respected Virgin Islands educators had begun their careers that way. The abrupt enforcement of the new policy led to some of the elementary schools in the 1960s having a large number of teachers who were new arrivals, largely white, from the U.S. mainland and who often had very little in common with their young students. The cultural and linguistic differences, therefore, posed special problems for some students and even some teachers.

The achievement of his administration of which Gov. Paiewonsky became proudest was the establishment of the College of the Virgin Islands in 1962. From as far back as the mid-1940s, the Progressive Guide Party had a plank advocating a junior college in its platform, but the widespread poverty in the V.I. at that time made it simply a pipe dream. Then, during his short administration, Gov. Merwin had asked Ralph Paiewonsky, as one of Merwin's advisers, to look into the need for a local college. Paiewonsky's research convinced him that it was definitely time for such an institution, as economic betterment over time was enabling more students to go away to college after high school and many never returned, resulting in a substantial brain drain of Virgin Islanders. Thus Paiewonsky was ready, from the first day of his administration, to champion the establishment of a college. After all of the preparatory conferences, meetings, and reports had been completed, the Governor submitted to the Legislature a bill containing a charter for the new institution; the bill was passed by the Legislature, then signed into law by the governor on March 16, 1962, now referred to as the institution's Charter Day. It established the College of the Virgin Islands (CVI) as a publicly-funded, two-year liberal arts institution. Its main campus was located at Bourne Field on St. Thomas, on 125 acres of land that that had been a naval base during World War II, and which was relinquished by the U.S. to the government of the Virgin Islands for use as a college. Having been a naval base, the land came with the advantage of having a number of buildings—barracks, officers' residential quarters, and a hangar, all of which would be well utilized.[22]

CVI commenced classes on St. Thomas in July, 1963, with an enrollment of forty-five full-time students. Classes began on St. Croix one year later, in 1964, on a campus which was also a gift from the federal government. At the institution's first commencement in 1965, at which eleven degrees were awarded, the esteemed speaker was Lady Bird Johnson, the wife of U.S. President Lyndon Baines Johnson. By 1967, the full-time enrollment on both campuses was 272, with a part-time enrollment of over 1,000 persons, taking classes

The College of the Virgin Islands' first graduating class in 1965, with President Lawrence Wanlass and Lady Bird Johnson, the speaker and wife of U.S. President Lyndon B. Johnson. Courtesy of the Virgin Islands Government's Archival Collection at the Charles W. Turnbull Regional Library.

in the evenings after work to upgrade their skills or to study part-time for an eventual degree.[23]

Achievements in Economic Diversification— Tourism, Light and Heavy Industries

Another area of special attention by Gov. Paiewonsky was the transforming of tourism into a year-round industry. It became a reality and tourism became a major financial support of the growth in housing, education on all levels, and the general modernization of the Virgin Islands. However, Paiewonsky and the Democratic coalition owed thanks to Fidel Castro and the revolution he orchestrated in Cuba after his takeover in 1959. Cuba had been the most popular destination for American tourists prior to 1959; after its break with the U.S., much of the old Cuban traffic was diverted to Puerto Rico and the Virgin Islands.[24]

White entrepreneurs and investors were the keys to the development of the infrastructure that a booming tourist industry needed, and had been at work substantially before the 1960s. What is considered the beginning of the era of modern tourism in St. Thomas took place in 1950 with the opening of the Virgin Isle Hotel, the first luxury hotel in the V.I. Located on a hill west of Charlotte Amalie, the huge white complex of 130 rooms was an imposing sight and was the first building in the V.I. to have elevators. Built by two white Americans from the mainland, Sydney Kessler and Benjamin Bayne, it was without peer during its first few years and was the site of the most important social functions on St. Thomas. It employed a substantial number of local St. Thomas residents, not only adults but even high school students (part-time) such as Elmo Roebuck and Roy Schneider, both of whom would become political leaders in the V.I. decades later. In 1980 the hotel changed management and became the Virgin Isle Hilton.[25] (In 1995 it was destroyed by Hurricane Marilyn.)

In 1954 Bluebeard's Castle Hotel (which was first developed as a federal project in the 1930s) was reopened and, after extensive renovations and enlargement, became quite a competitor to the Virgin Isle Hotel. Then, in 1956 Laurance Rockefeller opened an attractive resort on the Caneel Bay Plantation on St. John that he had bought in 1952, It became a well-known retreat for U.S. Presidents, Vice-Presidents, Congressmen, and other prominent persons whose stays were outstanding advertisement. In 1954, Rockefeller had also embarked on a land-acquisition program in St. John, and presented to the U.S. National Park Service in 1956, to become the Virgin Islands National Park, over 5,000 acres of land, embracing most of the land area of St. John and several beautiful beaches. Campgrounds were established, attracting campers from throughout the nation. Tourism in St. John formed a part of St. Thomas's tourist traffic, as St. Thomas was the usual port of entry and departure for St. John and its tourists also often shopped in St. Thomas.[26] The same benefits rebounded to St. Thomas from a hotel which opened on Water Island (located in Charlotte Amalie's harbor) in 1954, and from residential sites being sold on that island.[27]

There was, therefore, a substantial amount of hotel development already in place when Gov. Paiewonsky took office in 1961. What really mushroomed during his administration was cruise ship traffic. No longer able to go to Cuba, cruise itineraries from the U.S. went further east, with St. Thomas becoming within a decade the No. 1 port of call in the Caribbean. St. Thomas presented no language or currency differences from the U.S., no need for passports or visas. Even television entertainment played a role, with the ABC television "Loveboat" series increasing the popularity of cruising. In 1962, the year after Paiewonsky took office, 131 cruise ships visited St. Thomas; by 1968, the year before he left office, cruise ship visits numbered 342. Similarly, in 1962, cruise ship passengers to St. Thomas had numbered 57,368; by 1968, they numbered 166,117.[28]

Another great objective of the Paiewonsky/Democratic coalition of the 1960s was the diversification of the economy. By clever use of federal legislation that permitted entry into the U.S. of items containing a restricted percentage of foreign materials, Paiewonsky encouraged the expansion or establishment, in both St. Croix and St. Thomas, of many small factories in which hundreds of workers assembled textiles, watches and costume jewelry, thermometers, and chemicals. However, the two major events of economic diversification took place on St. Croix, where the cultivation of sugar was still a substantial, but non-profitable, part of St. Croix's economy. The Paiewonsky/Democratic coalition's plan to phase out sugar led to great opposition from some of the big landowners of St. Croix and the old Democratic faction. Despite the opposition, the federal corporation that had managed the sugar industry was phased out, with federal approval, and agreements were negotiated with two large industrial corporations to establish plants on St. Croix. In fulfilment of the agreements, Harvey Alumina Virgin Islands, Inc. (1962) and the Hess Oil Virgin Islands Corporation (1965) both constructed huge complexes on St. Croix that employed hundreds of workers, both residents and imported employees who possessed needed skills and experience. The two corporations brought modern industrial operations and high incomes to St. Croix, and generated substantial governmental revenues. In 1962, the year after Paiewonsky took office, the estimated per capita income of the U.S. V.I. was $1,153.00; by 1967 it had become $2,133.00, the highest in the Caribbean.[29]

By 1967 also, Governor Paiewonsky had been in office for six years and, unless something very unusual happened, could expect his term to last an additional two years. His major plans for improvement in education, social, economic, and political conditions were proceeding successfully and 1967 presented him with another highly anticipated privilege—presiding over the 50th or semi-centennial anniversary celebration of the Virgin Islands becoming a part of the United States. In addition to all of the programs and commemorative activities that usually characterize such an occasion, Paiewonsky came up with an additional and unforgettable event: he persuaded the Annual National Governors' Conference to have its 1967 conference on a cruise ship that would cruise to the Virgin Islands.

In his *Memoirs of a Governor*, Paiewonsky explained that originally his thought was of having the conference solely in the Virgin Islands. But after considering all the details of accommodations, food preparation, and adequacy of utilities for all of the fifty-four state and territorial governors, their fami-

California's Governor and Mrs. Ronald Reagan during 1967 Governors' Conference in the Virgin Islands. Courtesy of the Virgin Islands Government's Archival Collection at the Charles W. Turnbull Regional Library.

lies, staffs, and reporters, it occurred to him that maybe the entire conference could take place on a large ship, and the central organization office of the Governor's Conference agreed. The SS *Independence* was contracted to sail from New York City to St. Thomas, then St. Croix, and return to New York. RCA Communications, Inc. was contracted to install a complete sophisticated communication center on the ship, along with the technicians, operators, and supervisory personnel needed. Arrangements were also made, with the permission of the President of the United States, which it was Paiewonsky's special task to obtain, to have large U.S Air Force helicopters stationed along the route of the cruise to get governors off the ship in case of emergencies. The helicopters were stationed in New York, Bermuda, and Puerto Rico, but no emergencies for their use occurred; they did, however, deliver and take away mail from the ship regularly. Another source of assurance for the governors was their knowledge that they were sailing under the escort of the U.S. Navy, which followed the ship discreetly in the background.[30]

The cruise began and ended in New York City, from October 16 to 24, 1967, with three days—the 19th through the 21st—at St. Thomas and St. Croix.

Most of the business of the conference was conducted during the days at sea, so that the time in the Virgin Islands could be devoted to seeing and experiencing the islands. As would be expected, the islands had been cleaned and beautified in every way, and the visitors were treated to all the usual and special amenities—welcoming flotillas and bands, special receptions and beach picnics, shopping tours, and fireworks displays. On St. Thomas, the climax of one of the programs was a presentation by Henry Reichhold, the then-owner of the Bluebeard's Castle Hotel on St. Thomas and who had become a friend of Gov. Paiewonsky, of his second one-million dollar check to the College of the Virgin Islands for the construction of a center for the performing arts. On St. Croix, Governor and Mrs. Ronald Reagan of California delighted everyone by joining a quadrille dance group for a few moments, and the visitors were then taken to the Fountain Valley Golf Course where the owners, Laurance and David Rockefeller, had arranged a dinner fete for them.[31]

Governor Paiewonsky stated in his memoir that in addition to the joy and specialness of having the nation's governors visiting to join in the semi-centennial celebration of the V.I.'s ties with the United States, he expected the conference to accomplish two other objectives. One was that the publicity about the conference would increase tourism to the islands. Secondly, the governor thought that with race relations then at a low ebb in the U.S., due to the efforts of the Rev. Dr. Martin Luther King, Jr. and other civil rights leaders to obtain more opportunities for Blacks and the resistance it was causing in many white communities, the Virgin Islands could present a different picture to the visiting governors: that "blacks and whites lived together in harmony here." The governor had also tried to mirror that harmony in a practical way as the conference guides and chaperones, who had each been assigned to interact with a visiting governor (who were all white) and their families, included both black and white Virgin Islands natives.[32]

The 1967 visiting Governors' Conference and other semi-centennial celebrations were successful and inspiring, and most residents seemed to feel that the Virgin Islands had come a long way during the Paiewonsky administration and in the half-century of. U.S. sovereignty. However, in spite of those sentiments and the relative truth of Governor Paiewonsky's statements that race relations in the Virgin Islands were much better than on the U.S. mainland, there were existing local racial conditions that were far from ideal and that were causing a great deal of concern among some groups. The last year of his governorship and the years following would reveal some of them.

Notes

1. Paiewonsky, *Memoirs of a Governor*, pp. 9–19.

2. Ibid., pp. 41, 47, 35.

3. Ibid., pp. 50–127.

4. Ibid., pp. 130–131.

5. Ibid., pp. 155–158. This author has also been a beneficiary of the Paiewonsky family's kindness. After meeting me as a young instructor of history at the College of the Virgin Islands, the Governor always made sure that I got an autographed copy of any book the family published, whether authored by him, his brother Isidor—who was a dedicated historian, or Isidor's son, Michael.

6. Paiewonsky, *Memoirs of a Governor*, pp. 481–485.

7. Paiewonsky, *Memoirs of a Governor*, pp. 278–287; Ottley, *Trials and Triumphs*, pp. 234–248.

8. Personal information about Earle B. Ottley was taken from his eulogy by his nephew, Basil Ottley, Jr., in Earle Ottley's Funeral Booklet, dated September 4, 1999.

9. Carl Midgall, "Caribbean: One More Sea of Trouble," *U. S. News and World Report*, Vol. 51, No. 19 (May 8, 1961), p. 92.

10. "Racial Trouble in Islands? Legislators Discuss Problem," *Daily News* (St. Thomas, V.I., May 3, 1961, p. 1; Editorial, *Home Journal* (St. Thomas, V.I.), May 4, 1961, p. 3.

11. "Gov. Paiewonsky Pledges to End Possible Racial Discrimination," *Daily News* (St. Thomas, V. I.), May 5, 1961, p. 1.

12. "UN hears charge of Race Bias in Virgin Islands," *Daily News* (St. Thomas, V.I.), May 11, p. 1.

13. "Paiewonsky Appoints Commission," *Home Journal* (St. Thomas, V.I.), May 23, 1961, p. 1; Louis Shulterbrandt, editor, *Messages of the Governor of the Virgin Islands: Governor Ralph M. Paiewonsky* (Oxford, New Hampshire: Equity Publishing Company, 1962–1969), pp. 106–107.

14. "Civil Rights Bill would end possible Race Discrimination," *Daily News* (St. Thomas, V.I.), May 27, 1961, p. 1; "New Civil Rights Act Designed to Prevent Discrimination Here," *Home Journal* (St. Thomas, V.I.), June 3, 1961, pp. 1, 5, 8.

15. "U.N. Hears Charges of Race Bias in Virgin Islands," *Home Journal* (St. Thomas, V.I.), May 11, 1961, p. 1.

16. Ibid., December 14, 1961, p. 1.

17. Ibid., January 25, 1962, p. 1; February 1, 1962, p. 1.

18. *"Monsanto Plans No Resignation,"* *Daily News* (St. Thomas), February 8, 1962, p. 1.

19. *"Legislature Asks Paiewonsky to Fire Monsanto,"* Daily News (St, Thomas), February 9, 1962, p. 1; February 10, 1962, p. 1.

20. Ottley, *Trials and Triumphs*, pp. 201–202; Paiewonsky, *Memoirs of a Governor*, p. 203.

21. Paiewonsky, Memoirs of a Governor, pp. 323–333.

22. Ibid., pp. 353–367.

23. Ibid., 370–377.

24. Martin Garson Orlins, "The Impact of Tourism on the Virgin Islands of the United States" (Ph.D. dissertation, Columbia University, 1969), pp. 89–96.

25. Ibid., pp. 100–101.

26. "Over 500 Attend Benefit Ball at V.I. Hotel." *Daily News* (St. Thomas, V.I.), December 17, 1954, p, 1; November 20, 1854, p. 1; Orlins, "The Impact of Tourism," pp. 100–101.

27. "Completion of Waterfront Before March Unlikely," *Daily News* (St. Thomas, V.I.), January 21, 1952, p. 1.

28. "Editorial—Virgin Isles Hotel," *Daily News* (St. Thomas, V.I.), April 28, 1951, p. 3.

29. Morris Kaplan, "L. S. Rockefeller Offers U. S. a Virgin Islands Park," *Daily News* (St. Thomas, V. I.), November 20, 1954, p.1; Ottley, *Trials and Triumphs*, pp. 206–211.

30. Paiewonsky, *Memoirs of a Governor*, pp. 388–393.

31. Ibid., pp. 392–399.

32. Ibid., pp. 387–388, 390–391, 396, 434.

Part 3

The Second Half-Century of United States Sovereignty, 1967–2017

"Jamaican tourism, in the final analysis, reflected a colossal contradiction. On the one hand, postwar tourism development was meant to relieve the problems of Jamaica's colonial past. On the other, tourism reinforced many essential features of that original condition and entrapped the island in the clasp of neocolonialism."
— *To Hell With Paradise*, Frank Fonda Taylor (1993)

At the end of 1967, with the semi-centennial celebration, including the Governors' Conference, having been completed successfully, Governor Paiewonsky seemed to have earned the right to look forward to spending the remainder of his term peacefully, in a thriving jurisdiction that he, and strong legislative support, had done much to bring about. In the 1983 and 2010 editions of his book, *America's Virgin Islands*, University of Delaware political scientist, Dr. William Boyer, labeled the 1960s as the Development Decade of the Virgin Islands. V.I. legislative leader Earle B. Ottley's first book, *Trials and Triumphs*, published in 1982, was subtitled "The Long Road to a Middle Class Society in the U.S. Virgin Islands." Truly, the 1960s were a decade in which development transformed the Virgin Islands substantially and effected the creation of a sizeable local middle class.[1]

Chapter 14

A Troubled Atmosphere, 1968–1972

What also came to characterize the late 1960s was a somewhat troubled atmosphere, in which there was one incident after another of racial discord. The year 1968 proved to be an extremely eventful year for race relations in the Virgin Islands. By the end of that year no one who had spent the year locally could make a credible claim that there were no race relations problems, as some theretofore had been inclined to do.

The events began in January 1968 with the news that racist literature was being disseminated in Christiansted, St. Croix. The literature was reported to declare that there must be "supremacy or slavery" and called upon black islanders to fight the attempt of Continentals to take over the economic and political direction of the islands. It led to much public discussion and a debate in the Legislature. While one senator, for example, proposed the naming of a 'committee on race relations,' another declared, "We have no need for such a committee here. We have one of the tightest Civil Rights Acts on the books." No race relations committee came about, but due to the rapidly rising crime rate, a group was proposed to study crime and juvenile delinquency.[2]

The assassination of Martin Luther King on April 4, 1968, was deeply felt in the Virgin Islands. In common with people of color in many places, black Virgin Islanders had been deeply touched by the 1963 March on Washington and King's stirring "I Have A Dream" speech. In fact, there were even Virgin Islanders who had attended the march. Then, compounding the shock and grief of King's loss, was the murder in a St. Croix restaurant, a few hours after King's slaying, of a white man by a black Continental for no apparent reason other than revenge for King's death.[3]

On the afternoon of King's funeral, Monday, April 9, a memorial march, organized by the Student Council of the College of the Virgin Islands, was held on the Main Street of St. Thomas. Hundreds of persons took part in the march and over 2,000 persons gathered at the terminal point of the march, the Market Square, for a program that included the singing of the Negro National Anthem and "We Shall Overcome," along with a speech by the V. I. Assistant Commissioner of Education, Charles W. Turnbull. All of the Main Street stores, mostly white-owned, closed. It was known that this was due to the shop owners' fear of violence, a great deal of which was taking place on the mainland, but a Gift Shop Association spokesman said that the early closings were out of respect for Dr. King and to allow their employees to participate in the march. The event was totally peaceful, but the Department of Public Safety had stationed an unusually large number of policemen along the route of the march.[4] (The Virgin Islands would later become the first place in the U.S. to make King's birthday a public holiday.)

A couple weeks later, in late April 1968, Allen Grammer, a white continental businessman and journalist who had resided on St. Thomas since the mid-1950s was shot dead outside his home. Grammer had had his business license revoked in 1956 for discriminatory practices, and had been identified by some persons ever since as a racist. Even though the native black young man charged with the murder was judged insane and sent to a mental institution, it touched off a wave of fear in the white community as the perpetrator had had anti-white slogans on his car previously and also made anti-white declarations at his trial. The murder had been committed just prior to the annual carnival in St. Thomas, at the end of April, and it generated a host of rumors about various anti-white activities that were "supposed" to take place during the carnival festivities. The carnival, however, took place without any unusual incident, but some Whites remained a little fearful after that year about their presence in Carnival activities.[5] (One of Grammer's children, Kelsey, who was born on St. Thomas, would later become an award-winning television and Broadway actor on the U.S. mainland.)

In early May 1968, Governor Paiewonsky accused black power militants from the mainland of having responsibility for the increasing tensions in the V.I. "A few of these crazy people have come down from New York to stir up the natives," the New York Times quoted him as saying.[6] There were widespread public and private discussions regarding whether outbreaks of racial violence, similar to the riots which had occurred on the mainland after Dr. King's death, could happen in the Virgin Islands. One point of view, propounded publicly by Associated Press correspondent Oeveste Granducci, a Continental who had lived in the V.I. for eight years, answered in the negative. He said that the chances of racial violence in the V.I. were "at least ten to one against" and gave four reasons for his conclusion. Granducci argued that: (1) the causes of stateside violence did not exist in V.I.—there was "equal opportunity—in education, jobs, housing, everything?"; (2) the islands were "as near non-segregated as a bi-racial society can be"; (3) the "native Virgin Islander considers himself a 'West Indian.' He is proud of his history, of his heritage and of the fact that he has lived successfully in peace and harmony with men of other races for many years"; and (4) the "white mainlanders who emigrate to the Virgin Islands are fully aware—when they come here—of the non-segregation and of the fact that they are 'the minority.'" Granducci admitted there were a "handful of exceptions" in both races but reasoned they were not enough to turn any minor racial incidences into widespread violence.[7]

Another point of view was put forth in a *Daily News* editorial a few days after Granducci's analysis. It defended the need for the committees which had recently been appointed by the Governor to assess the crime situation and the potential for violence. Some persons had said the committees were unnecessary. The editorial read, in part:

> It is ignorance and hypocrisy to say 'It can't happen here.' 'It' can happen here or anywhere else. There have been stories of shiploads of guns apprehended by the U.S. Coast Guard ... machetes concealed in taxicabs; the purchase of great numbers of ice picks; a declared war on 'hippies'; a merchant reserving chairs in her store for pet dogs, but not for patrons of a certain color; ... during the memorial march of Martin Luther King, rumors were circulating through the islands charging that 'continentals' are monopolizing choice property to the detriment of the native population. We hope that the committees will not pretend that problems do not exist.[8]

On Monday, May 6, 1968, President of the Legislature Earle B. Ottley, one of the most influential political figures in the V.I. and himself a newspaper editor, delivered a major address on the racial temper of the islands. He urged islanders to speak up and not allow those who wished to stimulate racial discord to be the only audible voices. He warned that racial discord and violence would mean economic suicide as "investors would pullout, visitors would stay away, and our major industry go into a tailspin." A poll of several St. Thomas political and economic leaders showed that they greatly applauded the speech and thought it timely and very much needed.[9]

The reactions to Senator Ottley's speech and to the weeks of discussion and rumors which had preceded it were quite varied. They showed how divided opinions in the islands were regarding the sources of the growing racism. In

mid-May 1968, the Legislature passed a bill to restrict drastically the possession of firearms. The senators also considered proposals for strict regulation
of all publications in the V.I., as a means of controlling racist literature. A public letter to Senator Ottley expressed what seemed to be the feelings of many
Whites. The writer was a recently-arrived Continental who signed as "A Friend
of the Virgin Islands" because of his expressed fear of unpleasantness if identified. He expressed great approval of the Senator's speech and declared that
since Blacks were a large majority in the V.I. and controlled the Legislature, it
was difficult to understand why prejudice against Whites was developing. The
only discrimination the writer had witnessed in St. Thomas was on the parts
of Blacks against Whites and he cited the booing of a white carnival queen contestant by an audience as an example. The writer's opinion was that much of
the prejudice was being generated by the schools, which he supported by a recent newspaper report of the singing of "We Shall Overcome" by the children
of a public elementary school during a Music Week program. The writer's reaction was:

> With the schools of the Virgin Islands instilling this philosophy in
> the children, it won't be many years before the Virgin Islands will
> be having racial incidents, riots and finally a disintegration of the
> whole economy when tourists stop coming and Congress takes
> reprisal actions.[10]

On the other hand, a segment of public opinion seemed to feel that the
great concern with weapons, racist literature, and anti-white acts, though understandable and worthy of attention, overlooked the real roots of the problem—those aspects of life in the V.I. which were turning some Blacks, especially
the young, into anti-white advocates. One public letter (May 1968) to Senator Ottley stated:

> The dark skin person is an underdog on the mainland—must he be
> an underdog in the V.I. also in order to accommodate bigots from the
> outside? I believe that a different approach should be used in regards
> to the correction of racism in the V.I. and that is first and foremost
> the protection of the local people from the 'so called' industrialists and
> business people from the mainland.[11]

One of the most comprehensive public utterances came from William S.
Harvey of St. Croix. His correspondence to the St. Thomas *Daily News* (June
1968) stated that he was happy to see people speaking out against racism and
concurred that the islands should be free of race hatred. He continued:

However, there is an inconsistency in our islands as regards to racism which concerns me. We seem to condemn the fact while at the same time we condone its cause.

One of the reasons for the smoldering resentment among some natives, which has served as a potential hotbed where a hate group might flourish, is the failure of many erstwhile continentals ... to participate in native-led community activities.

In the interests of improved racial harmony, we should attempt to ferret out the cause of this seeming inability to live together. Well-meaning phrases and high sounding clichés will not help. Nor will it help to condemn racial hatred when it emanates from blacks, and condoning it when the source is in the white segment of the community?[12]

Even from the mainland there came similar expressions. One possessed special poignancy because the magazine editor to whom it was addressed was the continental journalist, Allen Grammer, who had been murdered on St. Thomas in late April, and thus he was already deceased by the time the letter appeared in the newspaper in late May. The writer was Rosalyn L. Spitzer of New York and she was debating certain points the deceased journalist had expressed in a recent issue of his magazine.

You complain that relocated Continentals are misunderstood by oversensitive Virgin Islanders. Have you noticed that recent arrivals who have come to live in the Islands because they have been charmed by the life there, immediately upon arrival set out to change the very attraction that drew them in the first place? So that life can be more like the "at home" from which they have fled? Have you considered that this is why the "obvious" Continental runs into difficulty with his "most casual remark?"[13]

The second half of 1968 was not marked by any dramatic events, but discussions continued concerning the reasons and offering solutions for continuing racial tension. Occasional reports told of incidents in which white Continentals acted in very rude or discriminatory ways toward Blacks and accused such persons of being the cause of the islands' racial problems. Sporadic verbal and/or physical harassment of white tourists or residents by young Blacks also continued to take place.

Early 1969 saw renewed calls for governmental action to curtail acts of racism against Whites. What apparently was not being understood or addressed by some of the most influential voices in the community was that a goodly portion of young Blacks were feeling that they were in, or were rapidly approaching, the same position as Blacks in the ghettoes of New York, Newark, Detroit, or Los Angeles. Feelings of total economic powerlessness, similar impotence in determining the political future of the islands, and a future which indicated a worsening of these conditions were some of the major anxieties of young Blacks. And the fact that Blacks formed the majority, in contrast to the mainland, served to make their feelings of impotence even more searing and frustrating.

Not only were such aspects not emphasized as much as demands for prevention or punishment of anti-white racism, but persons who attempted to steer discussions and make suggestions in such directions were often maligned from various quarters. When the Reverend Robert Rierson, a white Continental pastor of the Nisky Moravian Church on St. Thomas, spoke on a television program in late 1968 of white domination of the Virgin Islands economy and its effects, a storm of protest ensued. He was severely criticized by some business interests and accused of creating racial disharmony and meddling in non-religious affairs. Undaunted, however, another prelate called in early 1969 for a greater sharing of economic power by Blacks and Whites. The Right Reverend Cedric E. Mills, Episcopal Bishop of the V.I. and a black Continental, told a diocesan convocation that white economic control was causing great resentment and not talking about it would not make it go away. He broached that people in the V.I. were hiding their heads in the sand in regard to black-white relations, and that the Church should become active "for the welfare of all," and more in particular "for the black people in our several communities."[14]

On September 23, 29, and 30, 1969, the New York Times published a series of three articles on the V.I., assessing how the prosperity of the 1960s had affected the islands and asking if its price may have been too great.[15] They were very much discussed in the Virgin Islands. A couple weeks later, J. E. Kean, a Black resident of St. John, put forth in a letter to the Daily News a very strong case for Blacks, so cogent that it deserves extensive space:

> To expect an island people, 85 per cent black, to remain supinely indifferent while a generally continental and white minority acquires most of their land, controls their banks, dominates their industry, obtains political power by corruption of government officials, and scarcely troubles to disguise their contempt for the majority in their culture and in their persons, is to ask too much of human, even black, forbearance.
>
> One needn't stupidly bother to invoke some vague wave of Black Nationalism engulfing the Caribbean, or mindlessly denounce non-existent outside agitators. The present virulent form of racial tensions

in the Virgin Islands has no other source than in the rapid and accelerating dispossession of the hapless native by white continentals and the exploitation of the black alien by all.

The evil takes place within a framework of laws in themselves often unexceptionable, but which, since they fail sufficiently to favor and protect the native in his economic competition with the better educated, experienced, trained and more resourceful continentals, condemn him to defeat and future servitude in his own country.

Racial tension will increase and not be aggravated until the day the Virgin Islands Government move to redress the situation by enacting laws capable of eventually changing the present situation of wealth along racial lines to a distribution not racially weighted.[16]

During the early 1970s the local newspapers received correspondence regularly from persons concerned with the racial situations that the economic progress of the 1960s had accelerated in the territory, and it was also reflected in mainland publications.

In October 1970, *Ebony* magazine published an article on race relations in the V.I., entitled "The Struggle for Paradise." One of its foci was the differences in awareness and outlook between many of the older Blacks and the younger. It mentioned, for example, that awareness of exploitative racist techniques had hardly been developed in some older Blacks, who thus made statements such as, "We're in the majority here so white people have to treat us right." But, as attorney Alexander Farrelly was quoted as saying, "Some of the whites came here with their prejudices in their suitcases. Unlike some of the older blacks here, these younger kids are quick to spot racist tendencies and they aren't going to put up with that these days."[17]

About the middle of 1970, there appeared in the local press the first letters from Continentals who had resided in the V.I. for some time and were wondering if they should stay or leave. Race relations continued to be a main topic of discussion in St. Thomas throughout 1970 and 1971. In early June 1970, there was a three-hour debate in St. Thomas on the racial situation which supposedly pitted "Black Power" against the "Establishment." It was carried by all television and radio stations in the V.I. and, at the time, was said to have had the greatest audience in the history of electronic media in the V.I. A few days later, Governor Evans, the last appointed governor, appointed a seventeen-member Advisory Committee on Community Relations.[18]

In December 1970, a black Virgin Islander resident in New York, but who had recently visited the islands, wrote back and brought up a matter which had begun to be a secret worry of a number of Blacks. He wrote that during

his two decades in New York he had suffered every known form of discrimination, but he had not become "anti-white … only decidedly pro-black." His
great concern was:

> One is hiding his head in the sand to believe that when white conti-
> nental Americans gain control over the American Virgin Islands, as
> indeed they will someday, that they will adopt a magnanimous atti-
> tude towards the blacks. Black Virgin Islanders will run up against the
> same barriers, the same bigotry which they encounter on the main-
> land, north or south.[19]

As Blacks had observed the growing influx of Whites and realized the local
inability to regulate this migration, some had begun to realize that the day
might arrive when the current demographic pattern could change to the degree that Blacks would be outnumbered by Whites, and thus the economic and
other disadvantages of Blacks would most likely be greater. When it was mentioned at black gatherings, there were those Blacks who scoffed at the idea and
considered it practically impossible. But there were also Blacks who were aware
that such a reversal had already taken place in the early history of the many
West Indian islands, with Whites having been dominant before the wholesale
utilization of the slave trade. Some also thought of Hawaii where, from having been a small minority a few decades earlier, Whites had become the largest
single ethnic group by the late 1960s.[20]

The year 1972 began with several warnings that race relations in the V.I.
were on a very perilous path. In February, 1972, an open letter from a black
St. Thomian resident, a businessman originally from St. Kitts and known locally as Doris King, expressed concern about the public mood. Mr. King stated
that he was on the street (as a popular food van owner) and knew how people felt, and there was great displeasure with big business, the spread of condominiums on the eastern area of St. Thomas, and the injustice of Water Island
[to be discussed later in Chapter 18]. He asked officials to act or things could
be "very explosive if conditions remain as they are."[21]

Clearly, by the summer of 1972 no knowledgeable person could characterize St. Thomas or the Virgin Islands as a racial paradise. Not only were Blacks
dissatisfied with their status, but the aggressive anger in some young Blacks
created a climate in which many Whites had become fearful for their physical
safety.

Notes

1. William W. Boyer, *America's Virgin Islands: A History of Human Rights and Wrongs* (Durham, North Carolina: Carolina Academic Press, 1983 and 2010 editions), Chapters 10; Earle B. Ottley, *Trials and Triumphs: The Long Road to a Middle Class Society in the U.S. Virgin Islands* (St. Thomas, V.I., 1982).

2. Editorial—"Signs of Danger," *Daily News* (St. Thomas, V.I.), January 20, 1968, p. 7.

3. "Widespread Violence Hits U.S. as King is Slain," *Daily News* (St. Thomas, V.I.), April 6, 1958, p. 1.

4. "Acting Governor King, Students Pay Tribute," *Daily News* (St. Thomas, V.I.), April 9, 1968, pp. 1, 5, 8; "Final Tributes Paid to King," Associated Press, "Students Hold March Honoring Dr. King," Ibid., April 10, 1968, p. 1, 5.

5. Oveste Granducci, "Part-time Cabbie Held in Slaying of Editor," *Daily News* (St. Thomas, V.I.), April 29, 1968, p. 1; "Committee Named to Investigate Rumors," Ibid., May 1, 1968, p. 1.

6. *New York Times*, May 4, 1968, p. 23.

7. "Leaders Mourn Loss of Dr. King," Daily News (St. Thomas, V.I.), May 3, 1968, p. 1, 5.

8. "It Can Happen Here, Rumors or Fact?", *Daily News* (St. Thomas, V.I.), May 6, 1968, p. 7. The reference to a white merchant practicing discrimination was based on an incident that had gained wide publicity. Mrs. Jean Robinson had written to the Governor to inform him of what had happened to her family on the day of Martin Luther King's funeral in the John Bell Importer Store in St. Thomas. When one member of the family had attempted to sit on a stool while another was trying on clothing, the proprietress of the store had said she provided the chair for her dog, not customers. The proprietress had further said she did not understand the reason for all the fuss over King's death because he was just another man. When a member of the Robinson family had attempted to explain how King was perceived, the proprietress had expressed her opposition to open housing and legislation to improve the position of Blacks, and ended up telling the family, "If it takes 300 more years to get what you want, then you'll just have to wait." The Robinsons had expressed their opinion that such behavior, especially on an emotionally charged day, showed extreme insensitivity and could have touched off a major racial incident. (Daily News, St. Thomas, V.I., April 17, 1968, p. 7.)

9. *Home Journal* (St. Thomas, V.I., May 14, 1968, p. 3; "Warning Issued At Opening Of Senate," *Daily News* (St. Thomas, V.I.), May 7, 1968, p. 1.

10. Editorial—"A Dangerous Bill," "Possession Of Firearms Regulated By Measure," *Daily News* (St. Thomas, V.I.), May 10, 1968, p. 1; May 16, 1968, p. 7; *Home Journal* (St. Thomas, V.I.), May 31, 1968, p. 5.

11. Letter to the Editor, "Correspondence", *Daily News*, (St. Thomas, V.I.), May 11, 1968, p. 7.

12. Letter to the Editor from William Harvey of St. Croix, *Daily News*, (St. Thomas, V.I.), June 1, 1968, pp. 7, 14.

13. Rosalyn L. Spitzer, "Letter to the Editor from Rosalyn Spitzer of New York," *Daily News*, (St. Thomas, V.I.), May 29, 1968, p. 7.

14. Copy of a letter sent to Mr. Robert Moss, TV Station WBNB, St. Thomas, December 2, 1968; *Daily News* (St. Thomas, V.I.), March 4, 1969, p. 8.

15. Martin Waldron, author of articles on the Virgin Islands in the *New York Times* on September 28, 1969, p. 1, September 29, 1969, p. 38, and September 30, 1969, p. 72. "Civil Leaders Meet to Air Times Story", *Daily News* (St. Thomas, V.I.), October 4, 1969, p. 7; 1; "Keep the Record Open", October 14, 1969, p. 147; "Evans Claims Times Story 'Erroneous'", October 1, 1969, p. 1.

16. Letter J.E. Kean, "Letters to the Editor from J. E. Kean of St. John,", *Daily News* (St. Thomas, V.I.), October 6, 1969, p. 14, 15.

17. Charles L. Sanders, "The Struggle for Paradise," *Ebony*, Vol. 25, No. 12, October, 1970, pp. 66–72.

18. "3-Hour Debate Conducted on Racial Situation in V.I.; 17 Named to Race Relations Panel," *Daily News* (St. Thomas, V.I.), June 4, 1970, pp. 1, 6.

19. Letter from Clifford Rabsatt, "Letter to the Editor," *Daily News* (St. Thomas, V.I.), December 2, 1970, pp. 7, 13.

20. Bryan H. Farrell, *Hawaii, The Legend That Sells* (Honolulu: The University Press of Hawaii, 1982), pp. 212–216.

21. Open Letter from Doris King, *Home Journal* (St. Thomas, V.I.), February, 16, 1972, pp. 6, 15.

Chapter 15

The Tragedy of Fountain Valley and After, 1972–1975

On September 6, 1972, a type of explosion that some persons had come to expect finally took place on the island of St. Croix. On that Wednesday afternoon, one day after the Olympic slayings at Munich had shocked the world, the Virgin Islands provided another shock. Eight persons were shot to death at the clubhouse of the Rockefeller-owned Fountain Valley Golf Club on St. Croix. Seven were white; one was black. Four of the Whites had been two couples on vacation from Miami—they had received free transportation to St. Croix from Eastern Airlines as one of each couple had been an Eastern employee. The four slain St. Croix residents were all workers at the Golf Club—the temporary pro-shop manager, a groundskeeper, an electrician, and the electrician's assistant—the only Black. The three white St. Croix residents were all Continentals. Several other persons who had been at the clubhouse, all black, were injured but had escaped.[1]

The eyewitnesses who had escaped stated that the murders had been perpetrated by several masked men, wearing Army fatigues and carrying guns, who had appeared at the clubhouse at about 3:30 p.m. They were reported to have robbed the tourists and the clubhouse's cash register, and then to have started shooting after the uttering of an anti-white statement. A force of 100 armed men, including specially imported U.S. marshals and FBI agents assisted by aircraft, conducted an island-wide search for the killers. In less than a week, five black male Virgin Islanders, aged 21 to 25, were arrested and each charged with eight counts of first-degree murder and robbery. All five—Warren Ballantine, Beaumont Gereau, Raphael Joseph, Ishmael LaBeet, and Meral Smith—were native Virgin Islanders, some from very well-known families.

One had grown up on St. Thomas and another had recently lived there; three were Vietnam veterans.[2]

What happened on that Wednesday afternoon at Fountain Valley was the most shocking event in the twentieth-century history of the Virgin Islands. It imposed a new reality and a new fear as no non-violent deed or warning could have done. For a period of almost a year, from its occurrence until the middle of August 1973, when they were all found guilty and sentenced to eight life imprisonments each, the acts of the Fountain Valley Five were constant news items in the Virgin Islands. Aside from the infamy of the deed with which they were charged, the trial was long and dramatic, involving countersuits, obscenities, enthusiastic supporters of the defendants, and the presence of national figures such as noted lawyer William Kunstler, who served as one of the defense attorneys, and Roy Innis, head of the Congress of Racial Equality and a native Virgin Islander. The Fountain Valley slayings, trial, and close subsequent occurrences imparted wholly new dimensions to the Virgin Islands race relations atmosphere.

A couple things did not change. The Governor, then Dr. Melvin Evans who was a black native, and some other officials, insisted that the Fountain Valley deed had no racial motives. The Governor, noting the damage that labeling it a racial incident would cause, was quoted as saying: "There is not one shred of evidence that the robbery and shooting were racial." But the *Miami Herald*, in a story reprinted locally, countered: "ONE FACT, though emerges clearly; Gunfire killed all seven whites at the site. Eight of nine blacks escaped." Many local Blacks and some officials and other leaders agreed with the *Herald*. In an editorial entitled "Will We Face the Facts Now?", the *Daily News* declared that too many in the V.I., both in and out of government, had closed their eyes and ears to repeated warnings that the seeds for such a tragedy had been germinating. They had been critical of any who had dared to point out such developments. Robert Ellison, a Black and former Commissioner of Public Safety, asked:

> Who would you find as a rule at a rich resort of that type? White Continentals. The selection of the target was racially motivated.... I don't go for that robbery theory.... I think they went there to do what they did ... it seems to me over years we ought to have known we were not making any provisions for our young and sooner or later were going to pay the price.... It's time we got frightened and faced up to the reality of things.[3]

In the weeks following the tragedy, a number of Whites tried to highlight black racism in the V.I., revealed the frequent abuses they were subjected to and tried to determine their causes. Robert Cramer thought there was too much emphasis on phrases like "social disaffection among young blacks" and "a piece of the action." He suggested that people point to the positive and speak realistically:

> People need to be told that you don't get educated without study-
> ing, no one ever gives anything away, one has to work hard for what
> one gets, and no one owes anyone a living. Let's also tell them you
> can't work or shake hands with a clenched fist.[4]

Some worried about the economic effect Fountain Valley might have on the Islands. Just three days after, on September 9, it was announced that plans were being dropped for the Cabrita Point Resort on St. Thomas. The application had been for a large scale hotel, marina, and club and condominium resort on the easternmost point of St. Thomas. A couple days later, on September 12, a New York Times article spoke of a "cloud" over the V.I.'s economic future. However, less than a week later, on September 18, ground was broken for a new Sapphire Beach Resort, a $14 million dollar new condominium complex. Maybe the amount of preparation that had already occurred was a determining factor.[5]

Many Blacks felt especially uneasy and on the defensive about black racism following Fountain Valley. Vicki Gardine Smith, however, explained that though she was only in her twenties, she had witnessed the transformation of the islands from polite considerate places to what they had become. She thought many of the new ways had been brought by some of the same people who were wondering why they were hearing "Whitey go home." She wrote:

> I am not condoning the criminal acts that have been committed in
> the Virgin Islands, but I think one should really evaluate the reasons
> why these criminal acts have been committed....
> I agree that nothing can be solved by retaliation, but I want you to
> understand what is happening and why it is happening. The problem
> has to be understood before it can be solved. Everyone needs to ex-
> amine himself to evaluate how he may have contributed to the dete-
> rioration with the U.S. Virgins. Don't put all the blame on the
> "hoodlums." They are reacting to what is happening around them.[6]

An appreciable number of Whites, on St. Thomas and St. Croix, became sufficiently fearful that they left during the post-Fountain Valley period. And interviews later established that a substantial number who stayed had seriously considered leaving at some point. The chief source of fear was not just what happened at Fountain Valley, which one could argue was a unique occurrence, but the frequency of seemingly similarly racially-motivated brutal crimes during the year following the initial tragedy. Two months afterward, in November 1972, the governor felt it necessary to again request special FBI assistance in the murder of two Whites during a restaurant robbery on St. Croix. Eleven months after Fountain Valley, in August 1973, Governor Evans was, for a third time, asking the U.S. Department of Justice for help in the wake of the murders of several more whites on St. Croix. In October 1973, after additional slayings of Caucasians on St. Croix, the White House announced the creation of a special high level task force to help the V.I. government overcome its problems of social unrest.[7]

St. Thomas did not experience a pronounced wave of brutal murders such as took place on St. Croix during the post-Fountain Valley year, but there was always the lurking fear of its possibility. Moreover, there were enough lesser happenings on St. Thomas to maintain a somewhat tense and apprehensive atmosphere. John R. Schuller, a Continental who decided to leave St. Thomas in late 1972, reported that his family had been robbed five times in the four years they were there and that "St. Thomas made us decide that Paradise had turned into Hell." Pastor Ray Thompson of the Calvary Baptist Church in St. Thomas disclosed in January 1973 that the church had been vandalized three times in the previous three months and the last time there had been an attempt to destroy the church by fire. In March 1973, an editorial deplored the number of people in St. Thomas who were carrying around guns while claiming it was necessary for their protection.[8]

Very frightening for Whites in St. Thomas also was the emanation of various rumors regarding threats of violence to Whites. Some of these were discussed in December 1972 by local columnist Henry Wheatley, who appealed for common sense and a realistic perspective in dealing with the rumors. Some of the recent rumors had been that in late November 1972 many white-owned businesses would be burned; that on December 8 1972 a lot of Whites would be murdered or a Kill-a-Whitey-a-day campaign would be launched; that a leaflet was being distributed at the Charlotte Amalie High School calling on white teachers to leave by December 1 or else…. The sources of such rumors were hardly ever known but they spread with amazing rapidity among Whites; many Blacks were often unaware of them. None of these mentioned rumors or several others ever got beyond the rumor stage.[9]

On the other hand, some Whites noted very cordial relations between Blacks and Whites on St. Thomas in the post-Fountain Valley period—at least on the surface. Pastor Lawrence Baietti, of the Frederick Lutheran Church in St. Thomas, found that in 1973 many persons were going out of their way to prove that Fountain Valley had been an isolated occurrence and were extremely polite and gracious in dealings with others.[10]

There seemed to be general biracial agreement in the post-Fountain Valley years, at least as voiced, that overall soul-searching was needed to pinpoint the various causes of racism in the V.I., followed by genuine efforts to eliminate or reduce them. An interesting journalistic episode in late 1973, however, demonstrated the extreme difficulty of any such undertaking. Henry Wheatley was a native black St. Thomian who had gone to the mainland after high school in the 1940s and returned in 1969, after serving in such positions as Administrative Aide to Governor Nelson Rockefeller of New York and head of the Peace Corps in the Ivory Coast and Venezuela. Notably intelligent and sophisticated, Wheatley quickly became a unique type of leader in the community, equally in touch with Blacks and Whites. He had a weekly TV program called "Overview," a regular newspaper column, and in 1970 was elected president of the St. Thomas-St. John Chamber of Commerce. In the latter capacity, Wheatley had made a speech in December 1971, which had functioned as a focal point for a community debate. He had warned against black racism, white separation and insufficient business responsibility, and strongly disputed the assertions of many young Blacks that the V.I. was culturally African. Wheatley had asserted that the islands had a uniquely blended cultural heritage. In general, the speech had been applauded by Whites and older and more established Blacks, while a number of younger Blacks had decried his anti-African culture remarks and his seeming equation of black and white racism. Some Blacks had even come to view Wheatley as more pro-white than pro-black.[11] It was a great surprise, therefore, when after one of his columns, a number of Whites bitterly turned on Wheatley. It was his column of November 1, 1973, entitled "A Memorandum to White Virgin Islanders," and read in part:

> The first, and most obvious, commitment should be to the acceptance of a society in which people of all races and origins will be treated with friendliness, respect and dignity. We have never been perfect in our race relations but it is certain that the influx of many white Americans over the past two decades has led to a deterioration in mutual good conduct between ethnic groups. White people who came into this community and found a congenial relationship between the races should be willing to take on the burden of making the principal overtures toward reestablishing bridges of brotherhood that were broken in the process of their joining the community. Even if it means going out of your way, leaning over backwards, to make a personal contribution to the redevelopment of a multi-racial peace. White people who consider this extra effort too much of a burden would do themselves and the rest of us a favor by going somewhere else, someplace, if there is such a place, where they can keep to "their own kind" without becoming a social problem.[12]

The reaction and responses were so unexpectedly great that Wheatley's column was reprinted six days later, and again two and a half weeks later. The *Daily News* carried a special column just for letters addressed to Wheatley. The first printed public response came one week later in the form of another column — by Herman Luben, who was pastor of the Reformed Church in St. Thomas. It bore the title, "Memo to All Virgin Islanders" and read in part:

> Were the Virgin Islands to become a sovereign state, then the government could say quite clearly who are welcome foreigners and who are not. But are we not the people of one nation. As such we are accustomed to circulate freely. A Michigander by birth, I lived almost 30 years in New York. I have spent time in most of the 50 states, but no one ever said to before, that outside Michigan I am on probationary stay. I've never needed to earn a green card in America before. As soon as we limit Virgin Islanders from living on the mainland until they fulfill some statesider's expectations, or vice versa, we destroy the meaning of our common citizenship.
>
> A final presupposition is that mature human beings accept one another, warts and all. That the white race has been guilty of gross racism is known to us all. But now to charge our current racism here to white Americans and to call upon them to build alone the bridges of reconciliation many of us want thrown across the chasms, this is simply racism in reverse.... Who of us is qualified to order another group around?[13]

Eleanor Heckert, a white continental St. Thomian novelist and businesswoman, accused Wheatley of trying "to start a racial fight about who-did-what-to whom." She suggested that if his memorandum were edited by striking out the word "white" wherever it appeared and substituting "people" it would then be "constructive." Of course, that would not have remedied the objection voiced by the Reverend Luben and some others that no one should suggest to others that they might be better suited elsewhere. One letter from a John Meade, who said he had lived on St. Thomas for ten years, told Wheatley that he had previously agreed with him on many things, "then that last article really showed me how you think." He stated he was going to do as Wheatley advised and leave, but promised his first stop would be Washington, D.C., where he threatened to try to get the U.S. to abandon the V.I., whereupon he expected the economy of the islands to go to nothing. Dick Doumeng, another white continental St. Thomian, defended Wheatley by saying he knew him and he was not anti-white, but admitted that many Whites had come up to him (Doumeng) and said things like: "Did you read Wheatley's column? I can't believe him…. He is telling the whites to leave…. I thought his head was together.[14]

A couple of Whites—from St. Croix—did write to tell Wheatley that his memo had needed to be written. One felt reassured by the suggestion of Wheatley's that Whites should participate fully, including politically, and said some Whites may have previously thought that such participation would be resented as "taking over." Interestingly, one writer stated that her family had been in St. Croix since 1959 and wrote (in 1973!): "We are shy about asking natives to our homes, and they are diffident."[15]

Many Blacks noted the white criticisms of Wheatley's column with amazement. The reactions seemed to be saying that Whites thought they had a right to act exactly as they wanted to. While that was very true, as was the Reverend Luben's assertion that all Americans could settle wherever they wished under the U.S. flag, many Blacks had thought that the common concern had been the restoration of a better way of life—the kind which had once suggested for the Virgin Islands the "American paradise" label. But if that suggestion—that white V.I. residents should try to behave in ways other than those which had created the well-known racial problems of the mainland, and if they could not then maybe they should go elsewhere—met with such vehement resistance, what hope could there be for a better way of life in the islands?

In an effort to promote friendliness and good will among all residents, a well-publicized "Tramp Together" was held in St. Thomas on March 2, 1974, with Gertrude Dudley as its honorary chairman. In accordance with island custom, the tramp was a mass everyone-join-in parade with many bands to provide music. The actual "trampers" were reported to number several hundred while an estimated 5,000 turned out to watch the affair. It was judged a success by the numbers involved and its spirit.[16]

There were several other efforts and programs during the following years of the 1970s aimed at improving race relations on St. Thomas. In early 1974 a series of "People to People" parties were hosted by some persons to promote the mingling of residents and tourists. In the following years, Project St. Thomas, a business-promoted community movement, tried to boost friendliness among residents and to tourists by a "Good Day" campaign which utilized posters, buttons, and other media, and also sponsored special business-familiarization activities for high school students. They all produced some positive effects, but the key to effecting real change in race relations, however, seemed to depend on the effectuation of changes in underlying socioeconomic conditions in order to give young Blacks more hope for the future. That was not taking place to any noticeable degree, and reports from both tourists and residents through the 70s and beyond revealed that some young

Blacks were still seeking the nearest vulnerable victims, white or black, on whom to vent the socio-economic and political frustrations they felt.

The base for the overall state of race relations anywhere is probably the degree to which members of different races associate with and get to know each other in the conduct and maintenance of affairs in the several spheres of life. This research effort has discovered that in the decades before the 1970s and similarly in those since, there has been a noticeable absence in St. Thomas of significant contact between substantial numbers of Blacks and Whites, except in circumstances where people needed to meet in the business of making a living. Only a very small percentage of either Blacks or Whites had or have any sustained or voluntary non-economic contact with persons of other races. It may be argued that a large portion of such separation is a function of socio-economic stratification which is operative even in mono-racial societies. While that is true to some extent, the knowledge obtained in this research effort presented evidence that racial considerations have played a substantial role in the various forms of separation.

Notes

1. "8 Dead; 4 Injured in Golf Course Massacre," *Daily News* (St. Thomas, V.I.), September 7, 1972, p. 1–6; "Police Question 3 in Golf Course Killings," Ibid., September 8, 1972, pp. 1, 2, 4, 5; "125 Man Posse Seeks Fountain Valley Killers," Ibid., September 9, 1972, pp. 1, 6.

2. "Police Arrest Two Men in Golf Course Fillings," *Daily News* (St. Thomas, V.I.), September 11, 1972, p. 1–5; "Crowd Blocks FBI, Cops from Questioning Youth (Youth was younger brother of a FV suspect," Ibid, September 11, 1972, p. 1; "Three More Arrested in Golf Course Slayings," Ibid., September 13, 1972, pp. 1, 8; Boyer, *America's Virgin Islands*, p. 314.

3. Jon Nordheimer, "Gunmen Hunted in Virgin Islands," *New York Times*, September 8, 1972, p. 8; Nordheimer, "Pair Charged in Murder of Eight in Virgin Islands," September 10, 1972, p. 72; Nordheimer, "Economic Future Clouded by Virgin Islands Slayings," September 11, 1972, p. 7; September 18, 1972, pp. 8, 97.

4. The long quote is from Robert Cramer, in the *Daily News* (St. Thomas, V.I.), September 26, 1972, p. 7; also see *Daily News* issues of September 19, 1972, p. 7; September 25, 1972, p. 7; September 28, 1972, pp. 1, 2; September 27, 1972, pp. 7, 13.

5. "Group Drops Plans for Cabrita Point Resort," *Daily News* (St. Thomas, V.I.), September 9, 1972, pp. 1, 6; Jon Nordhimerr, "Time Sees Cloud Over Economic Future of V.I.," Ibid., September 12, 1972, pp. 1,8; "Ground Broken for new Sapphire Beach Resort," Ibid., September 18, 1972, pp. 1, 6.

6. "Letter to the Editor" from Vicki Gardine Smith, *Daily News* (St. Thomas, V.I.), September 27, 1972, p. 13.

7. "Police Press Search for Ballroom Killers," *Daily News* (St. Thomas, V.I.) November 9, 1972, p. 1; "Editorial— 'How Often Can We Call for Help?' " Ibid., November 13, 1972, p. 7.

8. "Letter from Pastor Ray Thomson, to the Editor," *Daily News* (St. Thomas, V.I.), November 16, 1972, p. 7; "Pastor Deplores Theft, Vandalizing of Church," January 22, 1973, p. 44; "Our Amateur Gun-Slingers," March 5, 1973, p. 7.

9. "Overview," Column by Henry U. Wheatley, "Rumors and Common Sense," *Daily News* (St. Thomas, V.I.), December 27, 1972, p. 6.

10. Interview with Pastor Lawrence Baietti, St. Thomas, February 24, 1983.

11. Wheatley's speech is in the *Daily News* (St. Thomas, V.I.), December 9, 1971, pp. 2, 4. Representative letters in the *Daily News* commending the speech were from Charles Current, December 13, 1971, p. 7; Glorida M. Lewis, December 14, 1972, p. 7; Mr. and Mrs. Warren Corning, December 15, 1971, p. 7; Charles Golt, December 15, 1971, p. 7; and Larry McEvitt, December 18, 1971, p. 7. McEvitt predicted that "If the proper authorities haven't read it or fail to act upon it, we are all in for a really *terrible* 1972."

Representative correspondence to the Daily News critical of Wheatley's speech were from Gerald E. Hodge, January 14, 1972, pp. 7, 13; Koko Simba U'ibi A'mdulla (Horatio Millin, Jr.), January 20, 1972, p. 7; Wayne Francis, January 26, 1972, p. 7; and Eugene Rasch, March 18, 1972, pp. 7, 13. Hodge's main point was that "black racism is the effect and not the cause of the existing problem. The cause is, white racism which has been prevalent within our community, however subtly, over the years." Francis asserted: "There was never a claim that the V.I. society or culture is totally African in origin. What has been said is that the underlying structure, the basic foundation is African. The European and American cultural features have been borrowed and worked into an African based but distinctly Virgin Islands [way of life]."

12. Henry Wheatley, "Overview—A Memorandum to White Islanders," *Daily News* (St. Thomas, V.I.), November 10, 1973, pp. 6, 16.

13. Herman E. Luben, "Memorandum to All Virgin Islanders," *Daily News* (St. Thomas, V.I.), November 17, 1973, pp. 6, 17.

14. Letter from Dick Duomeng, "Attorney Gen. Hodge Chides Bus. Group," *Daily News* (St. Thomas, V.I.), November 21, 1973, p. 7.1.

15. Letter from St. Croix couple, *Daily News*, (St. Thomas, V.I.), November 28, 1973, p. 15.

16. "'Tramp Together' Set to Show Friendliness," *Daily News* (St. Thomas, V.I.), February 12, 1974, p. 3; "Main Street Jammed for 'Tramp Together,'" *Daily News*, March 4, 1974, p. 1; "Editorial—'Tramp Together Shows the Way,'" *Daily News*, March 6, 1974, p. 7.

Chapter 16

Changing and New
Socio-Racial Groups

Despite the uneasy social atmosphere, by the 1970s, and continuing for decades after, there were substantial changes in the socio-economic positions of previous socio-racial groups on St. Thomas, and also the growing immigration of racial/ethnic groups that were new to the island. The French communities and the alien-status or previously alien-status black West Indian groups underwent noticeable positive changes, and the population of St. Thomas would be augmented by new arrivals from the Dominican Republic, the Middle East, and India.

French St. Thomians

By the late 1960s, the position of the French in St. Thomian society was undergoing remarkable change from what it had been a quarter-century before and earlier. Numerically, the French had fallen from first place among the white groups, having been eclipsed by the Continentals during the 1960s. However, their socio-economic position had soared. The term "Cha Cha" had fallen from favor and St. Thomians of French descent were spoken of as "the French" or, familiarly, "Frenchies." "Cha Cha Town" became properly "French Town" or Carenage. As the incoming white population from the mainland grew larger, it strengthened the position of the local French. In fact, intermarriage with white Continentals, either from having met in St. Thomas or from meetings on the U.S. mainland as a result of college attendance there, proved to be great for the French, as former marriages within their local population, which was preferred to marriage with Blacks, had been blamed for physical problems related to inbreeding.

Interracial family, Mr. & Mrs. Joseph Ledee and daughter Karel, in the 1950s. Mr. Ledee was a Frenchie and his wife, Laurita, was originally from St. John. Courtesy of Karel Ledee Daniel.

Contrary to the prevailing custom of the late nineteenth and early twentieth century, when some young French females did not remain in school after the primary grades, young French St. Thomians were pursuing secondary, higher, and professional education, and began filling positions at all levels of government service and private enterprise. In fact, their race seemed to favor their choice for certain types of positions in white Continental-owned industries. Thus, the former differences in styles of living between the French and the other white groups or any groups of the society had been erased, and many former French Town residents began living in wealthier residential areas of St. Thomas. Their former places in French Town were taken by Blacks and other residents, so French Town is now more mixed residentially, though 'Frenchies' still form its core. Thankfully, also, and to the great appreciation of many St. Thomians of all groups and races, some of the French families that had a tradition of fishing or farming (the Northside community) have continued to be major suppliers to the community of fresh fish and local fruits and vegetables, both very important to today's emphasis on healthy and balanced nutrition.

Queen Jessica (center) of the French Town Father's Day Carnival of 2011, flanked by her grandmother Karel on the left, her mother Laurita on the right, and the queen's little brother, J'Quan, in front. Grandmother Karel was the little girl in the previous picture of the inter-racial family. Courtesy of Karel Ledee Daniel.

In 2004 a French Heritage Museum was established in French Town, ex-hibiting and extolling the history and culture of the area's earlier residents. French Town has become also the location of several excellent restaurants, and some of its cake makers (a lucrative home industry) attract customers from throughout St. Thomas. Every year on Father's Day weekend, a reminder of the importance to the French of intact families with fathers, which is not as emphasized in some levels of black society, French Town hosts a carnival-like celebration that is well attended by all groups of St. Thomians. Then, about a month later, to honor the national holiday of France—Bastille Day, July 14th—the French of both local communities, French Town and the Northside area, celebrate French Heritage Week, with activities such as fishing tournaments and various other cultural events.[1]

Non-Citizen and New-Citizen West Indians

The position of Blacks from other West Indian islands, particularly those east of the Virgin Islands, who were first admitted as temporary alien-status workers, gradually became more secure and solid. In April and May of 1970, Congressional legislation and a new U.S. Department of Labor policy permitted the spouses and children of non-citizen workers to join them. Then in June 1970, a U.S. District Court of the Virgin Islands ruling by Judge Almeric Christian, a native black Virgin Islander, established that alien-status children were entitled to free public education. As a result of those rulings, both the general population and public school enrollment increased rapidly. In the fall semester of 1972, 80 percent of the new students enrolling in the public schools had alien status, and by December, 1974, non-citizen students accounted for one-third of public school enrollment.[2] The increased demands and strains on public funds and facilities caused greater-than-ever outcries from the native population, as would probably have taken place anywhere, but did not impede the needed progress.

However, in addition to the above-mentioned administrative and judicial decisions which led to the greater protection and inclusion of foreign-born West Indians in the Virgin Islands, by the early 1970s there were also other unifying factors at work among the native and the alien-status black groups. One was that of romantic involvements and marriages, which were taking place in substantial numbers. Another was the development of friendships among the young in residential neighborhoods, schools and sports, and among adults in churches and work settings. A third was the increasing number of former non-citizen West Indians who were being naturalized as U.S. citizens, creating a political force with which to reckon, and all of these processes have been ongoing.

Moreover, there had always been natives who advocated the necessity of greater racial consciousness and unity among Blacks, realizing that Blacks were losing economic ground and other community indices of well-being to other groups. With a number of the non-citizen or new-citizen Blacks attending CVI/UVI, many were encouraged that the new black Virgin Islanders were preparing themselves to become greater contributors to the society and economy. As a result, during the 70s, the term "Garrot" for alien-status Blacks was being replaced by the less offensive "Islo" (pronounced i-lo), which actually is descriptive of all West Indians. V.I. residents, of all types, were realizing that the once-temporary workers had become permanent residents of the Virgin Islands, and deserved to be treated inclusively in every way, without any condescending names or labels.

The St. Thomas Campaign Committee of Paul Alexander, originally from Dominica and wearing black in the center, supporting his 2014 candidacy for membership in the Virgin Islands Legislature. Courtesy of Paul Alexander.

Former alien-status workers and/or their children are now an integral part of Virgin Islands society, and are found at all levels of governmental, business, religious, and social settings. An outstanding example is former Senator, now present Lieutenant Governor of the Virgin Islands Osbert Potter. Not only were Lt. Gov. Potter's parents Antiguans, but instead of migrating directly to the U.S. Virgin Islands, they first went to the British Virgin Islands, and thus his birthplace was Tortola. However, he and his siblings all received from, and contributed bountifully to, the U.S. Virgin Islands—in areas as diverse as governmental administration, legislation, the calypso arts, and carnival pageantry. Interestingly, Lt. Gov. Potter has achieved something similar to what Gov. Paiewonsky did fifty years ago: he persuaded the National Lieutenant Governors Association to have its 2017 meeting in St. Thomas in November, just as the Governors were a part of the V.I. semi-centennial commemoration in 1967.[3] May it be successful and memorable!

Dominicans

Another new group in St. Thomas, which had not existed during the first half century of American rule, consisted of migrants from the Dominican Republic. Hispanics from Puerto Rico had begun to be a sizeable population group in St. Croix during the 1920s, due to their recruitment for the sugar industry there, and a few Puerto Rican families had settled in St. Thomas during the 1930s and 40s. However, it was not until after the assassination of the Dominican dictator Rafael Trujillo in 1961 and the American military intervention that substantial numbers of persons from the Dominican Republic started migrating to the United States, including the Virgin Islands.[4]

The migrants refer to themselves as "Dominicanos" but many of the other residents of St. Thomas call them "Santos." An interview was secured with one of the early Dominican arrivals to St. Thomas—Juana Corcino, who lives in the Hospital Ground area of St. Thomas. Her story is instructive regarding the lives and progress of many "Santos" in St. Thomas. She was born as Juana Alvarado in 1944 in the city of San Francisco de Macoris in the Dominican Republic, and is thus now a young-looking matron in her early seventies. She came to St. Thomas in 1968, when she was 24, and got a job at a restaurant across from the Charlotte Amalie High School. One of the persons who had lunch there regularly was a mechanic named Andres Corcino, who had been born in Vieques, Puerto Rico but had been taken to St. Croix as a child and had lived there before moving to St. Thomas. Andres and Juana fell in love and were married in 1969.[5]

At the time of their marriage, Andres had just bought a home for $500.00, a small one-room shack and lot, on a small part of their present property in Hospital Ground. When Juana saw the dilapidated wooden shack with holes in the roof through which water poured when it rained, she cried and did not want to live there as it could not compare to the room in Sugar Estate she had been renting. But they both made up their minds to work hard to make their lives successful. They made the shack as sturdy as possible and built a small adjoining garage for Andres's mechanic business, for which he became well known. Juana tried to learn mechanics and became very proficient in all but the most technical aspects; she mastered jobs such as changing various car parts and spray-painting. But she said it was very hard work, from early morning until night, and while relating her story, she had to stop at times to prevent tears from flowing. This especially happened when she spoke of their first child, a boy who died just before his birth, which she thinks was due at least partially to her over-working. She also regrets deeply that at the times of her

Juana Corcino and granddaughter. Courtesy of Juana Corcino.

mother's and sisters' deaths, she could not afford to go to the Dominican Republic to attend their funerals.

In 1976 their landlord, who lived in New York, offered to sell to Juana and Andres, for $10,000.00, the entire tract of land on which their little home and garage were located. The bank said it could not lend them more than $7,000.00, so Juana sold all of her jewelry, including family heirlooms she had brought with her, for $3,000.00 and got the rest from the bank. After saving as much as they could for several years and with Juana also selling V.I. lottery tickets, they started building their home in 1979. Over the years, with additional bank loans, it has become a substantial and very attractive two-story complex, including a couple apartments.

Juana is a devout Catholic, who attends Sts. Peter and Paul weekly, and thanks God greatly for His blessings in her life. However, her life has also included substantial griefs. Their second son was epileptic and died at age 36 after a grand mal seizure. Then their third son was attracted, as a substantial number of young men in the Virgin Islands, to drug use and dealing, and thus has had legal problems. She prays regularly for him.

Andres Corcino died in 2007. However, Juana says she has found St. Thomas people to be kind and helpful, and thinks of St. Thomas as her home where she wishes to stay, even though she has sisters and other relatives in New York. When asked if she considers herself as a white or black Hispanic, as it is reported that among Dominicans there is substantial variety as to how persons classify themselves racially, regardless of complexion, she says she knows she is brown-skinned and therefore black. In common with many other Dominicans who came to the V.I. after their school years, Juana has leaned to converse in English, but still not quite as fluently as she would like.

A substantial number of other Dominican migrants to the V.I. have also been enterprising. In the Downstreet area of St. Thomas, west of the Sts. Peter and Paul Cathedral, they have established a number of small businesses — mainly bars and restaurants. In the Savan area they have additional small groceries and beauty salons. In fact, there appears to be so great a presence of "Santos" in the area of Charlotte Amalie north of the Market Square and the Christ Church Methodist, that it is sometimes referred to as "Santo Dominguito" — meaning "Little Santo Domingo." There are also well-known enclaves of Dominicans in parts of Bovoni and the "Soto Town" area of Contant. Many work in services, maintenance, and construction industries, and many are quite active in Carnival, politics, and other areas of Virgin Islands life.

Arabs

Another relatively recent Virgin Islands migrant group is comprised of persons from the Middle East, who are called "Arabs" on St. Thomas. Actually, from about the 1940s/1950s, there were a few Arabs in St. Thomas who became well-known itinerant merchants, going from door to door selling various household items. According to U.S. immigrant statistics, most of those early Arab migrants (before the 1970s) were Christians who were fleeing from the Muslim countries of the Middle East. By the 1990s the pattern had changed completely, with more than 70% of new Arab migrants being Muslims and that has not changed, not even since the Trade Center attacks of 9/11, 2001. Additionally, many of the newer Arab immigrants are more educated and have a higher rate of business ownership.[6]

The higher rate of Arab business ownership is extremely evident on St. Thomas, and involves dominance of large and vital sectors of the economy. Arab businessmen now own most of St. Thomas's gas stations, furniture stores, department stores, neighborhood groceries, and supermarkets (the non-membership types—with the largest being the two Pueblos, the two Gourmet Galleries, Plaza Extra, Moe's, and Food Center). As would be expected, there are a number of persons of other races or ethnic groups who have great concerns about one group's control of so many vital sectors of the economy.

Success, however, did not arrive on a well-paved road for all of the owners, and the life of the owner of the two Gourmet Gallery stores illustrates that. Zakaria Suid was born in Palestine in 1954, and received only four years of formal schooling; he never got to the fifth grade. He simply tried to learn all he could by observation, listening to others, doing whatever he could to the best of his ability. He first went to St. Croix in 1968 and worked there for a few years. He came to St. Thomas in 1972, at the age of eighteen, and continued to engage in whatever he could to earn a living—he was a dishwasher, bartender, sold clothing from door to door, and did trucking—carrying luggage for tourists and taking cargo from the airport to grocers and homeowners. He worked at those activities long hours every day, with no vacations as, in addition to himself, he was also supporting his mother, sister, and ten brothers he had left behind, after promising his dying father that he would take care of them.

After years of saving whatever he could, Mr. Suid started the first Gourmet Gallery at Yacht Haven in 1983–84. A few years later, he was able to open another store at Wheatley Center in 1986–87. During a 1987 trip home to see his family, the mother of a young lady invited his mother and him for lunch, and he met the young lady, Keefah, who became his wife. He brought her to St. Thomas, and today they have a lovely home in Frenchman's Bay and six children: three boys—Yahia, Yossef, and Mohammed, and three girls—Yasmeen, Nour, and Fatima. The family attends the local mosque, Masjid Nur, in Sugar Estate.

Zak, as Mr. Suid is called informally, opened two additional Gourmet Gallery stores—one at Crown Bay in 1991 and another at Havensight Mall in 1998, and they are now his major businesses. As the owner of two well-known businesses, he meets and relates well to many residents of St. Thomas. His wife and the children, as they got old enough, helped in the stores as much as they could. He takes pride in having provided his children with good educations

Zakaria Suid and the female members of his family—his wife Keefah at the far left and daughters Yasmeen, Nour, and Fatima. Courtesy of the Suid family.

(four attended Antilles, and one each at All Saints and CAHS), and having tried to instill in them the values of working hard, being thankful, and being humble. He believes that all of the challenges and difficulties he encountered (at one time he was robbed and had to get 37 stitches) only made him stronger and he feels truly blessed. Arab presence in the Virgin Islands has truly changed the business and economic landscape of the territory.[7]

Indians

A third new group of immigrants to St. Thomas during the second half-century of American sovereignty was comprised of Indians. This reference is not to American Indians, who were misnamed by Columbus and his contemporaries, but persons from the Asian country of India, the seventh largest and second most populous country of the world. U.S. migration statistics show that since the 1990s, Indians have become the second largest group migrating to the U.S., surpassed only by Mexicans. Indian immigrants are generally well educated and have much higher average incomes than both the other foreign and the native-born American populations.[8]

The general U.S. description of Indian immigrants is demonstrated perfectly by the Indians in the Virgin Islands. Many are business owners, or are in business management or sales occupations. They are the proprietors of many of the major gift stores on St. Thomas that cater to the large tourist traffic of the island. Well-known Main Street establishments such as Boolchands, Brasilia Gift Shop, Dynasty, Paramount, Seven Wonders, and the Valentine Gift Shops are all Indian businesses.

Some Indian residents on St. Thomas have become known for living in small enclaves where Indians are the only or the major residents. As examples, there is one such community of condos in the Havensite area; another is at the Sugar Mill Hill Condos on Raphune Hill; and yet another is at the Yacht Haven Grande. In common with about one-third of all children on St. Thomas, most Indian children attend private schools. Initially, the parochial schools were most utilized, particularly All Saints Episcopal School on Garden Street or Sts. Peter and Paul Catholic School on lower Main Street, probably partly due to their proximity to the Main Street business sector, where many Indian parents worked. However, most Indian students now seem to attend the Antilles or Montessori Schools.

The concentration of Indians in gift shops intended mainly for tourists has tended to limit their acquaintance with broad spectrums of other St. Thomas residents to a greater degree than is true of the other more recently-arrived groups. Indians have tried to share their culture with other St. Thomas residents in some limited ways. One is having had a long-running Sunday radio program that features Indian music, and another is through occasional lectures by internationally-known Indian spiritual or intellectual leaders to which public attendance is often invited.[9]

Until the latter decades of the twentieth century, any discussion of race relations on St. Thomas or the Virgin Islands generally included only two groups—Blacks and Whites of European background. However, with the arrival of groups from various areas of Asia and changes made in the U.S. Census Bureau's standards of race classification at the end of the last century, there are now officially more racial groups involved. In 1997, the U. S. Office of Management and Budget Standards on Race and Ethnicity, which are followed by the Census Bureau, delineated the following five racial classifications in the United States, effective with the Census of 2010:

1. White—persons having origin in any of the original peoples of Europe, the Middle East or North Africa;
2. Black or African-American—persons having origins in any of the Black racial groups of Africa;

3. American Indian or Alaska Native—persons having origins in any of the original peoples of North and South America and who maintain tribal affiliation or community attachment;

4. Asian—persons having origins in any of the original peoples of the Far East, Southeast Asia or the Indian subcontinent, including, for example, Cambodia, China, India, Japan, Korea, Malaysia, Pakistan, the Philippine Islands, Thailand, and Vietnam;

5. Native Hawaiian or other Pacific Islander—persons having origins in any of the original peoples of Hawaii, Guam, Samoa, or other Pacific islands.[10]

Also, the new standards allow, for the first time, persons to report being of more than one race, and also to answer the question of race based on self-identification. The new regulations also state that the term of Hispanic or Latin or Spanish is an ethnic category that may be used in combination with any race. Thus, if a person from India wishes to be recorded as white in addition to Asian, that is acceptable. Similarly, if there are two "Santos" of the same complexion, recording that they are both Hispanic, but with one saying he is black and the other saying he is white, that is also allowable. (The results from the Virgin Islands Census of 2010 are in Appendix C.)

In addition to Indians, the last half of the twentieth century and since have also seen the arrival in St. Thomas of small numbers of Asians from the Philippines. Most of the early-arriving Filipinos were associated with the medical profession, but recent arrivals have been largely in the field of education. Haitians also constitute another group of recent arrivals, with many working in the construction and service industries. St. Thomas, from early in its recorded history, had always been a multi-racial, multi-ethnic society, and at the centennial of its American period, it has become even more so!

Notes

1. Roy Magras, "The French in the Virgin Islands," *Daily News* (St. Thomas, V.I.), July 14, 2016, pp. 10–11; July 15, 2016, p. 24/7–2.

2. Boyer, *America's Virgin Islands* (2nd edition, 2010) pp. 303–305.

3. "Halos & Pitchforks," *Daily News* (St. Thomas, V.I.), July 18, 2016, p. 24.

4. Chiamaka Nwosu and Jeanne Batalova, "Immigrants from the Dominican Republic in the United States"—https://www.migrationpolicy.org/article/immigrants-dominican-republic-united-states, July, 2014.

5. All information about Juana Corsino and her family were obtained in a long interview with her on July 23, 2016, at her home in St. Thomas. My special thanks!

6. Steven A. Camarota, "Immigrants from the Middle East"—article of the Center for Immigration Studies—https://cis.org/Immigrants-Middle East, August 2002.

7. Information about Zakaria Suid and his family was obtained in St. Thomas through interviews with him and his daughter, Nour, during the period of July 25 to August 5, 2016. Special thanks to both!!

8. Jie Zong and Jeanne Batalova, "Indian Immigrants in the United States"—article of the Migration Policy Institute.org—https://www.migrationpolicy.org/article/indian-immigrants-united-states, May 2015.

9. Public media, such as St. Thomas' radio station WSTA and the *Daily News* are usually utilized to publicize the lectures of esteemed leaders, and an invitation to take part in "The Moment of Calm" was carried in the *Daily News* (St. Thomas, V.I.), August 1, 2016, p. 7.

10. Results of the Virgin islands 2010 Census, based on these new guidelines, are listed in appendix C at the back of this book.

Chapter 17

Race Relations in Government and Politics, 1969–2017

While race and ethnic relations had become a topic of great concern in St. Thomas and the rest of the Virgin Islands by the late 60s and the early 70s, due to increased race consciousness and the coming of new groups, politics—as it had for about three decades—continued to receive great attention. With the Republican presidential victory on the mainland in 1968, Gov. Paiewonsky's term ended in February, 1969, when the new President Nixon accepted his resignation. A dearly longed-for Virgin Islands goal had taken place during the Paiewonsky administration—Congressional legislation in 1968 allowed Virgin Islands voters to elect their governor, beginning in 1970. It meant that any person appointed in 1969 by President Nixon would be the last appointed V.I. governor, as the first election of a governor would take place the following year.

The Era of Elected Governors

On accepting Gov. Paiewonsky's resignation, Pres. Richard Nixon replaced him with a provisional appointment, Acting Governor Cyril King, to hold the office until a permanent appointee was identified. King was a black Virgin Islander, born in St. Croix, a Democrat who had been Paiewonsky's Government Secretary (the # 2 position), but the two had not gotten along. In fact, King had been a leader in forming a new V.I. third party, the Independent Citizens Movement (ICM) in 1968, to oppose a proposed merger of the Ottley-

Paiewonsky dominated Democratic Party with an older "Donkeycrat" Democratic faction led by Ron de Lugo, a seasoned local white politician.

In March 1969, President Nixon appointed Peter Bove to the Governorship of the Virgin Islands. Bove was a white Continental who had been serving as the U.S. Comptroller for the V.I. and thus had lived in St. Thomas for over ten years. While many white continental residents approved the nomination, a number of black Virgin Islanders opposed it, arguing that it was too reminiscent of old-style colonialism to appoint a white Continental to the post a year before the first election for it would take place. There was also a published report by columnist Drew Pearson (the son of the first V.I. civilian governor) that Bove had made unwanted advances to female employees in the Office of the Controller. Before these issues were addressed, Bove suffered a heart attack and removed himself from consideration for the position. Nixon then appointed Dr. Melvin Evans, a black physician from St. Croix who had been a Democrat, but had become a Republican only in 1968, following a dispute with the Paiewonsky administration. Evans took office on July 1, 1969.[1]

As expected, Evans's appointment led to the beginning of a very competitive campaign for the first-elected-governor election in 1970. Some had assumed that Paiewonsky's great record of ultra-development during the 1960s would make him a shoo-in candidate, and he admitted in his *Memoirs* that he would have been willing to run and thought he would win as the electorate was predominantly Democratic. However, to Paiewonsky's surprise, none of the Democratic Party leaders ever approached him about running for the governorship. Instead, the leadership decided, after finding out that Ottley, the party's leader, was not interested in the position, that Alexander Farrelly would be the Democratic candidate for the history-making election. Paiewonsky, in trying to determine why he was overlooked, thought it may have been reasoned that the two terms he had already served were sufficient, as that was all the Elective Governor Act allowed a governor; or that maybe there was jealousy about his accomplishments and a desire to prove that someone else could do as well; or that it was thought fit for a black Virgin Islander to become the first elected governor of the Virgin Islands, in view of its black majority. Of the latter supposition, Paiewonsky wrote:

> That kind of thinking was well in keeping with the temper of the Black Power movement then current in the United States and the Virgin Islands. I would have had no problem with understanding it. I only wished that someone had come to me and explained that I would not be the party's candidate.[2]

It would probably be hard for most persons not to empathize with the degree of hurt Paiewonsky felt from the total lack of communication with which he was treated by the Democratic Party's leaders. On the other hand, his position pointed out the gulf that existed between him and many black Virgin Islanders in his thinking that only "the temper of the Black Power movement then current" could explain the desire of local Blacks to want the first elected governor to be a black person. After three hundred years of governors, all of whom had been white except four (Hastie, Alexander, Gordon, and the last-appointed Evans), would not the people of any society wish to use the new opportunity to choose leaders who were more reflective of the current society than of the old order? However, it is a well-known phenomenon of history that even leaders who try to bring about the kinds of progressive changes that Paiewonsky did—more education, greater economic security and freedom—do not truly understand or welcome the changes that these transformations cause in human societies.

Alexander Farrelly, the Democratic candidate, was a black, also St. Croix-born, resident of St. Thomas. He was very well known and very accomplished, with a background as a lawyer who had served as a Caribbean specialist at the United Nations, a judge of the Virgin Islands Territorial Court, and a member of the Legislature of the V.I., to which he was elected at-large in 1966 with the greatest number of votes any V.I. elected official had ever received to that time.[3]

The newly-formed third party, the Independent Citizens Movement (ICM) was represented in the gubernatorial contest by its leader, Cyril E. King. King was also black and St. Croix-born, and had spent a number of years in the Washington office of Democratic Senator Hubert Humphrey of Minnesota as an aide, the first Black to achieve such a Congressional position. In 1961 King was appointed by President Kennedy to be the Government Secretary in the Paiewonsky administration, a position he maintained throughout the administration, despite great friction between him and the Governor. In February, 1969, the new President Nixon accepted Paiewonsky's resignation and appointed King as the Acting Governor, a position he held for the next four and one half months.[4]

The third gubernatorial candidate in 1970 was Dr. Melvin Evans, a physician who had also served as the V.I. Commissioner of Health during most of the 1960s. In common with the other two candidates for governor, he also was black and St. Croix-born, but had been a member of the Charlotte Amalie High School Class of 1935, as St. Croix's school system did not go beyond grade 10 at that time. As a result of a dispute with the Paiewonsky administration in 1968, he left the Democratic Party and registered as a Republican. It proved to be great timing as it led to his appointment by President Nixon as the expected last appointed governor of the V.I. in 1969, and presented him with the advantages of incumbency in the 1970 first-ever gubernatorial election.[5]

Five leaders relaxing! L-R: Governors-to-be Juan Luis, Alexander Farrelly, Cyril King, with Governor Melvin Evans and Lt. Gov. Athniel Ottley. Courtesy of the Virgin Islands Government's Archival Collection at the Charles W. Turnbull Regional Library.

In spite of the absence of former Governor Paiewonsky in the campaign, race became one of its issues. David Maas, a white continental lawyer and tourism entrepreneur who had been living on St. Thomas since the mid-1940s, was appointed to the second administrative spot when Evans was appointed governor in 1969, and Evans retained him for the election campaign. A prominent Democrat was reputed to have stated that if Evans won, "Maas would be but one heartbeat away from the governorship." That reputed remark was used during the campaign by non-Democrats to convince white voters not to support the Democrats.[6]

The importance of race as an issue in 1970 and any other subsequent election campaigns with a racial issue was due to the substantial percentage of voters that white Continentals had become by 1970. With the black vote divided, Whites were considered to possess the deciding balance. Each of the two parties appeared in time to be labeling its opponents as black power advocates or racists of some type. Both Democrats and Republicans were accused of trying to associate the ICM candidate, King, with black power. As early as 1969, the *Home Journal* newspaper, of which Senator Ottley was editor, had reported that King had flown to Washington "to confer with Black Power militant, Roy Innis" and that King had had previous meetings with Innis.[7]

The V.I. Elective Governor Act 0f 1968 stipulated that the winning candidate must receive a majority of the votes cast. If no candidate achieves that in the general election, a run-off election is held two weeks later between the two highest vote-getters. In 1970, in a shocking reversal of the Democratic political dominance of the 1960s, the Democratic candidate, Farrelly, was eliminated in the general election. The Republican incumbent, Evans, faced the ICM candidate, King, in the run-off. During the run-off campaign, Evans was reputed to have called King a "racist" and a "bigot." King, who did have a number of supporters who were very vocal regarding their concerns about Blacks in the V.I. felt it necessary to make a statement of his racial views. He declared:

> I am not now nor have ever been a racist. The Independent Citizens Movement does not advocate any radically oriented programs, plans, and policies. We are not involved in any Black Power movement, as the term is emotionally used …[8]

Evans won and remained in office, transitioning from the last appointed to the first elected governor. The major reason for his victory over King was the fact that many Democrats, with memories of the rivalry of King against the Democratic-Paiewonsky coalition of the 1960s, threw their support to Evans. One of the auxiliary factors, however, was that Evans enjoyed a much larger percentage of white votes as many Whites were afraid that King did have black power leanings or at least that a number of his supporters did.

Governor Evans experienced an abundance of racial troubles during his elective term. Growing black resentment of white racism and economic control and other factors combined to make crime the greatest problem of his administration. Foremost, of course, were the Fountain Valley tragedy in September 1972 in St. Croix and the spate of murders during the following months. Whites appeared to be the chief victims of the crime wave. They became incensed over Evans's reluctance to admit that many crimes seemed to have racial motives, as he never did with Fountain Valley, and they charged the Evans administration with ineffectiveness in law enforcement and criminal apprehension. Some Whites, both residents and tourists, charged that there were even policemen (the police force was overwhelmingly black) who displayed active hostility toward Whites. Some policemen complained, in turn, that they were stymied at times by the white personnel in the V.I. Attorney General's Office when they attempted to enforce the law against white lawbreakers.[9]

Two incidents indicated clearly that a deterioration of race relations was affecting even the highest circles of V.I. government. In November 1972, two months after Fountain Valley, two Whites were killed in a restaurant in St.

Croix. A third White, who was injured at the scene, was admitted to the hospital. A fourth White, fearful for his injured friend's life, went to the hospital with an unlicensed gun to keep watch over the patient. The man with the gun was apprehended by the police, who had been notified by hospital authorities. However, Evans' Attorney General, a white Continental named Ronald Tonkin, refused to authorize prosecution of the self-appointed defender. Afterward, on the advice of the Governor, he reversed his position and authorized filing of charges.[10]

Many Blacks became incensed. There was sympathetic understanding for a man who had felt so strongly about his ill friend, but there was also the realization that he had been guilty of a crime. That the Attorney General could have contemplated ignoring the crime was widely disapproved. A Committee to remove Tonkin, co-chaired by Gaylord Sprauve and Rena Rhymer, was formed on St. Thomas. On November 2, 1973, it led a march of about 100 persons on Government House and the Legislature in St. Thomas. At Government House the marchers presented a petition for removal of Attorney General Tonkin "for conduct while in office which further threatens an already brittle race relations situation in the Virgin Islands." One sign carried by a marcher read "Racist Policies Are Dangerous." Even a group of Virgin Islanders resident in Washington, D.C., wrote to urge the removal of Tonkin.[11]

A few months later when Tonkin finally appeared before the Legislature (he had failed to show for a previously-scheduled session), other serious charges regarding discrimination in employment in the Attorney General's Office were also probed. It was disclosed that of the twenty-five attorneys on the staff, only nine were black or Puerto Rican. Tonkin resigned in May 1973.[12]

A second affair within Governor Evans' official circle took place in December 1972, less than a month after the beginning of the Tonkin affair. David Maas, the Lieutenant Governor, submitted his resignation. Maas simply cited "personal considerations" and the matter was never publicly discussed by the principals. It was widely believed, however, that Maas had become disgusted because he had no significant role in the administration and was never knowledgeable about what was happening at Government House. Some Whites felt that Evans had used Maas simply to get the white vote and then ignored him after the election. Some Blacks, on the other hand, insisted that Evans had learned to be wary about Maas due to alleged attempts of the latter to overturn, during the Governor's absence, decisions that had been made in the best interests of the black majority. In February 1973, Governor Evans, although a Republican, offered the Lieutenant Governorship to Athniel "Addie" Ottley, a young black Democratic senator who was also a well-known radio personality. Some Whites pointed out that after the resignations of Maas and Tonkin, both of whom were replaced by Blacks, there were no Whites in Evans' cabinet.[13]

The 1974 gubernatorial campaign featured the same three candidates as the first campaign in 1970, but had very different results. Evans, due to the racial upheavals and simply being thought of as too conservative and out-of-touch for the times, had lost a great deal of support and was eliminated in the general election. The ICM's King then won the run-off against the Democrat's Farrelly, who had placed first in the general election. King seemed to have credibly impressed a number of Whites, since the 1970 election, that he was not at all a dangerous black power advocate. Additionally, in 1974 he chose a St. Croix running mate of Puerto Rican descent, Juan Luis, thus ensuring for his ticket most of the votes of that ethnic bloc. Above all, he consistently stated to the electorate that to place a Democrat in Government House would lead to the resurgence of what had been labeled as the Ottley-Paiewonsky Machine.[14]

The greatest period of growth in the Virgin Islands during the twentieth century had been the Sixties, the period dominated by the Ottley-Paiewonsky alliance, or machine as its critics called it. In view of the economic growth and the positive transformations in the lives of so many, why did the threat of the resurgence of that alliance become an effective campaign cry? Why did many persons by the mid-1970s, even some who had personally benefited from the alliance, come to think that in spite of the beneficial changes it had brought about, it had also perpetrated a great deal of harm? Different groups had different answers, but many of the answers seemed to be connected to race, reflective of the increasing importance race had assumed in V.I. life by the last decades of the twentieth century. Many Whites and some Blacks seemed to think that the machine had turned government service into a large employment agency for native Blacks, a number of whom were not qualified for posts they held. Not only was this considered corrupt and a great financial burden, but it was thought to have given some Blacks the idea that the government (and by extension, other entities) owed them a living regardless of their performance. This attitude of Blacks was held by many Whites to be the major explanation for many of the ills of the islands, ranging from the poor functioning of school children to corruption and inefficiency at the highest levels of government.

West Indian non-citizens and those who had naturalized thought that the machine, in appealing to black and white citizens, the groups that had possessed the vote, had completely overlooked contributions of non-citizens to the community. They claimed that the machine had often appeared unaware of the fact that alien-status West Indians, racially and culturally, had more in common with the majority of the native population than did white Continentals. The machine was thus seen as having failed to act in a way promotive of full assimilation of the new West Indians into the V.I. community. They pointed to several issues to substantiate their charges, the chief one being the fact that it had taken a court decision in 1970 to permit most alien-status children to attend public schools.

To the contrary, some Whites felt that Ottley had purposely fostered the importation of alien workers to preserve Blacks as a racial majority in the V.I. This thought was conveyed by Michael Paiewonsky, a nephew of the former Governor, to Professor William Boyer in 1978, and it was also told to this writer by two continental Whites who requested anonymity. Additionally, some white Continentals complained of their group being victims of employment discrimination, unable to secure governmental employment in proportion to their new numbers in the population.[15]

Many Blacks, of all origins, resented most those operations of the alliance and of any subsequent governments which they regarded as economic giveaways to continental Whites and which had resulted in continental Whites gaining economic control over the islands. Summarizing what many Blacks thought, St. Thomian Larry Sewer wrote to Governor Evans in 1970: "There is no sense in saying the people of the Virgin Islands have totally black representation when our public servants merely represent a chosen few, and cater to the incoming white Americans."[16]

Some black St. Thomians thought they could point to too many examples of economic beneficence for Whites. In 1962, a firm connected with Sydney Kessler and Ben Bayne, the two white continental developers of the Virgin Isle Hotel, won a bid to construct a housing development for the government. A native black contractor, Luther Benjamin, who had also entered a bid, subsequently charged that the winning bid had been awarded unfairly. Investigation by the Daily News substantiated Benjamin's claim that the winning bid had not been mentioned or listed at the time of the formal opening of the bids. Even though, as mentioned earlier, Virgin Islanders had not traditionally thought in terms of religious groupings, the blatant irregularity of the awarding of the bid caused some persons to wonder if the Paiewonsky administration might have influenced the award of the bid to the firm connected with the governor's co-religionists (Jews) and known friends. Some Virgin Islanders went beyond wondering. In his book, *Redemption*, Mario Moorhead of the United Caribbean Association of Black People in St. Croix, asserted that the Paiewonsky administration had "delivered the economy to the Jews."[17]

The land on which the Altona housing development was built had also been purchased by the Paiewonsky administration from Kessler. The same land had been rejected, earlier, in 1957 for a public housing project by the V.I. Housing Authority. One reason for its rejection had been that Kessler and Bayne were asking up to $43,000 per acre for a tract of nine acres, when they had purchased the entire tract of over 100 acres for $29,000.[18]

It was no wonder, then, that when the Legislature passed a resolution in 1970 to honor Sydney Kessler for his role in pioneering a large private housing development, it met with widespread criticism. The resolution would have changed the name of the residential area from Estate Tutu to Kessler Town. St. Thomians were not unmindful of the benefits of the enterprise Kessler had undertaken. Hundreds of homes had been constructed and had offered to many their first chance to own a home. What they thought, however, was that Mr. Kessler had already been amply rewarded by the economic returns he had made on his various transactions in St. Thomas. A number of petitions were therefore circulated asking the Legislature to undo its actions. Kessler, noting the reaction, wrote to the Senate and asked them to allow Estate Tutu to retain its old name. The Kessler Town Resolution was repealed by the Legislature in May 1971.[19]

A notorious case, after the machine was no longer in power, which Blacks frequently pointed to as one example of the "easy" riches many Whites attained in the V.I. was that of the Gramboko lease. In May, 1969, the Port Authority, a semi-autonomous agency of the V.I. Government, leased the Gramboko Hotel to the Bay Corporation, whose president was Eleanor Heckert, a white continental resident on St. Thomas. Mrs. Heckert was also a writer and one of her novels, *Muscavado*, was based on the famed St. John slave rebellion of 1733. The property her company leased included a large building which had been erected at the Submarine Base in St. Thomas by the U.S. Navy in 1942, and after the war turned over to the V.I. government. The 1969 agreement leased the property to the Heckert company for thirty years at an annual rate of $8,000 for the first ten years. Sixteen months later, in September 1970, when the government urgently needed classrooms to accommodate the increased enrollment due to the Court decision on alien-status children, the Heckert company leased the property back to the government, for use as a school, at a rate of $72,000 a year for three years. Thus, the same property that the Heckert Company was leasing from the government for $8,000 a year, it was leasing back to the government for $72,000—a profit of $64,000 per year![20]

Most Virgin Islanders were aghast that such a transaction could have taken place. The government kept trying to have the original contract annulled on a legal technicality, but to no avail. While admitting that the second contract was clearly an injustice to the people of the V.I., the District Court in 1975 declined to void the lease. However, knowledge of such happenings made it difficult to convince some black Virgin Islanders that government employment of persons who needed jobs, often paying no more than a few thousand dollars per year, was in any way corrupting or wasteful, especially with residence on an island not affording the option of being able to drive to a nearby city or state in search of work, as mainland residents could.[21]

It was, therefore, a convergence of a number of factors, some old and some new, that led to the victory of the Independent Citizens Movement and its leader, Cyril E. King, in the election of 1974. Gov. King tackled his duties energetically and tried to improve governmental functioning in various ways, such as cracking down on the use of government cars for personal reasons, and by showing up at various departments early in the mornings, to promote punctual attendance by employees. He also laid off hundreds of employees in what he described as a fiscal necessity, but which made him very unpopular. Unfortunately, late in the third year of his term, King was diagnosed with stomach cancer, so advanced that treatment on the mainland was to no avail. His illness occasioned a very sad 1977–78 Christmas/ New Year season in the Virgin Islands, as he lay gravely ill at St. Thomas's Knud-Hansen Memorial Hospital, so named after a former beloved Danish physician. St. Croix even cancelled its annual Christmas Festival. Governor King died on January 2, 1978, four days before the third anniversary of his inauguration.[22]

Governor King was succeeded by his chosen Lieutenant Governor, Juan Luis, who served what would have been the last year of King's term, plus two terms of his own (elected in 1978 and 1982), for a total of nine years. Gov. Luis had been born in Vieques, Puerto Rico, but his parents moved to St. Croix, where he grew up, when he was only one year old. He has been, to date, the only Hispanic lieutenant governor or governor of the Virgin Islands. David Maas, who was white and served with Governor Evans, holds the same double distinctions as Evans—he was both the last appointed Lieutenant Governor and the first elected.[23]

All of the governors to date since Juan Luis (Governors Alexander Farrelly, Roy Schneider, Charles Turnbull, John de Jongh, and Kenneth Mapp) have been black and non-Hispanic. However, just a quick genealogical or geographical consideration of them reveals the fascinating mosaic of the African, European and West Indian strains that comprise the Virgin Islands population today—a continuation of the pattern the Danish colonizers established. As examples, Governor Farrelly was of both Irish and African descent. Governor Schneider's father, as one might guess from his name, had both German and African ancestry and had been born on St. Croix, but moved to St. Thomas, where the future governor was born and grew up. Governor Turnbull was a first-generation U.S. Virgin Islander, as his parents, who were both of African and British ancestry, had migrated to St. Thomas from Tortola, British Virgin

Islands during the decade before the governor was born. Governor de Jongh's mother was a black Continental, but his father was a member of a mixed and prominent St. Thomas family; his grandfather had been Commissioner of Finance in the Merwin and Paiewonsky administrations, and his father was a well-known lawyer who had been an administrative assistant to Gov. Paiewonsky.[24] The centennial governor, Kenneth Mapp, was born in Brooklyn, New York, to a St. Croix family which also had roots in Barbados and the British Virgin Islands; the family returned to St. Croix during Mapp's childhood.

The first two gubernatorial elections (1970 and 1974) involved racial issues due to Gov. Evans's 1970 running mate being white, and due to a charge by some opponents of candidate Cyril King's connection with "black power" in 1974. The third gubernatorial election in 1978 was the only one that had a white gubernatorial candidate to date—Delegate to Congress Ron de Lugo, whose running mate was Senator Eric Dawson of St. Thomas. However, with de Lugo's popularity and down-to-earth personality, his race never became a real issue. What seemed to weaken the ticket on St. Croix was the charge that Senator Dawson was against an international airport on St. Croix, as he was reported to have once stated that he would rather fly from Puerto Rico to St. Thomas, instead of having to go to St. Croix to fly to St. Thomas. Thus Governor Luis remained as governor and Rep. de Lugo went back to Washington two years later.

Other than the first two elections, therefore, the only other gubernatorial election to date that had outright racial sentiments as an issue was the election of 1986. That election featured five teams: attorneys Alexander Farrelly and Derek Hodge as the Democrats; Senator Adelbert Bryan and Dr. Gilbert Sprauve as the ICM team; Drs. Roy Schneider and Roderick Moorehead as Independents; and Lt. Gov. Julio Brady and Sen. Lilliana Belardo de O'Neal for the Republicans, all of whom were black. The fifth team, which apparently never completed all the steps to make their candidacies official and sometimes did not even bother to show up for the gubernatorial forums, had William Crow as its gubernatorial candidate and Ernest Daniels as his running mate. The *Daily News* identified Crow, a white Continental, as a 43-year-old lifeguard at Magens Bay and described him as looking like an ageing hippie, with gray-streaked blonde hair that extended to his neck. Daniels, a 61-year old black Continental, was reported to have become a candidate by answering Crow's newspaper ad for a running mate, and was a warehouse employee at the University of the Virgin Islands, St. Thomas campus. Both men had been living on St. Thomas for a number of years, having come from the U.S. mainland. Crow and Daniels seemed to have had no effect on the campaign, except that their candidacies provided a little humor.[25]

U.S. Virgin Islands Civilian Governors

Name	Socio-racial classification	Term of office	Method of selection
Paul M. Pearson	White Continental	1931–1935	Appointed
Lawrence W. Cramer	White Continental	1935–1941	Appointed
Charles Harwood	White Continental	1941–1946	Appointed
William H. Hastie	Black Continental	1946–1949	Appointed
Morris F. de Castro	White "Native"*	1950–1954	Appointed
Archibald A. Alexander	Black Continental	1954–1955	Appointed
Walter A. Gordon	Black Continental	1955–1958	Appointed
John David Merwin	White Native	1958–1961	Appointed
Ralph M. Paiewonsky	White Native	1961–1969	Appointed
Melvin H. Evans	Black Native	1969–1975	Appointed '69–'71 Elected '71–'75
Cyril E. King	Black Native	1975–1978	Elected
Juan F. Luis	Hispanic	1978–1987	Elected
Alexander A. Farrelly	Black Native	1987–1995	Elected
Roy L. Schneider	Black Native	1995–1999	Elected
Charles W. Turnbull	Black Native	1999–2007	Elected
John P. de Jongh	Black Native	2007–2015	Elected
Kenneth M. Mapp	Black "Native"*	2015–	Elected

(The first seven U.S. governors (1917–1931) were all white naval officers.)
* Both Governors de Castro and Mapp were born abroad (de Castro in Panama and Mapp in Brooklyn, New York) to Virgin Islands families, who returned to the Virgin Islands during their childhood, and they are thus popularly considered as "natives."

The team that generated a substantial racial debate as part of the campaign was the ICM's, specifically the gubernatorial candidate, Senator Adelbert Bryan of St. Croix. A white businessman, Dick Doumeng, who was the owner of the Bolongo Bay Beach Resort on St. Thomas, publicly charged that Bryan was an anti-American and anti-White racist, and urged his employees and others not to vote for Bryan. Bryan, in turn, reminded Doumeng of his act in the 1970s of extending a fence across the beach at Bolongo Bay in order to separate the

L-R: Former Gov. Roy Schneider, Former Gov. Charles Turnbull, Gov. John de Jongh, and Gov.-elect Kenneth Mapp at Government House, St. Thomas, December, 2014. Courtesy of the Office of Gov. Kenneth Mapp.

hotel's guests from Virgin Islands residents. Additionally, Duomeng and some other Whites were not the only ones who publicly accused Bryan of racism. George Goodwin, originally from Antigua and a leader of the former Alien Interest Movement, charged that "division, hate, prejudice and bigotry" were being intentionally fanned by Senator Bryan in an attempt to divide and conquer. He maintained that Bryan had a history of prejudice against anyone who was not born in the Virgin Islands and had pushed for a native-born governor requirement in a proposed V.I. constitution. Additionally, even some native-born black Virgin Islanders who had had workplace contact with Senator Bryan wrote to the *Daily News* and described Bryan as a "wild madman" who the people of the territory should reject.[26]

As would be usually expected of an election with several gubernatorial teams, a run-off election was needed between the two teams that were the top vote-getters—the Democrats' Farrelly and Hodge and the ICM's Bryan and Sprauve. The run-off election on November 18, 1986, resulted in the Democratic candidates getting almost two-thirds of the votes, 16,553 (65%) to 9,742 (34 %), and Alexander Farrelly thus became the fourth elected Governor of the Virgin Islands.[27]

Eight years later, at the end of his second term, Gov. Farrelly unexpectedly became embroiled in a very emotional racial issue. On December 22, 1994, the local press reported that Farrelly had done what governors often do at the end of their service—he had issued pardons to ten imprisoned Virgin Islanders by commuting their sentences to the times they had already served. One was Raphael Joseph, one of the five young men sentenced to eight life sentences each for the 1972 Fountain Valley murders of eight persons, seven of whom were white. Another was Keith Comissiong, a local black male who had been convicted in 1988 of murdering a young white woman, and sentenced to life without parole. A third pardoned prisoner was a murderer who had also been sentenced to life without parole; the other seven prisoners had been convicted of lesser offenses and did not cause the uproar the murderers inspired. Residents territory-wide, both Blacks and many Whites, expressed shock and began various types of protest. U.S. Attorney David M. Nissman was quoted as saying the actions were "a horrible injustice to the victims of these criminals." Steven Bornn, a St. Thomian who was identified as a local tourism and travel marketer, stated that the actions would have a devastating effect on the territory's tourism efforts, as he had been working on promoting St. Croix, and mainland travel agents always asked about Fountain Valley.[28]

At 3 p.m. on the afternoon of December 23, 1994, the day following the news of the commutations and just two days before Christmas, there were simultaneous marches on St. Thomas and St. Croix. The Women's Coalition of St. Croix coordinated the march on that island, and St. Thomas's was organized by the Women's Resource Center. The marches went to the respective Government Houses; the one on St. Thomas had about 400 persons and was filmed by CNN for later broadcast. The matter was considered so grievous that even cabinet members and other close associates of Gov. Farrelly disavowed involvement, according to the *Daily News'* reports. His legal counsel, Atty. Jesse Bethel, and Lt. Gov. Derek Hodge both said they had nothing to do with the decision. Hodge had been away at a relative's funeral and thus was not consulted; he did sign the documents when he returned, but said he did so only to attest to the authenticity of the Governor's signature. Attorney General Rosalie Simmonds Ballentine said she had recommended release for only two of the ten prisoners for humanitarian (medical) reasons; she had not reviewed or made recommendations for the three whose releases sparked the great uproar. At the St. Thomas march, attorney Edith Bornn received loud applause when she announced that several stores would have petitions demanding the removal of the Governor's name from the Alexander A. Farrelly Justice Center, a large structure on Charlotte Amalie's waterfront named in his honor and which housed the offices of the V.I. Police Department and the then-Territorial (now Superior) Court.[29]

On December 27, Governor Farrelly held a conference and stated publicly that he had made a mistake in pardoning Joseph and Comissiong. He admitted that, due to the unusual demands of the pre-Christmas period, he had lacked the staff to conduct a proper review of the issues, so he went ahead, acted on the basis of goodwill as a Christmas gift, and gave those who had strayed a chance for rehabilitation. He also said that Joseph had an unusual number of strong recommendations for release based on his conduct and accomplishments (such as earning a college degree) while in prison. Apparently, however, someone had not waited for the collection of the petitions, but over the Christmas weekend had painted the letters "IN" before the word "Justice," so that the nameplate of the center on the 27th read "Alexander A. Farrelly IN-Justice Center." The illegally painted letters were quickly removed and, despite the continuation of criticisms for quite a while, the Center has retained Farrelly's name. However, the experience must have been very painful—both for the memories of the deceased and the tragedy and for the way the Farrelly administration ended.[30]

Legislative Representation and Political Parties

The Office of the Virgin Islands Delegate to Congress has had a substantially different racial record than the office of the Governor. The first holder, Ronald "Ron" de Lugo, was born in New Jersey to an "Old White" Puerto Rican family that had attained retail and real estate success in St. Thomas during the late decades of Danish rule. De Lugo grew up in St. Thomas and became a radio personality who sparked the first modern-day carnival in St. Thomas in 1952. He afterward moved to St. Croix, where he served as the island's administrator and a senator. He first went to Washington in 1968 on an initiative of the Virgin Islands Government to have a spokesperson, as the V.I. had not been granted a delegate position in Congress, even though Puerto Rico had had one since 1917. There was a widespread feeling in the V.I., among both Whites and Blacks (based on the well-known racial attitudes of white Americans), that the powers in Washington would be more inclined to listen to a white person than to a Black, so that made de Lugo an obvious initial choice. Shortly after, the Congress finally passed legislation establishing the position of Delegate to Congress from the Virgin Islands, to be elected every two years and to serve as a member of the House of Representatives, but without the ability to vote on the final passage of bills.[31]

From 1972, when it took effect, de Lugo was elected every two years through 1994, with the exception of 1978, when he left the position to run for V.I. Governor, but lost to the incumbent, Juan Luis, then returned to Washington two years later. Thus, de Lugo served as the V.I. Congressman for twenty years, from 1973 to1979 and again from 1981 to 1995. One of de Lugo's successors as the V.I. Delegate to Congress, Dr. Donna Christensen, successfully sponsored a Congressional bill to honor his long period of service by giving his name to a federal building on Charlotte Amalie's waterfront—the Ron de Lugo Federal Building/United States Courthouse. All of de Lugo's successors to date have been black (former Gov. Evans, 1979–81; attorney Victor Frazer, 1995–97; Dr. Donna Christensen, 1997–2015; attorney Stacey Plaskett, 2015–), but there have also been white candidates for the position who were unsuccessful.[32]

In the Legislatures of the Virgin Islands during the last five decades (1967–2017), the seven St. Thomas senators of the fifteen-member body have generally been reflective of the island's racial and geographical pluralities. (The Revised Organic Act of 1954 was amended in 1966 to allow fifteen senators— seven elected from the St. Croix district, seven from the district of St. Thomas-St. John, and one elected at large who has to be a resident of St. John.) One St. Thomas senator alone, Lorraine Berry of the Northside French community, guaranteed white representation for half of the period as she was a member of twelve consecutive Legislatures—from 1983 to 2007, two of which she served as president. However, even before Senator Berry began running, Michael Paiewonsky, also white and a nephew of Governor Paiewonsky, had been a member of two consecutive Legislatures (1979–83), and three other white senators—Clement Magras, also a French St. Thomian; David Puritz, a brother-in-law of Governor Paiewonsky; and Allan Paul Shatkin, a Continental—were all elected to multiple terms between the early 1980s and the early 1990s. And interestingly, in the Seventeenth Legislature (1987–89), Senators Berry, Magras, Puritz, and Shatkin actually constituted a white majority of St. Thomas' seven senators. The three black St. Thomas senators in that Seventeenth Legislature were Virdin Brown, Bingley Richardson, and Iver Stridiron, with Stridiron becoming president in March 198**7**.[33]

Interviews and election results have indicated that most Blacks on St. Thomas have been willing to vote for white as well as black legislative candidates, as long as they knew them and thought they would work in the public's interest. A number of Whites have also been willing to vote for Blacks they knew and trusted, though some Whites at times followed a policy of "bullet-voting" for Whites (voting for only one White or only for Whites) in order to ensure their election, in view of the larger number of black voters. Also elected from St. Thomas to the legislature, during the latter decades of the twentieth century and the first decade and one-half of the twenty-first, have been Senator Virdin Brown, a black Continental, and a number of black senators who had first come to St. Thomas from other West Indian islands as alien-status residents—Senators George Goodwin, Osbert Potter, Roosevelt David, Donald Cole, Louis P. Hill, and Tregenza Roach.

On the eve of the centennial year, the political party system of the Virgin Islands was an interesting and often puzzling picture. All three parties have existed for the last half-century. The Democratic and the Republican Parties were both formally organized in the 1950s as the local branches of the U.S. national parties, while the Independent Citizens Movement (ICM) was organized in 1968 as a Virgin Islands third party by local Democrats who had become a minority faction in the Democratic Party due to its legal reorganization. (Before being formally reorganized in the 1950s, however, there had been a "Republican Club" from the 1920s, due to Republican national dominance then, and a "Democratic Club" from the 1930s due to national Democratic dominance at that time, but neither had been active in local politics.)[34]

The V.I. Democratic Party reorganization that took place in 1963 is usually difficult to understand for persons not having an acquaintance with Virgin Islands society prior to the 1950s. The older political groups were somewhat class-selected groupings and persons could not necessarily affiliate with a party by simply going to an office and registering. Prior to the 1960s, a person desirous of joining a political group usually had to apply for membership and was admitted or not based on the decisions of the existing leaders. As most Blacks and other poor Virgin Islanders could not vote prior to the implementation of the first Organic Act in 1938, they had had nothing to do with organized politics. With the organization of the first local Virgin Islands political party on St. Thomas in the late 1930s, the Progressive Guide, and its successor parties in the 1940s and 50s, the Liberal and Unity Parties, Blacks grew to understand the power of political organization and realized that Virgin Islands power could be greater through affiliation with the national parties. Of course, the national party that most wished to be a part of, based on the same sentiments that Blacks on the mainland had developed due to President Franklin Roosevelt's New Deal policies of the 1930s, was the Democratic Party. However, after the rejections of a number of persons who had applied to the local Democratic Party, some local political leaders realized that a special strategy would be needed to permit the enrollment of local persons who were not well-connected, but desired to be Democrats in order to align the local party system with the national.[35]

As discussed in the chapter on the Paiewonsky administration, the plan for allowing national party membership by locals was introduced in the Legislature as the Election Code of 1963. It allowed qualified Virgin Islands residents to register as they wished, and the newly-registered Democrats, by virtue of their numbers, became the majority of the party and were able to select its leaders. Though bitterly denounced by the older Democrats as immoral and illegal and challenged in courts, the new majority's control was upheld by the U.S. Third Circuit Court as being in keeping with the American system of politics and party registration. The Independent Citizens Movement (ICM), which will be 50 in

2018, was formed by those older Democrats who refused to accept the new alignment; but there were also older Democrats, such as Ron De Lugo, who eventually decided on the importance of local alliance with the national parties.

As of June 13, 2016, political party registrations in the Virgin Islands overall and in the District of St. Thomas and St. John were:[36]

	Democratic	Republican	ICM	No Party
Virgin Islands	29,659	1,688	1,275	12,358
St. Thomas-St. John	15,028	627	604	7,006

As figures often do, these tell quite a story, and it is even more compelling with additional information. As examples, not one of the fifteen senators elected to any of the last two V. I. Legislatures (the 30th Legislature, 2013–2015, and the 31st Legislature, 2015–2017) ran as a Republican. And the listed affiliations of persons who most recently sought office show similar inequalities. Of the forty (40) candidates who registered in May 2016 to compete in the November 2016 election in the District of St. Thomas and St. John for the Thirty-Second Legislature (2017–2019), the Boards of Education and Election, and the position of Delegate to Congress, twenty-four (24) candidates registered as Democrats, two (2) as Republicans, one as ICM, and thirteen (13) as having no party affiliation.[37] The party system in the Virgin Islands is apparently not at all healthy.

However, the Virgin Islands parties do reflect substantially the racial preferences which are associated with their national organizations. Therefore, the largely black character of the Virgin Islands population is reflected by strong V.I. identification with the national Democratic Party. Its political programs, aimed at uplifting and sustaining the poor and the middle class, such as Social Security, greater health care, housing and educational benefits, are valued greatly by most Virgin Islanders and form the basis for the strength of the local Democratic Party.

Similarly, the Republican Party in the Virgin Islands, in common with the national party, does not enjoy any substantial degree of black support. Though possessing some strong black supporters, the Virgin Islands Republican Party is thought by many to be mainly the party of Whites or persons who are not considered as having strong affinity with the interests of the non-wealthy, and thus is supported by relatively few local Blacks. Maybe, then, it should not have been a great surprise that, in connection with the 2016 election year, which saw so many unprecedented actions in mainland Republican politics, a handful of white professional Republican operatives from the mainland came to the Virgin Islands to attempt to effect control of the local party's support of presidential candidates at the national convention, in case the nomination ended being hotly contested and close. It led to rival groups of local party officials who almost came to physical confrontation, and they had a number of court battles.[38] At times, many Virgin Islanders were left wondering whose antics were zanier—the national Republicans or the locals?

However, on the eve of the Republican National Convention in Cleveland, Ohio in July, 2016, one local Republican Party official took a surprising stand. Former Senator Holland Redfield, a white Continental with residency in the Virgin Islands for decades and a record of election to several terms in the Legislature as a senator from St. Croix, announced that he would not attend the Republican Convention, even though, as National Committeeman for the local party, he had an assured vote. According to the *V.I. Daily News*, Redfield thought that as "a Caucasian representing a predominantly black community, he 'wouldn't sleep at night' if he supported Trump, who has been vocal in his attacks on Muslims, Mexicans and other minority groups."[39] However, the other eight delegates who represented the Virgin Islands in Ohio, six of whom were white, voted solidly for Trump. Thus, many Virgin Islands residents were left wondering, even more than usual, about the genuineness and goals of the local Republican Party, and its leadership.

The Independent Citizens Movement (ICM) supporters, in common with V.I. Democrats, are mainly Blacks, and both have backgrounds of ties to the national Democratic Party and its philosophies. The historical record indicates that the ICM was founded in 1968, not because of deep philosophical differences with Democrats about social progress, but mainly because of differences over leadership and the sharing of power at the time. The takeover of the old Democratic Party by a majority of new Democrats took place because of the failure of the old system to provide for membership by choice. It was, naturally, a very painful and humiliating experience for the previous Democratic leaders and members, and some refused to accept the change. However, it is amazing that even though the takeover happened over half a century ago, in 1963, that most of the old players are now gone, that the schism at that time has little or no relevance for today's millennials, it is still being used by some politicians as a basis for trying to organize political behavior. The present challenges of the Virgin Islands require greater realistic thinking to face current problems and conditions effectively.

Constitutional and Political Status Issues

Two other political issues in the Virgin Islands in the last half-century have involved substantial differences in racial thinking and in some native versus newcomer aspirations. They have been the efforts to write a new constitution for the Virgin Islands and attempts to fashion or define a new political status for the territory in regard to its relationship with the United States.

Thoughts about the need for a new constitution began shortly after the enactment by the Congress of the Revised Organic Act of 1954, which still remains today—with a number of amendments such as the Elective Governor Act—as the constitution of the Virgin Islands. The Organic Act's most disliked features then included the continued appointment of governors by the President, the continued power of the President to veto locally-passed legislation, the continued lack of a delegate to the Congress, and St. Croix's dislike of the unification of the government—with only one legislature headquartered on St. Thomas.

Therefore, a decade later, in 1964–65, a locally-initiated Constitutional Convention formulated a new constitution for the territory, and sent it to the Congress. Its major proposals were: 1) an elected governor and lieutenant governor; 2) an elected delegate to the Congress; 3) the right to vote for the president and vice president; 4) no presidential veto of local laws. The Convention also adopted a resolution dealing with the status of the islands, which declared that there was unalterable opposition to the attachment of the Virgin Islands to any other state or territory of the United States, but that the people of the Virgin Islands were also unalterably opposed to independence from the United States. They thus wanted to remain an unincorporated territory with the fullest measures of internal self-government and close association, and proposed a designation as an "autonomous territory" of the United States.[40]

The U.S. Congress chose to work only on the proposals it favored, and after two years of trying to reconcile differences between the Senate and the House of Representatives, finally passed the Virgin Islands Elective Governor Act in 1968. It provided for the election of a governor and lieutenant governor for four-year terms, beginning in 1970. It also ended the Presidential veto of local legislation, and provided for the legislature's ability to override a gubernatorial veto by a two-thirds vote. It additionally extended to the Virgin Islands some parts of the U.S. Constitution which had not been granted before, such as most of the Bill of Rights and parts of some other amendments. However, many Virgin Islanders have recently been surprised to find out, as a result of recent federal decisions, that the first sentence of the Fourteenth Amendment—the citizenship clause which reads "All persons born or naturalized in the United

States, and subject to the jurisdiction thereof, are citizens of the United States and of the State wherein they reside"—had not been extended to the Virgin Islands by the Elective Governor Act. Thus, being born in the Virgin Islands bestows Congressionally-granted U.S. citizenship (based on Congressional legislation for the V.I. in 1927 and 1932), but not Constitutional U.S. citizenship. This means, for example, that a Virgin Islander born in the Virgin Islands, of non-mainland born parents, may not be judged eligible to be president of the United States, based on recent rulings.[41]

A Second Constitutional Convention in 1972 produced a draft constitution and document on status that were very similar to those of the First Convention. Because many voters cast blank ballots, the positive votes did not constitute a majority, and thus the documents were not sent to the Congress. However, as the first two constitutional conventions had been undertaken without federal authorization, V.I. Delegate to Congress de Lugo sponsored a Congressional bill directing Virgin Islanders to write a new constitution, that the Governor would then send to the President and Congress for approval, after which V.I. voters would have the final vote of approval. Also specified was that the proposed constitution should have a republican form of government and a bill of rights and was not to include provisions dealing with political status or the relationship with the U.S.

Thus, the Third Constitutional Convention began in 1978 with sixty elected delegates. Their draft included a 17-member legislature, with thirteen district senators who would have 2-year terms and four at-large senators with 4-year terms. It also included a system of local government districts, with elected mayors and district assemblies, and provisions for the protection of Virgin Islands culture and the environment, declaring that all beaches and shorelines would be open to public use. In March 1979, when it was the voters' turn to approve it, less than 38 percent went to the polls, and of those 56 percent voted against it. Well-publicized disagreements between St. Croix and St. Thomas delegates over the aspects of local governmental districts were thought to have been significant in affecting both the convention's proceedings and the public vote.[42]

The Fourth Constitutional Convention met just a year later—in March 1980—and voting on its draft took place one year and eight months later, in November 1981. The big issue that embroiled the public was its initial provision that the governor had to be a "native" of the Virgin Islands. Practically all non-native groups of the population—White Continentals, Black Continentals, natives of elsewhere in the Caribbean and of practically anywhere else on the planet—attacked the provision as discriminatory, un-American, and divisive. Even a substantial number of natives also disapproved of it as being unrealistic and inflammatory. Even after its Convention supporters broadened the definition and pointed out that it conferred no other special privileges, public opposition was so agitated that a Convention delegate characterized the proposal as having "created a schizophrenic atmosphere." Only 47 percent of voters went to the polls, and over 60 percent of them voted against the proposal.[43]

As if the unsuccessful outcomes of several constitutional conventions did not suggest some change in strategy, there were calls for another convention as soon as possible. However, strong arguments were made for a different strategy, pointing out that it may have been more logical to decide on a status with the United States, and then write a constitution consistent with that status, rather than writing a constitution first. However, status determination would also have a checkered history. President Jimmy Carter in 1980 had reminded the Congress and the Democratic Party Platform Committee that, in keeping with the revered democratic beliefs of the U.S., options for their political development should be available to the nation's territories. Spurred by that, the V. I. Legislature created a V.I. Status Commission in late 1980 and asked retired Senator Earle B. Ottley to be its executive director. However, Carter's defeat in late 1980 and the new presidency of Ronald Reagan dimmed chances of federal interest in that area, and Ottley resigned after realizing that most local politicians also had very little interest in political status determination.[44]

Another attempt to deal with political status took place in 1984 when the Fifteenth Legislature created a Select Committee on Status and Federal Relations, with Senator Lorraine Berry as its chair. However, the matter died when the committee was not continued by the next Legislature. Then, in 1988, the Seventeenth Legislature established the U.S. V.I. Commission on Status and Federal Relations and it was signed into law by Governor Farrelly. It was composed of fifteen members, whose work was substantially predetermined by the work of a legislative committee that had been chaired by Senator Berry, one of the two Commission chairs, the other being UVI history professor Marilyn Krigger (this author). Thus, Commission members were presented with a list of seven status options, on which they had to educate the public. The options, listed alphabetically, were: 1) Commonwealth, 2) Compact of Federal Relations, 3) Free Association, 4) Incorporated Territory, 5) Independence, 6) Statehood, and 7) Status Quo—Unincorporated Territory. Some Commission members thought the choices were definitely too many, with statehood, for example, not even being a realistic option. However, as they were legislatively mandated, it was decided that the best the Commission could do was to group them into three broad categories for a first round of voting, and then winnow them down to a choice in the chosen category for the follow-up vote. The three broad categories were: 1) Continued Association with the U.S., which included Commonwealth, Compact of Federal Relations, and the Status Quo; 2) Integration with the U.S, which included Incorporated Territory and Statehood; and 3) Removal of U.S. Sovereignty, which included Free Association and Independence.

Unfortunately, Nature also ended up being a determinant of the Commission's activities. The date for the initial status vote had been set for November 14, 1989, with the follow-up vote on November 28. However, Hurricane Hugo visited the Virgin Islands on September 17–18, and its destruction was so great that there was no question as to the necessity for postponing the status referendum, and for quite a while. After substantial recovery from the hurricane and the renewal of the educational campaign, the first-stage vote of the referendum was finally held on October 11, 1993. Instead of the 50 percent voter turnout that was required to go on to the second vote, only 27.4 percent of voters took part, bringing the process to an end.[45]

The voter turnout on St. Thomas-St. John had been 31.4 percent, and on St. Croix only 22.6 percent. The category of Continued Association with the U.S. received the most votes in both districts: 84 percent on St. Thomas-St. John and 75 percent on St. Croix. The category of Integration with the U.S. received 20 percent of the vote on St. Croix and 11 percent on St. Thomas-St. John. The category of Removal of U.S. Sovereignty received the same percentage of votes, 5 percent, on both St. Croix and on St. Thomas-St. John.[46]

Interestingly, the final days surrounding the status referendum had produced some of the most prolific reactions of voters regarding their status choices. Well-known examples were educator Glenn Davis (also known as the cultural artist Kwabena) and retired UVI professor Linda Benjamin, who both had articles in the *Daily News* recommending their choice of the commonwealth option. On the other hand, UVI professor Gene Emanuel was reported to be the leader of an independence faction that had been organizing a boycott of the referendum. Many public officials had seemed hesitant to reveal their choices earlier, but the *Daily News* had contacted them and revealed their choices in this chart on the day of the referendum.

Who's for What (Status Referendum of October, 1993)

Free associated state—Sen. Osbert Potter, Sen. Arturo Watlington, Jr., Allie-Allison Petrus (potential senatorial candidate).

Commonwealth—Sen. Celestino A. White, Sr., Sen. Almando "Rocky" Liburd, Sen. Judy Gomez, Sen. Lilliana Belardo de O'Neal, Senator

Gerard Luz James 11, Sen. Mary-Ann Pickard, Sen. Bingley A. Richardson, Sr., Dr. Roy L. Schneider (potential gubernatorial candidate).

Compact of federal relations—Gov. Alexander A. Farrelly, V.I. Delegate to Congress Ron de Lugo, Lt. Gov. Derek M. Hodge, Sen. Lorraine L, Berry, Sen Holland M. Redfield 11, Sen. George Goodwin, Sen. Edgar D. Ross.

No reply—Sen. Alicia "Chucky" Hansen, Sen. Kenneth E. Mapp.[47]

It may have been good for their choices to have been publicly known earlier, but the final results suggested that such knowledge would not have made a substantial difference. For as the *Daily News* pointed out in an editorial two days after the voting, the usual V.I. voter turnout for gubernatorial and legislative elections had normally been 64 percent or higher, so the status turnout showed other strong factors at work.

It took several years before the Virgin Islands again attempted to establish a new framework for self-government through the medium of a Fifth Constitutional Convention, which met during 2008 and 2009. In view of the results of the prior conventions and the status referendum, Former Governor Charles Turnbull, the only person to have served on all five constitutional conventions, reminded his fellow delegates of the results produced by provisions involving "native only" policies. However, it would be done again and to a greater degree!

Previously, nativity had been considered only for one's eligibility to become governor or lieutenant governor. In the Fifth Convention's draft, there were two special categories—"native Virgin Islanders" and "ancestral Virgin Islanders." The native category included persons who were born in the Virgin Islands and the "ancestral" included those who could trace their bloodlines to persons born in the Virgin Islands prior to 1932. Both were entitled to special economic benefits—such persons would not have to pay property taxes on their primary residence or on undeveloped land they owned, in addition to their exclusive entitlement to the top two executive offices. Twenty of the Convention's thirty delegates voted in favor of the draft document.[48]

The Fifth Constitutional Convention draft also did not become a reality, but not because of rejection by the voters, as was the fate of previous drafts and which many had expected also for this draft. However, the 2010 draft never got to the voters. The procedure had called for it to go to the governor, who would then transmit it to the president and the Congress, after which it would return to the V.I. for submission to the voters. However, Governor de Jongh thought that some of the special features (including the native and ancestral provisions) to be so illegal that he decided not to transmit the document to

Washington. While some delegates agreed with the governor, other decided to go to court to force its transmission. De Jongh's response to the delegates pointed out that some provisions of the draft actually challenged the sovereignty of the U.S., and poignantly stated that as one of only three black governors in the nation, he was ashamed to send to its first black president a draft that insisted that even though he was president of the U.S., he would be ineligible to become the governor of the V.I. if he moved there. However, the suing delegates won as, in accordance with the enabling legislation, the Court ruled that the document had to be sent to Washington.[49]

Both President Obama's Justice Department and the Congress had the same opinion of the illegalities de Jongh had pointed out in the draft, and sent it back to the islands at the end of June, 2010, asking the convention to meet and produce a revised draft by October 31st. The meetings of the convention were characterized by much disagreement and arguing, and no revised document was produced by the end of October 2010. Thus ended another attempt to produce a new constitution for the U.S. V.I.[50]

The failures of the work of the five Constitutional Conventions and the Commission on Status and Federal Relations made clearly visible the two great social divides in Virgin Islands society. One was racial and had had a long history, as long as the permanent settlement of the colony. Whites, even those with a long history in the Virgin Islands, were afraid of the possibility of Blacks getting powers that might be used against Whites, as Whites had historically used their vast powers against Blacks. The other divide was a relatively recent one—that of geographical origin, and that fear was not limited to Whites. It was shared by all persons who were not native, whether white, black, or of other racial categories, some of whom had come to the Virgin Islands relatively recently, in most cases since the 1950s, and were equally in dread of the possible implications for themselves and their progeny if a new constitution or a new political status allowed natives, who were largely black, more powers than non-natives.

The constitutional attempts and the status referendum had provided a very easy method by which voters could show their disapproval of the processes, as they all stipulated that a majority (50 percent plus one) of the electorate had to participate in the approval process. Thus, all that voters who were wary of any possible outcomes had to do was not go to vote, and that knowledge was effectively circulated and employed by concerned persons and groups. Thus, the outcomes of the majority of the six events were not surprises to many persons who had closely followed the events and the public campaigns. Maybe the sizes of the voter turnouts were even less than had been expected, but most studious followers of letters to newspaper editors, radio talk shows (which are very popular in the Virgin Islands), talk on the streets, and simple common sense had very good ideas of how various voters felt and why.

White Americans, and also most Blacks from the United States, wanted no status or provisions which would diminish, in any way, the power or influence of their native country. Similarly, Whites who were not U.S. citizens had also come to the Virgin Islands knowing that the laws of the United States were in force and would protect their lives, property, and investments as they expected. Even Blacks from elsewhere in the Caribbean and from Africa, while understanding the psychological pain of colonialism and of having been branded the "inferior" race, may have been sympathetic in wishing to see some historic inequities amended, but were also aware of the deprivations they may have suffered when public services were earlier unavailable to them, and of the general knowledge that discrimination is terrible under any system of inequality, regardless of the identity of the oppressor. And even while equally hating the alienation of land and beach resources, and the discriminatory traditions that some white Americans had brought to the Virgin Islands, a sizeable number of black natives have been equally afraid of the "corrective" measures and their consequences that they think some native Blacks might be willing to employ. The Virgin Islands may be at a crossroads where, in view of its increasingly diverse population and economic challenges, only a rare combination of political genius and herculean efforts may be able to bring about some of the solutions the society desperately needs.

Notes

1. Harold W. Willocks, *The Umbilical Cord* (St. Croix, V.I., 1995), pp. 365–367.

2. Paiewonsky, *Memoirs of a Governor*, pp. 444–445.

3. Moolenaar, *Profiles of Outstanding Virgin Islanders* (3rd ed., 1992), p. 68.

4. Ibid., pp. 133–134.

5. Ibid., pp. 66–67.

6. *Edward A. O'Neill, Rape of the American Virgins* (New York: Praeger Publishers, 1972), p. 188. O'Neill's version of the reputed quotation was that Evan's election would "put a white man a heartbeat away from the governor's chair."

7. See, as examples, various articles and comments in the following Daily News (St. Thomas, V.I.) editions: February 20, 1969, pp. 1, 7; December 4, 1970, p. 7; *Focus* (The Sunday magazine of the *Home Journal*—St. Thomas, V.I.), March 9, 1969, p. 5.

8. "King Rebukes Evans For Racism Charges," *Daily News* (St. Thomas, V.I.), November 13, 1970, p. 2.

9. "Correspondence to Glenn 'Kwabena' Davis from an abused White," *Daily News* (St. Thomas, V.I.), April 6, 1972, p. 7.

10. "Asks Probe of AG's Gun Order," *Daily News* (St. Thomas, V.I.), November 21 1972, p. 7; "Gov. Says Tonkin Move In Harris Case Ill Advised," November 24, 1972, p. 1.

11. Letter from Leon Casey, *Daily News* (St. Thomas, V.I.), November 18, 1972, p. 7; a letter from Virgin Islanders in Washington came from Dana Orie, Ibid., November 17, 1972, p. 7.

12. "Backs Down On Employee Rating," *Daily News* (St. Thomas, V.I.), January 5, 1973, p. 1; "Tonkin Fails to Show For Legislative Probe," February 14, 1973, p. 1; "Tonkin Questioned on Hiring Policies," March 22, 1973, p. 1; "Tonkin Resigns Post As Attorney General," April 18, 1973, p. 1.

13. "Maas Resigns Post As Lt. Governor," *Daily News* (St. Thomas, V.I.), December 7, 1972, p. 1; "The Lt. Governor Takes Leave," December 7, 1972, p. 7; "Maas Term Extended For Month," December 23, 1972, p. 1; "Selection of Ottley Irks Governor's Aide," February 21, 1973, p. 1; May 4, 1973, p. 1; also an interview with a government official who requested anonymity.

14. Both the 1972 and 1974 senatorial campaigns were marked by racist literature, in which fake letters were distributed with the aim of making some candidates appear antiwhite. Most of the public seemed to have realized that the letters were fakes. See *Daily News* of November 7, 1972, p. 1; November 7, 1972, p. 5; November 4, 1974, p. 18; and *Home Journal* (St. Thomas. V.I.), of November 7, 1972, p. 3.

15. Boyer, *America's Virgin Islands*, p. 290—footnote 14.

16. "Letter to the Editor," *Daily News* (St. Thomas, V.I.), September 25, 1970, p. 7.

17. "Kessler-Bayne Company Wins Housing Bid," *Daily News* (St. Thomas, V.I.), July 10, 1962, p. 1; "The Altona Scandal," May 14, 1965, p. 11; "The Big Silence," June 23, 1965, p. 11; Mario Moorhead, *Redemption* (St. Croix, V.I.: UCA, 1981), p. 93.

18. "Abandons Altona Area For Public Housing," *Daily News* (St. Thomas, V.I.), May 29, 1957, p. 1.

19. "Tutu is now Kesslertown," *Daily News* (St. Thomas, V.I.), December 23, 1970, p. 1; "Women's League Marks 25th Anniversary in Virgin Islands," May 14, 1971, p. 8. Kessler

was also rumored in St. Thomas to have spoiled one of the best beaches, John Brewers Bay, by stripping it of its sand, which was used in the building of the Virgin Isle Hotel.

20. *Daily News* (St. Thomas, V.I.), August 30, 1970, p. 1; August 25, 1972, p. 1.

21. "Dept. Asks Action on Gramboko School Suit," *Daily News* (St. Thomas, V.I.), May 19, 1975, p. 18; Letter from Joseph Maronna, saying he did not understand the Government's legal argument for nullifying the Gramboko lease, Ibid. May 23, 1975, p. 1.

22. Willocks, *The Umbilical Cord*, p. 424.

23. Moolenaar, *Profiles of Outstanding Virgin Islanders* (3rd ed., 1992), p. 143.

24. Paiewonsky, *Memoirs of a Governor*, pp. 181–182.

25. "Lifeguard, warehouse man say they are serious," *Daily News* (St. Thomas, V. I.), October 19, 1986, pp. 1, 15.

26. "Bryan, hotelier point fingers at each other," *Daily News*, October 10, 1986, page 3; "George Goodwin stumps for Farrelly," *Daily News*, October 14, 1986, pp. 3, 13; "Letter to the Editor from Dick Doumeng," *Daily News*, October 18, 1986, p. 6; "Guest Editorial" by Vincent Frazer and Garry Sprauve, Daily News, November 1, 1986, p. 6.

27. Bernetia Akin, "Voter Turnout of 83 percent expected," *Daily News*, November 4, 1986, p. 1.

28. Ibid., Hal Hatfield, "Farrelly frees three murderers," December 22, 1994, pp. 1, 7.

29. Ibid., Hal Hatfield, "Furor over releases continues," December 24–26, 1994, pp. 1, 2.

30. Ibid., Hal Hatfield, "Farrelly: I made a mistake," December 28, 1994, pp. 1, 2.

31. Willocks, Harold W. L., *CIVICUS: Virgin Islands of the United States Civic and Character Enhancement* (2009), pp. 121–123.

32. Ibid.

33. Willocks, *The Umbilical Cord*, pp. 484–490.

34. Valdemar A. Hill, Sr., *Rise to Recognition: An Account of Virgin Islanders From Slavery to Self-Government* (St. Thomas, V.I.: St. Thomas Graphics, 1971), pp. 102–103.

35. Paiewonsky, *Memoirs of A Governor*, pp. 279–281.

36. Figures received from the Office of the Election System of the V.I., St. Thomas, from Sheri Richardson, Election Assistant, on June 13, 2016.

37. "Candidates for Office 2016," St. Thomas Source, May 18, 2016. Accessed on October 5, 2016 at http://stthomassource.com/content/news/local-news/2016/05/18/candidates-office-2016.

38. Suzanne Carlson, "Police step in as fight breaks out at GOP meeting," *Daily News* (St. Thomas, V.I.), April 8, 2016, p. 8; Carlson, "Canegata: V.I. Republican delegation backs Trump," Ibid., May 24, 2016, p. 4; Carlson, "Local GOP slammed for 'soap opera' shenanigans," Ibid., July 1, 2016, p. 6.

39. Suzanne Carlson, "V.I. GOP delegate says he'll skip Trump's nomination," Daily News, Ibid., July 16, 2016, p. 2.

40. William W. Boyer, *America's Virgin Islands*, pp. 273–274.

41. Boyer, Ibid., p. 275; Neil Weare, "We the People loses battle, will continue fighting for V.I....," *Daily News* (St. Thomas, V.I.), June 15, 2016, p. 29; The Constitution of the United States of America, 1787, Amendment XIV.

42. Ruth Moolenaar, *A Student's Resource Guide on the Third Constitutional Convention of the Virgin Islands* (St. Thomas, V.I. Department of Education, 1978), pp. 146–178; William W. Boyer, *America's Virgin Islands*, 2nd Edition, p. 389.

43. Boyer, Ibid., p. 390.

44. Ibid., p. 394; Ottley, *Trials and Triumphs*, pp. 427–428.

45. William W. Boyer, *America's Virgin Islands*, 2nd Edition, pp. 395–396.

46. "VOTE: Referendum is VI's first on political status," *Daily News* (St. Thomas, V.I.), October 11, 1993, p. 1.

47. "Who's for What," *Daily News* (St. Thomas, V.I.), October 11, 1993, p. 2.

48. "Editorial," *Daily News* (St. Thomas, V.I.), October 13, 1993, p. 11.

49. Megan Poinski, "Governor Rejects Constitution Draft," *Daily News* (St. Thomas, V.I.), June 12, 2009, p. 3; "Constitutional Convention Delegates Oppose Lawsuit," *Daily News* (St. Thomas, V.I.), June 19, 2009, p. 2.

50. Aldeth Lewin, "Obama Signs V.I. Constitution Legislation," *Daily News (St. Thomas, V.I.)*, July 1, 2010, p. 1; Lou Mattei, "Constitutional Convention Meetings marred by arguments, technical snarls," Ibid., Sept. 29, 2010, p. 5.

Chapter 18

Race Relations in Economic Affairs

At mid-twentieth century, St. Thomas was a fairly typical West Indian island—characterized by widespread poverty, lack of substantial economic opportunity, a slow pace of life, and a population which was predominantly
native-born and consisted largely of native Blacks. Less than two decades later,
by the celebration of the semi-centennial of United States ownership in 1967,
St Thomas was boasting of being one of the busiest tourist ports in the world;
the Virgin Islands had the highest per capita income in the Caribbean area;
and the once-dominant native population was seemingly about to be outnumbered by persons from elsewhere.[1]

At the core of many of the significant changes that have taken place in St.
Thomas during the last seven decades was the transformation of the economy,
accomplished mainly under the direction of and by the investments of Whites.
It should be no wonder, therefore, that the relationship between the trans-
formers of a society and the persons whose lives were transformed should be
a topic of great concern. When such great changes, astounding in themselves,
are intermixed with differences of race and cultures, it often demands all possible elements of constructive thought and discipline to ensure a society of
peace and comfort.

The Landscape and Impact of Tourism

This centennial decade finds most of St. Thomas's largest and best-known
tourist accommodations located in the eastern part of the island. However, for
most of the American century, the eastern part of St. Thomas was relatively

Cruise ships at both of St. Thomas's docks: Havensight Dock in the foreground and Crown Bay Dock at Sub Base in the distance. Courtesy of Larry Benjamin.

undeveloped and most tourist facilities were located in and around Charlotte Amalie. The oldest of St. Thomas's hotels was the Grand Hotel, which was built as the Commercial Hotel in the 1830s in the heart of the city, on the northern side of the square known today as the Emancipation Garden. It was representative of the great wealth of the "Golden Days" of St. Thomas (1830s–1850s) and remained, after its acquisition by Alfred H. Lockhart early in the twentieth century, as the center of special social activities on St. Thomas. (Grand Hotel is now no longer a hotel; the first floor houses several gift shops and other businesses, and a recently opened Children's Museum occupies the second floor.) Another old hotel was Hotel 1829, so named because it was erected in that year as the home of a wealthy merchant; it became a hotel around the beginning of the twentieth century and is still in business.[2]

Bluebeard's Castle Hotel was erected in 1934, with federally-granted funds, and may be considered the precursor of the modern tourist accommodations in the Virgin Islands. Then at the midpoint of the twentieth century, the Virgin Isle Hotel was opened in 1950 as the first luxury hotel in the territory, owned by white Continentals Sidney Kessler and Benjamin Bayne. Located on a hill west of Charlotte Amalie, the huge white complex had 130 rooms, a swimming pool, and was the first building in the V.I. to have elevators. It was without peer during its first several years and became the site of the most important social functions on St. Thomas. Then in 1954, after undergoing enlargement and renovations, Bluebeard's was ready to rival Virgin Isle in hosting glittering events on St. Thomas. In July 1960 the Virgin Isle changed management and became the Virgin Isle Hilton, while Bluebeard's was purchased in the 1960s by Henry Reichhold, a non-resident white Continental.[3] The changing of management and names became a regular feature of the hotel scene.

In addition to those old or sizeable hotels, St. Thomas had a substantial number of other hotel or guesthouse facilities prior to the big tourism decade of the 1960s. The pretty large places, whose number of rooms ranged from at least 20 to 50, included the Caribbean Hotel on western Lindbergh Bay; Flamboyant Beach Hotel on the present site of Frenchman's Reef; Gramboko Inn, in Sub Base; Island Beachcomber on Lindbergh Bay; Trade Winds Hotel, overlooking Brewers Bay, on UVI's present campus; Water Isle Beach Hotel, built in 1954 across from Sub Base in St. Thomas' harbor; and Yacht Haven Cottage Resort on Long Bay, near to the West Indian Company Dock.[4]

Smaller guesthouses, which had from 5 to 20 rooms, included Adams Guest House, about two blocks east of Government Hill; Estate Contant Guest House on Contant Hill; Galleon House on western Government Hill; Harbor View Guest House, upper Frenchman's Hill; Higgin's Gate Guest House on Back Street; Hilltop Guest House on lower Contant Hill; Mafolie Hotel on Mafolie Hill; Midtown Guest House on lower Garden Street; Miller Manor on Frenchman's Hill; Morningstar Hotel and Beach Club, now the lower portion of Frenchman's Reef; Mountain Top Hotel, the highest at over 1,000 ft.; Sapphire Bay Beach Club, in the eastern countryside; Smith's Fancy, near to Synagogue Hill; and Villa Santana on Denmark Hill.[5]

Even though the great majority of these accommodations were owned by Whites, a few were owned by Virgin Islands natives with black ancestry. They included Bandmaster Alton Adams of Adams Guest House, Omar Brown of Midtown Guest House on Garden Street, the Millers of Miller Manor on Frenchman's Hill, Lockhart family members who owned the Grand Hotel and the site of Harbor View on Frenchman's Hill, and the Schakelton family of Hilltop Guest House in Contant. These were quite unusual individuals as, unfortunately, those Blacks who were not working for the government or private employers were generally restricted, due to lack of available capital from banks or other lenders, to very small businesses. Most business-minded Blacks, therefore, were usually in such undertakings as small variety shops; taxi driving; cooked food and/or liquor shops; home-based ventures of selling baked goods or candies, sewing or tailoring; or hair-cutting and styling. For the average poor person in the Virgin Islands, life before 1960 was still quite challenging financially.

Then came the 1960s! The victory of the Cuban Revolution in 1959 was followed by the nationalization of all U.S. property and businesses in Cuba in 1960. That ended the relationships between the two countries, including visits by Americans to Cuba, which had been their #1 destination in the Caribbean. Puerto Rico and the Virgin Islands (especially St. Thomas) became the new choices and their tourism industries soared. In addition to its own direct traffic, studies showed that over half of all U.S. Puerto Rican visitors took the short side-trip to the V.I., just half an hour flying time away.[6]

The decades of the 1960s through the 90s, therefore, were marked by continuous tourism accommodation expansion on St. Thomas. The earlier hotels had demonstrated the needs and opportunities, and more and more tourists kept arriving. Entrepreneurs thus built, enlarged, renovated, or leased facilities to enable them to host a portion of the ever-increasing throng of visitors. Human enterprise was also needed to acquaint potential visitors with the natural and other attributes of the islands, to cater to visitors once they got here, and to lobby for special economic benefits, such as the greater customs exemptions for American tourists on liquor purchased in the Virgin Islands.[7] White continentals were important in all three, and the providing of those larger facilities for the tourists and related services brought great change to the landscape and to St. Thomas's way of life.

The largest of the post-1960 hotels, Frenchman's Reef, opened in 1973 as a member of the Holiday Inn chain. Now, combined as the Marriott's Frenchman's Reef and Morningstar Beach Resort, it totals 478 rooms plus suites, and includes 15 meeting rooms and multiple restaurants. The Sugar Bay Resort and Spa in the Smith Bay area has 294 rooms and 6 suites. The Ritz-Carlton, on the southern side of eastern St. Thomas, has 180 rooms and suites, plus 4 restaurants, and is especially known for luxury and pampering its guests. Best Western Emerald Beach Resort on eastern Lindbergh Bay has 90 rooms. In addition to the hotel overlooking Charlotte Amalie, Bluebeard's Beach Club and Villas on Frenchman's Bay has 74 rooms. Bolongo Bay Beach Resort has 65 rooms and 12 suites; and Secret Harbor Beach Resort has 68 rooms—beach front and hillside. Margaritaville Club Resort is in the Smith Bay area. Palm Courts Harbor View is on upper Frenchman Hill, and Windward Passage Hotel, once but no longer a Holiday Inn, is centrally located on Charlotte Amalie's Veterans Drive or waterfront.[8]

However, hotels were only one aspect of the tourist accommodations business. Many corporations or entrepreneurs came to realize that as much money, or more, could be made by erecting hotel-type accommodations and selling

Selected Growth and Tourism Statistics for St. Thomas, 1950–2010

Year	1950	1960	1970	1980	1990	2000	2010
Population	13,813	16,201	37,285	44,372	48,166	51,181	51,634
Cruise ship arrivals	15	126	500	821	1,140	949	680
Cruise ship passengers	7,692	49,700	230,000	635,100	1,117,200	1,719,800	1,751,300
Air arrivals	9000	88,000	401,624	392,700	510,500	481,100	530,900

Sources: V.I. Department of Commerce, *Annual Economic Review, 1980*, pp. 34–35, 65, 68, for 1950–1970; "U.S. Virgin Islands Annual Tourism Indicators," Bureau of Economic Research, Office of the Governor, U.S. V.I., 1990 & 2010; *1995 U.S. Virgin Islands Statistical Yearbook*, Eastern Caribbean Center, University of the Virgin Islands, April, 1998.

the units to guests who might usually occupy them only for a couple weeks or months of the year, and allow their rental to others for the remaining periods. There is therefore a sizeable list of such condominium resorts, including Anchorage Condominiums at Nazareth (30 suites); Elysian Beach Resort at Nazareth (65 villas); Crystal Cove Beach Resort on Sapphire Beach; Point Pleasant Resort; Sapphire Village Resort; and Sapphire Beach Resort (117 units).[9] In fact, there are also local residents who find some of these developments to be great places for living and reside in them year-round. The long-term residents are usually Whites, but there are also some Blacks, usually Continentals.

As would be expected, there are also smaller hotel facilities that went into business in the post-1960 period. Some examples are the Bellavista Scott Hotel in Sugar Estate; the Bunker Hill Hotel; and the 5-room Crystal Palace, the old Lockhart family residence with its historic furnishings and memories, at the western end of Synagogue Hill in Charlotte Amalie.[10]

In addition to living accommodations, many other businesses have been spawned by tourism. Numerous gift stores and malls, restaurants, taxis and tours, wedding planning, public beach accommodations, marinas, ferries for side trips to St. John and the British Virgin Islands, and real estate agencies are all well-developed entities. Coral World provides great marine vistas, there is the Mahogany Run golf course, and there are other attractions such as sailing, sea and air sports, cable and zip-line rides, and even a butterfly farm.

However, a major complaint about tourism by Blacks is that, for them, tourism has not delivered as had been hoped. It was understood that tourism meant inviting and entertaining visitors to share in the beauty, culture, and natural resources of the island, and that some of the tourists might decide to move and establish permanent residence. Tourism did, therefore, generate many jobs, the greatest number of jobs in the overall economy, and the resulting governmental expansion also led to positions that paid enough to enable a substantial number of residents to build or buy homes and to provide education for their children. In the process, however, the overall effect has been a loss of control of the land, resources, and thus of the future development of the Virgin Islands. Many Blacks have come to feel that in the Virgin Islands, tourism has been and is used as slavery was—a vehicle for getting Blacks to supply the needed labor while Whites maintained or gained control of the land. However, in the post-slavery period, when sugar cane cultivation proved to be no longer the cheapest way of building wealth, many of the Whites left to seek better returns elsewhere. Today Blacks are the main ones leaving the Virgin Islands, as the high costs of living in a tourist economy, with its diminished possibilities of having a home and employment in certain areas, lead them to the mainland.

The research projects of the Eastern Caribbean Center of UVI thus found that 58,786 native-born Virgin Islanders were living on the U.S. mainland in 2008, substantially more than the 49,719 that the Census of 2010 recorded as living in the Virgin Islands. Of the native Virgin Islanders on the mainland, one-fourth (25%) of them were living in Florida, followed by 15% in New York, 10% in Georgia, and 7% in Texas. Half of them were between 25 and 44 years old. The percentage of V.I. natives on the mainland who existed below the poverty level—18%—was 10% less than it was among V.I. resident natives. Therefore, as would also be expected, the V.I. Census of 2010 found that median family income in the Virgin Islands in 2009 was $34,612 for black families, which represented a small increase over the previous figure, while that of white families was $51,424, which represented a substantial decrease from what they had previously enjoyed, due to declining economic conditions on the mainland and in St. Croix's oil-refining industry.[11]

Real Estate and Business Ownership

The growing demands for facilities for tourists (short and long term), business sites, home sites, and land for speculation led to a thriving real estate industry on St. Thomas. Prior to the 1950s, the owners and prospective buyers of land had generally dealt with each other directly. In the 1950s the first real estate agencies in St. Thomas were established by white Continentals, and they

Marriott Frenchman's Reef Condos, next to the hotel. Courtesy of Larry Benjamin.

began acquiring control over a large portion of the available land on the island. In October 1960, the St. Thomas-St. John Board of Realtors was formed with 20 members. The names of its seven officers and its legal counsel were released to the press; all eight were white. After having organized as a professional group, the real estate interests over the next decade and a half tried as much as possible to keep the profession closed to others—through certain testing practices and by urging the enactment of high license fees and other restrictive requirements. By 1974 the racial composition of the profession had not changed very much in a decade and a half. An advertisement in celebration of Realtor Week in 1974 listed twelve realtor firms and their chief officers. Nine of the firms were owned and officered entirely by Whites.[12]

However, it should be known, as it gives a complete perspective of the land and economic history of St. Thomas, that substantially before there was a "white continental real estate industry," there were the achievements and holdings of Alfred Harris Lockhart. Lockhart, who was "mixed," was born in St. Croix in 1862 and migrated to St. Thomas as a young man. He apparently had a natural talent for business acquisition, which was truly important, but there was additionally a local story of his winning a lottery in his early years. He founded a number of businesses and, at a time when there were no banks that

The old Lockhart Bakery, between Back Street and the Dutch Reformed Church. Courtesy of the Virgin Islands Government's Archival Collection at the Charles W. Turnbull Regional Library.

made loans to poor Blacks, in the earliest decades of the twentieth century, he became known as a person who did, but who also was an unyielding bargainer who adhered to his terms even if it meant taking the property of a poor widow whose payment of a loan was slightly late because of the late arrival of a ship due to bad weather. By the 1920s, Mr. Lockhart had become the richest person in St. Thomas, to whom the Paiewonsky family, along with others, were indebted. By the time of his death in 1931, Mr. Lockhart's holdings included one-eighth (1/8) of all privately held real property on St. Thomas and even more, about one-fourth, of St. John's.[13]

For years after Mr. Lockhart's death, the various enterprises that had comprised his vast business empire—numerous parcels of land and occupied properties, a lumber yard, dairy, hotel, bakery, department store, gift and liquor store, insurance and financial companies—were at times overseen by various members of the family. Today, after certain strategic sales and adjustments, the assets have been combined, as Lockhart Companies Incorporated, under the management of two family members—attorney George Dudley, the son of Lockhart's great granddaughter Gertrude Lockhart Dudley Melchior; and the Rev. Dr. Wesley Williams, Jr., a black Continental lawyer and Episcopal priest who married Lockhart's great-great-granddaughter, Karen Hastie Williams. The assets they manage now comprise the largest amounts of developed commercial property in the Virgin Islands (shopping centers such as Drake's Passage, Lockhart Gardens, Fort Mylner, Red Hook Plaza, and Market Square East, plus the Guardian Insurance Company), and also the greatest amount of privately held undeveloped real estate (several hundred acres) in the Virgin Islands.[14] Even though A. H. Lockhart was greatly maligned and despised by ordinary St. Thomians of his time for the size and acquisition methods of some of his holdings, one wonders if the present situation of so much non-local ownership of land may not have been even worse without his activities. Of course, the eventual disposition of the present properties still remains to be seen!

After 1960, between Whites who were settling in St. Thomas and those who were utilizing property for tourism or speculation, large areas of land became practically unavailable to the major racial group of the islands. In 1973, for example, Arthur Witty, a major white developer, announced two new condominium projects. One, Harbor Ridge East, would be located on Skyline Drive and was planned for residents(?), while the other project would involve the addition of thirty units to the Secret Harbor Hotel and Condo Complex in the east, planned for non-residents.[15]

One of the major aspects of the heritage of slavery was that most Blacks in the Virgin Islands had never been the owners of the land on which they worked or lived. In January 1950, a Daily News editorial had stated that only five per cent of the people owned eighty per cent of the land of the Virgin Islands, and even that represented an improvement over the previous two decades.[16] Therefore, even though suffering from the many effects of a past of slavery, post-slavery oppression, and studied neglect of the many community actions that can bring about development of the disadvantaged, many black Virgin Islanders had lived with the hope that someday, through hard work and improved economic conditions, they would own at least a small plot of land. The alienation of land to new continental residents and even non-residents during the first quarter century of the tourist era seemed to turn the hopes of many Blacks into an impossible dream. In response to the advertised appeals and in the absence of local restraints, land and property values rose at unbelievable levels.

One of the most revealing of all public statements ever made by a white Continental in regard to the destiny of the V.I. came from the pen of real estate agent Roger Moran in 1968. Moran, whose family had built one of the largest real estate firms in St. Thomas at that time, wrote an article for the *Virgin Islands View* entitled "Read Estate Turns Tourists into Residents." It stated:

... probably 80% of the real estate sales made in the V.I. are of sites for retirement homes to couples who may be two or three years or many, many years from actual retirement. All realize that good land is selling rapidly.... Many areas that look like greenbelts are really hundreds of homesites ... that have been purchased and on which so many island homes are planned.

The Virgin Islands can't compete price-wise with Florida or Arizona; the islands are not the place in the sun for those of modest means.... Expensive? Sure. But imagine twenty years from now and consider how much what you buy today will be worth then.[17]

There it was—plainly stated! Mr. Moran was obviously writing mainly for white readers, and what some black Virgin Islanders may have realized fully only recently, was known by Moran and at least some other realtors from back in the 1960s. That is, these islands were being sold out under the noses of the majority of their people, who would simply have to move elsewhere where there was land for housing they could afford. The now-known fact, that there are more native Virgin Islanders living in Florida or other states of the U.S. than in the Virgin Islands may be news to some, but apparently had been expected and promoted by some realtors for many decades!

The real estate profession in St. Thomas continues to be fairly healthy, though not at all as robust as it was in its heyday, a couple to a few decades ago. In fact, the industry met with Governor Mapp in September of 2016, asking for governmental assistance in helping to keep it operating at high prices— unfortunately, the same prices that have been driving so many Blacks out of the Virgin Islands and encouraging the entry of land speculators into the local market.[18] The St. Thomas Board of Realtors' 2016 membership included a listing of 42 companies, ranging from fourteen companies which have just one realtor, many which have several realtors, to the largest company, John Foster Real Estate, which listed a total of 19 realtors. As there are now very few direct owner-buyer contacts, which prevailed in the pre-1960 era, almost all real estate sales today, whether involving Blacks or Whites, are done by professional agents. However, even though there are more Blacks involved today than before, especially in some of the one-person or small companies, the profession is still largely white![19]

The Virgin Islands involvement of one of its great businessmen in the last three and one-half decades apparently began accidentally. In 1980 John B. Anderson, a lawyer, came to St. Thomas at the request of two friends, Henry Kimelman and Elliott Fishman, to assist them in closing a transaction involving the sale of the West Indies Corporation. However, when the deal for the beverage distribution company did not materialize, Anderson decided to buy the company on his own, thus beginning a long and lucrative business relationship with the Virgin Islands. From the 1980s onward, he acquired several historic properties on Main Street in Charlotte Amalie and then the Bakery Square on Back Street. He also made acquisitions in St. John, such as a part of Mongoose Junction and part of Buccaneer Mall in St. Croix. His company, Topa Equities, Ltd., came to include more than 40 wholly owned subsidiaries. In addition to his Virgin Islands properties and distributorships, he owned properties in California and Hawaii, and holdings in insurance, real estate, financial services, automobile dealerships, manufacturing, and ranked in 2010 as the 9th largest beer distributor in the United States.[20]

A native of Minnesota, Anderson had attended the University of California at Los Angeles on a scholarship and never forgot it. He and his wife ended up donating over $42 million to the UCLA's business school, which is named in his honor. In 2006 he was ranked #189 on the Forbes list of 400 richest Americans, with a net worth of $1.9 billion. At the time of his death in 2011, Gov. de Jongh stated that Anderson had quietly contributed over the years to many V.I. charities and community organizations that had helped thousands of Virgin Islanders, including scholarships for teachers and the funding of Carnival activities.[21] A greater accounting of his contributory role in the Virgin Islands would definitely be in order!

In the early years of this century, St. Thomas was once again faced with two proposed grand developments that had been planned for the island by two American corporate groups. One proposed to turn Benner Bay, on the island's eastern end, into a large marina that would cover 400 acres; the beauty of the area and projected pictures of the occupied marina were displayed in stateside sources and the electronic media. The other development was a grand community of new estates at Botany Bay on St. Thomas' western end. Named "The Preserve at Botany Bay," it would feature new home sites on 397 acres which overlooked two half-moon beaches on the island's secluded western end.[22]

Conservationists and environmentalists urged publicly and at the Senate hearing that the Benner Bay Marina should not be approved. They noted that construction of the marina would have involved the dredging of a pond which provided a needed habitat for a number of plants and animals, some of which were endangered. Four members of the appropriate committee at the Legislature—Senators Donald Cole, Roosevelt David, Carlton Dowe, and Celestino White—agreed with the testifying scientists and voted down the permit for the marina at the Senate's hearing.[23]

However, both the environmentalists and the Department of Planning and Natural Resources had asked the Legislature to allow the Botany Bay project, but urged its limitation to the size that had initially been proposed rather than allow blanket development through rezoning of the entire area. Unfortunately, the four senators who had voted to preserve Benner Bay voted with seven other senators to allow all 400 acres of the Botany Bay project to be rezoned. Then in December 2001, Governor Turnbull signed the rezoning into law, explaining that it was "a difficult decision" but that the economic benefits to the territory were too important to ignore. The overcrowded east end of St. Thomas would finally be joined by a first resort in the west end.[24]

The Legislature's and Gov. Turnbull's decisions were no doubt based on worldwide economic news in the aftermath of September 11, 2001, that international tourism was down everywhere, as the terror attacks in New York had made persons wary about traveling and most were taking smaller trips nearer to their homes. Thus the Virgin Islands and other places dependent on long trips and international tourism all experienced declines in tourism in 2002. But even as St. Thomas *Daily News* reporter Hal Hatfield recorded the economic decline, he reminded readers that, in spite of such news, an important question always needed to be asked: "How much development is too much development?"[25]

The 2016 U.S. Virgin Islands Economic Review revealed that the average value of the sale price of a home in the V.I. fell to $508,811 in 2015, about $60,000 less than in 2014. The average cost was so high because a number of houses in the St. Thomas-St. John district had sold for over a million dollars. However, in St. Croix, on the contrary, the average home price had increased to $368,789. Territory wide, in both districts the sale price for condominiums was $215,142, far less than detached homes.[26]

The average salary in the Virgin Islands was $39,258 in fiscal year 2016. The private sector's average annual salary was $34,088, while the public sector's average annual salary was $52,572.00. Most jobs in the Virgin Islands are in the private sector, as tourism accounts for over 70% of wage and salary jobs. The unemployment rate, which is based on the number of persons actively seeking employment, was 11.4 per cent for St. Croix and 11.5 per cent for St. Thomas and St. John. The territory seems to be emerging from the losses caused by the national recession, but the 2012 closing of the oil refinery in St. Croix still affects very adversely the economy of St. Croix and overall governmental receipts. Additionally, St. Thomas is no longer the #1 tourist port in the Caribbean.[27]

U.S. Census Bureau figures show the hold that white businesses exert on the Virgin Islands. In the 2012 Economic Census for Kinds of Business and Ethnicity Status of Ownership, the Virgin Islands listing included 161 construction businesses. Of those, 73 were white-owned, 24 were black-owned, and 9 were Puerto Rican-owned; however, 51 did not report ethnicity, which is a sizable percentage of the 161 companies and could distort the picture substantially. Similarly, 57 establishments were listed as manufacturing companies, of which 29 were white-owned, 9 were black-owned, 1 was Puerto Rican, 4 were "other ethnicity," and 14 did not report ethnicity. Of the 64 establishments in wholesale trade, 27 were white-owned, 6 were black, 1 was Puerto Rican, 4 of "other ethnicity," and 26, again a considerable amount, did not report any ethnicity. One last example, which is widespread in the Virgin Islands and the figures so indicate, is the area of retail trade: 560 such businesses comprised the total, of which 161were white-owned, 60 were black-owned, 13 were Puerto Rican, 86 were "other ethnicity," and 231 (by far the largest group) did not report any ethnicity.[28] Though the existence of so many who prefer no ethnic identification (one wonders why) clouds some of the reports, the continuing dominance in key industries of those who identify themselves as white, as opposed to those who identify as black, is overwhelming.

The Need for Greater Governmental Regulation of Economic Activities

It seems as if the regulation of economic activity, which is so very important to the life and well-being of any community, is often relegated to much lesser importance in the Virgin Islands that it rightly deserves. Of course, planners, developers, and builders want to have their ways in doing things in the easiest and most profitable ways for themselves, but the residents of a community who will have to abide with the results every day, for all their lives and their children's lives, should be even more diligent than visiting developers and their agents in insisting on what they need and want. This has been a weakness in Virgin Islands development that should be monitored and exercised very carefully for future well-being. Four examples—the old "Free Beach" movement, Water Island development, the once-proposed Magens Bay Resort, and the newer Mandahl Bay proposed development should serve to illustrate the great need for and the moral imperative of protecting the Virgin Islands to a much greater degree.

N
↑

ST. THOMAS

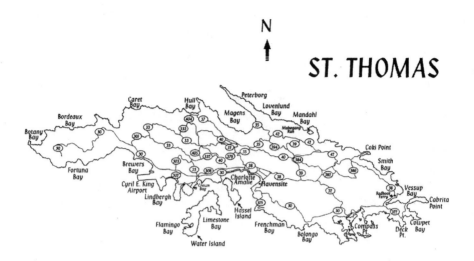

The major bays and roads of St. Thomas. Courtesy of Pyles Publishing and *Houses* Magazine.

Free Beaches

Most beach areas in St. Thomas (the island has over fifty beach areas) had traditionally been available for public use. However, the various developers who bought beachfront land during the 1950s and 1960s tended to close the beaches to the public. Thus, by the late Sixties, there were only a few beaches on St. Thomas to which the public had clear access.[29]

Concern about the problem had emerged early. In 1960 a bill had been prepared for introduction in the Legislature, asking for the creation of a special committee to study ways in which the beaches "can be utilized in the best interests of the people of the Virgin Islands." An editorial in 1963 urged the adoption of a policy like Puerto Rico's, where legislation had declared that all beach property belonged to the Commonwealth and was reserved for the enjoyment of all. Even though complaints were made to the government in the early 1960s about the fees and/or other policies at Dorothea Beach Club, Bluebeard's Beach Club, Morning Star Beach Club, and other restricted beaches, their management always appeared able to convince government officials of the openness of their practices. Therefore, no decisive action was taken during the 1960s.[30]

In late 1970, a tri-island Citizens Committee for Free Beaches for all was formed. It was headed in St. Thomas by Mrs. Marva Sprauve Browne and Edwin Hatchette. The Committee drew up a five-point petition, asking the

Governor and the Legislature to take steps to affirm that all sandy beaches and the entire shoreline of the V.I. were the property of the people and should remain forever free and open to all. The petition also asked for effectuation, by negotiation, gift, or eminent domain, of means to establish public access to all sandy beaches, and for the repudiation of any previous legislation which may have allowed private titles or entrance fees to beaches. The document was presented in early February 1971, with over 2,500 signatures. During the following weeks, hundreds of additional signatures were added. Almost all senators expressed agreement and promised quick action.[31]

The Legislative Committee on Conservation held public hearings on the islands about the beach issue. At the St. John hearing, Dr. Gilbert Sprauve, a black professor at CVI, said to the senators: "If we lose this one, we are finished," and he told of private owners who had used guns to drive persons away from beaches. Of course, a number of private owners and the hotel interests vigorously opposed any changes and constantly warned of the high costs to the government which beach access would entail.[32] However, others decided that the bad publicity was not worth it, and decided to comply. Thus, in March 1971, several establishments—Bolongo, Sapphire Bay condos, Morningstar, and Bluebeard's Bay Beach Club—were added to a list of properties to which persons could go for free and experience no restrictions.[33]

In May 1971, the Legislature passed a bill which "confirms the right of the public to use and enjoy all beaches and shorelines of the Virgin Islands." The Citizens Committee was greatly disappointed with the Open Beach Bill. The Committee wrote to the Governor, explaining that the bill was "ambiguous and misleading" because it had failed to distinguish "between the right to use beaches upon payment of a fee to private person from the right to use beaches free of any fee to any such a person." The Committee also lamented the bill's silence on the practice of selling so-called "beach rights," which left open the possibility of "developing exclusive enclaves around desirable beach real estate." In June 1971, Governor Evans allowed the Open Beach Bill to become law without his signature.[34]

Ever since the petitions had been presented, the Citizens Committee had been sponsoring "swim-ins" at restricted beaches and public rallies to educate residents on the beach issues and to urge free use of the beaches. A member of the Committee, St. Thomian poet Corey Emanuel, wrote a poem on the issue which became the popular theme of the movement. Bingley Richardson, a member of the Citizens committee, urged "all Virgin Islanders, this year and forever henceforth to go and swim on any beach in these Virgin Islands." The Committee had done so at several beaches without any resistance. Anyone who encountered harassment or attempted intimidation was urged to contact the

Committee. Late in 1971, the Lime Tree Beach Hotel on St. Thomas declared its beach free and open to the public.[35]

In January 1972, members of the Citizens Committee again appeared before the Legislature to urge passage of a stronger bill on beaches than the one passed the previous May. Spokeswoman Marva Browne accused the senators of "lack of commitment and sincerity" and said the law which had been passed was more representative of the opinions expressed by the hotel interests and the Chamber of Commerce than those of the people. On the question of access to the beaches, which the private interests had posed as a great problem, the Committee recommended that access routes be the same as those used for commercial purposes and which were also utilized for public services such as police and fire protection. The inadequacy of the previous legislation was demonstrated when, in February 1972, a Girl Scout group was prohibited from swimming by the management of the Sapphire Beach Resort unless each scout and their leaders paid a $3.00 fee. Still, the Legislature did not act, even though one or two individual senators were trying to secure a stronger bill.[36]

In April 1974, a St. Thomas resident, Charles C. Hull, brought to the attention of Attorney General Verne Hodge the case of Bolongo Bay Beach and Tennis Hotel in southeastern St. Thomas. The Hotel had actually erected along the sides of its property two chain fences nine feet in height, one of which extended thirty feet into the sea and the other fifty feet. It thus had completely enclosed its property and prevented access to its beach even from the sea along the shore. Mr. Hull thought that "the fence is there to keep out citizens of the Virgin Islands." At a meeting between the attorney general and representative of the Bolongo Hotel, the Hotel's vice president and general manager, Richard Doumeng, a white Continental, explained that the fences had been erected for security and not to exclude the public from the beach. He thought the club's membership fees of $350 per family and $150 for individuals were enough to permit wide public membership. Even though V.I. legislation confirmed the right of all to use and enjoy all beaches and shorelines, Doumeng said he would take down the fence "when the Department of Public Safety can do its job or when conditions change." The V.I. government decided to file suit against the Bolongo establishment, and the federal government decided to join the territorial government as a party to the suit.[37]

Shortly after, in mid-May 1974, Mrs. Browne, Mrs. Wilhemina Lewis, Dale Carty, and Darwin King of the Citizens Committee went to use the beach at Bolongo Hotel. After they refused to pay the entrance fee, Doumeng approached them accompanied by a policeman. When they told Doumeng of the open beach provisions of V.I. law, he replied: "the Virgin Islands Code does not govern the V.I." After listening to both Doumeng and the group, the officer refused to arrest the group as Doumeng had requested and the officer also refused to support Doumeng, who then wanted to make a citizen's arrest of the group.[38]

The V.I. government based its suit on the V.I. Open Shorelines Act. It thus did not challenge the right of the hotel to restrict access to the beach through the property, but confined itself to the question of access from the sea or from adjoining beaches. The Act defined the shoreline, for most areas, as extending from the low tide to fifty feet inland. The Government also secured affidavits from persons, including Whites and a previous owner of the beach that the beach had previously be open to the public for bathing and recreation for at least fifty years. In December, 1974, Judge Almeric Christian of the U.S. District Court in St. Thomas upheld the constitutionality (which the hotel challenged) of the V.I. Open Shorelines Act and ordered the permanent removal of the two fences blocking access to the Bolongo Bay Beach. Citing the historical documentation of public use, the Judge said that Bolongo Bay's property rights "have always been subject to the paramount right of the public to use the beach."[39]

The Bolongo Hotel appealed the ruling. It was not until one year later, in December 1975, that the Third Circuit Court of Appeals upheld the District Court ruling and the hotel finally removed its fence. Even while the fences were being removed, Doumeng was considering an appeal to the Supreme Court. And, at about the same time, the St. Thomas-St. John Hotel Association showed just how sensitive it was to public concerns by electing Doumeng as its president. In a letter to the press about Doumeng's selection, a black Virgin Islander, Darwin King, asked: "... is it any wonder that the tourist industry has perpetuated so much social unrest in the islands?"[40]

The last legislation on beach access, passed in 1993, still did not make it absolutely clear that the public has the right of access to beaches, free of fees or any other unreasonable encumbrance. That remains pending and should be enacted as soon as possible.[41]

The Once-Proposed Magens Bay Resort

A great example of how Virgin Islanders should control development, making it a helpful tool for their existence rather than being the master of their lives, took place in regard to the proposed Magens Bay Resort in 1985. It was planned as a 300-room hotel above Magens Bay, to be developed by the Criswell Development Company of Texas, along with James Armour, a white Continental who had become a resident and major developer in St. Thomas. However, the zoning of the proposed area needed to be changed for the hotel to be built there. The St. Thomas-St. John Chamber of Commerce endorsed the proposal, and so also did the Magens Bay Authority, which is charged with managing the Magens Bay beach area on behalf of the people of the Virgin Islands. The Authority's stand, however, became very controversial. It caused the resignation of member Guido Moron, who said that the beach would become "a genteel Coney Island," and member John Maduro also voiced a strong dissent.[42]

When substantial opposition developed, Armour, saying that his name had become "a lightning rod for controversy," withdrew from the two resorts with which he had been connected—not only the proposed Magens Bay Resort, but also the Mahogany Run Resort. A Criswell Company spokesman said the firm would continue with the plans to improve Mohogany Run and to get the required zoning for the proposed Magens Bay Resort, saying that the firm had built hotels and office buildings throughout the United States.

The plans for the Magens Bay Resort, above St. Thomas's most beloved and popular beach, created a community uproar. Armour, who was a principal in the Royal Dane Mall in Charlotte Amalie and also one of the owners of the well-known Mountain Top tourist stop, walked out of a meeting with several concerned groups, saying that groups such as the V.I. Conservation Society and the St. Thomas Historic Trust preferred a "combative role" to dialogue. On December 2, 1985, there was a protest rally at Magens Bay Beach, attended by members of the two groups already named, in addition to members from the League of Women Voters, Virgin Islands 2000, and Virgin Islanders United. Also in attendance and against the proposal were Senators Lorraine Berry, Cain Magras, Iver Stridiron, Adelbert Bryan, and Virdin Brown.[43]

In spite of such opposition, the Planning Office, whose director was Roy Adams, recommended in late January 1986 that 56 acres behind Magens Bay beach be rezoned to allow the planned resort. Mr Adams explained that Governor Juan Luis had favored the hotel's request, so he felt obligated to do so.[44]

A day for the hearing on the re-zoning, Tuesday, February 18, 1986, was set at the Legislature, where many business tycoons probably looked forward to emerging victorious. However, the request for the re-zoning was withdrawn on the day of the hearing, as the hotel's developers and friends realized that they did not have the votes to get their wish. For in addition to the Senators who had attended the rally—Berry, Magras, Stridiron, Bryan, and Brown— additional senators, such as James O'Bryan, Lilliana Belardo de O'Neal, and Derek Hodge, as least eight of the fifteen senators, were known to be opposed to the rezoning. Their personal morality and listening to the voices of the people have preserved, at least up to the present, one of the great natural beauties

Charlotte Amalie Harbor with Hassel Island, foreground, and Water Island behind. Courtesy of Larry Benjamin.

and assets of the Virgin Islands.[45] May the leaders and the people of the Virgin Islands continue to rise and fight for such causes whenever such actions are necessary!

Water Island

The case of Water Island represents a special possibility for the Virgin Islands. The 500-acre island, the fourth largest of all the U.S. Virgins, is located in St. Thomas's harbor. It is three-eighths of a mile and a few minutes by ferry away from the Sub Base pier of St. Thomas. During World War II it had been bought from a private company by the U.S. Department of Defense and used as an army base. In 1950 the Army vacated the island and it was transferred to the Department of the Interior in 1952. Interior leased it that same year to Water Island, Inc. for twenty years, with a twenty-year renewal option. The major principal in Water Island, Inc. was a white Continental named Walter Phillips, who developed the island as a tourist resort. The Water Island Hotel opened for business in 1954, and bare homesites or sites with cottages were available for sale. By 1973, of over 100 property owners on the island, only three were black. Thus, at the entrance of St. Thomas' harbor, clearly visible, was an almost all white colony.[46]

Water Island was a great example of the dilemmas that growth as a tourist economy brought to the V.I. Admittedly, when the developers leased the island in 1952, it was an uninhabited, uncultivated place with only some old military buildings. It took a great deal of foresight, faith, hard work and money to turn it into the beautifully-landscaped, well-developed tourist resort that part of the island had become by the early 1970s. In 1972, Water Isle Hotel and Beach Club, Inc., to which Mr. Phillips had assigned his lease, applied to the Department of Interior for its twenty-year lease renewal option. Phillips and the other principals involved thought that their efforts and expenditure more than justified renewal of the lease.

However, St. Thomas of 1972 was a very changed society from 1952. Even though the work of the developers was appreciated, Water Island, as a virtually white colony in the midst of a mainly black society, had become a source of social discontent. Moreover, because this island was federal property, its residents paid no property taxes to the V.I. government. Yet they voted on St. Thomas and used various facilities there. In 1972, the V.I. legislature, therefore, sent a resolution to the President and the Congress asking, instead of the renewal of the private lease of Water Island, for the transfer of the island from the Department of the Interior to the jurisdiction of the government of the Virgin Islands.[47]

The 1972 Audit Report of the federal comptroller of the V.I. also questioned whether Water Island was being developed in the best interests of the federal and V.I. governments. Additionally, a citizens group petitioned President Nixon in June 1972 to turn Water Island over to the V.I. government for residential and recreational use. A Water Island Commission established by the V.I. government in late 1972, after studying the matter, also recommended that the V.I. government be made administrator of the Water Island lease. The Commission also recommended an investigation into possible civil rights violations by the island's developers. However, the St. Thomas-St. John Chapter of the V.I. Hotel Association filed a petition with the federal government, asking that it honor its lease with the Water Island interests and "take no steps to transfer Water Island to the Virgin Islands." Some other Continental and business interests felt similarly. On January 1, 1973, much to the disappointment of many Islanders, the Department of Interior renewed its lease with the private interests on Water Island for another twenty years—until December 1992.[48]

In 1992, both the Virgin Islands Government and the private corporation that had been leasing Water Island conducted campaigns again for the control of the island. This time the lease was finally given to the local Government, and a public ceremony of thanks and appreciation was conducted by the Farrelly administration. Unfortunately, the popular hotel was destroyed by Hurricane Marilyn in 1995, and rebuilding did not take place until 2016. The other, maybe even sadder, aspect is that the Virgin Islands government has not done anything to make the island different. It remains a white bastion in St. Thomas' harbor so, hopefully, additional plans are being formulated. Meanwhile, thanks to a white Continental who lives on Water Island, UVI Communications professor and Radio Station WSTA "Good News" announcer Alexander Randall, for periodically hosting at his home very much appreciated musical concerts.

Mandahl Bay

A fourth example of governmental action that could make a big difference deals with Mandahl Bay. The public's knowledge of plans for the Mandahl Bay area were revealed mainly at Government House in St. Thomas on Wednesday, November 6, 2014, when Governor John de Jongh signed a 99-year lease agreement with Mandahl Bay Holdings, according to the story published in the local *Daily News* and other media outlets. Mandahl Bay had been a V.I. government-owned property, located on St. Thomas's northern shore, east of Magens Bay, and which business entities had tried to develop before without success. According to the Mandahl Bay Holdings (MBH) president Karl Blaha, MBH was a wholly owned subsidiary of a publicly traded corporation on the New York Stock Exchange, and which also purchased St. Thomas's Mahogany Run Golf Course during the Government House signing. The signing was also attended by a small group of "Friends of Mandahl Bay," who were heard murmuring about "signing away our lives."[49]

During the following week, the public was treated to repeated full-page newspaper advertisements, complete with attractive artists' conceptions, emphasizing that the MBH's proposed Hyatt Regency hotel would be St. Thomas's first new hotel in 20 years, and that the MBH project was not "just a new hotel, it's a new community." The features of the "new community" would include the 300-room Hyatt Regency Hotel, a 50-slip marina, private estates and marina town houses, three restaurants, a full-service spa and fitness center, 17,000 square feet of meeting and conference space, multilevel interconnected pools, and a commercial "town center." Afterward, the second phase of the project, in partnership with the Mahogany Run Golf Course, would include an expanded and improved golf course, a much larger conference center, another 200-room hotel, and 158 vacation club units. It was promised that over a 15-

year period, the project would generate more than 700 permanent and part-time jobs and V.I. tax revenues of $272 million dollars.[50]

On November 20, 2014, the Friends of Mandahl Bay initiated a civil suit against Gov. de Jongh, seeking to stop the proposed development on the grounds that the governor violated the public's trust by signing the lease. Within months, there were several newspaper commentaries on the Mandahl Bay proposal. The first was an op-ed, in the March 23, 2014, *Daily News* by local attorney George H. T. Dudley, who argued that the V.I. economy was weak and needed more jobs, as had been offered by the Mandahl Bay development, to bolster its poor attraction rate of young educated persons. Dr. Gwen-Marie Moolenaar, a retired UVI faculty member and administrator, responded, two days later, that she agreed with the concern of not attracting young Virgin Islanders, but that construction and hotel jobs were not the means of doing so. One day later, on March 25, David Silverman, a member of the Save Coral Bay organization of St. John, opined on the need, not only for sustainable growth but for a "quality of life and respect" that had made the Virgin Islands special. Then, attorney Dudley, again in the April 10th newspaper edition, urged that "it is time to stop wringing our hands over the territory's current condition and seize the opportunity to improve our economy by participation in the growth in hotel tourism occurring throughout the Caribbean." An accompanying note by the newspaper, on April 10, pointed out that Dudley was the attorney for the developer who negotiated the agreement for the development of the Mandahl Bay area. Finally, in the April 13 *Daily News* issue, there were two letters. One from William J. Demetree, known as a local contractor, stated that he thought the Mandahl Bay development was a good idea, and he wished the principals well. Then another letter from David Silverman argued that places interested in the quality of life could thrive with smaller types of development.[51]

On Tuesday, February 11, 2015, a meeting with ten of the fifteen senators, representatives of the proposed Mandahl developers, preservationists and environmentalists took place at Mandahl Bay. The Senators included Jean Forde, Novelle Francis Jr., Justin Harrigan, Sr., Almando Liburd, Terrence Nelson, Nereida Rivera-O'Reillly, Clifford Graham, Tregenza Roach, Kurt Vialet, and Janette Millin Young. They looked at the site, at maps and projected drawings of the development, and listened to all. When Mandahl Bay Holdings president Karl Blaha asserted that "The environment is going to be improved," and someone from the "Friends of Mandahl Bay" shouted that the land is meant for the people, Blaha responded, "We own this land."[52]

The Mandahl lease extension is not now before the government of the Virgin Islands because, after being signed by Gov. de Jongh, it had to be ratified by the 30th Legislature, which did not do so before its expiration in January, 2015.[53] The lease would therefore need to be re-submitted by the Mapp or a future administration for ratification by a future legislature. It will be up to the people of the Virgin Islands to make their wishes known to legislators of the future.

The V.I. Director of the Office of Management and Budget, Nellon Bowry, issued warnings for much of the 2016 year about the dire economic situation of the Virgin Islands government. In June he was cited as saying that economic growth is the only salvation for the deep financial hole the government is in, and there were other governmental and business leaders making similar statements. Moreover, in the centennial year of American rule, the Virgin Islands Government Employee Retirement System does not have funds to meet its obligations beyond a few years, and the Government is unable to sell bonds as experts have warned against their purchase.[54]

One thus wonders if a project such as the Mandahl Bay development which, in its own words, is not just about a new hotel or hotels, but about "a new community," will end up being approved, as presented, for the sake of our economic "well-being." Our main business is tourism, so it is accepted that another hotel or two would accommodate more tourists. But if the Mandahl proposal is approved as presented, with a new "community" of scores of boat dwellers and hundreds of costly homes, it would be a case of assisting with a transformation of our islands that is not truly beneficial to most of our population. The government of the Virgin Islands should *always use its powers to effectively regulate and ensure the kinds of development that may be shared beneficially by all of its peoples and not just certain segments.*

Notes

1. Paiewonsky, *Memoirs of A Governor*, pp. 416–417. The estimated per capita income in 1950 was about $600, in 1967 it was $2,133; cruise ship arrivals in 1950 had been fewer than 30, but by 1967 numbered 296.

2. "Sample Guest Room at New Hotel Completed," *Daily News* (St. Thomas, V.I.), January 19, 1950, p. 1; Suzanne Carlson, "Children's Museum plans opening on Friday," *Daily News*, March 17, 2016.

3. Orlins, *The Impact of Tourism*, p. 101.

4. Jeanne Perkins Harman, *The Virgins: Magic Islands* (Appleton-Century-Crofts, Inc., New York: 1961), pp. 236–240.

5. Ibid., pp. 237–240.

6. Orlins, *The Impact of Tourism*, pp. 93–98.

7. Ibid.

8. *St. Thomas Source*—https://stthomassource.com/source-guide-to-st-thomas-accommodations/. "Source Guide to St. Thomas Accommodations," Visitor's Center, August 2, 2016; INNOVATIVE, *2016 United States Virgin Islands Telephone Directory*, pp. 33, 108–110.

9. Ibid, INNOVATIVE 2016 Telephone Directory.

10. Ibid.

11. Mills, Dr. Frank, "Native-Born Virgin Islanders Living in the States," from "Research News from ECC," Volume 2, Issue 1, a publication of the Eastern Caribbean Center of the University of the Virgin Islands, January, 2010; U. S. Bureau of the Census, Characteristics of Population: Virgin Islands of the United States, 2010 Census.

12. "Real Estate Brokers Form V.I. Board Here," *Daily News* (St. Thomas, V.I.), April 21, 1960, p. 1; "Realtors Board Formed For St. Thomas, St. John," November 17, 1960, p. 8; "Territorial Board of Realtors," September 11, 1961, p. 5; April 16, 1962, p. 1; Donald Stanford, et al., "Letter to the Editor," August 9, 1972, pp. 7, 13; Gerald E. Hodge, St., "Letter to the Editor," August 12, 1972, pp. 7, 14; "Celebrate Home Ownership: Realtor Week, April 29–May 4, 1974," April 30, 1974, p. 15.

13. "Alfred H. Lockhart, St. Thomas," Bing Images; Jarvis, J. Antonio, *Brief History of the Virgin Islands*, pp. 212–213; Ralph M. Paiewonsky, *Memoirs of a Governor*, p. 25.

14. Interview with Rev. Dr. Wesley Williams, St. Thomas, September 1, 2016; " Alfred H. Lockhart, St. Thomas," Bing Images; www.Lockhart.com.

15. *Daily News* (St. Thomas, V.I.), January 13, 1973, p. 1.

16. Editorial, *Daily News* (St. Thomas, V.I.), January, 1950, p. 5.

17. Roger F. Moran, "Real Estate Turns Tourists into Residents," *Virgin Islands View*, Vol 3, No. 8, (January, 1968), pp. 23–25.

18. Bernetia Akin, "Undercurrents: V.I. Real Estate Market Continues Subdued Recovery," *St. Thomas Source*, Internet Explorer, September 12, 2016.

19. "St. Thomas Board of Realtors," Internet Explorer, consulted on September 5, 2016.

20. Lynda Lohr, "V.I. Philanthropist John Anderson Dead at 93," *St. Thomas Source*—Internet Explorer, August 4, 2011.

21. Lynda Lohr, "V.I. Philanthropist John Anderson Dead at 93," *St. Thomas Source*, August 4, 2011. John Anderson, attorney—Bing—Internet Explorer.

22. Chris Larsen, "2 Developments stir opposition," *Daily News* (St. Thomas, V.I.), January 2, 2002, p. 7.

23. Ibid.

24. Ibid.

25. Hal Hatfield, "Sept. 11 sent V.I. economy reeling," *Daily News* (St. Thomas, V.I.), February 2, 2002, p. 8.

26. "U.S. Virgin Islands Economic Review," May 2016, Bureau of Economic Research, Office of the Governor, St. Thomas, V.I., pp. 5–6.

27. Ibid., pp. 6–7, 1.

28. U.S. Census Bureau, Island Area Series: Geographic Area Series: General Statistics by Kind of Business and Ethnicity Status of Ownership for the U.S. Virgin Islands, 2012. pp. 2, 3.

29. "Public Beaches," *Virgin Islands View*, Vol. 3, No. 9 (February, 1968), p. 19.

30. "Bill Would Study Public Beach Use," *Daily News* (St. Thomas, V.I.), May 21, 1960, p. 1; "No Discrimination At Beach Clubs is Said," July 22, 1961, p. 1; "Toward a Sound Beach Policy," September 16, 1963, p. 9; "Hotel Petitions To Have Fence Removed," June 12, 1963, p. 1.

31. "Public Beaches Asked," *Daily News* (St. Thomas, V.I.), December 28, 1970, p. 1; "Committee Pushes Free Access To All Beaches," February 4, 1971, p. 1.

32. "200 Jam Sprauve School For Free Beach Hearing," *Daily News* (St. Thomas, V.I.), March 15, 1971, p.1.

33. "3200 sign Free Beach Petition," *Daily News* (St. Thomas, V.I.), March 27, 1971, p. 3.

34. "Open Beach, Voting Age Bills Pass Senate," *Daily News* (St. Thomas, V.I.), May 15, 1971, p. 1; "The Seashore Belongs To Everyone," June 4, 1971, p. 7.

35. "Committee On Free Beaches To Hold Rally," *Daily News* (St. Thomas, V.I.), February 24, 1971, p. 3; "Free Beaches For All," March 11, 1971, p. 10; "3200 Sign Free Beach Petition," March 27, 1971, p. 3; Bingley G. Richardson, "Letter to the Editor," July 27, 1971, p. 7; "Free Beach Group Urges Passage of Strong Law," January 25, 1972, p. 1.

36. "Free Beach Group Urges Passage of Strong Law," *Daily News* (St. Thomas, V.I.), January 25, 1972, p. 1, 7, 16; "Correspondence from Edwin Hatchette and Marva S. Browne, Chairmen of the Citizens Committee," *Daily News*, March 4, 1972, p. 7; "Sapphire Bay Swim-in-Site," *Daily News*, March 10, 1972, p. 3; March 22, 1972, p. 7.

37. Editorial—"Let's Cut Out the Noise," *Daily News* (St. Thomas, V.I.), April 18, 1974, p. 7; "Free Beach Test Case Looms," "Gov't to Challenge Bolongo Resort Fence," *Daily News*, May 17, 1974, p. 1.

38. "Letter to the Editor" from Dick Duomeng of Bolongo Bay, *Daily News* (St. Thomas, V.I.), May 21, 1974, p. 7.

39. Associated Press, "Judge Rules Bolongo Beach Fences Illegal," *Daily News* (St. Thomas, V.I.), December 28, 1974, p. 1.

40. "Judge Denies Bolongo Bay Motion for New Trial," *Daily News*, January 24, 1975, p. 1; December 11, 1975, p. 1; December 23, 1975, p. 7; December 30, 1975, p. 1.

41. Olasee Davis, "Public access from land to V.I. beaches is the law, but we should put all beaches into V.I. parks system," *Daily News* (St. Thomas, V.I.), January 7, 2016, p. 25.

42. Jon Nordheimer, "Many Virgin Islanders Outraged Over Plans For Resort at a Pristine Beach," New York Times, December 16, 1984. Accessed on October 5, 2016 at http://www.nytimes.com/1984/12/16/us/many-virgin-islanders-outraged-over-plans-for-resort-at-a-pristine-beach.html.

43. "Plans for resort above Magens Bay made more waves," *Daily News* (St. Thomas, V.I.), January 11, 1986, p. R-8; "*Magens Bay Rally aims at control issue*," Ibid., January 18, 1986, pp. 1–10.

44. "Recommendation from Planning Director for Hotel," *Daily News* (St. Thomas, V.I.), January 23, 1986, pp. 1–15.

45. Jonathan Glass, "Magens Bay Rezoning bid is withdrawn," *Daily News* (St. Thomas, V.I.), February 19, 1986, p. 1.

46. Island Resources Foundation, "Water Island Study: Economic Development Options" (St. Thomas, V.I.: mimeographed report, 1980); Island Resources Foundation, "Water Islands Study: Summary Report and Fiscal Analysis" (St. Thomas, V.I.: mimeographed report, 1980); Home Journal (St. Thomas, V.I.), January 21, 1952, p. 1; *Daily News* (St. Thomas, V.I.), May 6, 1972, pp. 6, 13; May 2, 1973, p. 1; August 1, 1975—45th Anniversary Edition, pp. 67, 68.

47. Island Resources Foundation, "Water Island Study: Report and Fiscal Analysis," p. 7; *Daily News* (St. Thomas, V.I.), June 21, 1972, p. 1.

48. Island Resources Foundation, "Water Island Study: Report and Fiscal Analysis," pp. 8, 9; *Daily News* (St. Thomas, V.I.), March 15, 1973, p. 1; June 20, 1972, p. 1; *Home Journal* (St. Thomas, V.I.), June 20, 1972, p. 1.

49. Jenny Kane, "Mandahl Bay development plans are back, bigger," *Daily News* (St. Thomas, V.I.), November 7, 2014, pp. 6–7.

50. Mandahl Bay Holdings advertisement, *Daily News* (St. Thomas, V.I.), November 12, 2014, p. 35; November 17, 2014, p. 27.

51. George H. T. Dudley, Opinion—"The Case for developments like Port of Mandahl," *Daily News* (St. Thomas, V.I.), March 23, p. 23; Gwen-Marie Moolenaar, Opinion—"Yes, V.I. needs a job, economy boost; no, we don't need enviro-destruction to get there," *Daily News*, Ibid., March 24, 2015, p. 18; David Silverman, Opinion—"A rebuttal to the statistics and argument cited by Mandahl Bay developer's attorney," *Daily News*, Ibid., March 26, 2015, p. 23; George Dudley, Opinion—"Attorney's reply to development critics: New resorts address needs of V.I. economy," *Daily News*, Ibid., April 10, 2015, p. 23; William J. Demetree, "Opinion—Mandahl Bay resort was a good idea for economy," *Daily News*, Ibid., April 13, 2015; David Silverman, "Opinion—V.I. economy can thrive with smaller development," *Daily News*, Ibid., April 13, 2015, 2016, p. 22.

52. Aldeth Lewin, "Senators, developers, preservationists meet at Mandahl," *Daily News* (St. Thomas, V.I.), February 11, 2015, pp. 1, 2, 3.

53. Aldeth Lewin, "Mandahl lease extension expired with 30th Legislature," *Daily News* (St. Thomas, V.I.), February 11, 2016, p. 3.

54. Suzanne Carlson, "Bowry: Economic Growth only salvation for V.I.," *Daily News* (St. Thomas, V.I.), June 7, 2016, p. 2; Joy Blackburn, "GERS at Risk-Who's to Blame?", Ibid., March 9, 2017, Special Supplement; Jonathan Austin, "Analysis: USVI poised for a financial collapse," Ibid., January 25, 2017, p. 3.

Chapter 19

Race Relations in Education, 1967–2017

Race relations in education, while quite controversial at times in St. Thomas during the second half of its first American century, on the whole were not as conflict-laden as educational developments on the U.S. mainland. That was because some American practices, such as racial segregation in the American South from kindergarten through higher education, did not exist in the Virgin Islands. However, some local issues such as white domination of the economy, along with educational developments such as a substantial importation of white continental teachers and the appearance of de facto-like segregation at some private institutions, resulted in youth resentment and actions that became key factors in influencing the evolution of race relations in St. Thomas during the last half-century.

Non-Public Schools

Non-public or private education has had a long history in St. Thomas. Concerns related to social class and to the quality of education had always led a sizeable number of residents who could afford it to send their children to private or parochial schools. A 1976 study by Dr. Charles Turnbull, a St. Thomas historian-educator who later served as the V.I. governor from 1999 to 2007, found that the percentage of students in St. Thomas who attended non-public schools in the decade from 1960 through 1970 hardly differed from the percentage who had done so in the decade from 1920 through 1930. The 1920s figure was 28.4%; in the 1960s it was 29.1%.[1]

Therefore, with a traditional enrollment of almost one-third of all children on the island, non-public schools had always existed in substantial abundance. The Catholic school—Sts. Peter & Paul, adjacent to the Church—had a long history and by 1950 had both elementary and secondary divisions. By 1950, there were also at least three other private elementary schools which had been in existence for several years—the Goodwill (or Oliver) School in the Upstreet (Goat Street) area, Mrs. Millin's Private School in Savan, and the Boynes' Private School in Garden Street.[2] Additionally, in 1950 another parochial school opened—the Episcopal Church's All Saints Parish School, adjacent to the Church on Garden Street; it would eventually be extended to the twelfth grade. During the 1950s also the Lutheran and Seventh Day Adventist congregations opened schools, and were joined by the Moravians in the 1960s. In 1950 a nonsectarian Antilles School had also opened, and so in the 1960s did a Montessori School.[3] In addition to these, which were well-recognized institutions, there were some smaller private schools, a couple of them even in private homes. Indeed, the fact that alien-status children were not admitted to public schools until after the District Court ruling of 1970, made private school attendance a necessity during the 1950s and 60s for those children whose parents could at all afford it in any way.

However, what came to be a very much resented symbol of de facto racial segregation in St. Thomas from its founding in 1950, and for a few decades after, was the Antilles School. A private institution, it was founded through the efforts of Howard Jackson, an industrialist and financier from Tennessee, who had recently moved to St. Thomas. Most elementary teachers in St. Thomas at that time were Blacks without college degrees, and it was felt that persons moving down from the mainland would be interested in an institution which offered an education for their children by college-trained teachers. The announcement of the Antilles School in 1950 read:

> The School has been organized to meet the demand for a Private School, which, through limited enrollment, can offer the highest academic standards and constructive cultural activities. The School is a membership, non-profit-making organization whose entire income must be devoted to maintenance and improvement of its educational facilities.[4]

Antilles School began with thirteen pupils. Its location was at Villa Santana, a historic site overlooking Charlotte Amalie, which had been the home of the Mexican dictator, Santa Anna (hence its name), during a period of exile he spent in St. Thomas in the mid-nineteenth century. Its initial program provided for children from the age of four through the eighth grade.[5]

By the beginning of its sixth year of operation, in 1955, it had outgrown its original site and moved to Estate Poinciana in the Havensight District, overlooking the entrance of the St. Thomas Harbor. By 1959 the school had 110 students and its program had been extended to the tenth grade; by 1964 there were 204 students. In September 1966, a senior class was added; the school thus had a complete program and graduated its first twelfth grade class in 1967. In 1971, the school moved to a new campus at Frenchman's Bay, a 26-acre site which had been donated by a continental resident of St. Thomas.[6]

What made Antilles School different, therefore, was not the fact of its being private, as there were already several such schools on St. Thomas. However, it was almost in a class by itself because of the composition of its enrollment due to its cost. Its tuition was much higher than that of any of the other non-public institutions, so high that only persons with incomes well in excess of "good salaries" could even consider sending their children there. It soon became regarded as "the white school" because, except for very few black students and one, at times two, black faculty members, it was a white institution. As no locally available pool of college-trained teachers existed, early newspaper announcements told of the arrival of its faculty members from various parts of the mainland, even from as far away as Alaska. Its student roster in the late 1950s read a lot like a list of the most prominent or well-off white continental families of St. Thomas, including the children of novelist Herman Wouk, along with representatives from the Old Whites and a few representatives from leading black families—native and continental. Its enrollment would not have been representative of the population even if it had been located on the mainland, because the black students constituted fewer than ten per cent of its enrollment.[7]

Similar to Antilles, the faculties of several of the parochial schools—the Catholic, the Episcopal, and the Lutheran—tended to be mainly white continental. However, the student enrollments of the other private and parochial schools were much more representative of the island's population than that of Antilles. Some of the least expensive schools had a smaller white percentage than that of the island's population, while a more expensive or well-reputed one—such as the Episcopal All Saints School—generally had an enrollment whose white population at times exceeded that of the island's population. None of the others, however, presented quite the image of elitism and racial separation that Antilles presented during its early decades. But, with the increasing influx of white Continentals, many of whom patronized "the white school" to the exclusion of others, and some of the older private schools eventually closing, the Antilles School, Inc. continued to grow. By the early Sixties it had become the third largest non-public school on St. Thomas, with an enrollment at the end of the 1961–1962 school year of approximately 140, as compared to 230 for All Saints School (Episcopal) and 700 for Sts. Peter and Paul (Catholic).[8]

Many black St. Thomians had looked with critical interest as the Antilles School grew during with Fifties with very little change in its racial composition. In May 1959, Albert Keep, its new headmaster, announced that he had spoken with the Commissioner of Education about the possibility of Antilles pupils using the public schools' athletic fields as Antilles had no such facilities. He said Antilles wanted to develop athletic teams, which would challenge other schools once they got good enough, for "what better way for the children to get to know each other?"[9]

There was objection to the headmaster's request. Some Blacks felt that it was bad enough that a white school had been established in a mainly black community; for it to solicit the use of the facilities of the public schools was considered brazen effrontery![10] Various other occasions brought out the fact that many Blacks greatly resented the racial composition of the Antilles School. Thus, in September 1959, Antilles announced a scholarship program. The school's founders, Mr. and Mrs. Howard Jackson, whose children, of course, were students, donated $20,000 toward the scholarship fund drive "to help make available to Island children of superior intelligence" the educational resources of the Antilles School. V.I. Commissioner of Education Dr. Andrew Preston, a white Continental, announced his support of the Antilles campaign to provide at least three scholarships yearly to local children and said, "it surely reveals the desire of the school to become more closely identified with the community." Interestingly, Dr. Preston additionally stated: "the school [Antilles] also contributes to the economy of St. Thomas by eliminating a problem facing potential visitors who want to bring their children with them during the school term." The V.I. Commissioner of Education was thus voicing his perception that the "potential visitors" [white Continentals?] would not want to place their children into the public school system which he had been employed to supervise and improve.[11]

The isolation of the Antilles School from the rest of the St. Thomas community was a matter of concern not only to Blacks, but to some Whites who realized the overall effects the development of such institutions could have. Jeffrey Farrow, a white Continental who came to St. Thomas at the age of nine but whose socialization was "atypical" due to the extensive contacts he had with Blacks on the island, was concerned about the aloofness of Antilles while he was in attendance there in the early 1960s. As president of the Antilles Student Council, he remembered meeting with student council presidents of other schools to organize a football league and thinking how much such activities were needed.[12] Allen Grammer, a white Continental who was the publisher and editor of the *Virgin Islands View*, was a known critic of the school. In July 1967, his magazine commented; "Antilles School, St. Thomas' most expensive non-public school…, graduated its first 12th grade class, five boys and two girls, all continentals."[13]

Another concern about the Antilles School, after it had decided to increase its black enrollment by the scholarship program, was its practice of going after the most outstanding black students in the public schools. To many black St. Thomians, it was aiming at nothing less than "taking the cream of the crop," as Attorney General Verne Hodge referred to the practice in a speech in November 1973.[14] In his address at the Antilles Commencement of 1962, Dr. Alonzo Moron had warned precisely against that. He stated that some had advanced the idea of:

> … using the Antilles School as a sort of finishing school or college preparatory school for the brightest students in the public schools.
>
> I can think of nothing that would serve more effectively to increase the social and economic distance which affects adversely the present standing of your school in the community. But even more significant in terms of the number of students affected would be the denigration of the public schools which such a procedure would dramatize.[15]

In that belief, some black families who were offered the opportunity to have their children compete for an Antilles scholarship turned down the offer. However, as time went by, Antilles was able to build its scholarship program, and by the 1971–1972 school year, there were twenty-three students who had scholarships which totaled $18,402.[16]

What were the experiences of some of the black students who attended Antilles? Charlene O'Neal Henderson was one of the earliest students and spent about a decade there. The daughter of a St. Thomas physician, Dr. Eric O'Neal, she enrolled in the early 1950s as a preschooler and left in the early 1960s after the eighth grade because she was not comfortable. She remembers some of the teachers and students as having been very nice, but there were also others who appeared as distinctly prejudiced. She realized that as they got older, from about the fifth grade on, a Black was invited to birthday parties and other social occasions less and less. The Antilles School was the only place where she has ever been called "nigger" (it was done by a white student)![17]

Jasmine Gunthorpe entered Antilles on scholarship in 1968, a brilliant black student who was "skimmed" after completing the seventh grade at the public Wayne Aspinall Junior High School (now named Addelita Cancryn).

She remembers that her great-aunt, Mrs. Eulalie Petersen who was a public elementary school principal, was very much opposed to her acceptance of the scholarship and argued that good students should remain in the public schools and could get a good education there. Her parents ended up deciding that Antilles would be a good challenge for her and tried to prepare her for any problems that might occur. She therefore did not enter with the expectation of being comfortable, which she was not for the first year or two; she simply expected to do the work. However, after the first couple years, she became involved in sports, which brought about a more complete relationship with other students and she felt totally accepted and comfortable by her senior year.

Jasmine Gunthorpe did have some experiences similar to those which young Charlene O'Neal had had some years earlier. One day when she was walking past the kindergarten classroom, one of the little boys said, "Oh, look at that black nigger!" In another negative experience of the early years, she unexpectedly received a report card grade of "F" in a math class, a first and shocking experience for her, even though her test grades had been good. In the consequent conference with the headmaster, the teacher and her parents, the teacher admitted that her test grades had been ignored. Her report card grade had been based on her oral participation in the class, and he had been unable to understand her because of her island accent! Her grade was changed and the teacher later departed before the end of the school year. Jasmine Gunthorpe eventually graduated as the valedictorian of the Antilles Class of 1973.[18]

Miss Gunthorpe had two main thoughts concerning attendance of Blacks at Antilles School. She thinks the academic program was good, but does not believe it was without peer in St. Thomas, as some have said or implied. She believes that other institutions had been comparable, some at their particular stages of offerings, and she referred to at least one other competing institution that she thought offered an education equal to that of Antilles. The other thought she had has been expressed by a number of persons: that attendance at Antilles cut off black students socially from the majority of their racial peers on the island. This was true to some degree of all the non-public high schools, but it was a much greater isolation for those who attended Antilles, as a large percentage of the students who attended Antilles have traditionally not returned to St. Thomas after college, so those who do have very few high school friends with whom to associate. Miss Gunthorpe thought it important that children have many local contacts in school, especially at the primary levels.[19]

In 1968, at a conference held on St. Thomas by the College of the Virgin Islands on political and other problems of development in the Virgin Islands,

Philip Gerard of St. Croix, then Vice Chairman of the V.I. Board of Education, presented a paper in which he asked:

> What are the implications for the future of the fact that the Virgin Islands boasts two school systems, one which is private with high achievement and a student population that is largely white and another which is public with low achievement and a student population that is largely black?[20]

The same concern was addressed by Governor Evans when he declared in November 1973 that as a result of self-segregation, the Virgin Islands had as segregated a school system as perhaps existed in the South at any time.[21] The exaggeration aside, the problem was extremely serious, more so because it reflected a synthesis of racial and class prerogatives. For in addition to Whites, many of the children of black leaders in the V.I. also attended non-public schools, including a sizeable percentage of the children of public school administrators and teachers. In 1970 Raymond Moorhead, the president of the St. Croix Teachers Federation, found it necessary to request legislators who were on the governing boards of private schools which their children attended to disqualify themselves from voting on a bill which would have granted government aid to non-public schools. Morehead declared: "All of our government leaders send their kids to private schools.... It is no coincidence that we have a double system here ..."[22]

However, by the 1960s the private non-parochial elementary schools (Boynes, Millin, and Oliver) had all closed, and the growing economy of that decade enabled more parents to afford to educate their children privately. A second non-parochial private school was opened on St. Thomas in 1964—the Montessori School in the Vessup Bay area of eastern St. Thomas. Its early history was quite similar to Antilles', but at least parents were able to state that their interest was in the special progressive methods of the Italian educator whose name the school bears, and which were being popularized worldwide. Also added to the private school count during the last few decades have been a number of parochial elementary schools, many affiliated with Fundamentalist Christian churches, such as the Calvary, Zion Assembly, and Wesleyan Academies in Contant; and the Church of God and New Testament Academies in the Tutu area.

In 2009 the Montessori School added a full high school, the Peter Gruber International Academy, named in honor of an international philanthropist who was its benefactor. The Academy touted that, in addition to the demands of a regular high school diploma, its graduates would have to complete a rigorous academic, cultural and linguistic course of study aimed at providing them with the global skills of a prestigious International Baccalaureate program.[23]

During the last years of the twentieth century and the early years of the twenty-first, several factors led some parents who could afford their tuitions, along with some who received strategic offers of scholarships, to choose the Antilles and Montessori Schools over All Saints and Sts. Peter and Paul, which had been their main rivals. One great public relations factor was that the Antilles School teams, based on vigorous efforts, started doing very well on the various math, science, and general knowledge high school quiz bowls that had become very popular in the Virgin Islands; they were generally broadcasted on radio or TV. When the quiz bowls had first started in the 1970s and 80s, they had often been won by the Charlotte Amalie High School or All Saints, but that did not remain the norm.[24] Another factor was that Antilles worked hard also at developing a good sports program, something that had not been typical of private schools on St. Thomas. In fact, its sports program now not only includes the traditional sports, but also a sailing team which seems to go almost anywhere in the world to compete, and is ranked as one of the best in the U.S. Wealth is obviously a great factor in the Antilles' sailing team's existence.[25] Thirdly, the two major parochial schools, located in older residential areas of St. Thomas, did not have the extensive campuses of the private ones and, unfortunately, the Garden Street area near to All Saints developed a reputation for drug dealing and other crimes, thus scaring some parents into withdrawing their children, but both the neighborhood and school are working on rebounding.

By the Centennial decade, therefore, Antilles and Montessori had student populations that were quite mixed racially, and their enrollments had grown to surpass the parochial schools. At the end of the 2015–16 school year, Antilles' enrollment was 472. Antilles reports that their students are not recorded by race, but by origin, based on which, 40% of their students were of U.S. continental origin, while the remaining 60% were a combination of "local and international" origin. However, faculty members were mainly Caucasian, with 40% having taught at Antilles for over five years and 10% for more than 30 years.[26]

The numbers of the 12th grade graduating classes of 2016 illustrated the new order: Antilles had 35 graduates; the Montessori School and Peter Gruber International Academy had 17; All Saints had 14; Sts. Peter and Paul had 12; and the St. Thomas-St. John Seventh Day Adventist School had 10. Both the valedictorian and salutatorian of Antilles, Amanda Engeman and Paige Clark, respectively, were white, and one of the members of the class was the son of former Governor John de Jongh. Montessori's valedictorian, Marcus Norkaitis, was white, and its sal, Naren Advani, was Indian. All Saint's valedictorian, Sidharth Parwani, and its sal, Yash Bajaj, were both Indians. Sts. Peter and Paul's val and sal, Camille Emanuel and Promise Walker, respectively, were black. The val of the Seventh Day Adventist School, Kenique Liburd, and the sal, Jair Smith, were also both black.

To illustrate contrast with the two public high schools of St. Thomas, the Charlotte Amalie High School Class of 2016 had 243 graduates, while the Ivanna Eudora Kean High School, in the eastern Red Hook area of St. Thomas, graduated 188. The racial composition of both schools was overwhelmingly black, but they also had Arab, Dominican, Haitian, and Indian students. The CAHS val was Asel Mustafa, an Arab, while its sal, Kera Smith, was black. The val and sal of Kean, Micaiah Bully and Sherkquan Henry, respectively, were both black. The schools of St. Thomas, both the private and the public, attest to the variety of racial and ethnic mixtures that comprise the island's Centennial population.[27]

The Public School System

The most striking development in the public school system of the V.I., during the last half-century of U.S. rule, was its tremendous growth which during the early decades was so rapid and intense that it was actually overwhelming. The two most imposing facets of that growth were those of student enrollment and the consequent necessity for a larger teaching force. Considerable growth took place in the late 60s and was greatly magnified after 1970, when the U.S. District Court of the V.I. ruled that alien-status children legally resident in the V.I. could not be denied entrance to the public schools. Consequently, between 1965 and 1975, public school enrollment in St. Thomas rocketed form 5,717 to 11,543! While the 1970s on the mainland were marked by declining school enrollment, the situation in the V.I. was exactly the opposite.[28]

It was the concomitant growth of the teaching staff that has special relevance to this study. The number of public school teachers in St. Thomas went from 114 in 1955 to 625 in 1975! However, the sources of the student and the faculty growth were from two different directions. Student-wise, the great increase resulted from the public school attendance of children of non-citizen black West Indians. Thus, by May 1974, non-citizen children amounted to 27.7% of the total public school enrollment in St. Thomas. New teachers, on the other hand, were recruited mainly from the U.S. mainland. The V.I. public school teaching staff thus went from being about ten per cent continental in 1960 to about fifty per cent in 1970, with the great majority of the Continentals being white.[29]

The major reason for the importation of so many mainlanders was based on the adoption by the V.I. Department of Education, in 1962, of a college degree requirement as the minimum educational requirement for certified class-room teachers. Ever since the American assumption of the islands in 1917, there had been the importation of some mainland teachers due to the lack of opportunity for higher education locally and the resulting deficiency of local persons with such training. For the first four decades the practice had been to use persons with college training on the secondary level and to restrict non-college trained teachers to the elementary level. By 1955, therefore, the great majority of the teachers at the Charlotte Amalie High School in St. Thomas had college degrees, while the great majority at the elementary schools did not (though a number had varying amounts of college credits). However, the Department of Education's Annual Report of 1961–62 stated: "While some of the best teachers in the system are non-degreed teachers, the times demand that no less than a college degree will be the minimum requirement for all new teachers," and certification requirements to that effect were published. The report further stated that until the College of the Virgin Islands (which had just been legislated into being that year) could start supplying teachers, "It will be absolutely necessary to draw upon the mainland for our teaching staff."[30]

In retrospect, it appears amazing that such a profound decision, with such wholesale applicability, was made at a time when the islands did not even have a functioning college. One wonders if the major educational policymakers had been Virgin Islanders, whether such a consequential policy would have been initiated so cavalierly. However, as was frequently the case in the islands, they were not Virgin Islanders. The Commissioner of Education, Dr. Pedro Sanchez, a Guamanian, and a New York University Survey Team, which studied the V.I. public elementary system at the request of the Commissioner, both thought that the wholesale importation of trained teachers was the best solution, as did also many Virgin Islanders at the time. Even though the New York University Survey reported that the turnover rate of elementary continental teachers was five times greater than that of native teachers and that the continental teachers were less experienced than the natives, the better training of the continental teachers was apparently considered the most important factor. So, in 1965, when the Legislature passed a bill aimed at establishing a special program for the rapid training of Virgin Islanders to teach, it was vetoed by Governor Paiewonsky, whose action was solidly backed by the St. Thomas Teacher's Association. The *Daily News* editorialized that it was better to have standardly trained teachers than a special program to train teachers quickly.[31]

From 1962, therefore, a massive program of mainland recruitment started (even though utter necessity at times occasioned the hiring of a limited number of local non-degreed persons on the elementary level). For the 1962–63 school year, 121 new teachers were recruited; 105 were from the mainland. For the 1963–64 school year, the V.I. Department of Education was even aided by the U.S. Department of Defense by having access to the files of hundreds of already-screened teachers who had applied to Defense for overseas positions. The result was that by the late 1960s, the largely-black public school system had a teaching staff which was considerably white (usually forty to fifty per cent) and new to the islands and to the culture of most of their pupils. A couple of the new public schools on St. Thomas had mainly white faculties. At times, the faculty of the Charlotte Amalie High School, the oldest and largest secondary school on St. Thomas, was about equally divided between Whites and Blacks, and some departments, such as the social studies, were at times predominantly white.[32]

The ramifications of such racial configurations were considerable and some islanders came to question the recruiting policies of the Department of Education. From 1966 on, the recruiting was done by Mrs. Rita Martin, a black Virgin Islander and the Department's Director of Personnel Services. Mrs. Martin visited many colleges and employment agencies on the mainland each year. The Department's Annual Report for 1967–68, for example, stated that fifteen mainland colleges had been visited, nine of which were historically black campuses in the South. Mrs. Martin found that even though she spent more time at black colleges than white, the response from the mainly white institutions was much greater. Of course, an appreciable number of Virgin Islanders did not like black mainland teachers any more than white. In fact, some preferred the Whites, as a number of people—black and white—came to think that black continental teachers were teaching black consciousness and held them responsible for some of the increasing racism among young Blacks in the late 1960s and the 1970s.[33] However, there were also persons who pointed out that black consciousness was not necessarily promotive of black racism; a lot depended on how individuals chose to use their knowledge.

Educationally, the most significant questions were: (1) what was the relationship between the large body of continental teachers and their young island students, and (2) what was the educational impact they had on those students. There was a substantial amount of popularly-expressed opinions in St. Thomas that the wholesale importation of continental teachers contributed significantly to the decline in standards of discipline and of academic achievement which the public school system was thought to have experienced during the Sixties and Seventies. The popular feeling was that most white teachers could not realistically have been expected to have had the genuine interest in the achievement of black students that most black teachers would have. Unfortunately, there has been very little professional research on those issues. Lay research done for this study revealed varied opinions and also some points of underlying consensus from a sampling of native or long-term educators who were administrators and teachers. They felt that the majority of white teachers taught well and showed commendable interest in their students. A few even pointed out that some white teachers engaged in extracurricular activities with their students more than native teachers because they were less tied down with family and community activities than were the natives.[34]

In spite of those overall opinions, there was nevertheless also an expression from several of the educators that the massive outside recruitment policy had "ill effects" for the islands. Its "timeliness" in relation to the higher education capability of the V.I. at that time was viewed as having been severely misguided. There were expressions that the policy should have made provision for also recruiting good local high school graduates for elementary positions and aiding them in acquiring college training.

Some of the misgivings about the results of the mainland recruitment policy stemmed from the educational malfunctioning and disruptions the public school system experienced, especially in the late Sixties and the early Seventies, because of the performance of some of the continental teachers. Almost everyone admitted that there were those who performed miserably which, of course, applied across the board as there were also native teachers who proved to be great disappointments. But there was substantial agreement that there was a higher percentage of continental teachers who did not act in a dedicated manner; some appeared to have come to the islands mainly to enjoy the beaches and other aspects of the tropical environment. Along with poor classroom performance, there was an appreciable number of continental teachers who departed the islands (sometimes without notice or even bothering to resign) during the first school year. The Director of Personnel stated frankly that in the early 1970s the need for teachers was always so great that the Department of Education could not afford to be selective; there were always classroom vacancies as some teachers would only stay a month or two before leaving. The Annual Report for 1971–72 noted that three of the four music teachers at the Aspinall Junior High had resigned during the second semester and music activities simply had to be curtailed. However, there was also agreement among the administrators and teachers interviewed that most of the continental teachers who had remained in the system after the early Seventies functioned in a more dedicated and stable manner than had been the case in former years. In a 1974 newspaper photograph, for example, of eleven persons who were "Teachers of the Year" in St. Thomas, eight were continentals, five of whom were white.[35]

In response to criticisms, continental teachers explained that the conditions they found were often quite different to what they had expected. The high housing and food costs of the V.I. seemed astronomical compared to their salaries. In fact, cognizance of this problem had caused the Department of Education to resort to the expedient, in 1962, of leasing an old hotel and boarding thirty continental teachers there at what were considered very reasonable rates. Even that was not completely successful. Two of the teachers said they could not afford the rates, and broke their contract and returned to the mainland even before the school year started.[36]

Moreover, in the V.I., some cultural differences between black public school students and white continental teachers were even greater than such differences were on the mainland, in speech especially. There was substantial public discussion on St. Thomas about the effects on children of being taught by persons who often could not even understand them for the first several weeks. There were teachers and other observers who noticed that some children were afraid to ask questions or recite in class for fear they might not be understood by the teacher. And some teachers were in a genuine state of confusion regarding whether they should have allowed their students to use the local Creole speech in the classroom or if they should have insisted on standard English. During the early Seventies, a College of the Virgin Islands professor, Dr. Lezmore Emanuel, and a few other academics publicly promoted the use of Creole as a classroom tool for teaching standard English. However, such a plan could only be utilized by teachers who possessed facility in both forms of speech, and it was also never clear what the official policy of the Department of Education was on the matter. One of the teachers interviewed said she had used Creole very successfully in her classes, but never included it in her lesson plan as most administrators seemed to be against it.[37]

The most discomforting feeling some Blacks had about the presence of so many white teachers in the public school classrooms of the V.I. was the thought that, on the whole, they could serve to retard or even reverse black progress in the islands. Third World societies, of which the V.I. was one by many socioeconomic characteristics, regardless of its association with the United States, have traditionally hoped for education to play a key role in transformation of the societies. In the Virgin Islands, conceived of as a traditionally black society, many Blacks hoped for a future where Blacks would increasingly possess the attitudes and skills to perform many of the higher functions and services which Whites had traditionally been imported to perform. With a large white teaching staff, some Blacks sadly expressed the opinion, usually in small private groups, that any such goal was becoming more and more unlikely as they thought Whites simply were not going to train Blacks to take over a white-run society. The thought, though difficult to document, is supported by the fact that scholars have more and more realized the importance of group power and group position in maintaining and reinforcing racism, regardless of the overt actions of individual persons. The economic status quo in the V.I. was definitely racist in that Whites held the economic power that was often exercised in ways oppressive to Blacks. However, since many Whites experienced difficulty in even recognizing that, to expect any sizeable portion of them to be interested in altering the pattern did not seem likely. Thus, many Blacks who were concerned about education and the future of the islands feared that many white continental teachers would think of the status quo as perfectly normal (as it was simply an extension of that on the mainland) and program their students, however subconsciously, to function only in the traditional black roles.[38]

In many ways, the criticisms and bad reputations which continental (especially white) teachers suffered collectively were very unfair. They were a group of people who often had been recruited personally and who had been practically begged to come to the V.I. despite the general knowledge that they were of a different race and cultural background from most of the children they would teach. Then after arriving, they were thought inadequate for not being able to communicate fully with the children and for not understanding the new culture, even though there was generally not much in the way of orientation sessions or literature which might have been helpful in easing their transition. Supportive sources of a material nature (help in finding housing and in receiving initial paychecks within a reasonable period) also left much to be desired. Some of the criticisms undoubtedly stemmed from the fact that continental workers were a highly visible group in an overall politico-socio-economic system which was causing more and more people, by the late 1960s and the 1970s, to wonder in whose interest that system was really functioning.

An interesting issue demonstrated how long it often took for deserving matters to get attention. In 1960 the Legislature established the Edward Wilmot Blyden Scholarship program, which granted a $4,000 college scholarship each year to a V.I. high school graduate. The scholarship was named in honor of the noted African scholar who had been born in St. Thomas in 1832, and later became known as the "Father of Pan-Africanism." The scholarship winner was selected by competitive examination—the highest scorer on the Scholastic Aptitude Test among the valedictorians and salutatorians of the graduating classes of all the high schools, public and non-public, in the Virgin Islands. During the first eight years of the awarding of the scholarship, 1961–1968, five of the recipients were white. Seven of the eight awardees had been non-public school students; the only public school student to win it was one of the five Whites. Most of the white winners had migrated to the V.I. only a few years prior to their recipiency of the scholarship and thus could not be thought of as true products of V.I. schools—public or non-public.[39]

In May 1969, when the ninth Blyden award was announced, it went to a white, non-public school student, who had been on St. Thomas for only three years. A black St. Thomian who was a history instructor at CVI, Marilyn Krigger (this author), wrote to the press that the matter was one with which the public should be concerned as Dr. Blyden, in his life and writings, had stressed "the themes of pride in the achievement and promise of the Negro race." She contended that the history of the program "robbed the scholarship of its significance and the encouragement that it should be to youths of these islands." She then proposed that one of two steps be taken for the future:

> (1) Because of what Dr. Blyden's life symbolizes there should be a stipulation that recipients of the scholarship be Virgin Islanders of African descent; or (2) if it is thought best to maintain the present method of choosing recipients solely on the basis of competitive examinations, which pit Virgin Islands students against products of other and maybe better school systems, then Dr. Blyden's name should be detached completely from the scholarship, and a more meaningful way be found to honor this great Virgin Islander.[40]

No public school official reacted publicly to the issue. Even though there were substantial concerns among many Blacks about the unforeseen results of the scholarship program, there were those who believed that the Virgin Islands should maintain a stance of official non-recognition of the matter of race and do nothing, regardless of the consequences. The *Daily News* acted as a leader of those so minded. An editorial totally disagreed with the suggestion that a change was needed in the administration of the Blyden awards and stated, "we hope that no rules changes will be made in the years to come."[41]

Mrs. Krigger wrote again to the *Daily News* and suggested the alternative of a substantial residential requirement as an additional basis for the award, iterating that some type of change was definitely needed.[42] Lloyd L. Williams, a young black St. Thomian, wrote of the "signs of shortsightedness" which the scholarship issue had revealed and lamented the tendency of some to ignore the racial aspects of such problems and their ability to polarize the community.[43]

Ironically, less than two months after the latest (1969) award had served to highlight the workings of the Blyden scholarship program, the father of the 1969 awardee resigned his three-year pastorship of the Frederick Lutheran Church in St. Thomas in what was partially a racial controversy. Pastor William Hartman said he had decided to resign after hearing a member of his church council say, "I know how to handle white men." On the other hand, James O'Bryan, a black Virgin Islander who was vice president of the parish, countered that Reverend Hartman had been unable to get along with various church committees and noted: "He is from Georgia, was educated there, and all his parishes have been in the deep South."[44]

On knowledge of the resignation of the Blyden awardee's father and the announced intention of the family to leave St. Thomas shortly, Marva Samuel Applewhite, a black Virgin Islander, asked publicly:

> ... have you ever stopped to consider that the recipient of the $4,000 scholarship may never return to these islands as indicated by her father's statement.... I suggest that since the scholarship is named in honor of Mr. Wilmot Blyden, we should specify that the recipient must be a student who plans to come back and be of service to this community—not a transient.[45]

The winner of the next year's Blyden scholarship was again a white continental student from a private school in St. Croix. Then again the following year (1971) it was won by a white continental student—from the private Antilles School on St. Thomas. At the same time of that announcement, the V.I. Board of Education, which administered the award, finally announced that it had recommended to the Legislature revisions of the scholarship's requirements to include such additional factors as length of attendance in schools in the V.I., ties to the community and the likelihood of an applicant's return to the V.I., and financial need. But yet another white Continental received the award in 1972, the third year after it had become a matter of public controversy. By 1973, finally, the recommended changes had been legislated and placed into effect. The scholastic test score was used in combination with the other factors in the selection process, and the next few winners were black.[46] Interestingly, though, the winner of the Blyden scholarship in 1973, the first black winner in several years, was a student from St. Croix named Gerard Emanuel, and he had actually earned the highest score on the test! However, the fact that corrective action took so long on a matter that many Virgin Islanders considered grievously in need of amendment is illustrative of many processes in the V.I. which have caused black discontent and distrust of persons in positions of power and influence.

The unionization of public school teachers early in the last half century of American rule was also a matter which came to have racial perspectives. During the later 1960s, a teachers' union was formed in the V.I., affiliated with the American Federation of Teachers. A number of strong union actions in the years which followed were thought by some to have been unduly influenced by white continental teachers. The "dress code" issue of late 1975 was a good example. In September 1975, after a number of reported incidents of unbecoming school attire on the part of teachers, Governor Cyril E. King (a black

Virgin Islander who won the second gubernatorial election in 1974) requested all male teachers to wear ties and females to wear coordinated pants suits if they wore pants. Union officials urged teachers to ignore these dress requirements. A number of the most vocal teacher dissenters were white Continentals and when twenty teachers were suspended for violating the requirements, thirteen of the twenty were Continentals. Some members of the public expressed the opinion that the dissenting teachers were "rebellious to this society" and had a "public be damned attitude."[47] An editorial on the matter thought the administration's dress codes were unrealistic, but also criticized the dress of many teachers:

> A casual walk past almost any of our public schools will show that great many of their teachers are dressed more for play than for teaching. Skimpiness of many of the females' attire goes far beyond what may be required for comfort in a tropical climate.... We can hardly expect Eton or Cambridge style dress for teachers in a climate such as this, but we can expect them to dress as if they came to teach and not to orgy. The teachers and their union would improve their image with the community, and most important of all with the students ..."[48]

That continental teachers were considered the greatest offenders is clear from the editorial, and the sentiment was shared by much of the community. In this, as in other union issues, many came to fear that, even though the local leadership of the union was in black hands, white Continentals were the real force in the union. Glen Smith, a black Virgin Islander who was a member of the executive committee of the union at the time of the 1975 dress controversy, denies that the union was directed mainly by Whites, although union officials had realized there was public opinion to that effect. He explained that in some matters like the dress issue, Whites often had had more experience with unions and were more willing to stand up for their rights than were natives.[49] The general feeling of some in the community, however, was that not only in the classroom but also in some other areas, such as union activities, Whites exercised disproportionate influence in determining the educational direction of the islands.

In a 1980s book on Hawaii, the author asserted that the United States' educational system, of which Hawaii's is a part, is oriented toward middle-class Caucasians and the system neither trains Hawaiian students for a mainland vocation nor has relevance for life on the islands. He spoke of the generally poor performance of many Hawaiian school students, and said the public school system was actually accentuating the separation of Haoles (the Hawaiian term for white Continentals) and non-Haoles and indicted the V.I. public educational system for being an unimaginative carbon copy of mainland education without sufficient modification for relevancy to the V.I. milieu.[50] And at a time when the society was becoming more and more competitive, the educational system was actually functioning to make its graduates less competitive. V.I. educator Charles Turnbull found that the "system of public education generated negative consequences in the economic sector," as the percentage of graduates who were trained for jobs in commerce, business, trade, and industry declined during the latter decades of the twentieth century while the percentage of graduates who were not specifically trained for any vocation or profession increased.[51]

The public school system, in many ways, was both a victim of and a contributor to the new racial configurations and relations which had developed in St. Thomas by the second half-century of United States sovereignty. It contributed to a sizeable increase in the white population by the decision of its policymakers to rely to a large extent on an imported teaching staff. The system, however, became a victim of that same decision because its large continental staff was often cited as a factor which generated a number of problems.[52] Some of the young people who were in the system developed strong racial antipathies in response to what they viewed as the grossly disproportionate continental nature of the teaching personnel and instructional programs to which they were exposed. A number of young Blacks greatly resented the "whitewashing" which they thought was being perpetrated on them. Some seemed to have become dropouts after reaching the decision that their education was counterproductive as they were being programmed for failure or to succeed in only those areas in which Whites desired their success.[53] Research on the mainland had established that some young Blacks there become dropouts based on similar reasoning.[54]

The last years of the twentieth century and the first decade and a half of this century have brought about many changes. Mrs. Jeanette Smith Barry, the former Superintendent of Education for St. Thomas-St. John and, before that, the principal of the Charlotte Amalie High School, the largest on St. Thomas, and now recently retired, gives assurance that the teaching staffs of the public schools have stabilized greatly and there are no longer the great racial imbalances that had characterized the system during the latter decades of the last century. Mr. Stefan Jurgen, the immediate past principal of the Charlotte Amalie High School and presently the principal of the Ivanna Eudora Kean High School in eastern St. Thomas, provides a similar report, and so does Dr. Lois Hassel Habtes, the recently retired principal of the E. Benjamin Oliver Elementary School and, before that, of the Joseph Sibilly Elementary School. The student bodies of the public schools of St. Thomas also demonstrate a great deal of similarity, with their students being mainly black, along with small numbers of other racial or ethnic groups. Mr. Jurgen, of the Kean High School, provided the following racial breakdown of the Kean student body during the 2015–2016 academic year: 91% Black, 7.7% Hispanic, 0.7% White, and 0.1% Asian.[55]

Research had also raised the question of whether V.I. high school students are being prepared for the highly technological nature of many work places today. Mr. Jurgen began to answer that query with this statement: "It is very hard to find a blackboard at Kean today." He explained that most classrooms are computerized and have electronic smart boards, with students using interactive laptops and other electronic equipment. Dr. Hassel Habtes' additional wishes, based on her knowledge of educational developments elsewhere, are that music and the other arts should be utilized more in the teaching of other academic subjects, and that parents should be more regularly involved with their children's schools, as she experienced particularly during her principalship of the Sibilly School.[56]

It is always important to remember that, as a society grows, many of its demands for trained persons to fill professional and skilled-level positions will also be growing, and it is imperative to provide whatever resources are necessary for the cultivation of the minds, character, and overall well-being of the large numbers of students who are the responsibility of the public school system of any society. Some of any group's greatest minds and greatest achievers will always come from the public school systems and that should always be remembered and acted upon.

Research for this work led to the knowledge of some public school students who are equal to or better than many students of non-public institutions anywhere. One was Shinnola Alexander, whose mother, Martha Alexander (a single mother), was originally from Dominica; Shinnola was born in St. Thomas. Shinnola attended the Lockhart Elementary School and the Cancryn Junior High School, and was the valedictorian of her graduating classes at both institutions. As often happened, there was an attempt to get her to attend a private high school, which she resisted, stating that she wanted to continue in the public school system. And she did it again! Shinnola was the valedictorian of the Charlotte Amalie High School Class of 2009, a class of 287 graduates.

In preparing for college, Shinnola had been abundantly industrious and applied to 14 institutions, all of which granted her admission, including Harvard, Yale, Princeton, Brown, Dartmouth, and Stanford! She attended Yale on full scholarship, graduating in 2013 with a degree in political science. She then spent two years travelling in Europe and teaching English in Spain. In 2015 she started studying for her master's at the London School of Economics and Political Science. She recently completed her thesis on Environmental Policies and Regulations, and her degree was granted in December 2016. After a current internship in South Africa and additional travel in Germany and Italy, Shinnola plans to work with the United Nations World Food Bank in Rome. Without doubt, Shinnola Alexander ranks with the best of students, of any institution, anywhere![57]

The University of the Virgin Islands

The capstone of the educational system of the V.I. is the University of the Virgin Islands. UVI, as it is known, was created as the College of the Virgin Islands (CVI), a two-year institution, by action of the Legislature of the V.I. in 1962. It admitted its first students in July 1963 on its St. Thomas Campus, and a year later opened a second campus on the island of St. Croix, 40 miles away. As the only institution of higher education in the territory, CVI grew rapidly: by 1970 it was offering four-year baccalaureate degrees, and its first master's degrees by the late 1970s. In 1986, by virtue of its great growth in the number of baccalaureate and graduate degree programs and community and research services, the institution was renamed the University of the Virgin Islands. In 1986 also, UVI was also designated by the U.S. Congress as one of the nation's Historically Black Colleges and Universities (HBCU), a designation that allows such institutions to receive special federal funds. UVI is the only HBCU outside of the United States mainland.[58]

UVI was a source of controversy even before it came into existence. A poll in 1961 showed that eighty-five per cent of adult respondents and ninety-six per cent of students in the Virgin Islands favored its creation so that higher education would be available locally, becoming possible for many whose financial or family situations had prevented study on the mainland or in Puerto Rico. In the decade of the 1950s, prior to its opening, only about one-fifth of V.I. high school graduates went on to college. But there had been those, such as the vocal Continental Allen Grammer, who had been against a college, citing reasons such as the inbreeding it would cause and the poor quality of the existing public school system, which would be supplying most of its students. Grammer and other similar thinkers thought that the upgrading of the public school system and the establishment of a good trade school were more important priorities. Many thought that some of those who were opposed to a college were showing the same racist and class prejudices of those who had traditionally opposed any institutions which would be of special benefit to the masses. However, hopes for such an institution were kept alive, and would become a key agenda item for Governor Ralph Paiewonsky when he assumed office in 1961.[59]

After the enabling legislation for the College was enacted in March 1962, Governor Paiewonsky appointed a Board of Trustees for the new college. In October 1962, the Board announced its choice of Dr. Lawrence Wanlass from over forty applicants as the first President of the College of the Virgin Islands. Dr. Wanlass was a white political scientist, originally from Utah, and prior to his appointment to the CVI presidency, had been serving as Assistant to the President at Sacramento State College in California. The Board of Trustees cited his Fulbright professorship at the University of the Philippines in the mid-1950s, providing exposure to international and interracial living, as one of the factors in his selection.[60] Dr. Wanlass retained the presidency of CVI for sixteen years, from 1963 until 1979, and was very influential in determining the character and direction of the young institution.

By 1970, CVI had come to have two opposing images. For many of its students and certain portions of the community, it became a symbol of white racism because of its predominantly white administration and faculty. However, to a large number of other persons, CVI was seen in the late Sixties and the Seventies as a major hotbed of black power ideology, interpreted by some as black racism. CVI's faculty recruitment policies became a matter of controversy within a few years of the college's opening. Its policy was to attract "highly qualified" mainland professors and educational experts even if they were unable to stay for more than a year or two. New faculty members received air fare for themselves and their families plus a relocation allowance of up to one thousand dollars. In an audit released in June 1967, the federally appointed Comptroller of the V.I., Peter Bove, criticized the high costs involved in the employment of many faculty members who stayed only for an academic year of nine months. In addition to the financial cost, the Comptroller's report wondered if the frequent turnover could be "a healthy situation, if only because it may be difficult for staff and faculty members to become genuinely interested in the school and its students if their tenure is of such short duration."[61]

The recruitment policies of CVI led to a substantial majority of white Continentals on its faculty and professional staff. In 1967, of the thirty-nine persons who comprised the faculty and professional staff, only nineteen were black. In 1975, of a teaching faculty of sixty-four, only twenty-two were black. Additionally, persons who were employed from within the V.I.—black and white—were often compensated far below those brought from the mainland by being denied initially the monthly housing allowance, which was essential to placing the remuneration at a standard level.[62]

The student body at CVI, as would be expected, was quite the opposite of its faculty—it was overwhelmingly black. However, it also had, from the earliest years, an appreciable number of white students—some whose families were residents of the V.I. and a greater number who came directly from the mainland. In a 1970 newspaper article which featured a group of CVI white continental students, they admitted that their greatest challenge was the adjustment to being the racial minority, and it was thought to be a factor in the decision of some of those who dropped out of the institution. No statistics on the race of students were kept until 1976, when it became necessary for federal reporting and at a time when Whites were found to comprise about ten per cent of the student body, which probably was about the figure it had been in former years. In addition to local Blacks and Whites and continental Whites, CVI also attracted a substantial number of students directly from other West Indian islands—they were almost all black and by 1975 made up over twenty percent of the student population.[63]

Differences in the level of work and the maturity of the students place less emphasis on faculty-student interpersonal relations at the college than at the high school level. CVI, nevertheless, experienced some of the same problems of the public school system based on its mainly white faculty versus mainly black student body configurations. A 1966 article in the *Virgin Islands View* on CVI was concerned that "many teachers readily admit they cannot understand their students ... and one result appears to be a great reluctance on the part of students to speak out in class." Dr. Frank Mills, who was a member of CVI's third class (1967) and returned to join its faculty in 1974, remembers that some of the V.I. and British West Indian students had the feeling that the white students were treated with favoritism. It was believed by students from the various islands that they were sometimes judged culturally on academic matters. There were cases of students who were excellent readers being placed in remedial reading classes after oral testing—with their Creole speech having seemingly been the determiner of the result. And students in such cases felt there was no one they could protest to for a fair hearing, as the entire academic power structure—president, dean, tester, and most other faculty members—was white. Erva Denham Greer, a White who grew up in the V.I. and was a member of CVI's second two-year class in 1966, had not been aware at the time that black students had any specially-perceived problems with the white professors. She remembers, however, that there was self-imposed segregation of various groups—evident in the choice of separate tables in the dining room and at some other occasions. But, in spite of the varying perceptions and the segregationist tendencies, she thought race had not been an overriding issue during the first few years of CVI's history.[64]

After the middle 1960s, several factors combined to make racial concerns a dominant aspect of the CVI experience. On being approved as a four-year institution, but before it had the full capability of providing complete preparation for the bachelor's degree, CVI entered into an agreement with New York University, whereby certain CVI education students spent their junior year at that university. Several of the students who spent the 1966–67 and 1967–68 school years in New York were apparently shocked by the institutional racism they observed there and returned to CVI with very militant feelings that the white racism of the mainland should not be allowed to gain further ground in the V.I. Some showed their new racial consciousness very visibly on their return by wearing Afros, dashikis, calling each other "Brother," and using other Black Power symbols and slogans.[65]

At about the same time, in an attempt to construct a good basketball team, CVI offered athletic scholarships, several of which went to black students from the mainland. Some appeared to have brought a well-developed sensitivity to certain matters which black islanders might have overlooked or excused, and became known for their adept use of mainland Black Power rhetoric. They came to be perceived as among the leading campus agitators, and the athletic scholarship program was afterward canceled. The ostensible reasons for the ending of the program were that too large a number of the scholarships had gone to non-Virgin Islanders and that some of the imported athletes had gotten into trouble with the law.[66]

Kwame (formerly Juan) Garcia, who graduated from CVI in 1969 and was a student who had spent his junior year at New York University, advanced another reason for the great concerns about racial justice which came to characterize CVI in the late 1960s. He found that students from St. Croix, such as himself, who were in attendance at the St. Thomas campus of CVI, gained clearer realization than they had before of the extent of white economic control in the V.I. The concentration of white economic power on Main Street in St. Thomas was easily visible, while Garcia said that on St. Croix one had to go to the eastern end of the island to see such economic concentration and many people did not go there often.[67] Similar realization may have been attained by students from other West Indian islands.

Yet another reason for the noticeably increased racial consciousness among the students at CVI in the late 1960s was simply the more visible developments of some aspects of racism as the College developed. One notable area was in the Hotel and Restaurant Management Program. President Wanlass had worked to establish the program with the hope that it would develop along the lines of the well-known Cornell University program, and would help to provide managerial and supervisory personnel for the important and growing hotel industry in the Virgin Islands. Wanlass said he soon became aware, however, that many of the hoteliers in the V.I. did not think of CVI in terms of training top personnel, only lower level employees. George Goodwin, who received an Associate in Arts degree in 1968 in CVI's Hotel and Restaurant Management Program, revealed that he and some other black students in the program became convinced that it was not only the hotels that had that idea; their experience demonstrated to them that the white professor of the program at CVI felt similarly. Mr. Goodwin said that he and another Black, Otis Williams, were the two senior students in the program. Bypassing them, the professor took three white students who were behind them in the program and got positions for the three at the Virgin Isle Hilton Hotel. Additionally, the three Whites got room and board at the hotel, and thus actually lived there. When Goodwin confronted the professor with the unfairness of what he had done, Goodwin's grades—which had always been good before—plummeted. The Hotel and Restaurant Management Program was suspended in the mid-Seventies due to its inability to attract black students, who realized that the type of jobs the program should have led to would, in many cases, probably not have been available for them. As students became aware of such racism, both within and outside of the College, many felt that part of their obligation of becoming educated was to promote increased awareness of racism and encouragement in the struggle against it.[68]

As already stated, CVI students had been instrumental in organizing a large memorial march in St. Thomas in April 1968, on the day of Martin Luther King's funeral.[69] The next month, May 1968, saw the first public call for a change in the racial composition of the CVI faculty. A letter to the *Home Journal* from "A Virgin Islander at CVI" read in part:

> I'm not a racist but I doubt very seriously if you can find one predominantly white college with a faculty composed of 98 per cent Negro instructors.... We can only rely on our "soul brothers" and a few (3 to be exact) whites to give us a helping hand and let us talk to them but the vast majority of our teachers only care to give assignments, grade papers ...
>
> We so badly need to build a rapport between students and teacher.... We need this identification badly! The administration doesn't understand this or the why of it.[70]

The next day, May 22, 1968, the newspapers carried headlines of a student revolt at CVI and included pictures of students tearing down a fence which had been erected on the campus between the faculty housing and the student housing area. The students were engaged in a concerted drive for improved conditions at CVI. At a heated meeting on the night of May 21, chaired by Student Council President Raymond Joseph and at which President Wanlass was present, students, including white ones, spoke of the aloofness of the faculty, its gross racial imbalance, racism, and other problems at CVI. A petition was signed by 155 students asking for reforms in the areas of concern. It included a demand for the reinstatement of Registrar Gaylord Sprauve, a black Virgin Islander whose contract was not being renewed because of what was purported to be a private matter but what students felt was a racial matter, as the Registrar had been an outspoken critic of racism at CVI. In a speech at the meeting, the Registrar had said, "what we need to emphasize is a black power structure."[71]

Home Journal writer Roy Gottlieb made an extensive investigation and analysis of the turmoil at CVI, during which he met with student leaders Raymond Joseph, Otis Williams, Dana Orie, Roger Hill, Roland Roebuck, Valentine Penha, and others. He found that the criticism of CVI's lack of interest in acquiring black faculty was not limited to so-called "radicals" but was shared by many within and outside of CVI. Students cited cases of well-qualified Blacks who seemed to have been overlooked for faculty appointment, especially that of Herbert James, a V.I. scientist resident on the mainland. Gottlieb found also that President Wanlass showed willingness to try to meet most of the demands, except for the reinstatement of the Registrar, whose "black power structure" speech was reported to have caused panic in the administration. Wanlass and other administrators communicated their positions to the student body by memoranda dated May 24 and May 26, 1968. The Home Journal editorialized that the black power issues at CVI should not be swept under the rug, and that as long as there were so few black professors there would be dissatisfaction so everything possible should be done to find and employ more.[72]

President Wanlass asserted that he had always followed the Board of Trustees' guidelines of choosing the very best person available for a position, with the proviso that if two persons were equally qualified and one was a Virgin Islander, the latter was to be given preference. He said there was "never the slightest attention paid to an applicant's race or religion."[73] By the late 1960s, however, a number of persons had come to have doubts about Dr. Wanlass' ability to administer the College in regard to the hiring of faculty in a way compatible with the aspirations of most Virgin Islanders. Because he was from Utah, some even assumed that he was a Mormon and that the Church's exclusion of Blacks from the priesthood may have affected his perception of Blacks. Wanlass, however, declared that though they had both grown up in Utah, neither he nor his wife had ever been Mormons.[74]

A composite assessment of Dr. Wanlass, based on interviews with several persons who knew him well and/or worked with him, is that he was not a racist, but that his personality may have caused him to behave like one in certain matters. One White characterized him as an "old fashioned liberal" who did not know how to cope with black activism and black demands for power. Thus, he tried to seal the CVI community, especially the faculty, against the presence of persons he thought might be prone to such activities, and in so doing refused to consider some Blacks who otherwise were very well qualified. Dr. Wanlass had admitted that in trying to get Blacks for the CVI faculty, he did not particularly search for Blacks from the mainland; his efforts were aimed at getting black Virgin Islanders and CVI alumni. When one realizes, however, the size of the V.I. and CVI alumni populations at that time, and the consequently limited pool from which to choose highly trained people, the restrictions which his preferences imposed on black candidates for the faculty are obvious. Two black continental faculty members, Librarian Ernest Wagner and Dr. Herbert Hoover, a professor of education, both had realized that Dr. Wanlass was wary about hiring mainland Blacks because recommendations they had made of such highly qualified persons had usually not been seriously acted upon. Additionally, even black Virgin Islanders and other West Indians were avoided if they showed signs of black consciousness and activism.[75]

The President became so sensitive about activism by the early 1970s that similar yardsticks were applied to students. On August 4, 1970, Dr. Wanlass abruptly terminated the Upward Bound Program ten days ahead of schedule and ordered the 105 students to be off the campus by 5 P.M. The students had registered complaints about some of the conditions and personnel, and Dr. Wanlass explained that while Upward Bound was to help young people mature and improve academic skills, "We are not prepared, however, for the program to degenerate into a vehicle to teach confrontation politics." Federal officials who came to investigate the program's cancellation said they found no justifiable reason for its termination.[76] Dr. Wanlass' stringency finally extended to the point that, after a student protest in 1972, every student admitted to CVI had to be personally approved by him. Some mainland student applicants were even requested to fly down for interviews. Without doubt, such attempts to isolate CVI from the changing racial currents of the times served to keep the faculty much less racially proportioned than it should have been and, in the long run, may be have been counterproductive to the state of tranquility the attempts were meant to insure.

There were, of course, persons within and outside of CVI who agreed with the positions of Dr. Wanlass. Some interpreted every call for more black faculty as a demand for a 100% black faculty, without regard for academic or other qualifications, even though no responsible person ever advocated such a faculty composition. In fact, in an effort to promote some amount of the needed racial-cultural change in the composition of the faculty, along with insuring a faculty of high quality, CVI faculty members who were native Virgin Islanders formed a group during the early Seventies to study the matter and make constructive recommendations. They wrote a position paper on the composition of the faculty, noting past trends and making predictions for the future. They urged a specific program financed by the V.I. government to provide doctoral-level training for Virgin Islanders who were interested in teaching at the College. After meeting with the group and studying its proposals, President Wanlass and Provost and Dean Dr. Arthur Richards, a black Virgin Islander who had come to CVI in 1969, wrote to the V.I. Director of the Budget in February, 1972, and requested adoption of the suggested program of financial aid to prepare islanders to teach at CVI.[77]

The student uprising in May 1968 had simply been the beginning of a series of activities and movements, concerned with racism in the V.I. and on campus, which pervaded the institution for the next several years. Later in 1968, a group named the Black Cultural Organization (BCO) was formed on the St. Thomas campus. Its goals were to promote pride in the cultural heritage of Blacks, to develop greater awareness of racism and its effects, and to encourage activities aimed at improving the educational, social, and economic status of Blacks. In February 1969 it started publishing a mimeographed weekly called "The Black Revolutionary." Its masthead featured a clenched fist, the slogan "The Time Has Come for All Black Students to Stop Talking and Start Acting," and said it was published "by the Brothers and Sisters at C.V.I." BCO soon became thought of by many throughout the V.I.—black and white—as a dangerous Black Power organization.[78]

Business Administration professor George Applewhite (a black West Indian who had grown up in New York City) was the faculty advisor of BCO, and a few other members of the CVI faculty (including this author) and professional staff who shared the students' concerns about racism and its effects in the V.I. also attended meetings of the organization. The administration of the College tried to persuade the faculty advisor to exercise a strong steering influence on the affairs of the organization, but Professor Applewhite said he interpreted his role as mainly that of giving advice when the students asked for it or when he deemed it necessary. Even if Professor Applewhite had thought otherwise, it probably would not have made much difference. Some of the students involved were very strong-willed and, in youthful exuberance, often acted contrary to the suggestions of the advisor and other concerned faculty.[79]

Some of the students' decisions were counterproductive in a community as conservative as the Virgin Islands. For example, instead of designating the officers of the group by standard titles such as president or chairman, they adopted titles usually associated with sovereign states. Thus the BCO officers, and the initial holders were: Prime Minister (Edwin G. Russell, Jr.), Minister of Information (Juan Garcia, Jr.), Minister of Communication (Alexis Weatherhead), Minister of Economic Affairs (Andreas Tutein), Minister of Defense (Roy J. Davis), Minister of Education (Dianne Marshall), and several Deputy Ministers. Additionally, instead of using their given names, some students sometimes used adopted Arabic names. Even though the practice was later modified, the first issue of the organization's newsletter, "The Black Revolutionary," listed the following staff members:

> Editor-in-Chief............ Soni Andi Alli
> Assistant Editor............ Mal 'x Ali
> Advisor .... Admed Muhammed Ali[80]

Not many people in the Virgin Islands could have been expected to identify with those names and whatever cause they represented. By such actions, the group severely limited its potential to have substantial positive effects outside the boundaries of the campus, and made itself appear as threatening, even to many Blacks. A New York Times series on the V.I. in late 1969 reported:

> A black militant movement was started at the College of the Virgin Islands last spring with the stated aim of wrestling control of the islands' commercial enterprises from white people.[81]

Not even the most revolutionary of BCO's members ever mentioned any such aims. Their main aim was to educate the people of the Virgin Islands, and "The Black Revolutionary" did contain some impressive intellectual expositions on socio-economic phenomena such as tourism and racism. Other contributions, such as this excerpt from a section entitled "Black People Awaken!!" by Prime Minister Edwin Russell, Jr., were apparently meant to grab the attention of those who were thought racially nonchalant:

> Things that we have so carelessly taken for granted to be acceptable must be questioned and analyzed:—Why do schools having 90% black students have honky principals? Why is there any argument over whether the governor should be black or white when 75% (this figure is a questionable minimum) of the natives of these islands are black?— Why does a black college have 90% white administration and faculty? Why are we questioned in forming black organizations when white organizations are accepted and even encouraged?[82]

Criticism of the Black Cultural Organization came from many sources. Former Governor Paiewonsky accused it, in 1970, of "preaching discrimination against the white, and that's un-Virgin Islandish." Robert Moss, the manager of St. Thomas television station WBNB, denounced the group on his station. When three of the students were permitted to appear on television, letters to the press criticized their "large bushy hair-do" and their statement that since Blacks formed the majority, they should also have major economic control in the V.I. Some thought the existence of the group made the entire college suspect. Antonio Jimenez Bevenuti wondered what kind of teaching was going on at the College— was it being used "to foment subversion and eventual destruction of our way of life?" The group, however, was not without some outside supporters. St. Thomian Corey Emanuel wrote, in response to one of its critics:

> If people of your ilk and time had thought the way these young men are doing now, perhaps much of our land, our businesses, and our own scattered Virgin Islanders (people without a homeland), would have survived the inroads made upon us by the unscrupulous speculators.[83]

In April 1970, St. Thomas was shocked by a gunpoint robbery of over $36,000 from the Fort Mylner branch of the Virgin Islands National Bank. A month later, in late May, police arrested four persons in connection with the robbery. Two were CVI students, one of whom was the former Prime Minister of BCO. By a striking coincidence, at the same time those arrests were being made, the other big news story in the Virgin Islands was the violence and brutality which had taken place at the U.S. District Court in St. Croix. A physical melee had erupted at what was to have been the sentencing, for an old robbery charge, of Mario Moorhead, the Prime Minister of the United Caribbean Association of Black People (UCA)—a St. Croix-based organization which was thought of as the Black Power group on that island. The defendant, instead of being sentenced, had ended up being beaten by federal marshals and was then immediately flown off the island. Even though the charges against the two college students of complicity in the bank robbery were afterward dropped and the brutal treatment of the UCA Prime Minister by the federal marshals earned him a great deal of sympathy and occasioned public amazement at the brutality of law-enforcement officials, the conjunction of the two events helped to give black activism an even worse reputation than it may have had before. It seemed to many people that, somehow, black activist leaders had a proclivity for becoming involved in criminal activity. In fact, some were even saying that such activity was the common means of support for Black Power activism.[84]

The Black Cultural Organization continued for a few more years at CVI, although somewhat reduced in prestige. One of its main activities was the sponsorship at CVI of the Annual celebration of Black History Week each February, which usually featured prominent black speakers from the mainland or the Caribbean area and to which the community was invited. Some Whites and Blacks in the community often disapproved of the speakers or their topics, alleging that some were fomenters of racial hatred. Another of the organization's projects in the early 1970s was a campaign for a Black Studies program at CVI.[85] BCO leaders used various opportunities to promote their views of the racial reality in the Virgin Islands. Glenn Davis, who was also president of the student government and a member of the graduating class of 1972, delivered a scathing speech at that year's Commencement:

> We deal with disciples of deception.... They have their own interest at heart and they are economic mongrels. They brand us as black racists when we speak of hope.... They are attacking the nightmare they themselves have created.[86]

The biggest upheaval at CVI, the embodiment of everything President Wanlass had tried to prevent, took place late in 1972. CVI had employed in 1970, partly as a result of student pressure, a black Virgin Islander who had just earned a Ph.D. in African Studies at Howard University. Dr. Lezmore Emanuel proved to be very popular with many students and was named "Professor of the Year" at the end of the 1970–71 school year. He had been instrumental in formulating a proposal for a Black Studies major, which eventually was adopted. Professor Emanuel also was asked to speak frequently by various community groups on topics such as Virgin Islands culture and the Virgin Islands Creole English, which he advocated should be utilized in the schools to teach Standard English. Additionally, he was active in a number of movements in the community, most of which were promotive of the African cultural heritage and concerned about the destruction of various aspects of that heritage by the U.S. way of life.[87]

The cultural and political pursuits of Dr. Emanuel and his wife (a teacher at the Wayne Aspinall Junior High School who acted as a partner in several activities) seemed to have caused a number of people to feel threatened and to think that the Emanuels were fanning the flames of an already tense racial situation. An especially outspoken critic was Alfred Groverton, a resident of Scott Free Estates in St. Thomas. In one of his letters to the press about the Emanuels, he ended with: "Finally If Professor and Teacher wife will stop poisoning the students [sic] minds with racial hatreds we'll all have a Happy New Year." He insisted in future correspondence that he had heard from non-white students, at both the Aspinall Junior High and CVI, that racial hatred was being preached in both schools.[88]

CVI's St. Thomas campus with dormitories in the foreground and the library at the top. Courtesy of the Virgin Islands Government's Archival Collection at the Charles W. Turnbull Regional Library.

In response to Groverton, Mrs. Emanuel wrote: "It seems to be the general attitude that if a black person teaches other black persons about their origins, their cultural achievements and their destiny, that he is accused of teaching hatred."[89] Another response to Groverton, from "A Disciple of the good Professor, Cheryl Mason," asked: "What makes you think it is necessary to teach hate? Our people know what has been done to them."[90]

On Saturday, December 9, 1972, the *Home Journal* carried a big front-page story that Professor Emanuel was under fire at CVI and the students were concerned. According to the story, Emanuel's annual evaluation from the head of the Social Sciences Division, a white Continental, had recommended that Emanuel be given a "terminal" contract for the following school year (1973–74) with the stipulation that future contracts would be contingent on "improvement" in his performance. The concerned areas of his performance reportedly included his "teachings" as perceived by some faculty members and persons in the community, "poorly organized" and "repetitious" courses, lateness in submitting book orders and grades, and having given out an "excessive number of above-average grades." Professor Emanuel had reportedly informed some students of his evaluation, whereupon they held a meeting to which they invited the President and the Provost, neither of whom attended. Dr. Emanuel stated to the news reporter, and in a reply to his evaluation, that he felt he was being harassed because of his outspokenness and activities against white racism and on behalf of the recognition and preservation of Virgin Islands culture.[91]

Two days later, early in the morning of Monday, December 11, 1972, a group of students, apparently acting on a decision of the student council, started an occupation of the St. Thomas campus library to protest Dr. Emanuel's evaluation. As the library contained the offices of the President and the Provost and Dean, it was in effect also the administration building. Attempts were made to get other students to join the initial group in the library, so some of the protest leaders went to classes which were in session and demanded that they adjourn immediately so that their students could join the protest in the library. Some of the protest leaders were quite mannerly in their actions (such as those who came to the class of this author), while others, such as the ones who went to disrupt classes in the science building, were quite rude to the instructors.[92] Most classes were thus dismissed, and a number of the students went to the library.

Students remained in control of the library all day, refusing entrance to some faculty who had offices in the building. Their leaders requested that the President and the Provost meet with them, but both refused on the ground that they would not enter the building as long as it was barricaded. A request that Dr. Emanuel be granted a three-year contract was also refused. At the height of the demonstration, there were about 125 students in the library. By late afternoon the number of occupying students had decreased, as students from the British West Indian islands had been advised that continued participation might jeopardize their student visas and they withdrew. Some others left for various reasons.[93]

As of 5:30 P.M., appeals from Provost Arthur Richards and Student Council President Eustace Arrindell (who had himself been a part of it earlier, but as a non-citizen student had withdrawn) had failed to persuade the remaining students to leave the library. Police officers who had been called decided to use tear gas to force the remaining students out. That effort took several hours as the students hid in the basement of the library and were not at first affected by the tear gas. It was not until 9:30 P.M. that those students were finally forced out of the building. Thirty-one students were placed on suspension, three of whom were arrested and taken to the police station but released on bond.[94]

The scene that night outside the college library before the siege ended was dreadful! There were lines of policemen ready for whatever may have confronted them; some had even been flown over from St. Croix. There was a sizeable number of persons who had gone to the campus from the town; some were shouting racist slogans. President Wanlass, apparently fearful, remained in the background and let Provost Arthur Richards (a black Virgin Islander) act as the head and spokesman for the College throughout the protest. Dr. Richards was physically threatened and told he would be killed; police officers guarded his home for several days following the protest. Ironically, the last round of tear gas which forced the students out might not have been necessary, if those outside had known what was happening inside the building. Senator Athniel (Addie) Ottley, Chairman of the Legislature's Committee on Education, had been in the library for a few hours trying to persuade the students to leave and was just about to succeed when the final round of tear gas was used. Both Senator Ottley and Dr. Herbert Hoover believed that within half an hour the students would have left peacefully. The problem was that they had no way to communicate with the authorities outside. Dr. Hoover, a black continental professor of education, had gone to the library that night to stay with the students. He had feared for their safety and felt that the presence of a faculty member might avert a Kent State-type situation.[95]

The occurrence of the protest just three months after the Fountain Valley tragedy added to its impact. However, while some viewed the protest as a racial issue, others considered it more as a matter of procedure and order. How most Virgin Islanders felt was not known with certainty, but the opinions of three of four persons (the fourth was Dr. Emanuel himself in a local newspaper opinion column) were probably the most common. Each of the three had somewhat divided sentiments, expressing sympathy for the students' right to protest and/or for Dr. Emanuel. Yet, each felt definitely that the students had gone about their protest in the wrong way and thus had left the college little choice but to act decisively. A commonly-heard expression of opinion was that other methods of appeal and protest should have been tried and exhausted by the students and Dr. Emanuel before resort to the drastic action that was undertaken. Most people were especially regretful that tear gas had been used, but in view of the seeming obstinacy of some students to the very end, some realized why the authorities may have thought that less offensive methods would not have been effective. Moreover, the college was faced with a very crucial timetable: the protest took place at the beginning of the final examination week. If it had lasted for several days, it could have had profound adverse effects on the academic functioning of the institution, such as possibly preventing the completion of the work of students who were finishing that semester or others who were not planning to return.[96]

Repercussions from the occupation of the library and the defeat of those involved lingered for a long time. Dr. Emanuel's teaching relationship with the college was immediately terminated, though the college fulfilled its financial obligations under the contract he had at the time. At the request of the college, the Department of Law dropped the charges against the three students who had been arrested on the night of the protest. However, Dr. Norwell Harrigan, a black British Virgin Islander who was the Associate Director of CVI's Research Institute, was appointed to conduct individual hearings for each of the thirty-one students who had been suspended and to present his findings and recommendations to Dr. Wanlass, who decided on the final disposition of each case. All but a couple of the students were readmitted to the college. A number of people—alumni and others—argued that the college needed more community surveillance than it had previously had and more community input into its policies. In February, 1973, the Committee on Education of the Legislature began a wide-ranging investigation into the affairs of CVI.[97]

In February 1973, two months after the protest, the *Daily News* noted that the pendulum seemed to have swung very swiftly from "descriptions of CVI as a hotbed of black revolutionary radicalism" to suggestions that CVI was "really a citadel of white bourgeois repressiveness." In actuality, the College had contained elements of both and each had served to reinforce the other. President Wanlass' desire to safeguard the institution from racial concerns and activism had made him reluctant to employ some Blacks—Continentals and others—whom he had though might be prone to such activities. This, in addition to the reasons the administration always gave—the smaller pool of highly qualified Blacks and the inability of CVI to compete with the salary offers of some mainland institutions at a time when Blacks were being eagerly sought to meet federal guidelines—led to a faculty whose overwhelming white and continental character seemed gross to students who had come of age during a time of heightened racial consciousness. Attendance at CVI, therefore, played a key role in transforming some young Blacks into activists (as the college experience anywhere often does) as they became more intimately aware of the fact and methods of white control in the islands and as they became more desirous of wanting to do something about it. In turn, Dr. Wanlass became ever more resolute in aspects of his position, as evidenced by his insistence after 1972 of personally approving each applicant for admission.[98]

The Emanuel issue, therefore, was tailor-made for a conflict. Given the administration's poor record of hiring Blacks, its known abhorrence of black activism, and its history of releasing the Registrar in 1968 and prematurely terminating the Upward Bound Program in 1970, both of which were thought to have racial issues involved, its credibility on any issue even remotely connected with race was non-existent. It did not matter to some, therefore, that some of the criticisms in Dr. Emanuel's evaluation may have had validity. All that most of the concerned students saw was another attempt to rid the College of a person who had become known for black activism.

By 1975, three years later, though the campus was much quieter, there remained an underlying feeling of discontent among many of the students and some of the faculty. Practically everyone acknowledged that, in many ways, President Wanlass had done a tremendous job of building a college from scratch. He was a dedicated and effective administrator and a great deal had been accomplished. CVI was an accredited institution. It had established master's degree programs. It had an impressive physical plant. Some of its alumni had attained outstanding records in various fields, and it had contributed significantly to the growth of an educated middle class in the Virgin Islands. However, the feeling continued to grow among some alumni, some students, and some other black Virgin Islanders that Dr. Wanlass had done his job, and that CVI's future development as an institution responsive to the needs of most of the people of the V.I. would be best served by a different type of person at the helm. Dr. Wanlass had probably long been aware of the sentiment, for in late 1971 he had submitted his resignation as president and had requested an assignment to the St. Croix campus as provost. However, the Board of Trustees had asked him to withdraw the resignation, which he had done early in 1972. With that vote of confidence, he remained.[99]

Concerns about the future character of the faculty were also being expressed by the mid-70s, as it began to appear that the tenure system might function to insure the permanency of the faculty in its state of severe racial imbalance. Strains even developed between black and white faculty members because of their differing viewpoints on that and other related matters. However, no one wanted another confrontation of explosive magnitude, and measures were agreed upon to provide for many of the needed changes over time in faculty employment and tenure policies.[100]

The appointment of Verne A. Hodge (the then-Presiding Judge of the V.I. Territorial Court) to the CVI Board of Trustees in 1978 was the beginning of a new era in Board affairs. Judge Hodge was an unapologetic advocate of students' rights and of greater employment of qualified Virgin Islanders and other local underrepresented groups at CVI, matters which he thought had not received sufficient consideration by the institution. Judge Hodge thus proposed late in 1978 that during the next five years, which was the term of trustees, the Board should set in place policies aimed at the identification and determination of the availability of qualified Virgin Islanders for the future presidency and other positions. The proposal was eventually approved by the Board at a later meeting in 1979, but apparently President Wanlass was so displeased by the proposal presented to the Board in late 1978 that he abruptly relinquished the presidency and never returned to the campus. Dr. Richards became the Acting President. To date (2017), President Wanlass has never been back, even

Governor Cyril King, center, with UVI Presidents-to-be Orville Kean, left, Arthur Richards, right, and President Lawrence Wanlass between Richards and Governor King. Courtesy of the Virgin Islands Government's Archival Collection at the Charles W. Turnbull Regional Library.

though he has been invited many times, including to UVI's big 50th Anniversary Celebration of 2012.[101] President Wanlass played a truly dynamic role in establishing the College of the Virgin Islands, and it would be laudable of him to visit the institution and see all that has resulted from his leadership and strenuous efforts!

Since Dr. Wanlass' departure, all presidents of the institution have been black; however, many white candidates have been in competition for the positions. In fact, Former Gov. Ralph Paiewonsky, who had become a member of the Board of Trustees and was chosen to head the Presidential Search Committee which was seeking a successor to President Wanlass, reported to the Board at a meeting in February 1979 that he had received 313 applications for the presidential position, and they had come from every state in the union, plus other territories such as Guam and foreign countries such as Wales.[102]

Dr. Arthur A. Richards, a black Virgin Islander originally from St. Croix, was chosen to become the second president of CVI in 1980. He had been educated at Howard, Hampton, and New York Universities, and had a long career as an educator and administrator before becoming the Commissioner of Education for the Virgin Islands. After moving to CVI, he was the Vice President and Provost under Dr. Wanlass, and served for over a year as Acting President when Dr. Wanlass left. President Richards had the special job of presiding over the transition of the institution from a college to a university in 1986, with all of the accompanying adjustments. UVI also was granted in 1986 by the Congress the status of being a Historically Black College or University, the only HBCU outside the continental United States. Then in 1989, with the rest of the Virgin Islands, UVI suffered great destruction from Hurricane Hugo. Dr. Richards worked untiringly to get the institution back to functioning mode. After accomplishing that, Dr. Richards retired in 1990, having served in the presidency for ten years.

Dr. Orville Kean, also a black Virgin Islander, became UVI's third president in 1990. His higher education was obtained at Lincoln University, and the Universities of Michigan and Pennsylvania. He had started teaching mathematics at CVI in the late 1960s, and held every administrative position between teaching and the presidency, including Chair of the Science and Mathematics Division, Dean, and Executive Vice President. Among his special achievements as president were the recovery efforts following Hurricanes Hugo and Marilyn, including the installation of power generators on both campuses. He also presided over the erection of the Sports and Fitness Center on St. Thomas, a dormitory on St. Croix, and a Department of Information Technology and video telephone conference centers on each campus. Dr. Kean also initiated the summer programs for Caribbean global leadership of university students, and created the Research and Technology Park on the St. Croix campus, before retiring in 2002.[103]

Dr. LaVerne E. Ragster became the fourth president of UVI, and the only female to date, in 2002. Again, a black Virgin Islander, she was a specialist in marine science who had been trained at the Universities of Miami, San Diego State, and California at San Diego. The UVI marine science program especially attracted a number of U.S. mainland students. Before becoming president, Dr. Ragster had taught for years in UVI's Science and Math Division, had served as its chair, and as an administrator in the President's Office. She considers, as her special achievements in the presidency, doing all that was necessary to ensure UVI's reaccreditation; establishing closer links with Eastern Caribbean institutions of higher education, which led to a more diverse institution and student body; and strengthening the financial base of the institution.[104]

Dr. David Hall, who became UVI's fifth and present president in 2009, is a black Continental, originally from Savannah, Georgia, where he was born and received his elementary and secondary education. His college major was political science at Kansas State University, after which he spent two years in Italy playing professional basketball. On returning to the United States, he earned a masters in human relations and a law degree at the University of Oklahoma, leading to practicing law in Chicago and then teaching it at the University of Mississippi.

Prof. Hall then decided to add to his law studies and went to the Harvard Law School, where he earned masters and doctoral degrees in law, and wrote a book on spirituality and the practice of law. He then taught law at Northeastern University for several years, and became the Associate Dean of its Law school, where he was serving when he heard of the presidential opening at UVI.

President Hall is very proud of the types and number (8) of degrees that UVI has added during his presidency, and in 2016 also added a Ph.D. program in cooperation with two other universities. His ambition is for UVI to promote not only new and needed programs, but also knowledge of the thought processes, skills, and understanding necessary for the ongoing improvement of programs. Of course, President Hall also hopes that the planned medical school will become a full reality, along with the continuing gifts and grants necessary for the sustaining and improvement of that and other activities.[105]

All of the presidents since Dr. Wanlass have aimed at ensuring that the UVI faculty would be more racially balanced than it was during the early decades. Admittedly, it has not always been an easy task, especially in areas such as the physical sciences, in which available Blacks with doctoral degrees were often far fewer in number than Whites, and the salaries offered by UVI, especially in relation to the local cost of living, were often not competitive. The latter remains a severe problem and the locally published list of UVI salaries, in July 2016, revealed how great a gulf exists between top executive compensation and the compensation of many faculty members.[106]

The numerical difference between black and white faculty members at UVI seems to have stabilized at about a 50/50 split. The most recent publically available data, compiled in the 2010–2011 academic year, revealed that the full-time instructional faculty was comprised of 60 Blacks and 56 Whites. The breakdown by campus showed St. Thomas as having 37 Blacks and 38 Whites, while St. Croix had 23 Blacks and 18 Whites.[107] More courses are being offered on St. Croix to meet the demands of persons residing there, and electronic technology is enabling some courses to be taught on both campuses at the same time by one instructor. Additionally, in the fall of 2016, UVI is offering its first Ph.D. Program, in Creative Leadership, in partnership with Fielding University and Buffalo State University. The program is already accredited, and many of the courses will be available through distance technology.[108]

A greatly welcomed and long delayed happening at UVI is a renewed Hotel and Tourism Management Program. The original program was discontinued in the 1970s, as black students stopped enrolling on realizing that black and white students were being treated very differently in being hired for management positions by some local hotels. The new program is headed by Professor Tamara

Lang, a black Virgin Islander who was trained at the University of New Haven in Connecticut and started working at UVI in 2011. She seems to have a great mix of the idealism and realism, the professionalism and practicality, that the program seems to need in order to succeed. It is a four-year, bachelor's degree program with more than 100 students, most of whom are Blacks from the Virgin Islands/West Indies, but also includes Whites and Blacks from elsewhere.

In structuring the program, Prof. Lang looked at similar programs on the mainland and also in Caribbean places such as Bermuda and Jamaica. She has been establishing relationships with local hotels and restaurants, and some of their personnel are serving as part-time instructors. Prof. Lang also realistically realizes that there are some West Indian cultural mores that may not match well with some of the concepts of the hospitality industry, and thus she and her students consider such issues and how best to bring about cooperation with hospitality principles. The program is also dedicated to practical training, and thus the preparation of some of the foods and management of the cafeteria at UVI are parts of the program. At the UVI commencement of May 2016 there were eleven graduates of the program; two of whom are presently employed as management trainees in local hotels, and some are employed in Anguilla and Tortola. There is great hope that this program may achieve the success that had been envisioned for it from the earliest days of CVI.[109]

It is great to be able to end this account of UVI's development in relation to racial affairs by noting that Blacks have become big donors to the institution. A white UVI professor once remarked that all gifts to UVI of which he knew had come from Whites. That can no longer be said. During Dr. Ragster's presidency in the first decade of this century, the Samuel Family of St. John donated land on St. John to UVI, and later added more during the Hall presidency, bringing their donation to about six acres. Miss Ruth E. Thomas, a well-known educator, former principal of the Charlotte Amalie High School and former UVI Trustee, has donated her home and its surrounding land at Estate Lindbergh Bay to UVI, to be used for the benefit of its faculty. Then in 2014, the Van Beverhoudt Family of St. Thomas gave UVI its largest private real estate gift, consisting of 65 acres at Estate Sorgenfri in St. Thomas. It includes rolling hillside, two freshwater guts, and a quarter mile of pristine beachfront. Leal Van Beverhoudt, speaking on behalf of the family stated: "We must encourage every Virgin Islander to contribute to this University, no matter how small, because that's the only way our future generations will prosper."[110] Profoundly stated!

Notes

1. Turnbull, "The Structural Development of a Public Education System in the Virgin Islands, 1917–1970," p. 205.

2. The Goodwill School was also known popularly as the Oliver School, because it was founded by E. Benjamin Oliver, a former public school principal after whom the elementary school at Estate Tutu is named today; Mrs. Lucinda Millin was also a renowned educator, who would later be elected to the Legislature; and Miss Boynes referred to Vitalia Boynes, a well-known educator, originally from of St. John.

3. "Bishop to Dedicate New Anglican School," *Daily News* (St. Thomas; November 4, 1950, p. 1; "Anglican School Re-opens September 15th," ibid., August 13, 1952, pp. 1, 4.

4. Announcement of the Opening of Antilles School, *Daily News* (St. Thomas, V.I.), September 18, 1950, p. 4.

5. "Head of Antilles School Returns from States," *Daily News* (St. Thomas, V.I.), September 1, 1950, p. 1.

6. "Antilles School New Location at Estate Poinciana," *Daily News* (St. Thomas, V.I.), September 3, 1955, p. 1; "Antilles Names College Dean as Headmaster," March 18, 1959, p. 1; "Local Private School Plans to Increase Grades," February 24, 1964, p. 1; "Antilles Building Fund Drive is Successful," November 4, 1970, p. 2.

7. *Daily News* (St. Thomas, V.I.), September 6, 1952, p. 3; "Antilles School Announces Full Plans," September 1, 1953, p. 1; "Teacher Added to Staff of Antilles School," December 2, 1958, p. 1; "Antilles School Elects Board for New Year," April 15, 1959, p. 1.

8. "Private School Enrollment Up, CHS Has Top Increase," *Daily News* (St. Thomas, V.I.), August 27, 1962, p. 1.

9. "Antilles School Head Hopes for Pupil 'Exchange'," *Daily News* (St. Thomas, V.I.), May 22, 1959, p. 1.

10. "Text of Hodge's Remarks to C and C," *Daily News* (St. Thomas, V.I.), November 6, 1973, p. 9.

11. "Antilles School Announces Scholarship Fund," *Daily News* (St. Thomas, V.I.), September 22, 1959, p. 1; "Howard Jacksons Give $5,000 more to Antilles School Fund," February 23, 1960, p. 1; December 21, 1959, p. 1.

12. Interviews with Jeffrey Farrow, St. Thomas-Miami airline flight, November 10, 1982; Helen Gjessing, St. Thomas, February 23, 1983.

13. "Commentary," *Virgin Islands View*, Vol. 3, No. 2 (July, 1967), p. 7.

14. *Daily News* (St. Thomas, V.I.), November 26, 1973, p. 9. "Text of Hodge's Remarks to C and C," *op. cit.*

15. "Moron Lauds Antilles Commencement Talk," *Daily News* (St. Thomas, V.I.), June 18, 1962, p. 1 pp. 4, 7.

16. *Home Journal* (St. Thomas, V.I.), June 30, 1972, p. 9.

17. Conversation with Charlene O'Neal Henderson, St. Thomas, February 23, 1983.

18. Interview with Jasmine Gunthorpe, Delaware-California telephone conversation, June 20, 1983; *Daily News* (St. Thomas, V.I.) July 7, 1972, p. 3; August 31, 1973, p. 3.

19. Interviews with Jasmine Gunthorpe, Delaware-California telephone conversation, June 20, 1983; Jeffrey Farrow, St. Thomas-Miami airline flight, November 10, 1982; Ruth Thomas, St. Thomas, October 14, 1982; Helen Gjessing, St. Thomas, February 23, 1983.

20. Philip A. Gerard, "Social Configurations and Some Problems," in Bough and Macridis, *Virgin Islands, America's Caribbean Outpost*, p. 162.

21. "Urges Residents Open Communication Lines," *Daily News* (St. Thomas, V.I.), November 20, 1973, pp. 1, 14.

22. "Farrelly Chided For Post On Private School Board," *Daily News* (St. Thomas, V.I.), March 20, 1970, p. 1.

23. Aldeth Lewin, "V.I. philanthropist Peter Gruber dies," Daily News (St. Thomas, V.I.), October 22, 2014, p. 4.

24. Two wins in 2016 were the Mathcounts Bowl and the Spelling Bee, which was for middle schools. See Daily News Staff, Antilles School wins St. Thomas-St. John Mathcounts contest," *Daily News* (St. Thomas, V.I.), February 24, 2016, p. 6; Ashley Mayrianne Jones, "Antilles student clinches St. Thomas-St. John bee," Ibid., February 13, 2016, p. 2.

25. See, for example, a picture labeled "USVI sailors competing in Argentina" on the back page of the Daily News (St. Thomas, V.I.), October 24, 2014, p. 42. The "sailors" were all young Antilles students taking part in a regatta in Buenos Aires, Argentina.

26. These figures were reported by Ananta Pancham of the Antilles School in a conversation of August 15, 2016.

27. Lori Abbotts, "V.I. Montessori graduates its largest senior class," *Daily News* (St. Thomas, V.I.), May 23, p. 3; Lori Abbotts, "10 graduate from St. Thomas/St. John Seventh-Day Adventist School," *Daily News* (St. Thomas, V.I.), June 13, 2016, p.2; Lori Abbotts, "35 graduate from Antilles School," *Daily News* (St. Thomas, V.I.), June 13, 2016, pp. 4–5; Lori Abbotts, "All Saints Cathedral School graduates 14," *Daily News* (St. Thomas, V.I.), June 18, 2016, p. 3; Lori Abbotts, "St. Thomas schools graduate 431 during momentous weekend," Daily News (St. Thomas, V.I.), June 20, 2016, pp. 2–3, 6–7.

28. V.I. Department of Education, "Annual Report, 1950–1951," Statistical Summaries— Tables 1, 2; "Annual Report, 1955–1956," Statistical Summaries—Tables 1, 2, 3, 19, 45; "Annual Report 1975–1976," Statistical Information—Charts 1, 2, 3, 4, 7; *Daily News* (St. Thomas, V.I.), March 5, 1974, p. 9.

29. V.I. Department of Education, "Annual Report, 1955–1956"; "Annual Report, 1975–1976"; "Annual Report, 1974–1975," Statistical Information—Chart 9; Pearl Ianthe Varlack, "Teacher Education in the Virgin Islands: A Strategy for Curriculum Design" (Ph.D. dissertation, University of Pittsburgh, 1974), p. 106.

30. Turnbull, "The Structural Development of a Public School System in the Virgin Islands," pp. 167–169; V.I. Department of Education, "Annual Report, 1950–51," p. 12, Statistical Summaries—Table 21; "Annual Report, 1961–62," pp. 27, 28; Edward L. Dejnoska, "American Educational Achievement in the Virgin Islands, 1917, 1963," *The Journal of Negro History*, Vol. 57, No. 4 (October, 1972), p. 391.

31. "The Virgin Islands: A comprehensive Survey Completed at the Request of the Commissioner of Education" (New York: Center for School Services, School of Education, New York University, 1963), Chapter 7, p. 2; Chapter 4, p. 24; Editorials, *Daily News* (St. Thomas, V.I.), December 13, 1965, p. 11; December 17, 1965, p. 4.

32. Turnbull, "The Structural Development of a Public School System in the Virgin Islands," p. 169; V.I. Department of Education, "Annual Report, 1963–64," p. 6; interviews with Ruth Thomas (Principal, Charlotte Amalie High School, 1969–1982), St. Thomas, October 14, 1982; Mary Francis (Chairman, Social Studies Division, CAHS, 1968–1981), St. Thomas, October 15, 1982.

33. Interview with Rita Martin, St. Thomas, February 24, 1983; V.I. Department of Education, "Annual Report, 1967–1968," pp. 39–44. As noted in Chapter 3, a sizeable number of persons interviewed believed that black continental teachers were teaching racism to their students.

34. Interviews with Dr. Arthur Richards (V.I. Commissioner of Education, 1966–1969), St. Thomas, February 1, 1983; Rita Martin (Department of Education's Director of Personnel Services, 1966–), St. Thomas, February 24, 1983; Ruth Thomas (Principal, Charlotte Amalie High School, 1969–1982), October 14, 1982; Mrs. Ulla Muller (Principal, Nisky Elementary School, 1953–1980), St. Thomas, February 16, 1983; Mary Francis (Social Studies Department Chairman, CAHS, 1968–1981), St. Thomas, October 15, 1982; Clarissa Creque (Teacher, Charlotte Amalie High School, 1960s–1981), St. Thomas, February 18, 1983; Erva Denham Greer (Public School Teacher, 1969–1976), St. Thomas, February 19, 1983; Gloria Alexander Statham (Guidance Counselor, Wayne Aspinall Junior High School, 1968–1971), Delaware-Pennsylvania telephone conversation, May 8, 1983; Marion Bray Hedrington (Teacher, Lockhart Elementary School, 1971–present), St. Thomas, February 13, 1983; Mrs. Vincent Bourne-Vanneck (Elementary School Teacher), St. Thomas telephone conversation, February 17, 1983; Margaret Quetel (Elementary School Teacher), St. Thomas, February 22, 1983.

35. Interviews with the educators listed in previous footnote; V.I. Department of Education "Annual Report, 1971–1972," p. 66; *Daily News* (St. Thomas, V.I.), May 25, 1974, p. 6.

36. Lewis, *The Virgin Islands: A Caribbean Lilliput*, pp. 277–278; *Daily News* (St. Thomas, V.I.), August 22, 1962, p. 1; August 29, 1962, p. 1.

37. "Notes on a Serious Local Problem," (Virgin Islands Forum, Vol. 1, No. 1 (May, 1973), p. 11; Daily News (St. Thomas, V.I.), February 9, 1973, p. 3; November 28, 1973, p. 6; January 11, 1975, p. 6.

38. An educational source which refers to the functioning of group power in maintaining racism is Atron Gentry, Byrd Jones, et al., Urban Education: The Hope Factor (Philadelphia: W. B. Saunders Company, 1972), pp. 1–3. See also sources listed in Chapter 3, footnote 246.

39. *Education Laws and Regulations of the Virgin Islands* (Oxford, New Hampshire: Equity Publishing Co., 1981), p. 61; *Daily News* (St. Thomas, V.I.), July 18, 1962, p. 1; August 2, 1963, p. 9; August 28, 1967, p. 3.

40. "Letter," *Daily News* (St. Thomas, V.I.), May 22, 196823, 1969, p. 5. See biographical note on Blyden in Chapter 1, footnote 45.

41. Editorial, "Unfair Criticism," *Daily News* (St. Thomas, V.I.), May 31, 1969, p. 7; also issue of "Student Gets Backing On Being Awarded Grant," May 29, 1969, p. 1.

42. "Letters to the Editor," *Daily News* (St. Thomas, V.I.), June 13, 1969, p. 7.

43. *Daily News* (St. Thomas, V.I.), June 30, 1969, p. 7.

44. "Pastor Resigns From Parish In Controversy," *Daily News* (St. Thomas, V.I.), July 30, 1969, p. 1; "Church Lay Official Challenges Pastor," August 5, 1969, p. 1.

45. Marva Samuel Applewhite, "Letter to the Editor," *Daily News* (St. Thomas, V.I.), August 2, 1969, p. 7. The Hartman family left St Thomas in the summer of 1969, Julia Hartman, the 1969 Blyden awardee, has not as yet returned to reside in the V.I.; neither have most of the other white Continental awardees.

46. "Antilles Student Wins Blyden Scholarship," *Daily News* (St. Thomas, V.I.), June 1, 1971, pp. 1, 6; "St. Joseph Valedictorian Wins Blyden Scholarship," August 18, 1973, p. 3;

"Wilma Lewis Awarded Scholarship," September 7, 1974, p. 3; *Education Laws and Regulations of the Virgin Islands*, pp. 81–82.

47. "Teachers To Defy Dress Code Order," *Daily News* (St. Thomas, V.I.), September 24, 1975, p. 1; "School Board Supports Dress Code Decision," September 25, 1975, p. 3; Marianne George, "Letter to the Editor," September 27, 1975, p. 7; September 30, 1975, p. 7; "Teacher Suspensions Recommended," December 2, 1975, p. 1; "20 Teachers Ordered Suspended," December 11, 1975, p. 1.

48. Editorial, *Daily News* (St. Thomas, V.I.), September 26, 1975, p. 7.

49. Interview with Glen Smith, Miami-St. Thomas airline flight, April 11, 1983; *Daily News* (St. Thomas, V.I.), November 24, 1975, p. 7.

50. Chapter Two of Turnbull's "The Structural Development of a Public School System in the Virgin Islands," provides a good review of such studies.

51. Turnbull, "The Structural Development of a Public School System in the Virgin Islands," pp. 222, 223.

52. The continental staff, however, was not considered a primary factor in the explaining public schools inadequacies. A survey in 1978 found that most residents of the V.I. believed poor student discipline and parental shortcomings to be the worst problems of the public school system. (Mills, "The Virgin Islands Household Survey," pp. 7, 28.)

53. Iran Hodge, Granville Hedrington, Jr., and Mali Kiambo (Lloyd David) were three young black interviewees who, while high school graduates themselves, said they knew a substantial number of young Blacks who had dropped out of school in the 1970s because of such beliefs. A few of the educators interviewed also support this. Hodge was interviewed in St. Thomas on February 1, 1983; Hedrington and Kiambo on February 15, 1983.

54. See, for example, Ronald L. Richardson and S. Craig Gerlach, "Black Dropouts: A Study of Significant Factors Contributing to a Black Student's Decision," *Urban Education*, Vol. 14, No. 4, (January, 1980), pp. 489–494.

55. Conversations with Mrs. Jeanette Smith Barry and Mr. Stefan Jurgen, St. Thomas, August, 2016; and with Dr. Lois Hassell Habtes, St. Thomas, September, 2016.

56. Conversations with Mr. Jurgen, St. Thomas, and with Dr. Hassel Habtes, St. Thomas, September, 2016.

57. Interviews with Martha Alexander and two former CAHS teachers of Shinnola, during August and September, 2016 and March, 2017, St. Thomas.

58. University of the Virgin Islands, *2010–2011 Catalog* (St. Croix, V.I., 2010), p. 1.

59. Isaac Dookhan, "The Expansion of Higher Education Opportunities in the United States Virgin Islands," *The Journal of Negro Education*, Vol. 50, No. 1, (Winter, 1981), pp. 15–25; Allen Grammer, "Correspondence," *Daily News* (St. Thomas, V.I.), August 2, 1961, p. 2; July 2, 1962, p. 1; interview with Ronald Walker, Delaware-Maryland telephone conversation; December 1, 1982.

60. "Trustees Named for College of the V.I." *Daily News* (St. Thomas, V.I.), April 25, 1962, p. 1; "Dr. L.C. Wanless is Named College Head," October 2, 1962, p. 1.

61. College of the Virgin Islands, "Self-Study Report of the College of the Virgin Islands" (St. Thomas, V.I.: Submitted to the Commission on Higher Education of the Middle States Association of Colleges and Secondary Schools, 1970), pp. 51, 56; "Wanlass Reiterates Policy on Faculty," *Daily News* (St. Thomas, V.I.), June 23, 1967, p. 1; "College Personnel Practices Criticized," June 26, 1967, p. 1.

62. College of the Virgin Islands, "Faculty Profile, 1967–1968"; "Faculty and Professional Staff, 1975–1976"; faculty figures compiled with the help of James Ready, Public In-

formation Officer at CVI, St. Thomas, February 14, 1983; compensation experiences of some faculty members at CVI, as told to this author.

63. "Mainland Students At V.I. College," *Daily News* (St. Thomas, V.I.), May 12, 1970, p. 15; College of the V.I., "Self-Study Report, 1970," pp. iii, 39–40; "Self-Study Report, 1975," p. iii; U.S. Department of Health, Education and Welfare, Office for Civil Rights, *Racial, Ethnic and Sex Enrollment Data from Institutions of Higher Education—1976* (Washington, D.C: U.S. Government Printing Office, 1978), p. 221.

64. "CVI," *Virgin Islands View*, Vol. 2, No. 2, (July 1966), p. 28; interviews with Dr. Frank Mills, St. Thomas, February 17, 1983 and Erva Denham, St. Thomas, February 19, 1983.

65. Interviews with Dr. Frank Mills, St. Thomas, February 17, 1983 and Professor Helen Gjessing, St. Thomas, February 23, 1983. (Professors Mills and Gjessing were also consulted again in September 2016, but on other topics, in accordance with the changing times.)

66. Interviews with Dr. Arthur Richards, St. Thomas, February 1, 1983; Prof. Helen Gjessing, St. Thomas, February 23, 1983; and Gov. Ralph Paiewonsky, St. Thomas, February 25, 1983. The trouble with the law usually centered on drug charges.

67. Interview with Kwame Garcia, St. Thomas-St. Croix telephone conversation, February 15, 1983.

68. Interviews with Dr. Lawrence Wanlass, Delaware-California telephone conversation, November 14, 1983; George Goodwin, St. Thomas telephone conversation, February 22, 1983; "Hotel and Restaurant Business," *Daily News* (St. Thomas, V.I.), May 18, 1967, p. 7. Also interviews with CVI alumni/students Iran Hodge, St Thomas, February 1, 1983; Glenn "Kwabena" Davis, St Thomas, February 25, 1983; Glen Smith, Miami-St. Thomas airline flight, April 11, 1983. (Glenn "Kwabena" Davis and Glen Smith have also been consulted (on other topics) during 2016.

69. "Acting Governor King, Students Pay Tribute," *Daily News* (St. Thomas, V.I.), April 9, 1968, p. 1.

70. *Home Journal* (St. Thomas, V.I.), May 21, 1968, p. 5.

71. *Home Journal* (St. Thomas, V.I.), May 22, 1968, pp. 1, 8, 9; May 23, 1968, p. 1; May 24, 1968, pp. 1, 8; "A Proposal for Immediate Reforms Within CVI," signed by 155 students ("Student Protest" File, Student Affairs Center, CVI, St. Thomas campus), May 21, 1968.

72. *Home Journal* (St. Thomas, V.I.), May 26, 1968, pp. 1, 3; May 29, 1968, p. 5; Memoranda "To Members of the Student Body" from Lawrence C. Wanlass, Roland Dickison, Jane E. Tuitt, and John H. Baker, May 26, 1968 (both are in the "Student Body Protest" File, Student Affairs Center, CVI, St. Thomas campus).

73. "Memorandum to Members of the Student Body" from Lawrence C. Wanlass, May 24, 1968, p. 1.

74. That Wanlass was of the Mormon faith is asserted in Lewis, *The Virgin Islands: A Caribbean Lilliput*, p. 266. Wanlass' denial of being a Mormon, which had already been made in St. Thomas, was reiterated in a Delaware-California telephone conversation with this author on November 14, 1982.

75. Interviews with Dr. Lawrence Wanlass, Delaware-California telephone conversation, November 14, 1982; Ernest Wagner, St. Thomas, February 1, 1983; Dr. Herbert Hoover, St. Thomas, February 16, 1983. Most of the information on how Dr. Wanlass thought and acted in regard to black activism came from persons who preferred anonymity in this area of discussion.

76. "College Discontinues Upward Bound Project," *Daily News* (St. Thomas, V.I.), August 5, 1970, p. 1; "Upward Bound to Continue," August 8, 1970, p. 1; "Federal Official Sees No Need to Cancel Program," August 10, 1970, p. 1; "Upward Bound End Termed Necessary," August 18, 1970, p. 1.

77. Norwell Elton Harrigan, "Higher Education in the Micro-States: A Theory of Raran Society" (Ph.D. dissertation, University of Pittsburgh, 1972), pp. 149–153 (pp. 150–153 contain a substantial portion of the position paper of the V.I. faculty group); copy of letter to Miss Magdalene Bryan, Director of the Budget, from Lawrence C. Wanlass and Arthur A. Richards, dated February 2, 1972.

78. Interview with Dr. George Applewhite, Delaware-New York telephone conversation, June 31, 1983. For issues of "The Black Revolutionary," dated February 21, March 3, March 19, and April 7, 1969, are in the "Black Cultural Organization" File at the Student Affairs Center, CVI, St. Thomas campus.

79. Interview with Dr. George Applewhite, Delaware-New York telephone conversation, June 30, 1983.

80. "The Black Revolutionary," February 21, 1969; March 3, 1969, p. 7.

81. Martin Waldron, "Racism Increases On Virgin Islands; Attack on Whites Linked to Black Nationalism," *New York Times*, September 30, 1969, p. 72.

82. "The Black Revolutionary," March 3, 1969, p. 3. The issues of March 19 and April 7, 1969, had some especially good articles. Faculty advisor Applewhite had advised against a negative reference to Jews in an article in the March 19th issue, but the student author insisted on retaining it.

83. "3-Hour Debate Conducted on Racial Situation In V.I.," *Daily News* (St. Thomas, V.I.), June 4, 1970, pp. 1, 6; Edwin G. Russell, "Letter to the Editor," March 10, 1969, p. 7; "Letter to the Editor," May 6, 1969, p. 8; January 16, 1970, p. 2; Corey L. Emanuel, "Letter to the Editor," May 8, 1969, p. 7.

84. "2 Held on $75,000 bond In Armed Robbery Of Bank," *Daily News* (St. Thomas, V.I.), May 20, 1970, p. 1; "21-Year-Old Coed Charged In Connection With Holdup," May 21, 1970, pp. 1, 4, 6; "Fourth Charged In Robbery," May 22, 1970, p. 1; "Jury Selected Rapidly For Bank Robbery Trial," December 2, 1970, p. 1.

85. *Home Journal* (St. Thomas, V.I.), February 19, 1972, p. 6; Kilner Worrell, "Letter to the Editor," *Daily News* (St. Thomas, V.I.), March 5, 1971, p. 7; "Black Studies Program Urged," September 21, 1971, p. 1.

86. *Home Journal* (St. Thomas, V.I.), May 30, 1972, p. 1.

87. "CVI Prof. To Speak On V.I. Culture," *Daily News* (St. Thomas, V.I.), May 28, 1971, p. 5; "CVI Students Salute Prof.," June 19, 1971, p. 3; "Anansi Story Telling Session Set At Beach," December 1, 1971, p. 3; "Creole Specialist To Address Antilles PTA," February 2, 1972, p. 3; *Home Journal* (St. Thomas, V.I.), January 13, 1972, pp. 3, 4; January 20, 1972, p. 1.

88. "Architect of our Problems," *Daily News* (St. Thomas, V.I.), January 13, 1972, p. 7.

89. Phyllis O. Emanuel, "Letter to the Editor," *Daily News* (St. Thomas, V.I.), January 22, 1972, pp. 7, 13.

90. *Home Journal* (St. Thomas, V.I.), January 20, 1972, p. 4.

91. "College Prof. Under Fire. Students Protest," *Home Journal* (St. Thomas, V.I.), December 9, 1972, pp. 1, 5; "Students Take CVI Library in Protest," December 12, 1972, pp. 1, 8.

92. *Home Journal* (St. Thomas, V.I.), December 12, 1972, pp. 1, 8; "CVI Protesters Claim Prof Treated 'Unfairly'," *Daily News* (St. Thomas, V.I.), December 12, 1972, p. 1; interview with Professor Helen Gjessing, St. Thomas, February 23, 1983.

93. "CVI Protesters Claim Prof Treated 'Unfairly'," *Daily News* (St. Thomas, V.I.), December 12, 1972, p. 1; December 15, 1972, p. 1; *Home Journal* (St. Thomas, V.I.), January 12, 1973, p. 1.

94. "CVI Protesters Claim Prof Treated 'Unfairly'," *Daily News* (St. Thomas, V.I.), December 12, 1972, p. 1; December 13, 1972, p. 1, 11; "Campus at College Quiet After Police End Library Siege," *Home Journal* (St. Thomas, V.I.), December 13, 1972, p. 1.

95. Interviews with Dr. Arthur Richards, St. Thomas, February 1, 1983; Dr. Herbert Hoover, St. Thomas, February 16, 1983; Former Senator Athniel (Addie) Ottley, St. Thomas, February 22, 1983.

96. "Six More Charged in Brauhaus Murders," *Home Journal* (St. Thomas, V.I.), December 16, 1972, p. 4; January 12, 1973, p. 1; February 7, 1973, p. 6; *Daily News* (St. Thomas, V.I.), January 4, 1973, p. 1.

97. "CVI To Drop Case Against Protesters," *Daily News* (St. Thomas, V.I.), December 15, 1972, pp. 1, 9; "Jucinto Lopez, "Letter to the Editor," December 23, 1972, p. 7; "Group Asks CVI Revoke Protesters Suspensions," January 5, 1973, p. 1; Glenn J. Smith, "Letter to the Editor," January 11, 1973, p. 7; "CVI Student Hearings to Finish Next Week," January 13, 1972, p. 1; "Senate Panel Drops CVI Investigation," January 24, 1973, p. 1; "Senate Education Panel To Probe CVI," February 5, 1973, p. 1; Benita Cannon, "CVI— Sacred Bull," February 16, 1973, pp. 6, 14; February 20, 1973, p. 3; "Says Students Afraid To Talk At CVI Probe," March 17, 1973, p. 3; "Brown, King Disagree On C.V.I. Investigation," March 24, 1973, p. 1; August 8, 1975, p. 1.

98. "The CVI Investigation," *Daily News* (St. Thomas, V.I.), February 7, 1973, p. 6; Richard D. Shingles, "College as a Source of Black Alienation," *Journal of Black Studies*, Vol. 9, No. 3 (March, 1979), pp. 267–289.

99. Interview with Dr. Lawrence Wanlass, Delaware-California telephone conversation, November 14, 1982; *Daily News* (St. Thomas, V.I.), January 13, 1972, p. 6.

100. Interviews with Dr Frank Mills, St Thomas, February 17, 1983; Professor Helen Gjessing, St. Thomas, February 23, 1983.

101. Minutes of the 1978–79 meetings of the CVI Board of Trustees, located in the Board of Trustees Room, President's Office, UVI, St. Thomas, V.I., were read on August 1, 2016; and telephone conversations with Judge Verne Hodge took place on August 1 and 30, 2016. (Only the general minutes, which are available to the public, were able to be seen. Executive committee minutes, which contain more information, are off-limits to the public.)

102. CVI Board Minutes of February 18, 1979, located in the Board of Trustees Room at UVI.

103. Telephone conversation with Dr. Orville Kean, August 20, 2016.

104. Telephone conversation with Dr. LaVerne Ragster on September 26, 2016.

105. Telephone conversation with Dr. David Hall, September 24, 2016; Jonathon Austin, "University puts medical school on hold," *Daily News* (St. Thomas, V.I.), July 28, 2016, p. 2.

106. Jonathan Austin, "University of the Virgin Islands salaries," *Daily News* (St. Thomas, V.I.), July 22, 2016, p. 4; July 23, 2016, p.5; July 25, 2016, p.4; July 26, 2016, p. 6; July 27, 2016, p. 7; July 30–31, 2016, pp. 6–7.

107. Information is from www.uvi.edu — Factbooks on institutional research and planning; with special thanks to Henville Pole, Executive Assistant to the Provost Camille McKayle.

108. "UVI enrolls school's first Ph.D. candidates," *Daily News* (St. Thomas, V.I.), August 30, 2016, p. 6.

109. Conversations with Prof. Tamara Lang, in August 2016, and also viewing of a PowerPoint presentation of the program that was developed by Prof. Lang.

110. Conversations with Marva Samuel Applewhite and Ruth E. Thomas, September, 2016; Jenny Kane, "Family donates Sorgenfri land to UVI," *Daily News* (St. Thomas, VI), October 13, 2014, p. 3.

Chapter 20

Race Relations in Religion

The great economic and population growth that St. Thomas (and the entire Virgin Islands) experienced in the 1960s and after affected every sphere of life. Even the area of religion, which some may have hoped would have been less subject to the baser human actions that were affecting other institutions, was affected by human racial prejudices.

Judeo-Christian Faiths

Until about the 1850s, the religious congregations in St. Thomas were mainly those of the European groups that had established the colony or were present during the first century and one-half of the colony's history. They were, somewhat in order of official recognition, the Lutheran, Dutch Reformed, Moravian, Hebrew, Roman Catholic, and Anglican congregations. Then, later in the 1800s and during the early decades of the American period, a large number of other denominations would establish themselves in St. Thomas. They included the Methodists, and later, a number of faiths founded in the United States such as the Seventh Day Adventists, Churches of God, Apostolic Faith, Baptists, and Assemblies of God. This research has found that, with the exception of Roman Catholics (and of course Jews, who are often also classified by ancestral heritage), many of the church-going white Americans who moved to St. Thomas from the 1950s onward seemed to have been motivated more by race than by former denominational membership in their determination of a St. Thomas place of worship.

The actions of the Catholics and the Protestants were in accord with sociological research findings that the theology and organization of the Roman Catholic Church (such as its assertions of being "the only true church," the doctrinal infallibility of the Pope, and the complete uniformity of each Sunday's service-mass throughout the world) do not generally allow members who are properly conditioned to feel free to leave the church for any other, regardless of the differences between them and other members. Protestants, on the other hand, tend to think of their denominations more in terms of voluntary groupings based on compatibility and find it easier to switch accordingly.[1] New continental Catholics in St. Thomas were additionally facilitated by the fact that there were several Catholic congregations to choose from, and they were of varying racial compositions. The congregations of St. Anne's in Frenchtown and at Our Lady of Perpetual Help at Mafolie were located in French residential areas and thus were much "whiter" congregations, for persons who preferred that. Sts. Peter and Paul, however, though located in Downstreet Charlotte Amalie, a black residential area, maintains special attraction as the oldest Catholic church on St. Thomas and as the Cathedral. Additionally, in the latter half of the last century, a new Catholic church, Holy Family, was built in eastern St. Thomas.

The absence of white Continentals from many of the local Protestant congregations demonstrated the tendencies and practices of racial separation which accompanied the movement of Whites to St. Thomas, even in the 1950s when there was little overt racial tension. The Methodist Church in Charlotte Amalie, Christ Church Methodist at the Market Square, had one of the largest congregations on the island—about 900 members in 1975 and did not then have a single white member! The Reverend Neville Brodie, a black West Indian who became pastor of the congregation in 1977, stated that the Church had a sizeable file of transfers from Methodist churches on the mainland in regard to members who were relocating to St. Thomas, but never actually joined the church. A similar absence of white members remains true presently at the large Wesley Methodist Church at Estate Tutu in St. Thomas.[2]

The membership was very similar at the Memorial Moravian Church in Charlotte Amalie, St. Thomas, whose membership of several hundred by the mid-1970s made it the largest of the eight Moravian congregations in the Virgin Islands. During the pastorate of the Reverend Norman Prochnau, a white Continental, from 1967 to 1974, there were only two white members (excluding the pastor and his family). The tenure of his successor, the Reverend Rawle Belle, a black West Indian who became pastor in 1974, was marked by a fifty per cent reduction in the white membership—there was only one! At present, there is a total absence of white members at Memorial Moravian, and also at New Herrnhut in eastern St. Thomas, the oldest Moravian Church in the Virgin Islands and in the Western Hemisphere, and at the Nisky Moravian congregation.[3]

In 1975 Pastor Lawrence Baietti, the white Continental pastor of the Frederick Lutheran Church in St. Thomas, one of the oldest congregations on the island, disclosed that there were hundreds of Lutheran members, of whom about two dozen were Caucasians. Pastor Baietti said the general experience was that when continental Lutherans first moved to St. Thomas, they attended the church. However, on finding out that the membership was overwhelmingly West Indian (meaning black) and that the congregation used a common chalice for communion, they did not return. The Frederick congregation had specifically adopted the use of the chalice, instead of individual cups, as a measure of complete integration; the motion had been made by a white member.[4]

At the other extreme from the great majority of all-black or almost all-black Protestant congregations stood the Reformed Church, which had had a long history on St. Thomas as the Dutch Reformed Church.[5] (It was the congregation from which young Edward Wilmot Blyden was sent to the U.S. in 1850, but his rejection there led him to Africa and fame.) In the pre-1950 decades the Church had acquired a reputation of exclusivity. Even though its membership was mostly black, it was generally thought to be "not for dark-skinned people." In the 1950s, therefore, it had a very small membership, comprised mainly of several old "mixed" families. The congregation was so small that it did not even have a resident pastor from the late 1940s through the late 1950s.[6]

In 1958 the Reformed Church finally got a resident minister, the Reverend Donald Lam, who actively set out to increase the size of the congregation. The movement of substantial numbers of white continentals to St. Thomas at the time facilitated his efforts, and during his five-year tenure, 1958–1963, the congregation almost doubled in size.[7] The sizeable number of new white members gave it a reputation as the church where Whites would be most at home. Thus, during the 1960s and 1970s, many churchgoing white Protestants, on moving to St. Thomas and learning of the racial composition of the various churches, tended to go to the Reformed Church, regardless of their previous denominational affiliations. By 1980, therefore, the Reformed Church had developed substantially and had quite a large congregation.

Some persons affiliated with the Reformed Church, both white and non-white, have been reluctant to acknowledge any racial basis for the great attraction the church has had for white Continentals. The Reverend Jack White, its white continental pastor in the mid-1970s, was known to be aggressively critical of persons who suggested possible racial motives. June A. V. Lindqvist, who was a member of a well-known mixed V.I. family with ties to the Reformed congregation and is now deceased, theorized that the Reformed Church had its roots in North America more so than denominations such as the Methodist and Lutheran, thus accounting for its large white continental membership. It

St. Thomas' Dutch Reformed Church congregation in 1929. The word "Dutch" is no longer used and the congregation is now mainly white, based on white continental membership. Courtesy of the Virgin Islands Government's Archival Collection at the Charles W. Turnbull Regional Library.

has also been pointed out that it is the closest equivalent on St Thomas to the Presbyterian and Congregationalist denominations of the U.S.[8]

That such religious rationales accounted for a portion of the white membership the Reformed Church gained in the 1960s, 1970s and since is not disputed. What is also clearly evident, however, is that some Whites who went to the Reformed Church did so for racial reasons. Pastor Baietti, himself a white Continental, revealed that some of his white Lutheran parishioners had told him that other whites had urged them not to attend the Lutheran church, stating that the Reformed was the congregation for Whites. There was even the case of an administrator at the College of the Virgin Islands who, even though he had attended a Methodist seminary and pastored Methodist churches on the mainland during the 1960s, affiliated with the Reformed, and not the Methodist Church, when he moved to St. Thomas in the mid-1970s. The Reverend Brodie of the Methodist Church acknowledged that he and some other Protestant clergymen were very much aware of the practice of some white Continentals in St. Thomas to go to the Reformed Church, regardless of their previous religious affiliations.

Actually, one of the most common religious perceptions of white Continentals in St. Thomas during the late twentieth century was that most of them did not go to any church. There were also occasional complaints by some Con-

tinentals and natives that most local congregations did not try to attract continental membership and thus did not foster integration. Attorney Edith Bornn,
a mixed St. Thomian who was Episcopalian and is now deceased, believed that
some Whites went to the Reformed Church because they were sometimes made
to feel not wanted in other churches. In 1974, a white teacher on St. Thomas,
asked by a newspaper roving columnist why so many newcomers did not belong to a church, stated: "In the Virgin Islands, some churches have had difficulty adjusting to the fast changing lifestyle here, and are too defensive about
reaching out to the new residents to participate."[9]

If it is true, as has been claimed in explaining the great attraction of the Reform Church for white Americans, that its American connection appeals to
them more than European-origin churches such as the Anglican and Methodist,
then the newer American churches should also be attractive to more white
Americans. However, recent contacts with pastors or members of some Amer-
ican-origin local faiths, such as the Baptist, Seventh Day Adventist, and Pentecostal Church of God in Christ, have revealed that many such congregations,
except for occasional visitors vacationing in St. Thomas, also have none or
only very few white members.[10]

The present pastor of the Reformed Church, the Rev. Jeffrey Neevel, has
been its leader since 2010, and the church now has hundreds of white members along with a lesser number of Blacks. While not explicitly denying that
there may be some white members of his congregation who simply preferred
white to black fellow church members, he believes that denominational switches
made by Whites to his church after coming to St. Thomas have been due mainly
to matters such as styles of worship, lifestyle issues, and the degree to which
they felt welcomed by other churches. Pastor Neevel has increased the Church's
ministry to the community's Blacks, needy and young through its expansion
of contributions to the Salvation Army's lunch program and its support of My
Brother's Workshop in its vocational training of young unskilled persons.[11]

A similar recent concern (of about ten years) on St. Thomas has been the
Nazareth by the Sea Episcopal Church or Fellowship, whose membership is
mainly white. The concern stems from the fact that there are four developed
Episcopal (the West Indian term is usually Anglican) churches on St. Thomas—
All Saints Cathedral (the oldest) on Garden Street, St. Andrews in Sugar Es-
tate, St. Luke's in the east, on a hill in the Smith Bay area, and the newest is
Holy Spirit in the western part of St. Thomas. It would therefore seem that
Episcopal churches are quite available on St. Thomas; if one does not prefer
the nearest one, which at one time was a frequent complaint in one parish,
another one is always available.

Because of the well-known concerns, an interview was secured with the Vicar of the Nazareth Episcopal Fellowship, the Rev. Dr. Wesley Williams—a gentleman of many professions and talents. He is presently also Priest of the All Saints Cathedral of St. Thomas and an accomplished musician. He had a stellar legal career on the mainland before moving to St. Thomas, where he now also serves as one of the two leaders of the Lockhart Companies Incorporated, a huge economic conglomerate of the Virgin Islands. The fellowship meets in the Inspiration Hall of the Paradise Cove Resort at Nazareth. Dr. Williams, who is called "Father Wes" by many of his members, explains that it is not possible for some of his parishioners to attend the morning services of other congregations because many of them make a living by the sea—as owners of boats which do a lot of business on the weekends, and are thus not available until after midday on Sundays. In fact, he says many are so fatigued on Sunday afternoons that they often sit in services at times when standing would be the normal behavior.

Dr. Williams seems to truly believe that, were it not for the Nazareth ministry, many of its attendees would not have much of a church life. The first leader of the fellowship was the Rev. Frank Johnston, who had a background of ministry in Long Island and at All Saints, and after he died, Episcopal Bishop Ambrose Gumbs took Dr. Williams to the fellowship and urged his ministry. Dr. Williams says members of the fellowship speak of the need to love others every Sunday, frequently have guest singers and choirs from other congregations, and are trying to encourage others to join.[12]

There has been another interesting aspect to the historical development of race relations on St. Thomas. Though their congregations were mainly black, the 1970s pastors Reverends Baietti (Lutheran) and Prochnau (Moravian), as examples, were both white Continentals. There were similar situations in several other congregations. Contrary to a substantial segment of Blacks on the U.S. mainland who had historically formed their own churches and supplied the manpower for them, religion among Blacks in the Danish West Indies/ U.S. Virgin Islands had developed differently. Most V.I. Blacks had become members of European or U.S.-headquartered denominations which viewed the local churches as missionary outposts and thus supplied pastors for them. The tradition of black congregations with white pastors became so established that some Blacks viewed it as the natural and best configuration. Frederick Lutheran Church, with a history of over 300 years in St. Thomas by the 1970s, had never had a black pastor to that time, even though that has since changed.[13] Those circumstances would also explain why Blacks in the Virgin Islands and other similar West Indian islands did not develop their own "Negro spirituals"-type hymns or any distinctive preaching style as some U.S. mainland Blacks did.

It was not until the 1950s or 1960s that most of the major denominations in St. Thomas got their first black ministers, and some members of the congregations experienced difficulty in adjusting. However, some Blacks also realized that it was past time for Blacks to set aside the white biases from a long history of colonialism that had generally caused them to devalue anyone or anything black. The Reverend Father James Moody, a black Virgin Islander who was ordained as a Catholic priest on St. Thomas in 1973, found that in the observances attendant to his ordination, he heard the phrase, "it's so nice to see another black face up there on the altar," almost as often as he was told words of congratulation.[14] Having black pastors, and even from the African continent, is no longer unusual in most St. Thomas denominations.

In 1974, asked by a St. Thomas public opinion columnist, Peter Goodwin, whether Jesus was black or white, Episcopal Bishop Edward Turner, himself white, answered that the false Sunday school image of a blond blue-eyed Jesus supported racism and could lead to a rejection of Christianity by aware black youths.[15] Such a rejection had already become noticeable in the late 1960s with the arrival of Rastafarianism on St. Thomas.

Rastafarianism and Islam

Even though Rastafarianism and Islam have very different worldwide histories and numbers, they are being discussed similarly in this study as they both became noticeable in St. Thomas during the 1960s decade. (St. Thomas also has several additional non-Christian religious faiths, but they are relatively very small, do not usually stand out in their dress as Rastafarians and Muslims often do, and are not usually considered as controversial in the discussion of racial or religious issues).

The Rastafarian movement had developed in Jamaica in the 1930s in the poorest areas of its capital, Kingston. It denounced many of the major tenets and institutions of Western culture (derogatively referred to as "Babylon"), and erected in their place a religious-cultural philosophy which viewed Emperor Haile Selassie as divine, Blacks as the chosen people—with eventual repatriation to Africa, and a lifestyle characterized by vegetarianism, the ceremonial use of marijuana, and allowing the hair to grow in a long fashion (referred to as wearing "locks" or "dreadlocks"). The Rastafarian movement is thought to have been spawned by the frustrations of economic and political powerlessness and the white-biased denigration of African-descended people and culture. For about three decades, the movement had grown but had remained confined to Jamaica.[16]

Dr. Klaus de Albuquerque, a deceased former faculty member at the College of the Virgin Islands who did a great deal of research on Rastafarianism, thought that the original Rastas (a shortened form of Rastafarians) on St. Thomas in 1967 or 1968 had arrived from Antigua or Trinidad. Conditions in St. Thomas at that time furnished fertile ground for the philosophy. Many young people were feeling that the islands were being taken over by white Continentals and Blacks appeared powerless to halt the march of events.[17]

By the early 1970s a number of converts had been made and the Rasta movement was becoming a matter of some concern among authorities on St. Thomas. Ethiopia Tamara I (formerly Anthony G. Leroy), who claimed the title of Commander-in-Chief of the Rastafari Union, arrived on St. Thomas in 1973. He was born in Haiti, became a Rasta in Brooklyn in 1971 (after having thought seriously about it during his service in Vietnam), and decided to reside in St. Thomas because his maternal grandmother had been from there. That same year, influenced by Bob Marley, he decided that the wearing of locks showed greater commitment and started to let his hair grow. He also thought that St. Thomas Rastas were languishing due to the lack of a strong adult leader, and in 1974 started the organization of a Rastafarian nation. However, all Rastas did not affiliate with the "nation"; many remained independent.[18]

Rastafarians had acquired quite a mixed reputation and had become a major topic of conversation in St. Thomas by the late 1970s. Definite figures are very hard to obtain, but it seems that there were at least a couple hundred by then, and the movement was growing rapidly. Contrary to the wishes of many who viewed them as being simply misguided, dirty, and/or dangerous, they gained some acceptance as a religious group. School officials, based on their claim of religious freedom, allowed requested modifications of school uniforms. Rasta students, for example, were allowed to wear large berets ("herb caps") at school to cover their locks. Some Rastas were known as very industrious and willing to work in areas compatible with their beliefs, such as gardening or retailing fruits and vegetables. Others were charged with stealing frequently, and often sought to defend their actions by their belief that anything that grew from the earth belonged to all people.

Many Whites had a special fear of Rastas, viewing the Rasta philosophy as anti-white, and were afraid Rastas might be particularly prone to violence against Whites, especially when under the influence of drugs. Some Rastas tried to explain that their philosophy was one of non-violence, but a common thought in St. Thomas was that most Rastas there really knew very little of the true Rastafarian philosophy. The Rastafarian movement in the 1970s thus added substantially to the racial tensions, and seemed as one response to the competitive economy that had come to characterize St. Thomas. An appreciable number of young Blacks felt that they had very little chance of succeeding in the new economy, and Rastafarianism, for some, was one way to avoid the stacked competition.[19]

Recent efforts to reconnect with Ethiopia Tamara I for the updating of this work were futile, and Hector "Hectito" Francis, also known by the Ethiopian name of "Alemu" (which means "God's world"), was chosen as the Rastafarian representative for the Centennial updating of this work. Contrary to many of the local Rastas in the 1970s, "Alemu" is a well-educated Rasta, who studied journalism at UVI and recently retired from the V.I. Legislature as its Director of Public Affairs (during which he worked for the establishment of the Legislature's television channel that so many Virgin Islanders view). He describes Rastafari as a dynamic and evolving faith, which has gained some of its beliefs and principles from studying religions such as Christianity, Judaism, Islam, and various indigenous African belief systems. As a result, there are various "houses" of Rastafari (somewhat comparable to the denominations of Christianity), such as the Nyabingi (to which some of the Bordeaux farmers involved with the "We Grow Food" organization belong), the Bobo Shanti, and the Twelve Tribes. In some "houses" there are places where believers get together and have sacramental ceremonies, while others do not congregate.[20]

At one time, some local Rastafari, such as now-deceased UVI Professor Gene Emanuel, UVI Administrator Louis "Akil" Petersen, Zebelge Izack, and "Alemu" himself established the Rastafari Improvement Association, Inc., but it did not materialize to the degree they had hoped and became dormant after they turned the organization over to younger members of the faith. The continuing beliefs of all Rastafari are that deceased Ethiopian Emperor Haile Selassie is the spiritual head (not necessarily "God" to all "houses") of the faith; Africa is the spiritual home; the diet is vegetarianism; and upright living—showing righteousness to all—is the guiding principle. No one knows the number of the local Rastafari population, but Alemu asserts that it is internationally known and acknowledged that the world's highest percentage of Rastafari per capita is found in the U.S. Virgin Islands.[21]

Another religious group that attracted many young Blacks in St. Thomas, beginning in the late 1960s and since, was the Muslim. Though originally not as feared as the Rastas, Muslims also were thought of by many as anti-white and thus contributed to generally increased racial consciousness and tension. Probably the most widely recognized Muslim in St. Thomas in the 1970s/1980s was Abdullah Muhammad (formerly Warren Venzen). A Virgin Islander who had gone to New York, he was converted there before returning to St. Thomas in 1973. On his return he started the operation of a fruit and vegetable stand and became a familiar figure in the Market Square area of downtown St. Thomas, distinctively dressed in an all-white outfit of a cap, tunic and pants. A problem that he resented from the beginning of his business was that of tourists taking his photograph without securing his permission, and he ran afoul of the law a few times for confiscating the cameras of tourists who did so.[22]

Contrary to what some other Muslims had been known to say, Abdullah Muhammad said he had no objections to Whites coming to St. Thomas; he welcomed them. However, he thought they had very little or no respect for Blacks as a people. Muhammad believed that by the mid-1970s St. Thomas had become bound by economic slavery, as Blacks had not taken opportunities that they could have utilized in the immediate decades before when they had been in a better position than they had realized.

When asked if there was any cooperation between Muslims and Rastas, Mr. Muhammad completely discounted any such thought. He said Rastas were a CIA group with no knowledge of what they were about. He gave as an example the fact that Rastas were supposed to be rejecting European culture but at the same time looked to the European Bible for guidance.[23]

Another black identified with the Muslim faith and who had returned to St. Thomas in 1973 after studying and working abroad prefers to be known only as Lamakalo (although his family's surname is Frett). He adopted his beliefs while studying at the University of Dar-Es-Salaam in Tanzania in the late 1960s and made a pilgrimage to Mecca in 1970–71. On his return to St. Thomas, Lamakalo became an active and respected worker among some young Blacks.[24]

Lamakalo believed that during the period from the 1950s through the 1980s, the black community had become more passive while the white community became more aggressive. To him the issue was ideological; he asserted there were really more black people in the Virgin Islands who thought white than there were white people. His concept of religion is that it is an opiate, though he said a strong belief is not, and he pointed to the growth of various religious groups during that period as signs of the growing desperation of the masses.

For the updated version of this work, both Mr. Muhammad and Lamakalo were interviewed again, after more than three decades, during late July and early August, 2016. Mr. Muhammad still dresses in his cap and tunic and now operates a very successful business, Muhammad's Halal Foods, making fruit smoothies in the Vendors Plaza on Charlotte Amalie's waterfront, along with his wife, the former Pamela Hoheb. While black and white tourists alike enjoy his pleasant personality and his delicious blender concoctions of mango/pa-

paya, banana/strawberry, or whatever other fresh fruits or combinations one wishes, philosophically he is just as serious as he was in the 1980s. He thinks local Blacks have gone backward in the last several decades. He asserts that Blacks did not capitalize sufficiently on the achievements of Martin Luther King and the so-called Black Revolution. He said black neighborhoods are mostly gone; drugs, killings, prostitution, and unemployment prevail, and others even control the food industry. When it was pointed out that his fellow Muslims control the food industry, he acknowledged that but said he is against what they have done to the neighborhoods as they sell liquor, cigarettes, other things that corrupt, and also Haram (unhealthy foods in Islam).

Mr. Muhammad worships every Friday at the Mosque in Estate Thomas, where he says all Muslims on the island—a few hundred—worship, regardless of their race, origin, or nationality. When asked what he thinks of ISIS, he said emphatically that he does not believe it has any connection to Islam, as there is no way anyone who follows the teachings of the Prophet Muhammed could do the things ISIS does. He thinks ISIS was formed to make Islam look bad, and while he does not know who is behind it, he suggests that the CIA or Jews are possibilities. Mr. Muhammad also asserts that in a matter of a decade or two, most European countries will be Islamic states, based on their democracy and their culture—as Europeans have very few children while Islamic families tend to have many.[25]

Lamakalo, the other Muslim who had been interviewed in 1983 and was interviewed again during August 2016 for this update, has travelled a different path. He converted to the Seventh Day Adventist faith about seven years ago and thus is now a practicing Christian, though some still identify him otherwise. He considers religion a personal matter, and is more interested in discussing socio-economic and political issues, which remain very similar to those he had had as a Muslim. He had grown up as a Methodist, with an extremely devout father and had always believed in the Bible. But he was very impressed with Malcolm X's autobiography, along with being disillusioned by Christians who were not living Christian lives, and was thus attracted to a structure where persons seemed more loyal to their faith. However, he now prefers the personal, extemporaneous prayers of Christians, and thinks Muslim prayers are more of a set pattern.

Lamakalo's political and social philosophies, however, are similar to his thoughts of three decades ago. He feels that laws and actions in the Virgin Islands are not sufficiently beneficial or suitable for a small society. He knows that, as a non-independent polity, there are limits to what can be done, but he believes that Blacks here can do much more to address local situations. As an example, he thinks there is insufficient knowledge and thus pride in local heroes and accomplishments. He thinks much of the violence and drug use stems from the daily stresses of life, which need to be minimized by measures such as increasing the minimum wage, revamping the educational system to present Virgin Islands history in a positive way, and to have teaching done with the aim of eliminating the impact of self-hate and tendency to violence many V.I. youngsters have, because if one hates oneself, one hates everyone looking like self. With the experience of having worked in the Department of Education, he believes it needs a strong cultural division, whose mandate would be to ensure that V.I. students understand and appreciate their special history and culture, and know how to use them in self-aggrandizement and moving forward.[26] With present Virgin Islands rates of shootings and drug use, his philosophical ideas may need much greater application.

Notes

1. For denominational histories in St. Thomas, see Isaac Dookhan, *A History of the Virgin Islands*, Chapter 11; for sociological aspects of church membership, see, for example, Thomas Ford Hoult, *The Sociology of Religion* (New York: The Dryden Press, 1958), pp. 311–312.

2. Interview with Reverend Neville Brodie, St. Thomas, February 18, 1983. Also interview with Reginald Davis, St. Thomas, February 19, 1983; Mr. Davis was a lay preacher in the Methodist Church for over fifty years. Telephone conversation with Mrs. Bernice Heyliger, of the Wesley Methodist Church in St. Thomas, August 31, 2016.

3. Conversation with the Reverend and Mrs. Norman Prochnau, Allentown, Pennsylvania, May 21, 1983, and Delaware-Pennsylvania telephone conversation, June 15, 1983; St. Thomas-St. Croix telephone conversation with the Reverend Rawle Belle, February 8, 1983; telephone conversations on August 31, 2016, with the Rev. Dr. Winelle Kirton-Roberts of the Memorian Moravian Church, the Rev. Anique Elms Matthew of the New Herrnhut Moravian Church, and the Rev. Dr. Errol Connor of the Nisky Moravian Church, St. Thomas, April, 2017.

4. Interview with the Reverend Lawrence Baietti, St. Thomas, February 24, 1983.

5. For obvious reasons, the Jewish congregation is not under consideration. Its membership would be expected to be mainly Hebrew.

6. Interview with Reginald Davis, St. Thomas, February 19, 1983.

7. "Rev. Lam Leaves For New Duties In Michigan," *Daily News* (St. Thomas, V.I.), September 19, 1963, p. 1.

8. Interviews with June A. V. Lindqvist, St. Thomas, February 3, 1983 and Attorney Edith Bornn, St. Thomas, February 24, 1983.

9. Interview with Attorney Edith Bornn, St. Thomas, February 24, 1983; *Daily News* (St. Thomas, V.I.), March 15, 1975, p. 6; 6; "What Can Churches Do to Help Reduce Crime?."

10. Conversations in March and April, 2017 with Dr. Dion Phillips and Dr. Whitman Browne, both Adventists; Retired Judge Audrey Thomas, a Baptist; Bishop Joseph Lewis of the Pentecostal Church of God in Christ; and others who preferred not to be mentioned.

11. Interview with Pastor Jeffrey Neeley, St. Thomas, August 23, 2016.

12. Interview with Rev. Dr. Wesley Williams, St. Thomas, September 1, 2016.

13. Campbell, *St. Thomas Negroes*, p. 35; interview with Pastor Baietti, St. Thomas, February 24, 1983.

14. Rev. Jerome Moody, "Letter to the Editor," *Daily News* (St. Thomas, V.I.), July 24, 1973, pp. 7, 18.

15. "Was Jesus Black or White?," *Daily News* (St. Thomas, V.I.), November 23, 1974, p. 6.

16. M. G. Smith, Roy Augier, and Rex Nettleford, *The Rastafari Movement in Kingston, Jamaica* (Kingston, Jamaica: Institute of Social and Economic Research, 1960); Leonard Barrett, *The Rastafarians: Sounds of Cultural Dissonance* (Boston: Beacon Press, 1977); Klaus de Albuquerque, "Rastafarians and Cultural Identity in the Caribbean," *Revista/Review Interamericana*, Vol. 10, No. 2 (Summer, 1980), pp. 230–247.

17. Interview with Klaus de Albuquerque, St. Thomas, February 23, 1983.

18. Interview with Ethiopia Tamara I (Anthony G. Leroy), St. Thomas, February 25, 1983.

19. Interviews with Klaus de Albuquerque, St. Thomas, February 23, 1983; Ethiopia Tamara I, St. Thomas, February 25, 1983; Van den Berghe, *Race and Racism*, p. 22; *Daily News* (St. Thomas, V.I.), June 14, 1973, p. 6.

20. Ibid.

21. Interview with Hector "Hectito" Francis (Alemu), St. Thomas, August 26, 2016.

22. Ibid.

23. Interview with Abdullah Muhammad (Warren Venzen), St. Thomas, February 18, 1983.

24. Interview with Lamakalo, St. Thomas, February 18, 1983.

25. Interviews with Abdullah Muhammad, St. Thomas, July 15 and 29, 2016.

26. Interviews with Lamakalo, St. Thomas, August 1 and 5, 2016.

Chapter 21

Race Relations in Social Activities

Social activities by members of a community, and the mutual enjoyment they generate, are among the greatest binders of human relationships. They may be effective destroyers of stereotypes and other obstacles that prevent persons and groups from seeing each other as common and equal residents of Planet Earth. This section focuses on a few social activities and how they may have helped or hindered the development of beneficial social relationships in St. Thomas during the last seven decades of the first American century of the Virgin Islands.

Carnival

The best known St. Thomas social activity, which started in the mid-twentieth century and still remains as the prime socio-cultural activity today, at least in terms of the number of participants, is the annual carnival. Actually, the first organized carnivals in St. Thomas's history were held much earlier in the century, in the pre-American years of 1912 and 1914. They were both organized by the white and mixed upper classes of St. Thomas' society, and five-year old Ralph Paiewonsky, who would become governor about half a century later, along with a little friend of about the same age and class, were the two pages in the 1912 carnival.[1] The outbreak of World War 1 in 1914 brought such activities to an end.

The present Virgin Islands Carnival, which was first held in St. Thomas in September 1952 and became an annual event, was thus the revival of a festivity that had not taken place for four decades, and the person mainly responsible for its rebirth was a young WSTA radio announcer, Ron de Lugo, a member of a local Old White family. De Lugo was a very likable and down-to-earth person, also well-known as the creator of a popular radio character, Mango Jones, who spoke in the local creole dialect. St. Thomians of all kinds were very grateful for de Lugo's role in promoting such an enjoyable and lucrative community celebration. To thank him, late in 1952 a special program to show the community's appreciation was held, and de Lugo received a scholarship from community-donated funds to pursue studies in radio and allied fields.[2] (De Lugo entered local politics in the late 1950s and later became the V.I.'s first Delegate to Congress in the early 1970s.)

After the 1952 carnival, it was decided that future carnivals should be earlier in the year, and in order to avoid competition with the Trinidad and other already established pre-Lenten festivals, the carnivals on St. Thomas from 1953 onward were scheduled for after Lent, therefore usually in late April. The carnivals of the first decade, the 1950s, were probably the best examples of interracial togetherness St. Thomas has ever known. People of all races and all walks of life took part in the parades, either by active participation or as onlookers, and joyfully tramped the streets to the calypso beat of the bands. A 1953 article in the *New York Times* stressed that Carnival in St. Thomas was notable for its idea of total participation and that even the tourists became a part of the celebration.[3]

By 1960, however, it was evident that substantial changes in the nature and organization of Carnival were taking place. For example, that year the Gift and Fashion Shop Association, whose membership was largely white continental, was responsible for raising funds by handling the sale of raffle tickets for a homesite, replacing the formerly-practiced sale of tickets by the carnival queen contestants. Thus, instead of the queen being the contestant who sold the largest number of tickets, the Gift Shop Association named a panel to select the queen based on beauty, personality, and other stated characteristics. The panel chosen by the Association was mainly white, even though most of the queen contestants were black.[4]

The feeling of many St. Thomians was that carnival was becoming too commercialized and slipping into the control of certain special interests. At the organizational meeting for the Carnival of 1962, Mrs. Gertrude Lockhart Dudley, a member of a prominent native family and herself a businesswoman, was quoted as saying that though she was a member of the Gift Shop Association, "business has ruined Carnival. It belongs to the people. Give it back to the people." Even though there was less direction of the carnival after that by white business interests, Carnival never quite returned to what it had been during the 1950s, as there was no curtailing of white business domination of the total community and the black resentment which that was causing, along with the other

A scene from the first modern St. Thomas carnival in 1952. Courtesy of the Virgin Islands Government's Archival Collection at the Charles W. Turnbull Regional Library.

effects of a burgeoning and more varied population. After the 1960s Carnival came to be viewed by many people as a time when one had to be very careful about activities such as street tramping, because some young Blacks seemed to use such activities as opportunities to vent their frustrations or seek revenge against rivals or enemies. More and more Whites began to withdraw from participation in Carnival. In fact, by the late 1960s Carnivals were often attended by scary racial rumors. Poppy Cannon White, a well-known civil rights activist on the mainland, who spent the carnival of 1968 in St. Thomas, wrote an article about the anti-white rumors of that year—that some Blacks were arming with ice picks and that a chartered plane of black power activists from the mainland was to land in St. Thomas just before the Carnival began. As she noted, the rumors amounted to nothing and "carnival was peaceful and fun."[5]

There was a vicious circle aspect of race relations in regard to Carnival that was also operative in several other areas of life on St. Thomas. Many Whites declared that it was the rumors and the discourtesies they sometimes experienced which caused them to lessen their participation in Carnival. James Ready, for example, a white Continental who moved to St. Thomas in 1967 and worked at CVI, explained that at first he used to go regularly to Carnival Village, a large, open area with music and booths selling food and drinks. However, he said teenagers would look at him and the other Whites he was with and call them "Honkies." He got to a point of discomfort and stopped going to Carnival Village at night, fearing an incident. Similar happenings and decisions have been told by a number of Whites, and even Blacks. However, some Blacks charged that instead of total non-participation in Carnival, which consists of many different kinds of activities over a span of two weeks, Whites who really wanted to be a part of the community could have chosen those activities more to their liking and comfort, as most Blacks did. Instead, it was not unusual, by 1970, that Whites who moved to St. Thomas made no effort to even find out for themselves what Carnival was all about. At the College of the Virgin Islands, where the major week of the Carnival was granted as the spring recess, some of the white continental professors would plan to leave the island during that week. Some Blacks thus charged that such Whites showed no interest in developing any appreciation of Virgin Islands or West Indian culture and that such attitudes accounted for some of the racial problems the island was experiencing.[6]

In 1973 columnist Henry Wheatley stated that Carnival, in many ways, had become a good idea gone sour—another victim of the crowding and ethnic separation of the past decade. He predicted that there would be more withdrawals along class and racial lines.[7] Certain institutions appeared to be actively working towards that end. Even though Carnival was considered a tourist attraction, some hotels on St. Thomas were known to discourage their guests from involvement with it. In 1975, Joan Burt, a Washington attorney who was staying at the Lime Tree Hotel, protested the hotel's failure to inform guests of a major Carnival event, and when it did, after the fact, compared the event to a "Zulu rebellion." The pertinent section of the hotel's daily information sheet, written by resident manager Mike Gaston, read:

> This morning at 4 a.m. there was a celebration called "Jouvert." This is an early morning tramp that winds its way through town. A tramp is a follow-the-leader type thing with drums and other percussive instruments dancing thru the streets. We didn't tell you about this happening yesterday cause we didn't think you would want to join in. At one time I lived in town and the tramp came directly under my bedroom window. I thought it was a Zulu rebellion.[8]

The hotel's manager admitted that there was "no good reason" for keeping guests uninformed about the event, but did not think that the writer had intended a racial slur, with which, expectably, the writer concurred.

It seems that a significant force in the history of socio-racial relations on St. Thomas since the 1950s was simply the factor of numbers. There is ample evidence that in the 1950s there was quite a bit of interracial socializing, more than there ever was afterward. The continental population was then rather small and practically needed to mix or else be quite hermitic. However, as more Continentals arrived, Blacks began to notice that there were fewer social affairs characterized by racial mixture. The perception of many Blacks and some Whites was that as white Continentals gained sufficient numbers to form their own social groups and socialize by themselves, they tended to do so more and more. There had come to exist on St. Thomas, though its population was almost eighty per cent black, a substantial number of white Continentals who had almost no real contact with Blacks. Dr. Aimery Caron, who worked at CVI and was also a member of a white family with a well-known business establishment on the Main Street of St. Thomas, witnessed this progression of separation with regret. However, while many Blacks believed that white racism was a major factor in the ever-widening chasm, Dr. Caron was not so sure. He tended to think that white Americans are simply not too adaptable to other cultures.[9]

In recent decades, nearing the Centennial, the separate self-sufficiency that greater numbers of Whites have enabled has spread and increased. There are social places of business, such as bars and restaurants, in which all or almost all employees are white and their patrons are similar. One area in which this is particularly noticeable is on the eastern end of St. Thomas, in the Red Hook area, and some Whites are speaking openly of their development of a new town in that area.

Another factor which affected socio-racial relations in St. Thomas was the general socio-economic level of the Whites who came at various periods. Many of the white arrivals of the 1950s and early 1960s were relatively well-to-do retirees, professional, or entrepreneurial-types, who were not engaged in economic pursuits which involved much competition with Blacks. A sizeable number seemed willing to engage in social activities in which Blacks were involved. Ronald Walker, who worked in St. Thomas as a journalist during portions of the Sixties and Seventies, recalled that about 1965, there was a great influx of Continentals: "They were a new kind of people—not affluent.... Many were very insensitive to the cultural nuances and way of life of the Virgin Islands." Edwin Hatchette, a black native St. Thomian, and Helen Gjessing, a white Continental who lived on St. Thomas from 1957 until the first decade of the 21st century, both cited the importation of white construction crews in the late 1960s and 1970s. Professor Gjessing noted that, on the whole, such new residents tended to be "less educated and less tolerant" than the type of Whites who had arrived earlier.[10]

At the same time, the black population was itself undergoing marked incremental changes due to the other incoming movement—of eastern Caribbean workers. They, too, on the average, were less educated and also less attuned to American culture than the native Blacks of the Virgin Islands. In general, then, neither the white nor black newcomers to St. Thomas in the Sixties and Seventies were amenable to the continuance of the type of interracial sociability of which the 1950s had given some promise.

In looking back at some events of the Fifties, however, there is reason to wonder if there was ever any real promise of more than token socio-racial interaction, even at that time. In July, 1957, for example, the Hands Across the Sea Committee held a gala affair at the Virgin Isle Hotel to raise funds for its college scholarship program. The affair was St. Thomas' first Debutante Cotillion and formally presented were twelve young ladies in their later teens. Even though most of the members of the Hands Across the Sea Committee were Continentals, and almost half of the committee was comprised of white Continentals, all of the debutantes were from native families (one was white). With several white Continentals on the committee and more and more Continentals moving to St. Thomas daily, would it not have been ideal to have at least one or two continental teenagers participate in that social event? Or was it their unspoken thought that, on the whole, white continental society and native (mainly black society) were really two different entities, whose debutante-age daughters were too different to be presented together?[11]

What came to prevail openly in St. Thomas from the 1960s and 1970s was the mainland American pattern of race relations. Though the few governmental records which noted racial differences, mainly birth and death certificates, did not change and retained their "White," "Negro," and "Mixed" classifications, the terms used in everyday speech were modified. In keeping with current terminology on the mainland, young people, with their elders following gradually, substituted "Black" for "Negro." "Mixed" became passé as a racial category; its use became mainly descriptive as mixed people came to be designated as black.

Except for a very small percentage of persons in both races, social life mirrored the American pattern of separateness. Even in those activities which brought together many persons of similar socio-economic status, such as the public schools where white and black teachers had the same levels of formal education, interracial relationships tended to be mainly professional and generally ended along with the workday. Of course, there were those individuals and groups of both races who consciously acted and entertained in ways promotive of interracial socializing. But such individuals, groups, and occasions constituted the exceptions rather than the customary.[12]

The later years of the twentieth century saw even greater reasons why social mixing became less than before. For example, in 1987, a combined band— the Jam Band/Eddie and the Movements, which was then the most popular of the orchestras among the young people of St. Thomas—produced a carnival hit tune which became the road march and had the name of "Legal." A small portion of the song had the lyrics "kill the rabbit," and without any special reason, except apparently that many rabbits are white, Whites in the community came to think that the song referred to them, and that they would be killed if they patronized the affairs of that year's Carnival. Efforts to dispel the rumor were unsuccessful and many of the Whites who had attended at least some of the activities of previous Carnivals refused to do so that year and often in the years after.[13]

Additionally, during the beginning decade and a half of this century, a number of incidents involving guns or knives have taken place during Carnival. A few of the early morning "J'ouvert" tramps on Charlotte Amalie's waterfront had to be stopped by police officials due to crimes or attempted crimes, and the Carnival of 2016 was marred at the end of its last night by a shooting at the Carnival village. As a result, a sizeable number of persons, especially the middle-aged and elderly, no longer attend the regular j'ouverts, parades and certain other carnival activities, but simply look at them on television. The Carnival Committee hopes, however, to present a very special 2017 Transfer Centennial and also 65th anniversary Carnival.[14]

Other Social Possibilities

St. Thomas has had and continues to have small numbers of notable groups interested in civic/cultural/academic/social/sports activities which regularly bring persons of different races and ethnic backgrounds into beneficial and enjoyable contacts. One early example was the Caribbean Chorale, which started presenting concerts in the 1960s and still continues, though seemingly not as racially integrated presently as it once was. A number of similar groups exist, often limited in size by the availability of persons with musical, dramatic, or other talent(s) that they emphasize.

However, the relative numbers affected by such groups are so few that they do not make substantial impact on the community. Maybe, for the near future, greater impact may be made by a campaign urging persons of good will to undertake greater efforts to perform, sincerely, actions that may lead to greater degrees of working together and bonding in the needed progress toward interracial thinking and living. The following are two examples of various cooperative endeavors toward the betterment of race and ethnic relations in St. Thomas that may serve as worthwhile examples for interested persons and groups. One involves an internationally known organization, while the other was born as a completely individual and local initiative.

Many of the Virgin Islands members of the Rotary Clubs in St. Thomas think these clubs truly foster brotherhood and bring about substantially better racial and social relations. Dr. Lawrence "Larry" Benjamin, a black Virgin Islander, who is an accomplished educator, musician, and boatsman, is a member of the Rotary Club of St. Thomas that was founded in 1957 and is the oldest of five Rotary groups in St. Thomas. Larry explained that, initially, Rotary clubs used to be considered as gatherings of only businessman and professionals, but they are open to anyone willing to live up to the motto of "service above self." The St. Thomas club meets weekly (every Thursday), has a mixed membership of Blacks, Whites, and others, and engages year-round in fund-raising and hands-on projects to assist worthy causes and groups, such as the Nana Baby Home, the Charlotte Amalie High School, the Boys and Girls Clubs, and keeping several students in college on scholarships.

Larry says that the cooperation and physical work members perform is truly heart-warming and bonding. In fact, Rotary goodwill goes beyond local settings, as members are urged to always attend weekly meetings and to contribute—wherever they are in the world. Thus, Larry, who travels a great deal, has never missed attending at least one Rotary meeting a week for the past thirty years—whether locally, elsewhere in the Caribbean, or on the U.S. mainland, Canada, South America, Europe, Africa, Asia, or Australia. He reports that the various projects on which Rotary members work often help them to bond, and members in many clubs sometimes form life-long personal and even family friendships.[15]

Another social example comes from the work of Mrs. Francine Penn-Scipio, a black St. Thomian, who has been the prime mover behind what is now known as the Penn-Scipio Thanksgiving Luncheon, held in St. Thomas's Emancipation Garden on Thanksgiving Day each November. Mrs. Penn-Scipio started the project in 1994, but could not continue for several years due to 1995's Hurricane Marilyn and its after effects. She tried again in 1999, after becoming even more aware of the need of many homeless and elderly persons for a good meal on Thanksgiving Day, and has organized it every year since. At first she was assisted by just a handful of family members and close friends, who did all the

Some of the many helpers of the Penn-Scipio Thanksgiving Luncheon, 2016. Courtesy of the Penn-Scipio Family.

cooking, setting up of the tables in the Garden, and they generally served about two to three dozen persons, who were usually elderly or homeless.

However, as news of the meal spread, other persons, such as Main Street employees on their lunch hour and cruise ship tourists who were shopping on Main Street, came and asked if they could be served, with some even offering to make a financial donation. As Francine is not a person to turn away any-one, she simply decided she would have to enlarge the offering. She asked for help from additional family and friends, such as some members of the Me-morial Moravian Church where her grandmother had worshipped and Francine is well known, and was thus able to serve more persons.

Then about ten years ago, shortly after 2000, Mrs. Penn-Scipio, whose hus-band, Clarence, is a deacon at the All Saints Episcopal Church, was asked by a group from the Nazareth Episcopal fellowship in eastern St. Thomas if they could contribute to the meal. Mrs. Penn-Scipio was delighted to accept the offer. The Nazareth group, whose members are white, has thus been a vital part of the luncheon for the past decade, bringing pastries and helping to serve the many more persons who are now availing themselves of the Thanksgiving luncheon. Francine was particularly impressed by the enthusiasm of Mrs.

Francine, in hat and madras, and additional helpers. Courtesy of the Penn-Scipio Family, 2016.

Ivanne Farr, a now-deceased elderly member of the Nazareth group, who always insisted on doing as much as she could, even when others were urging her to do less.

Then, Dr. Adam Flowers, a black Continental who is now a local orthopedic surgeon and had heard about the luncheon, asked if a group from his Reformed congregation could come to sing and help serve. The members of the Reformed Church group are mixed—black and white—and the group's singing is reported to be so good that it keeps many persons in the Garden long after they are through eating. The number of persons who are served is now approaching three hundred, and some high school students have received permission to use the activity to meet their community service requirement, thus many persons are involved and the services are shared so that no person is overburdened. The Penn-Scipio Luncheon is yet another great example of ways in which Blacks, Whites, and others may work together to meet human needs and improve interracial relations on St. Thomas.[16]

Needless to say, there are so many projects that need the contributions of many more persons. May such happenings continue to take place and to bear such abundant fruit that a day may arrive when the wonder will be why it ever took so long for persons, regardless of color, creed, geographic, or economic origins, to fellowship together and to conceive of and treat each other as we all would wish to be thought of and treated.

Notes

1. Ralph Paiewonsky, Memoirs of A Governor, pp. 39–41.

2. "Plans for Ron De Lugo Night Takes Shape," *Daily News* (St. Thomas, V.I.), September 20, 1952, p. 1; "De Lugo Gets Scholarship Fund Tonight," Ibid., October 17, 1952, p. 1.

3. Dorothy H. Harvey, "Spring Revels in the Virgin Islands," *New York Times*, March 22, 1953, Section II, p. 15.

4. "Queen Contestants Set For 'Coming Out' Events," *Daily News* (St. Thomas, V.I.), March 5, 1960, p. 1; "Carnival Queen Judges Revealed," March 30, 1960, p. 1.

5. *Daily News* (St. Thomas, V.I.), January 25, 1952, p. 1; *Home Journal* (St. Thomas, V.I.), May 23, 1968, p. 3.

6. Interview with James Ready, St. Thomas, February 14, 1983.

7. "Drunk And Disorderly," *Daily News* (St. Thomas, V.I.), April 18, 1973, pp. 6, 11.

8. "Hotel Guests Protest Content of Newsletter," *Daily News* (St. Thomas, V.I.), April 30, 1975, pp. 3, 17.

9. Interviews with Dr. Aimery Caron, St. Thomas, February 16, 1983; Zeathea Armstrong, St. Thomas, September 13, 1982; George And Marva Applewhite, Newark, Delaware, November 25, 1982; Edwin Hatchette, telephone conversation in St. Thomas, February 15, 1983; Mary S. Francis, St. Thomas, February 18, 1983; Helen Gjessing, St. Thomas, February 23, 1982; Louis Schulterbrandt, St. Thomas, February 25, 1982.

10. Interviews with Ronald Walker, Delaware-Maryland telephone conversation, December 1, 1982; Edwin Hatchette, telephone conversation in St. Thomas, February 15, 1983; Helen Gjessing, St. Thomas, February 23, 1983.

11. "'Debs' Social Bow At Benefit Here Thursday," *Daily News* (St. Thomas, V.I.), July 16, 1957, p. 1.

12. Interviews with Gloria Alexander Statham, Delaware-Pennsylvania telephone conversation, May 8, 1983; Beverly Bandler, Delaware-Washington, D.C., telephone conversation, December 7, 1982; Joyce La Motta, St. Thomas, February 19, 1983; Penny Feuerzeig, St. Thomas, February 21, 1983.

13. Interviews with retired educator and culturalist Glenn "Kwabena" Davis, St. Thomas, August 29, 30, 2016.

14. Interview with Carnival Committee Chairman Kenneth Blake, St. Thomas, August 29, 2016.

15. Interviews with Dr. Lawrence Benjamin, St. Thomas, July 1 and September 9, 2016; April, 2017.

16. Interviews with Francine Penn-Scipio, St. Thomas, July 1 and September 30, 2016.

Chapter 22

Centennial Thoughts and Prospects

A centennial is a very special milestone that usually inspires review of the past, evaluation of the present, and contemplation of future goals and dreams. The 2017 Transfer Centennial of the United States Virgin Islands is, as expected, comprised of all three perspectives. Much of this monograph and many of the other Centennial presentations focus on the past, and contemplate the future, based hopefully on honest, maybe even painful, evaluations of the present.

In common with the nation of which the Virgin Islands became a part in 1917, the Virgin Islands is a society of immigrants. Its Danish history exemplified that and United States rule, especially during the past five decades, has added amply to the tradition. Most Virgin Islanders, therefore, appreciate the richness and complexity of places where the population is made up of persons from different races, places, and traditions. The problem comes when one is or becomes strong enough, and has the desire, to exert undue control over the others. The history of slavery acquainted U.S. and V.I. Americans with that tradition, and thus there is also equally strong thinking that such unfettered control of one group over others should never happen again. That is the official doctrine of the United States, and Virgin Islanders are equally strong in their similar feelings. For in the United States and the Caribbean, the history of overarching white domination and the eras of slavery remain as constant reminders of what should never happen again. It is with this in mind that the matter of race relations is thought to be a very appropriate way of evaluating the last century and the present conditions of life in the Virgin Islands.

It is this author's very sad and very much thought-about opinion, after speaking with scores of persons that, on the whole, the state of race relations in St. Thomas, U.S. Virgin Islands, is far from good. On the other hand, neither is the state of race relations very bad. It is not bad in that persons of different races usually do not look at each other with hateful faces or thoughts; they usually do not hesitate to greet each other in appropriate circumstances; they usually do not hesitate to give assistance when needed; nor do they usually show any hesitancy in acknowledging that each person is special and deserving of the rights and dignity of civil living. And, as many can attest, there are admired interracial couples and families, and substantial numbers of persons of different races who have long and close relationships.

However, there is a feeling that these islands have changed so much, and are changing so rapidly, that no one seems to be sure of what the next five or even the next two years might bring and therein lie the anxieties. If, for example, a Mandahl Bay-type development really gets the go-ahead for the full "new community" they wish to create, what of the persons who now constitute the old communities? Will many be forced to move away in order to have a worthwhile way of life? And, for those who refuse to move, will some decide to make life miserable for the "new community"? Will the gun-carrying culture that seems to be gaining legal popularity in a number of U.S. states, and which stems from fear of gun crimes that have also become popular here, be adopted in the V.I. also? And, many Blacks now find it hard not to believe, as most of the new development proposals are made by Whites for the benefit of Whites, that their projected effects are not aimed at bringing about the intentional decrease of the black population of the Virgin Islands.

There seems to be no longer the understanding that lay behind the planning and projects of the 1960s, during which governmental concerns courted new and affluent members for V.I. society, realizing that their monies and investments were needed to help improve the historically-limited status of many of the older members of the society. However, the older black members were considered a vital element of the society (not just for labor, but to whom there was a historical and moral entitlement) and to whose well-being and physical continuance the society was committed. Thus, there was an understanding, or so many thought, that the new V.I. society would remain with multiple groups, but without any group totally dominating or eliminating others. This is the tradition that these islands have been living by, even though not everyone may have fully agreed. Now, even though it is not always stated outright, but a few have, a great deal of the proposals and projects today seem to advocate the takeover of the resources of the community so overwhelmingly by persons of wealth that very limited decent living space would be left for non-wealthy persons. Apparently, St. Thomas (and other parts of the Virgin Islands and similar places) are now considered by some to be so beautiful and conducive to good living that they should be best utilized by the wealthy, with others going elsewhere to live.

These uncertainties have led some to look at the past and the future in wistful contemplation of what might have been or what still could be. One such view, which seems to be the opinion of only a very tiny minority in the Virgin Islands, is that these islands would have been better off today had they remained under Denmark instead of being transferred to the Unites States. The rationale for that thought is that Denmark is presently, as is the U.S., a very well-off country, with the world's highest minimum wage, and it has two overseas areas— Greenland and the Faroe Islands in the North Atlantic—that are both self-governing, with full control of their domestic affairs. The thinking is that the Virgin Islands, under Denmark, would have been just as well off through tourism as it now is, and would also have received by now those degrees of broader political local control as the present Danish overseas areas. It is an interesting what-might-have-been thought, though some have pointed out that the populations of those Danish off-shore areas are much more similar to Denmark's population than is the major population group of the Virgin Islands, and also that the physical environment of those places may not be as pleasant as the Virgin Islands', so it is hard to know what different paths of development may have been taken based on different racial, physical, or cultural considerations.[1]

Other similar thinkers point out that many of the remaining English, Dutch, and French territories in the Caribbean are better off in some ways today than the U.S. Virgin Islands, because they have greater powers of self-governance or greater participation in their national governments. Martinique and Guadeloupe are departments of France, which make them equivalent to states of the United States, with full powers to vote for the French national political leaders. Similarly, Aruba, Curacao, and St. Martin have full status within the Kingdom of the Netherlands that enables them to take part in the elections for national leaders, contrary to Virgin Islands residents. British territories, such as the Caymans, Anguilla and the British Virgin Islands, do not participate in their national elections, but may set rules for their financial systems that allow them to operate some of the most lucrative banking systems in the world, and are also able to control immigration in order to protect their local citizenry and resources. As an example, based on governmental revenues, the British Virgin Islands had a 2010 average income per capita of $42,300, one of the highest in the region, second only to the Caymans. (The U.S. Virgin Islands' in 2011 was $40,500, and had fallen to $36,100 by 2013.) Of course, based on the recent "Brexit" from the European Union, there is presently some uncertainty as to how the Commonwealth Caribbean may be affected by the new order in Europe.[2]

Needless to say, there are also in the U.S. V.I. persons who now look forward to independence from the United States. There is no certainty about the number of such thinkers, but there are advocates who are well known to radio listeners as they sometimes make their wishes, and their arguments, known on the airwaves. One of their basic arguments is that it is the nature of mankind to want to be independent at some stage of development, as it is natural for children to grow up and become self-directing. They point to the substantial number of Caribbean islands that have become independent during the last six decades—Jamaica (1962), Trinidad and Tobago (1962), Barbados (1966), Bahamas (1973), Grenada (1974), St. Lucia (1977), Dominica (1978), St. Vincent and the Grenadines (1979), Antigua and Barbuda (1981), and St. Kitts and Nevis (1983), with two of them—Grenada and St. Kitts-Nevis—being smaller in land area than the U.S. Virgin Islands.

What is known about independence advocates is that their percentage of the population is smaller than it was three decades ago. What seems to have happened, both in the Virgin Islands and Puerto Rico, was that the destruction of 1989's Hurricane Hugo and 1995's Hurricane Marilyn convinced many of the great vulnerability of small places when faced with extreme acts of nature, and of the consequent need to be part of a greater unit. In the V.I. status referendum of 1993, of the 27% of voters who turned out, only 5% voted in favor of the removal of U.S. sovereignty. If that may be used as a guide, it indicates that a substantial percentage of Virgin Islanders, seemingly a substantial majority, seems to favor continued governance by the United States, even though some are apprehensive of changes that may thus result.

Probably the greatest motives behind sentiments for independence from the United States are the changes in population proportions that are taking place in the V.I. It is argued that continued control by the United States, with the V.I. having no ability to regulate incoming migration, will eventually result in a population much like the mainland's, with Blacks being a disadvantaged minority. It is thought that this may already have taken place on St. John and, without restrictions, will probably eventually take place on St. Thomas and St. Croix, simply taking longer because of their larger populations.

It is a main reason why many black St. Johnians and other Virgin Islanders have ambivalent feelings toward the U.S. National Park, which includes most of St. John. Everyone realizes the beneficial role national parks play in preserving nature for human use and enjoyment. However, in the case of St. John, where the park has obtained two-thirds of an entire island, the limited availability of the remaining one-third of its area has driven land prices in some areas to figures that only the rich can afford. Thus, many non-wealthy per-

sons—Blacks and Whites—have been priced out of St. John, partly accounting for its sizeable white population.

A number of white Continentals admit that the adjustment to being a racial
minority was one of the hardest they had to make on moving to the V.I. Some
Continentals, unable or unwilling to make the adjustment, leave after a period
of residence. Would most white Continentals, therefore, agree to any policies
or decisions which would keep Whites as a minority in the society? Most of
the Whites interviewed stated that they had not given the matter much thought
or did not envision any drastic population changes in the V.I. in the foreseeable future. However, a few Whites admitted that they had heard other Whites
speak in anticipation of a future when the V.I. would be mainly white.

In addition to the continental Whites, there are also the other white groups
in the V.I. that have benefited greatly from the great inflow of Whites since
1950. In addition to simply making them part of a much larger minority than
they had previously formed, the incoming continental Whites met some very
specific needs of the older white groups. The Jewish community of St. Thomas,
which had been a thriving community of over 400 in the mid-nineteenth century, had dwindled to about fifty persons in 1940. That began changing with
the arrival of Continentals in the 1940s and Jews in St. Thomas are once again
a thriving synagogue of hundreds.

Another older white group, the French, because of their unwillingness to
mix racially, had practiced intermarriage among themselves for decades, and
by the 1940s and 50s had a noticeably higher than average rate of mental re-
tardation and physical deformities. Since the 1950s a substantial amount of
intermarriages between French St. Thomians and white Continentals has served
to address the problem.[3]

Would the French and the Old Whites be willing to approve practices which
retain the V.I. as a mainly black society? And what about the opinions of some
of the newer groups in V.I. society—the Indians, the Middle Eastern Asians,
or the Dominicans? A diplomatic answer which many non-Blacks would probably give, if pressed, would be that nothing needs to be done—simply maintain freedom of migration between the mainland and the V.I., as there is now
and accept whatever results. Two of the Whites who acknowledged hearing
white anticipation of white dominance said it was thought that white dominance would simply come about naturally, in the course of a few decades of
unregulated migration. For with black West Indian immigration having been
curtailed and a sizeable number of Blacks regularly leaving the islands in search
of greater opportunities, the only regular source of population growth, other
than the net natural increase over emigration, would be immigration from the
mainland.

In the 1930s the American Geographical Society published a very interesting monograph entitled *White Settlers in the Tropics*. The author was a white Australian, A. Grenfell Price, and his research in the various tropical areas of the world had been partly supported by a Rockefeller Foundation Research Fellowship. His purpose was to determine whether Whites would be able, physically, to settle in great numbers and thus dominate numerically the tropical areas of the world as they had the temperate and subtropical zones. The author stated: "Behind everything lies a question of ethics. The white races command vast and sparsely settled areas of temperate country. Have they any moral justification for attempting to occupy the tropics as well?"[4]

The same ethical concern seems to lie behind the thinking of those Blacks who believe that the V.I. should not be subjected to extraordinary means to prevent it from being a mainly black society. For despite all of the labor which Blacks contributed to the development of large areas of the Western Hemisphere (the U.S. South, Brazil, various other countries in South and Central America, and the West Indian islands), Blacks now exercise numerical dominance over only a miniscule portion of the Americas—mainly some of the West Indian islands. A great many Blacks feel that historical justice obliges that Blacks remain the majority in the small portions of the Americas where they presently have dominance. Conversations with black Virgin Islanders who live on the mainland indicate that many of them, even though they have chosen for various reasons to live there, have a special pride in the fact that the Virgin Islands are a mainly black society and so even do some Continental Blacks. It is also of great recent concern to many Blacks, on noting how Blacks, especially young males, are treated in the U.S. by law enforcement officers. Would similar scenarios happen here?

There is also the question of the political position of the Virgin Islands, which are a territorial part of the United States. Specifically, the islands are an unincorporated territory of the U.S., which means that the territory is a part of the United States, but not 100% so—only to the extent that the Congress so agrees. Over the years, Congressional acts have incorporated the territory in most ways, but not completely. There has been, however, the same freedom of movement between the V.I. and the U.S. as there is among the states. As such, not only have the V.I. become a popular destination for mainlanders since the 1950s, but from decades before that, the mainland had functioned and continues to function as the chief provider of economic and educational opportunity for many Virgin Islanders. Would any serious proposal, with the intent or retaining a black majority in the V.I., need to involve imposing restrictions on the present mainland-island traffic?

Another issue is the political question of the meaning of being a territorial part of a nation. At the time the V.I. became a part of the U.S., both places already had long separate histories, and the islands' social composition had evolved in a way which differentiated them from the new parent country. May a territorial area, acquired under circumstances such as the V.I., justly insist on the preservation of those aspects of difference which the majority of its inhabitants hold dear? Or, does being a territorial part of a nation imply a process of complete integration, to the point that the major population group of a territory must be prepared to be replaced, if such is desired by the majority group of the national entity?

Another aspect in question is economic. Much of the present standard of living in the V.I. rests on the receipt of federal funding in many areas—education, health, welfare, transportation, and others. If any move is realized to limit migration from the mainland, there will probably arise the old dilemma about the inability to have one's cake and eat it too. Mainland taxpayers would probably question the sharing of tax revenues with a place, even though under the U.S. flag, to which their access would be limited. Of course, there is also a long tradition of great powers granting aid to strategic areas, regardless of special migratory rights. There is no guarantee, however, that the matter would be viewed in that light.

Concern with these matters has been partially responsible for the desire in the V.I. to acquire a constitution written and amendable in the islands, and/or a new status with the U.S. which would hopefully treat, and settle to some degree, some of these issues. However, the draft constitutions and status determination attempts to date have all failed.[5]

Two questions ultimately have to be settled as political ones, and the methods of their disposition will probably determine the course of the V.I. for the foreseeable future. There is no discernible sizeable realistically-based sentiment in the V.I. for independence. The economic, social, and cultural attachments to the mainland are very strong. Most people still feel that they enjoy a higher standard of living than many other places in the Caribbean because of being a part of the U.S. Most families—black and white—have many close relatives who live on the mainland. Most Virgin Islanders—Blacks and Whites—who have received higher education have done so at least partly on the mainland, and also use the U.S. for vacations, shopping, medical care, entertainment, recreation—in other words, as the national metropolis that it is. Only a small minority of people would willingly want these relationships interrupted or changed in any substantial ways.

On the other hand, some Blacks believe that none of the material benefits the U.S. offers would compensate for numerical subjugation of Blacks or their purposeful alienation from the lands on which their ancestors suffered en-slavement. Both are serious threats if the islands cannot maintain a political status which allows for some regulation of migration and for land protective measures. In 1980, then-retired Democratic Party leader Earle B. Ottley out-lined what he considered to be "the only realistic political alternative" for the Virgin Islands—"free associated statehood" with the United States. He men-tioned its chief features as complete internal self-government; the U.S. giving to the V.I. outright all local federal properties, except for some park lands and any properties needed for defense, security, and foreign affairs, for which the U.S. would remain responsible; and extensions of all provisions of the Social Security Act to the V.I.[6]

Some Blacks are also acutely aware of the historical attitudes of Whites to-wards Blacks on the mainland and of present national conditions, wherein there seems to be growing national acceptance of a large practically hopeless permanent underclass, a disproportionate percentage of which is black. They believe there would be a more promising future for most Blacks in the V.I. if the islands do not become simply a social replica of the mainland, but retain instead a society congruent with local historical developments and traditions.

Most of the Blacks who advocate this point of view do not appear to want independence. Neither do they desire statehood for the V.I., as statehood is a standard political status, which does not allow much in the way of special pro-visions. Many do want some type of negotiated status with the U.S. whereby the islands remain a part of the nation but have some control over immigra-tion and any other aspects of government deemed essential for the protection of the special Virgin Islands way of life. For, in addition to their connection to the U.S., the V.I. also enjoys historical, social, and cultural connections with the rest of the West Indies.

In March 1968, a conference was held in St. Thomas on the status of the V.I. One of its organizers was a distinguished white professor, Dr. Roy Macridis, of Brandeis University in Massachusetts, who was spending a semester at CVI as a visiting professor of government. In his concluding remarks at the con-ference, Dr. Macridis stated:

> Frankly, despite my admiration for the American Constitution, I am not sure that all its provisions provided guarantees and safeguards for the islanders. Some of them—and I have already mentioned the equal-protection clause and the privilege-and-immunities clause in connection with property rights—may be in the nature of straight-jackets. What was said about the unsuitability of parliamentary forms for the newly independent nations may apply also about the blanket

acceptance or rather the blanket application of the U.S. constitution to the islands. Yet there is no alternative unless new forms of association between the United States and the Virgin Islands are explored.... Ironically enough, the islanders see their full emancipation in the Constitution; and they pleaded to "contract in." The time may come for a careful and discriminating "contracting out." For as long as the Constitution is supreme, and Congressional legislation too, I cannot see how genuine self-government, adapted to the local needs, can be instituted, especially when the federal judiciary, sworn to uphold the Constitution, is the final judge.[7]

Virgin Islanders and Blacks, therefore, have not been the only ones to recognize a need for political changes aimed at the protection of the society and way of life of the Virgin Islands, and to recognize that special ways of crafting that need might have to be utilized. No reasonable person expects a society to remain the same forever; that happens only in isolated societies. On the other hand, change should take place at a pace that is beneficial for all, and does not injure and crush one group while aggrandizing another.

The reception of the demand for such a philosophy, if it becomes a sizeable and active sentiment in the islands, and some small indications are that it could, will determine the future of race relations and the society and economy of the islands. If Whites and the Federal Government can try to recognize the historical and spatial legitimacy of such demands, a status satisfactory to most Virgin Islanders (including Whites and others) may be achieved. However, if most Whites (and maybe others) and the Federal Government cannot make allowances for the aspirations of many islanders to preserve the differences of the society, the only alternative which may seem open to some might be an independence movement. Based on the amount of sentiment against it, it does not seem that such a movement would succeed. But, depending on the resolution of its followers, whether it gains ultimate success or not may almost be secondary for a time. Efforts which might be taken in its pursuit could inflict great damage on the social fabric and the economy of the islands.

There are probably those who would be willing to live through periods of turmoil and racial conflict, with the hope and confidence that the islands will eventually be as they prefer to envision them. The differing perceptions of the races in interpreting the present and, seemingly, in envisioning the future, remain the greatest barriers to the attainment of a desirable state of race relations based on mutual respect and understanding. The major perceptions of sizeable numbers of both groups are far apart and thus the goals of each may be incompatible with the perceived interests of the other. What has been a

major finding of this work—that the development of unpleasant race relations and black racism in the V.I. during the last half of the twentieth century
and since was due mainly to the incoming prejudices and practices of some
Whites—is not subscribed to by most Whites. Many Whites, not only in the
earlier research for this work, but also continuing into the present, place the
major blame for racial conflicts on the culture and actions of Blacks, not realizing, for example, the role that appropriating large areas of land and resources for incoming persons and "new communities" also play. A recent
example of such parallel, but contradictory, thinking on the U.S. mainland is
the charge by some Whites that the several deliberate attacks on white policemen during the summer of 2016 were due to the marches and protests of the
"Black Lives Matter" movement, rather than realizing that the movement
started in response to the rather prevalent cruelty that black men had been experiencing from some white police officers in their dealings with Blacks.

Thus, with some Whites unable to comprehend some white acts of racism
as such, and with some Blacks making no attempts to hide their anti-white behavior as they believe such acts to be justified, some Whites assert that it is
Whites who are now the chief victims, instead of perpetrators in any way, of
racism in the Virgin Islands. Unfortunately, almost everyone in the Virgin Islands today has some degree of fear of being a victim of crime—of having
one's home broken into, a car stolen, a bag or briefcase snatched, sexual as-
sault, or simply being physically present when guns are being fired or a robbery is taking place. As a minority, Whites probably do feel more threatened,
but it is Blacks who experience most of the ravages of crime as lawbreakers
usually commit most of their crimes in or near to their own neighborhoods,
with young black men being both the major perpetrators and the major victims of violent crimes in the V.I., such as gun shootings or murders.[8] And, unfortunately, one of the many difficulties in bringing about some of the changes
that are needed, is that it is very hard to give some young Blacks hope for the
future when they live in a place that is seemingly in line for transformation
into playground communities for the rich.

Therefore, even though most instances of race relations in St. Thomas are
characterized by at least seeming amicability, there are basic underlying differences in the groups that share the island, and in the conflicts those differences generate. A basic difference, which most persons (of practically all races
and ethnic groups) are reluctant to discuss, is that the persons who have moved
to the island from societies in which the population is mainly white are, probably naturally, more comfortable in such societies and thus most see nothing
disturbing in plans that would bring about that result in the Virgin Islands.
However, the majority of persons now in the Virgin Islands are black and are

also, again probably naturally, more comfortable with that population composition. They thus tend to resent seemingly deliberate projects that would lead to local population change, and consider their feeling justified in view of the history of racial discrimination in the United States, and despite the love that many black Virgin Islanders have for the United States.

Therefore, when a business conglomerate presents a plan for creating a new "community" in the Virgin Islands, consisting of hundreds of very expensive homes, the eventual effect of such an enterprise is immediately visualized. And there are substantial differences between such proposals for St. Thomas, as compared, for example, to any state in the U.S. One relevant factor is size: while mainland United States is one of the largest countries in the world and is comprised of adjoining states, the Virgin Islands is comprised of very small islands, thus making recreational and educational get-aways to other places generally less convenient and affordable than on the mainland, where persons may go in their own cars, or by bus or train, to other cities or states.

St. Thomas, as of the 2010 census, had a population density of 1,614 persons per square mile, making it one of the twenty most densely populated places in the world.[9] Thus, allowing large areas of St. Thomas to be allocated for residences for the rich from elsewhere works to deliberately increase the population density and to prohibit the possibility of the many local non-home owners—of any race or ethnicity—from ever owning a home.

This is not an argument against economic development, which is greatly needed now and always will be. With a tourist economy, St. Thomas definitely needs hotels, especially ones emphasizing conventions and other special attractions, as cruise ship passengers, now the majority of V.I. tourists, have no special need for regular hotels. St. Thomas is also in extreme need of developers willing to build houses for ordinary non-millionaire home buyers, and developers promoting new scientific and technological endeavors. However, it is understood that meeting any, or even all of these and other needs, will not necessarily prevent substantial change over time, as change is constant in most human societies. Thus, the Virgin Islands bicentennial population of 2117 might be quite different from the current 2017 centennial population. The ideal, however, remains that whatever changes take place over the years and decades should be the products of thoughtful and locally-relevant decisions, with the goals of providing a better life for all residents, rather than bowing to the economic designs of business entities which have no regard for the impact of their operations on the average Virgin Islands resident.

Interestingly, many mainland white Americans now seem to be similarly troubled by recent projections that imply possible changes in their domination of the U.S. population. History, of course, demonstrates the inevitability of change, and sometimes it takes place long after or even long before having been expected. As examples, when the United States bought the Virgin Islands in 1917, if anyone had predicted that a black American, and especially one with an African name, would have been elected its president in less than a century, the predictor would have been thought to be abnormally unrealistic. There would probably have been a similar evaluation of anyone who had predicted that a poor black boy named Terence Todman, born in St. Thomas in 1926, nine years after its purchase from Denmark by the U.S. would become, before the end of the century, the United States ambassador to white countries such as Denmark, Spain, and Argentina—but it happened! On the other hand, the current President of the United States, Donald Trump, recently made remarks that seem to imply that, had he been in Abraham Lincoln's position in 1860–61, slavery in the United States would probably have lasted longer than it did. What an interesting and great country we share!

Indeed, St. Thomas and the rest of the U.S. Virgins still comprise a special gem in the American family—a place that even after 100 years of being a part of the United States remains mainly black, yet multiracial and multiethnic—somewhat illustrative of the ideals (though not in substantial practice) of racial compatibility and cooperation. It is thus incumbent on all groups and persons who are truly interested in fostering such human relationships, to ponder, truthfully and critically, our attitudes and behaviors, racially and otherwise, to others, especially different others. These tasks are very difficult! However, based on the desire that most humans seem to have of wanting to make the world, before we leave it, better than we found it, the goal of working on the morality and respect that it takes to improve racial and other group relationships is probably among the most significant actions we can ever take. May our resolutions and efforts be abundantly fruitful!

Notes

1. "Denmark", *The World Factbook*, U.S. Central Intelligence Agency. Accessed on October 5, 2016, at https://www.cia.gov/library/publications/the-world-factbook/geos/da.html.

2. Articles on France, Kingdom of the Netherlands, British Virgin Islands, and Cayman Islands, and U.S. Virgin Islands, Ibid.

3. Waldo Evans, *The Virgin Islands of the United States: A General Report of the Governor*, 1928, p. 8; interview with William Quetel, St. Thomas, February 22, 1983.

4. A. Grenfell Price, *White Settlers in the Tropics* (New York: American Geographical Society, 1939), p. 9.

5. Julio A. Brady, "The Rocky Road to Self-Government," *Daily News* (St. Thomas, V.I.), 50th Anniversary Edition—August 1, 1980, pp. B15–17; Ottley, *Trials and Triumphs*, pp. 426–427.

6. Penny Feuerzeig, "Free Associated Status Statement for V.I. Is Urged by Ottley," *Daily News* (St. Thomas, V.I.), September 23, 1980, pp. 1, 15.

7. Roy C. Macridis, "The Evolution of the Islands—Some Concluding Remarks," in Bough and Macridis, *Virgin Islands, America's Caribbean Outpost*, p. 186.

8. "V.I. leads nation in murders," *Daily News* (St. Thomas, V.I.), October 1, 2016, p. 3. (The FBI's rating of the Virgin Islands as being # 1 in the nation's murder rate for 2015 was a jolting wake-up call for the V.I., but it was really skewed as it compared the V.I. and the other U.S. territories with the 50 states, as the chief political units of the nation. Therefore, the V.I., with a total of 44 murders for 2015 and a total population of just over 100,000, was compared with the states' populations, most of which were in the millions, so naturally the V.I. rate exceeded the states'. However, a number of cities had a higher rate (such the well-known situation of Chicago), but they were not used in the "national" figure; only the states and territories were.)

9. Information from Dr. Frank Mills, Director of the Eastern Caribbean Center of the University of the Virgin Islands, St. Thomas, V.I., 2017; "Population Prospects Table A-1," (2009), Department of Economic and Social Affairs Population Division, United Nations.

About the Author

Marilyn Francis Krigger was born in St. Thomas in 1940, twenty-three years after the Virgin Islands became a part of the United States. Virgin Islanders of her generation have generally been devoted United States citizens, but there is now great concern about some of the developments taking place in their beautiful home.

Dr. Krigger received her elementary and secondary education in St. Thomas, graduating from its Charlotte Amalie High School in 1955. She then attended Spelman College in Atlanta, Georgia, graduating with a B.A. in 1959, followed by an M.A. in history in 1960 from Columbia University in New York. Returning to St. Thomas, she taught at her high school alma mater, then in 1967 joined the faculty of the young College of the Virgin Islands. It became the University of the Virgin Islands in 1986, and Krigger remained on its faculty until her retirement in 2000.

In 1980, Krigger took leave to study at the University of Delaware, where she received a Ph.D. in history in 1983. Her doctoral dissertation was on race relations in St. Thomas to 1975, and race and ethnic relations have been her major research and writing interests.

Dr. Krigger has also served the Virgin Islands through membership on governmental bodies such as the V.I. Board of Education, the V.I. Humanities Council, the V.I. State Review Board for Historic Preservation, the V.I. Status and Federal Relations Commission, and the V.I. 150th Emancipation Commission.

Appendices

Appendix A
Official Population Figures for the U.S. Virgin Islands, 1773–2010

Year	St. Croix	St. Thomas	St. John	Total
1773	21,809	4,371	2,402	28,582
1796	28,803	4,734	2,120	35,657
1835	26,681	14,022	2,475	43,178
1850	23,720	13,666	2,228	39,614
1860	23,194	13,463	1,574	38,231
1880	18,430	14,389	944	33,763
1890	19,783	12,019	984	32,786
1901	18,590	11,012	925	30,527
1911	15,467	10,678	941	27,086
1917	14,901	10,191	949	26,051
1930	11,413	9,834	765	22,012
1940	12,902	11,265	722	24,889
1950	12,103	13,813	749	26,665
1960	14,973	16,201	925	32,099
1970	31,779	28,960	1,729	62,468
1980	49,725	44,372	2,472	96,569
1990	50,139	48,166	3,504	101,809
2000	53,234	51,181	4,197	108,612
2010	50,601	51,634	4,170	106,405

Source: U.S. Census Bureau, *Censuses of Population: Virgin Islands of the United States, 1917–2010*. After purchasing the Virgin Islands in 1917, the United States Census Bureau accepted the previous official Danish census figures.

Appendix B
Black, White, and Total Population Figures for
St. Thomas, V.I., 1890–2010

Year	Black	White	Total Population**
1890	10,519*	1,500*	12,019
1917	8,898	1,293	10,191
1930	8,256	1,578	9,834
1940	9,480	1,785	11,265
1950'	11,572	2,241	13,813
1960	13,278	2,923	16,201
1970	***	***	28,960
1980	35,641	7,330	44,372
1990	39,482	7,192	48,166
2000	41,286	6,456	51,181
2010	41,310	7,814	51,634

* Estimated.
** The figures for Blacks and Whites do not necessarily add up to the total figure, due to the presence of persons who classify themselves otherwise.
*** Unable to obtain.
Source: U.S. Census Bureau, *Censuses of Population, Virgin Islands of the United States.*

Appendix C
U.S. Virgin Islands Census of
Population, 2010

Racial Groups by Percent	
Black or African American	76.0%
White	15.6%
Asian	1.4%
Mixed	2.1%
Native Indian or Alaska Native	0.4%
Native Hawaiian or other Pacific Islander	0.1%
Some other race	4.5%
Two or more races	2.6%
17.4 % also identified as Hispanic or Latino	

(Racial groups are defined at the end of Chapter 16.)
Source: United States Census of 2010, United States Virgin Islands.

Appendix D
U. S. Virgin Islands Census of Population, 2010

Place of Birth Groups by Percent	
U.S. Virgin Islands	46.7%
Latin America and the Caribbean (Caribbean over 31%)	34.7%
United States born	15.8%
Asian-born	1.4%
European-born	0.9%
Other	0.4%

Source: United States Census of 2010, United States Virgin Islands.

Subject Matter Sources

Bibliography

A Look at Business Ownership in the Virgin Islands. (1974, August). *Virgin Islands Forum*, 2(7), pp. 5–6.

Adeyemi, S. *Engaging Freedom's Journey: V.I. Africans Struggle for Self Determination and Empowerment (1644–1993)*. Richmond, VA: Dejenne Publishing House, 2006.

Albuquerque, K. de. "Rastafarianism and Cultural Identity in the Caribbean." *Revista/Review Interamericana*, 10 (2), 230–247, 1980.

Albuquerque, K. de., & McElroy, J. L. "West Indian Migration to the United States Virgin Islands: Demographic Impacts and Socioeconomic Consequences." *International Migration Review*, 16 (1), 61–101. (1982, Spring).

Annual Reports of the Governors of the Virgin Islands (1917–1995). St. Thomas, V.I.: Government of the Virgin Islands.

Anthony Bottomley, M. H. (1976, March). Is Tourist Residential Development Worthwhile?—The Anegada Project. *Social and Economic Studies*, 25(1), 1–33.

Barnes, N. *Cultural Conundrums: Gender, Race, Nation, and the Making of Caribbean Cultural Politics*. Ann Arbor: University of Michigan Press, 2006.

Barrett, L. *The Rastafarians: Sounds of Cultural Dissonance*. Boston: Beacon Press, 1977.

Beckford, G. *Persistent Poverty: Underdevelopment in the Plantation Regions of the World*. New York and Mona, Jamaica: Oxford University Press and Institute of Social and Economic Research, 1971.

Beckles, H. and N. Shepherd, eds. *Caribbean Slave Society and Economy.* Kingston, Jamaica: Ian Randle Publishers, Ltd., 1991.

Benjamin, L. O. "Dates, Events and People in Virgin Islands History: 1493–1995." St. Thomas, V.I., 2005.

"Black Revolutionary" (St. Thomas, V.I.—published by the Black Cultural Organization of the College of the Virgin Islands.), 1969.

Blanshard, P. *Democracy and Empire in the Caribbean: A Contemporary Review.* New York: The Macmillan Company, 1974.

Bloom, L. *The Social Psychology of Race Relations.* Cambridge, MA: Schenkman Publishing Company, Inc., 1972.

Blue, J. T. "Patterns of Racial Stratification: A Categoric Typology." *The Phylon Quarterly,* XX (4), (1959, Winter).

Bough, James A. and R. Macridis, eds. *Virgin Islands, America's Caribbean Outpost: The Evolution of Self-Government.* Wakefield, MA: The Walter F. Williams Publishing Company, 1970.

Boyer, W. W. *America's Virgin Islands: A History of Human Rights and Wrongs.* Durham, North Carolina: Carolina Academic Press, 1983.

Boyer, W. W. *America's Virgin Islands: A History of Human Rights and Wrongs, 2nd Edition.* Durham, North Carolina: Carolina Academic Press, 2010.

Boyer, W. W. *Civil Liberties in the U.S. Virgin Islands, 1917–1949.* St. Croix, U.S. Virgin Islands: Antilles Graphic Arts, 1982.

Boyer, W. W. "Self-Determination for the U.S. Virgin Islands—Myth or Reality?" Distinguished Scholar Lecture, College of the Virgin Islands, December, 1982 (mimeographed).

Brathwaite, E. *The Development of Creole Society in Jamaica, 1770–1820.* Oxford: Oxford University Press, 1971.

Brathwaite, L. *Social Stratification in Trinidad: A Preliminary Analysis.* Kingston, Jamaica: Institute of Social and Economic Research, University of the West Indies, 1975.

Brathwaite, L. "Sociology and Demographic Research in the British Caribbean." *Social and Economic Studies,* 6(4), 523–571. (1957, December).

Brathwaite, L. The Role of the University in the Developing Society of the West Indies. *Social and Economic Studies,* 14(1), 76–87. (1965, March).

Brereton, B. *Race Relations in Colonial Trinidad, 1870–1900.* Cambridge: Cambridge University Press, 1979.

Bridenbaugh, C. A. *No Peace Beyond the Line: The English in the Caribbean, 1624–1690.* New York: Oxford University Press, 1972.

Brown, W. *Angry Men—Laughing Men: The Caribbean Caldron.* New York: Greenberg, 1947.

Browne, W. T. *From Commoner to King: Robert H. Bradshaw.* Lanham, Maryland: University Press of America Inc., 1992.

Bryden, J. M. *Tourism and Development: A Case Study of the Commonwealth Caribbean.* Cambridge: Cambridge University Press, 1973.

"C.V.I.", *Virgin Islands View*, 2 (2), p. 30. (1966, July).

"C.V.I. to Expand Hotel and Management Program", *Virgin Islands Forum*, II (5), (1974, June), 7–9. (1966, July).

Cahnman, J. W. "The Mediterranean and Caribbean Regions—A Comparison in Race and Culture Contacts." *Social Forces*, 22 (2), 209–214. (1943, December).

Camejo, A. "Racial Discrimination in Employment in the Private Sector in Trinidad and Tobago: A Study of the Business Elite and the Social Structure." *Social and Economic Studies*, 20 (3), (1971), 294–318.

Campbell, A. A. "Note on the Jewish Community of St. Thomas, U.S. Virgin Islands." *Jewish Social Studies*, IV (2), (1942, April), 161–166.

Campbell, A. A. "St. Thomas Negroes: A Study of Personality and Culture." *Psychological Monographs*, 55 (5), (1943).

Campbell, A., & Schuman, H. *Racial Attitudes in Fifteen American Cities.* Ann Arbor: Institute for Social Research, the University of Michigan, 1969.

Campbell, D. *St. Thomas: Sequent Occupance and the Development of Tourism.* University of Miami, 1977.

Campbell, E. Q. (Ed.). *Racial Tensions and National Identity.* Nashville: Vanderbilt University Press, 1972.

Caron, A. *The Danish Port of Charlotte Amalia (1790–1803).* St. Thomas, U.S. Virgin Islands, 2015.

Caron, A. "The Urgency for the Acquisition of the Danish West Indies". St. Thomas, V.I., 2014.

Carstens, J. L. *St. Thomas in Early Danish Times.* (A. R. Highfield, Trans.) St. Croix, Virgin Islands: V.I. Humanities Council, 1997.

Census, U. S. (1917–2010). *Censuses of Population: Virgin Islands of the United States.* Washington, D.C.: U. S. Government Printing Office.

Coates, B. "White Adult Behavior Towards Black and White Children." *Child Development, 43*(1), 143–154. (1972, March).

Cochran, H. *These Are The Virgin Islands.* New York: Prentice Hall, Inc., 1937.

Collins, J. (Ed.). *The History of the Legislature of the Virgin Islands.* St. Thomas, U.S. Virgin Islands: Amalie Printing, 1983..

Comitas, L., & Lowenthal, D. (Eds.). *Consequences of Class and Color: West Indian Perspectives.* New York: Anchor Press, 1973.

Corbin, Carlyle G. J. *Institutional Consequences of Imperial Education in the U.S. Virgin Islands.* Kingshill, St. Croix: International Institute, Caribbean Regional Office, 1975.

Coulthard, G. *Race and Colour in Caribbean Literature.* London: Oxford University Press, 1962.

Cox, O. C. *Caste, Class, and Race: A Study in Social Dynamics.* Garden City, New York: Doubleday and Company, Inc., 1948.

Cox, O. C. *Race Relations: Elements and Social Dynamics.* Detroit: Wayne State University Press, 1976.

Creque, D. D. *The U.S. Virgins and the Eastern Caribbean.* Philadelphia: Whitmore Publishing Co., 1968.

"Crime in the Virgin Islands As Discussed By the Governor's Commission on Human Resources." *Virgin Islands View,* 3 (11), pp. 24–33. (1968, April).

Cross, M. "Colonialism and Ethnicity: A Theory and Comparative Case Study." *Ethnic and Racial Studies,* 1 (1), 37–59. (1978, January).

Daily News. (The Virgin Islands Daily News–St. Thomas.), 1930–2017.

Dawson, E. E. *Down Street, St. Thomas and Beyond: A Dynamic Neighborhood.* Bloomingdale, IN: AuthorHouse, 2011.

De Booy, T. A. *The Virgin Islands: Our New Possessions and the British Islands.* Westport, Conn.: Negro Universities Press, 1918, reprinted in 1970.

Degler, C. N. "Slavery and the Genesis of American Race Prejudice." *Comparative Studies of Society and History,* 21, 49–66. (1959, October).

Degler, C. N. *Neither Black nor White: Slavery and Race Relations in Brazil and the United States.* New York: Macmilan Publishing Company, 1971.

Dejnozka, E. L. "American Educational Achievement in the Virgin Islands, 1917–1963." *The Journal of Negro History,* 57 (4), 385–394. (1972, October).

De Kadt, E. *Tourism—Passport to Development? Perspectives on the Social and Cultural Effects of Tourism in Developing Countries.* New York: Oxford University Press, 1979.

Demas, W. *The Economics of Development in Small Countries with Special Reference to the Caribbean.* Montreal: McGill University Press, 1965.

Diamond, J. "Tourism's Role in Economic Development: The Case Reexamined." *Economic Development and Cultural Change,* 25 (3) 539–553. (1977, April).

Donaghue, E. "British 19th Century Occupation of Danish West Indies Fueled Big Advance in Slaves' Quest for Freedom," *The Virgin Islands Daily News,* 27. (2015, November 23).

Donoghue, E. *Black Women/White Men: The Sexual Exploitation of Female Slaves in the Danish West Indies*. Trenton, NJ: Africa World Press, Inc., 2002.

Dookhan, I. *A History of the Virgin Islands of the United States*. Epping, Essex: Caribbean Universities Press in association with the Bowker Publishing Company for the College of the Virgin Islands, 1974.

Dookhan, I. "Civil Rights and Political Justice: The Role of the American Civil Liberties Union in the U.S. Virgin Islands. St. Thomas," 1982.

Dookhan, I. "The Expansion of Higher Education Educational Opportunities in the United States Virgin Islands." *The Journal of Negro Education*, 50 (1), 15-25. (1981, Winter).

Dookhan, I. "The Search for Identity: The Political Aspirations and Frustrations of Virgin Islanders Under the United States Naval Administration, 1917–1929." St. Thomas, V.I., 1978.

Du Bois, W. E. *The Souls of Black Folk: Essays and Sketches*. New York: The Blue Heron Press, 1953.

Dunn, R. S. *Sugar and Slaves: The Rise of the Planter Class in the English West Indies, 1624–1713*. Chapel Hill: The University of North Carolina Press, 1972.

Edmondson, L. "Trans-Atlantic Slavery and the Internationalization of Race." *Caribbean Quarterly*, 22 (2 and 3), 5–25. (1976, June–September).

Edwards, G. F., & Pettigrew, T. F. "Race Relations." In D. L. Sills (Ed.), *International Encyclopedia of the Social Sciences* (pp. 269–282). New York: The Macmillin Company and the Free Press, 1968.

Egerton, J. Education in the Virgin Islands. *Southern Education Report*, 3 (4), 18–22. (1967, November).

Elkins, S. M. *Slavery: A Problem in American Institutional and Intellectual Life*. Chicago: The University of Chicago Press, 1959.

Emancipator (St. Thomas, V.I.) 1921–1928.

Engerman, S. L., & Genovese, E. D. *Race and Slavery in the Western Hemisphere: Quantitative Studies*. Princeton: Princeton University Press, 1975.

Esh, T., & Rosenbaum, I. *Tourism in Developing Countries—A Trick or Treat? A Report From the Gambia*. Uppsala: The Scandinavian Institute of African Affairs, 1975.

Evans, L. H. *The Virgin Islands: From Naval Base to New Deal*. Ann Arbor: J.W. Edwards, 1945.

Fanon, F. *Black Skin, White Masks*. New York: Grove Press, 1967.

Fanon, F. *The Wretched of the Earth*. New York: Grove Press, Inc., 1967.

Fill, J. H., & Segal, I. Teacher-Child-Parent Interrelationships in the U.S. Virgin Islands ... Curaçao, Netherlands Antilles, 1963.

Fishman, K. *Paradise.* New York: Dell Publishing Co., Inc., 1980.

Flammang, R. A. (1979, October). Economic Growth and Economic Development: Counterparts or Competitors? *Economic Development and Cultural Change,* 28(1), 47–61.

Francis, A. E. "The History of Social Welfare and Foreign Labor in the United States Virgin Islands: A Policy Analysis." Columbia University, Dissertation, 1979.

Franklin, J. H. (Ed.). *Color and Race.* Boston: Houghton Mifflin Company, 1968.

Franklin, J. H. *From Slavery to Freedom: A History of Negro Americans* (5th Edition ed.). New York: Alfred A. Knopf, Inc., 1980.

Frazier, E. F. *Race and Culture Contacts in the Modern World.* Boston: Beacon Press, 1957.

Frazier, E. F. "Race Contacts and the Social Structure." *American Sociological Review,* 14 (1), 1–11. (1949, February).

Freedom's Flame—A Publication of Project "Emancipation: A Second Look." U.S. Virgin Islands: Department of Conservation and Cultural Affairs, 1981.

Girvan, N. (1973, March 1). The Development of Dependency Economics in the Caribbean and Latin America: Review and Comparison. *Sociological and Educational Studies,* 22 (1), 1–33.

Gjessing, F. C. and W. MacLean. *Historic Buildings of St. Thomas and St. John.* London, U.K.: Macmillian Caribbean, 1987.

Gladwin, E. *Living in the Changing Caribbean.* New York: The Macmillan Company, 1970.

Gore, H. A. *Garrotte: The Illusion of Social Equality and Political Justice in the United States Virgin Islands.* United States: Wadadli Press, 2009.

Goveia, E. V. *Slave Society in the British Leeward Islands at the End of the Eighteenth Century.* New Haven: Yale University Press, 1965.

Grammer, A. (1968, January). Island Immigrant. *Virgin Islands View,* 3(8), 39–43.

Grede, J. F. *The New Deal in the Virgin Islands, 1931–1941.* The University of Chicago, 1962.

Green, J. W. *Social Networks in St. Croix, United States Virgin Islands.* University of Washington, 1987.

Green-Pedersen, S. E. (1971). The Scope and Structure of the Danish Negro Slave Trade. *The Scandinavian Economic History Review,* 19 (2), 149–197.

Guirty, G. *Harlem's Danish-American West Indians: 1899–1964.* New York: Vantage Press, 1971.

Hall, N. A. "Anna Heegaard—Enigma." *Caribbean Quarterly,* Vol. 22, Nos. 2 & 3 (June–September, 1976), pp. 63–73.

Hall, N. A. "Establishing a Public Elementary School System for Slaves in the Danish Virgin Islands, 1732–1844." Paper delivered at the Caribbean Historians' Conference, St. Thomas, V.I., March 1978.

Hall, N. A. "Slave Laws of the Danish Virgin Islands in the Later Eighteenth Century," in V. Ruben and A. Tuden, eds., *Comparative Perspectives on Slavery in New World Plantation Societies*. New York: Annals of the New York Academy Sciences, Vol. 292, 1977, pp. 174–188.

Hall, N. A. *Slave Society in the Danish West Indies: St. Thomas, St. John, and St. Croix*. Mona, Jamaica: University of the West Indies, 1992.

Hall, N. A. "Slavery in Three West Indian Towns: Christiansted, Frederiksted, and Charlotte Amalie in the Late Eighteenth and Early Nineteenth Century." Mimeographed paper, Mona, Jamaica, 1981.

Hall, N. A. "The 1816 Freedmen Petition in the Danish Virgin Islands: Its background and Consequences." Paper delivered at the 11th Annual Conference of Caribbean Historians, Curaçao, Netherlands Antilles, April, 1981.

Hamilton, D. M. "A Study of the Virgin Islands Residential Real Estate Market and Mortgage Lending Analysis for 1980." St. Croix, USVI: Erikson, Schindler, Hamilton & Associates, 1981.

Hansen, A. C. *From These Shores*. Nashville Tennessee and St. Thomas, U.S. V.I.: Hansen and Francois, 1996.

Harrigan, N. and P. Varlack. "The U.S. Virgin Islands and the Black Experience." Journal of Black Studies, Vol. 7, No. 4 (June, 1977), pp. 378–410.

Highfield, A. R. (Ed.). *Emancipation in the U.S. Virgin Islands: 150 Years of Freedom*. The Virgin Islands Emancipation Commission, 1999.

Highfield, A. R. (Ed.). *Negotiating Enslavement: Perspectives on Slavery in the Danish West Indies*. St. Croix, U.S. V.I.: Antilles Press, 2009.

Highfield, A. R. *Sainte Croix, 1650–1733: A Plantation Society in the French Antilles*. Christiansted, St. Croix: Antilles Press, 2013.

Highfield, A. R. *The French Dialect of St. Thomas, U. S. Virgin Islands*. Ann Arbor: Karoma Publishers, Inc., 1979.

Hill, V. A. *A Golden Jubilee: Virgin Islanders On the Go Under the American Flag*. New York: Carlton Press, 1967.

Hill, V. A. *Rise to Recognition: An Account of U.S. Virgin Islanders From Slavery to Self-Government*. St. Thomas, V.I.: St. Thomas Graphics, Inc., 1971.

Hodge, W. A. "The Tasks of Public Education in the United States Virgin Islands." Ph.D. Dissertation, The University of Wisconsin, 1978.

Hoetink, H. *Caribbean Race Relations: A Study of Two Variants*. London: Oxford University Press, 1967.

Hoffman, A. *The Marriage of Opposites*. New York: Simon and Schuster, 2015..

Home Journal. St. Thomas, V.I., 1959–1973.

Hoult, T. F. *The Sociology of Religion.* New York: The Dryden Press: 1958.

Hughes, Allister. "The Disappearing Virgin Islander." Virgin Islands Forum, Vol. 4, No. 1, Jan.–Feb., 1976, pp. 10–11.

Jarvis, J. A. *Brief History of the Virgin Islands.* St. Thomas: The Art Shop, 1938.

Jarvis, J. A. *The Virgin Islands and Their People.* Philadelphia: Dorrance and Company, 1944.

Jordan, Winthrop. *White Over Black: American Attitudes Toward the Negro, 1550–1812,* Chapel Hill: University of North Carolina Press, 1968.

Knight, D. W. *St. Thomas 1803: Crossroads of the Diaspora.* St. Thomas: Little Northwest Press, 1999.

Knight, F. W. *The African Dimension in Latin American Societies.* New York: Macmillan Publishing Co., Inc., 1979.

Knight, F. W. "U.S. Cultural Influences on the English-Speaking Caribbean during the early twentieth century." Mimographed paper delivered at the Fourteenth Conference of the Association of Caribbean Historians, San Juan, Puerto Rico, April, 1982.

Knox, J. P. *A Historical Account of St. Thomas, W.I.* New York: Charles Scribner, (1852 (Reprinted in 1966 by CVI)).

Knud-Hansen, K. *From Denmark to the Virgin Islands.* Philadelphia: Dorrance and Company, (1947).

Krigger, M. "Thoughts on the Identity of Black American Virgin Islanders". Summer Seminar Paper, Brown University, 1976.

Krigger, M. (March, 1978). "Attitudes and References to Immigrants in the St. Thomas Press, 1936–1942." Annual Conference of Caribbean Historians, St. Thomas, V.I., 1978.

Krigger, M. F. "A Quarter-Century of Race Relations in the U.S. Virgin Islands: St. Thomas, 1950–1975," Ph.D. Dissertation, U. of Delaware, 1983.

Krigger, M. F. "Overview of the Struggle for Self-Determination in the U.S. Virgin Islands, 1848 and Beyond," in A. R. Highfield, ed., *Emancipation in the U.S. Virgin Islands: 150 Years of Freedom.* The Virgin Islands Emancipation Commission, 1999.

Krigger, M. F. "The Virgin Islands: A Kaleidoscope of People" in *The Daily News* (St. Thomas, V.I.), Fiftieth Anniversary Edition, August 1, 1980, pp. 149–151.

Kruvant, W. J. "Socioeconomic Development in the U.S. Virgin Islands." Ph.D. Dissertation, The American University, 1975.

Larsen, J. *Virgin Islands Story.* Philadelphia: Fortress Press, 1950.

Lawaetz, E. *Black Education in the Danish West Indies from 1732 to 1859: The Pioneering Efforts of the Moravian Brethren.* St. Croix, V.I.: St. Croix Friends of Denmark Society.

Leary, P. M. "The Virgin Islands' Political Status, 1917 and 1987" A Lecture Presented Under the Auspices of the Virgin Islands Humanities Council, 1987.

Leary, P. M. (Ed.). *Major Political Constitutional Documents of the United States Virgin Islands, 1671–1991.* St. Thomas: University of the Virgin Islands, 1992.

Leary, P. M. (Ed.). *Taking Bearings: The United States Virgin Islands 1917–1987.* St. Thomas, V.I.: UVI Bureau of Public Administration, 1988.

Lewis, G. *The Virgin Islands: A Caribbean Lilliput.* Evanston: Northwestern University Press, 1972.

Lewis, G. K. *The Growth of the Modern West Indies.* New York: Monthly Review Press, 1968.

Lewis, G. K. "The Myth of Danish Culture." *Virgin Islands View,* August, 1967, pp. 14–22.

Lewisohn, F. *St. Croix Under Seven Flags.* Hollywood, Fl.: The Dukane Press, 1970.

Lynch, H. *Edward Wilmot Blyden: Pan-Negro Patriot.* London: Oxford University Press, 1967.

Manley, M. *The Politics of Change: A Jamaican Testament.* Washington, D.C.: Howard University Press, 1975.

Maynard, G. O. *A History of the Moravian Church, Eastern West Indies Province.* Port-of-Spain, Trinidad: Yuille's Printerie Limited, 1968.

Mills, F. L. (1980, No. 6). Relationships of Ethnic Diversity and Residential Differentiation in the Virgin Islands. *The Journal of the College of the Virgin Islands.*

Mills, Frank. "Native-Born Virgin Islanders Living in the States." *Research News from ECC,* Volume 2, Issue 1, Eastern Caribbean Center, University of the Virgin Islands: St. Thomas, January, 2010.

Moll, V. P. *This Land: A Trust From God: The Environment and Related Topics.* British Virgin Islands, 2014.

Moolenaar, R. M. *Legacies of Upstreet: The Transformation of a Virgin Islands Neighborhood.* St. Thomas, V.I.: We from Upstreet, 2005.

Moolenaar, R. M. *Profiles of Outstanding Virgin Islanders, Third Edition.* St. Thomas, V.I.: V.I. Department of Education, 1992.

Moolenaar, Ruth M. *A Student's Resource Guide on the Third Constitutional Convention of the U.S. Virgin Islands.* St. Thomas, V.I.: V.I. Department of Education, 1978.

Moorhead, M. C. *Mammon vs. History: American Paradise or Virgin Islands Home.* St. Croix, V.I.: United People Party, 1973.

Moorhead, M. C. *Redemption*. St. Croix, V.I.: United Caribbean Association, 1981.

Moran, R. F. "Real Estate Turns Tourists into Residents." *Virgin Islands View*, Vol. 3, No. 8, January, 1968), pp. 23-25.

Murphy, P. G. "The Education of the New World Blacks in the Danish West Indies/U.S. Virgin Islands: A Case Study of Social Transition." Ph.D. Dissertation, The University of Connecticut, 1977.

Myrdal, G. *An American Dilemma: The Negro Problem and Modern Democracy*. 2 vols. New York: Harper & Brothers, 1944.

Naughton, E. "The Origin and Development of Higher Education in the Virgin Islands." Ph.D. Dissertation, The Catholic University of America, 1973.

Nettleford, Rex. *Mirror, Mirror: Identity, Race and Protest in Jamaica*. Kingston: LMH Publishers, 2001.

New York Times. Selected articles between 1931 and 2016.

Nicholls, R. W. *Old-Time Masquerading in the U.S. Virgin Islands*. U.S. Virgin Islands: V.I. Humanities Council, 1998.

Oldendorp, C. *A Caribbean Mission*. Ann Arbor, Michigan: Karoma Publishers. (English translation by A. Highfield and V. Barac.), 1987.

Olwig, Karen F. *Global Culture, Island Identity: Continuity and Change in the Afro-Caribbean Community of Nevis*. Chur, Switzerland: Harwood Academic Publishers, 1993.

Ottley, E. B. *The Hardball Years: A Chronicle of Politics, Progress, and Pain in the U.S.V.I.* St. Thomas, 1994.

Ottley, E. B. *Trials and Triumphs: The Long Road to a Middle Class Society in the U.S. Virgin Islands*. St. Thomas, U.S. Virgin Islands, 1982.

Ottley Family. "Funeral Booklet of Earle B. Ottley." St. Thomas, Virgin Islands. (1999, September 4).

Paiewonsky, I. *Eyewitness Accounts of Slavery in the Danish West Indies*. St. Thomas, V.I., 1987.

Paiewonsky, R. M. *Memoirs of a Governor: A Man for the People*. New York: New York University Press, 1990.

Patterson, O. "The Black Experience in the New World." (Speech delivered at the College of the Virgin Islands, St., March 7, 1975.

Patterson, O. "Toward a Future That Has No Past—Reflections on the Fate of Blacks in the Americas." *The Public Interest*, No. 27 (Spring), 1972, pp. 428–451.

Perry, J. B. (Ed.). *A Hubert Harrison Reader*. Middletown, Connecticut: Wesleyan University Press, 2001.

Price, A. G. *White Settlers in the Tropics*. New York: American Geographical Society, 1932

Roach, T. "A Virgin Islands History Capsule." St. Thomas, V.I., 2006.

Shepherd, V. *Working Slavery, Pricing Freedom: Perspectives from the Caribbean, Africa and the African Diaspora.* New York: Palgrave Press, 2002.

Shulterbrandt, L., ed. (1962–1969). *Messages of the Governor of the Virgin Islands, Ralph M. Paiewonsky.* Oxford, New Hampshire: Equity Publishing Company.

Skeoch, R. *Cruzan Planter,* 1972.

Smith, M. G. *The Rastafari Movement in Kingston, Jamaica.* Kingston: Jamaican Institute of Social and Economic Research, 1960.

Smith, M. G. *The Plural Society in the British West Indies.* Berkeley: University of California Press, 1965.

Smith-Barry, J. *"Our Educators, Our Schools."* St. Thomas, V.I.: Department of Education, Office of the Insular Superintendent, 2014.

Sowell, T. *Race and Economics.* New York: David McKay Company, Inc., 1975.

Sprauve, G. Toward a Reconstruction of Virgin Islands English Creole Phonology. Dissertation, Princeton University, 1974.

St. Croix Avis. Selected Articles, 2000–2015.

St. Thomas Source. (2015–2017). St. Thomas, V.I.—an on-line newspaper.

Tannenbaum, F. *Slave and Citizen: The Negro in the Americas.* New York: Alfred A. Knopf, 1947.

Tansill, C. C. *The Purchase of the Danish West Indies.* Baltimore: Johns Hopkins University Press, 1931.

Tatum, Beverly D. *Why are All the Black Kids Sitting Together in the Cafeteria and Other Conversations About Race.* New York: Basic Books, 2003.

Taylor, C. E. *Leaflets from the Danish West Indies.* London: Wm. Dawson and Sons, (1888, reprinted in 1958).

Taylor, F. F. *To Hell With Paradise.* Pittsburgh: University of Pittsburgh Press, 1993.

Thomas, R. E. *Sounding Offs, 1986–1989.* St. Thomas, Virgin Islands, 1995.

Thomas, R. E. *Sounding Offs, 1995–1998.* St. Thomas, Virgin Islands, 1998.

Thurland, K. C. "Ralph M. Paiewonsky: Economic and Social Reformer of the Virgin Islands." Master's Thesis, Adelphi University, 1979.

Thurland, K. C. *The Sugar Industry on St. Croix.* Bloomington, IN: AuthorHouse, 2014.

Turnbull, C. W. The Structural Development of a Public Education System in the Virgin Islands, 1917–1970: A Functional Analysis in Historical Perspective. Ph.D. dissertation, University of Minnesota, 1976.

Tyson, G. F. (Ed.). *The Kamina Folk: Slavery and Slave Laws in the Danish West Indies.* U.S. V.I.: Virgin Islands Humanities Council, 1994.

Tyson, G. F. (Ed.). *The St. Thomas Harbor: A Historical Perspective.* St. Thomas: St. Thomas Historical Trust, 1986.

Van den Berghe, P. L. *Race and Racism: A Comparative Perspective.* New York: John Wiley & Sons, Inc., 1967.

Van den Berghe, P. L. *The Ethnic Phenomenon.* New York: Elsevier, 1981.

Varlack, P. and N. Harrigan. *The Virgins: A Descriptive and Historical Profile.* St. Thomas, V.I.: College of the Virgin Islands, Caribbean Research Institute, 1977.

Virgin Islands Forum. 1973–76.

Virgin Islands View. 1965–1968.

Washington, J. R. (Ed.). *Jews in Black Perspectives: A Dialogue.* London and Toronto: Associated University Press, 1984.

Weinstein, E. A. *Cultural Aspects of Delusion: A Psychiatric Study of the Virgin Islands.* New York: The Free Press of Glencoe, Inc., 1962.

Westergaard, W. *The Danish West Indies Under Company Rule, 1671–1754.* New York: The Macmillan Company, 1917.

Williams, E. "The Historical Background of Race Relations in the Caribbean." Port of Spain, Trinidad, 1955.

Williams, Eric. "Race Realtions in Puerto Rico and the Virgin Islands." *Foreign Affairs*, Vol. 23, No. 2 (January, 1945), pp. 308–317.

Willocks, H. W. *CIVICUS: Virgin Islands of the United States Civics and Character Enhancement.* St. Croix, V.I, 2006.

Willocks, H. W. *The Umbilical Cord: The History of the United States Virgin Islands from Pre-Columbian Era to the Present.* St. Croix, V.I., 1995.

Willocks, H. W. and M. Allick. *Massacre in Paradise: The Untold Story of the Fountain Valley Massacre.* U.S.A., 1977.

Woods, E. D. *The Three Quarters of the Town of Charlotte Amalie.* London, Rome, St. Thomas: Mapes Monde Editore, 1989.

Wouk, H. *Don't Stop the Carnival.* Garden City, N.Y.: Doubleday and Company, 1965.

Zabriski, L. K. *The Virgin Islands of the United States of America.* New York: G. P. Putnam's Sons, 1918.

Persons Interviewed or Consulted, 1982–83

1. Liston Abbott, East Windsor, N.J.
2. Klaus de Albuquerque, St. Thomas, V.I.
3. George Amey, St. Thomas, V.I.
4. George Applewhite, Brooklyn, New York

5. Marva Applewhite, Brooklyn, New York
6. Zeathea Armstrong, St. Thomas, V.I.
7. Asta Aubain, St. Thomas, V.I.
8. Enid Baa, St. Thomas, V.I.
9. Lawrence Baietti, St. Thomas, V.I.
10. Beverly Bandler, St. Thomas, V.I.
11. Ada Battiste, St. Thomas, V.I.
12. Ruth Beagles, St. Croix, V.I.
13. Rawle Belle, St. Croix, V.I.
14. Edith Bornn, St. Thomas, V.I.
15. Victoria Bourne-Vanneck, St. Thomas, V.I.
16. Vincent Bourne-Vanneck, St. Thomas, V.I.
17. Neville Brodie, St. Thomas, V.I.
18. Leona Bryant, St. Thomas, V.I.
19. Aimery Caron, St. Thomas, V.I.
20. John Collins, St. Thomas, V.I.
21. Clarissa Creque, St. Thomas, V.I.
22. Darwin Creque, St. Thomas, V.I.
23. Kathleen David, St. Thomas, V.I.
24. Glenn "Kwabena" Davis, St. Thomas, V.I.
25. Reginald Davis, St. Thomas, V.I.
26. Jeffrey Farrow, Washington, D.C.
27. Richard Ferrelli, New York, N.Y.
28. Penny Feuerzeig, St. Thomas, V.I.
29. Halvor Francis, Sr., St. Thomas, V.I.
30. Mary S. Francis, St. Thomas, V.I.
31. Enid Frederiksen, St. Thomas, V.I.
32. Kwame Garcia, St. Thomas, V.I.
33. Alvion George, St. Thomas, V.I.
34. Helen Gjessing, St. Thomas, V.I.
35. George Goodwin, St. Thomas, V.I.
36. Peter Goodwin, St. Thomas, V.I.
37. Erva Denham Greer, St. Thomas, V.I.
38. Jasmine Gunthorpe, Pala Alto, Calif.
39. Edwin Hatchette, St. Thomas, V.I.
40. Granville Hedrington, Jr., St. Thomas, V.I.
41. Leslie Hedrington, St. Thomas,V.I.
42. Marion Bray Hedrington, St. Thomas, V.I.
43. Charlene O'Neal Henderson, St. Thomas, V.I.
44. Florence Hill, St. Thomas, V.I.

45. Iran Hodge, St. Thomas, V.I.
46. Hebert A. Hoover, St. Thomas, V.I.
47. Eric H. Jouett, St. Thomas, V.I.
48. Gwendolyn Kean, St. Thomas, V.I.
49. Mali Kiambo, St. Thomas, V.I.
50. Sydney Knight, St. Thomas, V.I.
51. Rudolph Krigger, Jr., St. Thomas, V.I
52. Rudolph Krigger, Sr., St. Thomas, V.I.
53. Lamakalo, St. Thomas, V.I.
54. Joyce LaMotta, St. Thomas, V.I.
55. Laurita Ledee, St. Thomas, V.I.
56. E. Maria Leerdam, St. Thomas, V.I.
57. June A. V. Lindqvist, St. Thomas, V.I.
58. Rita B. Martin, St. Thomas, V.I.
59. G. Olliver Maynard, St. Thomas, V.I.
60. Frank Mills, St. Thomas, V.I.
61. Abdullah Muhammed, St. Thomas, V.I.
62. Ulla Muller, St. Thomas, V.I.
63. Ras Nisha, St. Thomas, V.I.
64. Athniel "Addie" Ottley, St. Thomas, V.I.
65. Charlotte Paiewonsky, St. Thomas, V.I.
66. Isidor Paiewonsky, St. Thomas, V.I.
67. Michael Paiewonsky, St. Thomas, V.I.
68. Ralph Paiewonsky, St. Thomas, V.I.
69. Arona Petersen, St. Thomas, V.I.
70. Maria Prochnau, St. Thomas, V.I.
71. Norman Prochnau, St. Thomas, V.I
72. Margaret Quetel, St. Thomas, V.I.
73. William Quetel, St. Thomas, V.I.
74. James Ready, St. Thomas, V.I.
75. Arthur A. Richards, St. Thomas, V.I.
76. Dennis Richardson, St. Thomas, V.I.
77. Jim Samuels, St. Thomas, V.I.
78. Harriet Saxton, Newark, Delaware
79. Louis Shulterbrandt, St. Thomas, V.I.
80. O'Dean Skelton, St. Thomas, V.I.
81. Elma Davis Smith, St. Thomas, V.I.
82. Glen Smith, St. Thomas, V.I.
83. Viola C. Smith, St. Thomas, V.I.
84. Gloria Alexander Statham, Philadelphia, Pa.

85. Ethiopia Tamara I., St. Thomas, V.I.
86. Ruth E. Thomas, St. Thomas, V.I.
87. Emily Tynes, Washington, D.C.
88. Marjorie Vann, Hurst, Texas
89. Ernest Wagner, St. Thomas, V.I.
90. Ronald Walker, Bethesda, Md.
91. Lawrence Wanlass, Sacramento, Calif.
92. Edwin A. Weinstein, Bethesda, Md.
93. Werner Wernicke, St. Thomas, V.I.
94. Dawn Strong Wheatley, St. Thomas, V.I.
95. Maurice Wheatley, St. Thomas, V.I.
96. Henry Wheatley, St. Thomas, V.I.
97. Ivan Williams, St. Thomas, V.I.

Persons Interviewed or Consulted, 2015–17

1. Winston Adams, St. Thomas, V.I.
2. Martha Alexander, St. Thomas, V.I.
3. Paul Alexander, St. Thomas, V.I.
4. Myron Allick, St. Croix, V.I.
5. Marva Applewhite, Brooklyn, New York
6. Henrita Barber, St. Thomas, V.I.
7. Cecelia Barry, St. Thomas, V.I.
8. Ayishih Bellew, St. Thomas, V.I.
9. Lawrence "Larry" Benjamin, St. Thomas, V.I.
10. Elridge Blake, St. Thomas, V.I.
11. Kenneth Blake, St. Thomas, V.I.
12. William W. Boyer, Newark, Delaware
13. Mavis Brady, St. Thomas, V.I.
14. Whitman Browne, St. Thomas, V.I.
15. Fuller Campbell, St. Thomas, V.I.
16. Aimery Caron, St. Thomas, V.I.
17. Joyce Caron, St. Thomas, V.I.
18. Avna Cassinelli, St. Thomas, V.I.
19. Juan Christian, St. Thomas, V.I.
20. Vincen M. Clendinen, St. Thomas, V.I.
21. Dawn Comissiong, St. Thomas, V.I.
22. Errol L. Connor, St. Thomas, V.I.
23. Juana Corcino, St. Thomas, V.I.

24. Karel Ledee Daniel, St. Thomas, V.I.
25. Eric Dawson, Florida
26. Glenn "Kwabena" Davis, St. Thomas, V.I.
27. Donnie Dorsett, St. Thomas, V.I.
28. Gerard Emanuel, St. Croix, V.I.
29. Desiree Foy-Fisher, Atlanta, GA
30. Bernice T. Francis, St. Thomas, V.I.
31. E. Aracelis Francis, St. Thomas, V.I.
32. Halvor Francis, Jr., St. Thomas, V.I.
33. Ronald Harrigan, St. Thomas, V.I.
34. Edwin Hatchette, St. Thomas, V.I.
35. Hector "Alemu" Francis, St. Thomas, V.I.
36. Karl Frederiksen, Indiana
37. Stephen "Smokey" Frett, St. Thomas, V.I.
38. William "Bill" Frett, St. Thomas, V.I.
39. Helen Gjessing, Vermont
40. Grace Gregory, St. Thomas, V.I.
41. Dulcie Gumbs, St. Thomas, V.I.
42. Lois Hassel Habtes, St. Thomas, V.I.
43. David Hall, St. Thomas, V.I.
44. Edwin Hatchette, St. Thomas, V.I.
45. Bernice T. Heyliger, St. Thomas, V.I.
46. Verne A. Hodge, St. Thomas, V.I.
47. Brenda Hollar, St. Thomas, V.I.
48. Ruth DeMouy Hunt, St. Thomas, V.I.
49. Dexter Joseph, St. Thomas, V.I.
50. Eardley Joseph, St. Thomas, V.I.
51. Stefan Jurgen, St. Thomas, V.I.
52. Julie Kean, St. Thomas, V.I.
53. Orville Kean, St. Thomas, V.I.
54. Winelle Kirton-Roberts, St. Thomas, V.I.
55. Rudolph Krigger, Jr., St. Thomas, V.I.
56. Alphonso LaBorde, St. Thomas. V.I.
57. Tamara Lang, St. Thomas, V.I.
58. Paul Leary, Florida
59. Barry Leerdam, St. Thomas, V.I.
60. Joseph W. Lewis, St. Thomas, V.I.
61. Hollis "Chalkdust" Liverpool, St. Thomas, V.I.
62. Janet Lloyd, St. Thomas, V.I.
63. Ronald Lockhart, St. Thomas, V.I.

64. Susan Lugo, St. Thomas, V.I.
65. Manaazo Lamakalo, St. Thomas, V.I.
66. Ellen MacLean, St. Thomas, V.I.
67. Anique Elmes Matthew, St. Thomas, V.I.
68. Gwendolyn Meyers, St. Thomas, V.I.
69. Micheline Meyers, Maryland
70. Frank Mills, St. Thomas, V.I.
71. Juel T. R. Molloy, St. Thomas, V.I.
72. Gwen-Marie Moolenaar, St. Thomas, V.I.
73. Abdullah Muhammed, St. Thomas, V.I.
74. Jeffrey Neevel, St. Thomas, V.I.
75. Anantha Pancham, St. Thomas, V.I.
76. Dion Phillips, St. Thomas, V.I.
77. Beverly Plaskett, St. Thomas, V.I.
78. Margaret Quetel, St. Thomas, V.I.
79. William Quetel, St. Thomas, V.I.
80. LaVerne Ragster, St. Thomas, V.I.
81. Alexander Randall, Water Island, V.I.
82. Pamela Richards-Samuel, St. Thomas, V.I.
83. Letetia Penn Rodgers St. Thomas, V.I.
84. Gloria Samuel, St. John, V.I.
85. Francine Penn Scipio, St. Thomas, V.I.
86. Carla Donna Sarauw, St. Thomas, V.I.
87. Levron "Paps" Sarauw, St. Thomas, V.I.
88. Lawrence "Larry" Sewer, St. Thomas, V.I.
89. Gail Shulterbrandt Rivera, St. Thomas, V.I.
90. Beverly Smith, St. Thomas, V.I.
91. Glen Smith, St. Thomas, V.I.
92. Jeanette Smith-Barry, St. Thomas, V.I.
93. Gershwain Sprauve, St. Thomas, V.I.
94. Gilbert Sprauve, St. Thomas, V.I.
95. Alphonse Stalliard, St. Thomas, V.I.
96. Gail Steele, St. Thomas, V.I.
97. Mary-Louise Stern, St. Thomas, V.I.
98. Nour Suid, St. Thomas, V.I.
99. Zakaria Suid, St. Thomas, V.I.
100. Mervin Taylor, St. Thomas, V.I.
101. Audrey Thomas, St. Thomas, V.I.
102. Ruth E. Thomas, St. Thomas, V.I.

103. Charles W. Turnbull, St. Thomas, V.I.
104. Fred Vialet, St. Thomas, V.I.
105. Lloyd Williams, St. Thomas, V.I.
106. Cynthia Wallace, St. Thomas, V.I.
107. Lucien Wallace, St. Thomas, V.I.
108. Roy Watlington, St. Thomas, V.I.
109. Utha Williams, St. Thomas, V.I.
110. Wesley Williams, Jr., St. Thomas, V.I.
111. Jens Willumsen, Denmark

Index